TM

Course III ▪ Volume 2

21Book

Credits and acknowledgments appear on pages 342–345, which constitute an extension of this copyright page.

Copyright © 2010 by Scholastic Inc.

All rights reserved.   Published by Scholastic Inc.   Printed in the U.S.A.

ISBN-13: 978-0-545-11799-9
ISBN-10: 0-545-11799-2

1 2 3 4 5 6 7 8 9 10   58   18 17 16 15 14 13 12

D1403052

   Cover and pages printed on 10% PCW recycled paper.

2. Set Goals

...over's goal is to get his art form out
...ed to achieve

baseball signed by Ba...

In 1927, Charles Lin...
became the first pers...
fly solo across the Atla...
Ocean.

1998   Bringin' Funk...

2007   A Danci...

When Glo...
choreogr...
animated...
Mumble...
immedi...
directo...
be him...
dance...
the da...

Andy WARHOL

■SCHOLASTIC   Scholastic Inc. • 557 Broadway • New York, NY 10012

[expert 21] ™

Dear Reader,

Welcome to the *21Book*, Volume 2!

Get ready to explore four more expert questions, acquire amazing knowledge, examine essential ideas, get even more informed about the world, and maybe even change your mind about what's important to you.

There are many ways to express yourself through art. You can write, paint, dance, or take pictures. In **Workshop 5, "iShowcase,"** you'll meet artists who have put the "i" in individual expression. This workshop will showcase artists ranging from Vincent van Gogh—one of the best-known painters of all time—to teens who changed their lives by playing music. Their lives and work will inspire you to answer the question: **What makes art powerful?**

Space is a vast frontier to which a few brave explorers have traveled, discovering sights that amaze us and resources to use here on Earth. Space also threatens us: an asteroid strike could change our world forever. In **Workshop 6, "Space Invaders,"** you'll examine space from many angles: through science fiction, science fact, and the opinions of an outspoken astrophysicist. You'll form your own opinion about the question: **Should we explore outer space?**

History is more than just a series of names, dates, and events—it is made up of true stories about real people. What if you could step into the shoes of people who watched as important events unfolded? In **Workshop 7, "Eyewitness to History,"** you'll read firsthand accounts from victims of war, soldiers on the battlefield, and ordinary citizens who witnessed extraordinary events. You'll see that a real understanding of history starts with this question: **What was it like to be there?**

It's not always easy to determine right from wrong. And just when you're sure that you are doing the right thing, someone else might speak up and disagree. Whether it's leaving behind a life of crime, "borrowing" term papers from the Internet, or inventing new ways to use scientific knowledge, we all have choices to make—and we rely on our values to guide us. In **Workshop 8, "Do the Right Thing,"** you'll explore the question: **What values do we live by?**

Let the Expert 21 Team know what you think! Email us at: Expert21@scholastic.com

Sincerely,

the Editors

The Editors

TE...

Salvado...

Pablo PICASS...

front-page news

In 1923, baseball great Babe Ruth helped the Yankees win the World Series; in 1927, he became the first player to hit 60 home runs in one season.

Lindbergh's flight

National Geographic from December 1969

anti-war pins

1960s, as did protests against the war.

On July 20, 1969, more than 600 million people around the world watched astronaut Neil Armstrong on their TV sets, as he became the first man to walk on the moon.

In the 1960s, Barbie dolls marketed as to

Jeff KOONS

Jackson POLLOCK

ARTISTS
WHO CHANGED

CHAIM POTOK
AUTHOR OF *THE CHOSEN*

ZEBRA

AND OTHER STORIES

cent GOGH

Fri

L Reading 5 | **PLAY: CLASSIC RETELLIN**

Frankenste

By Mary Shelley, adapted by Sunita Apte

ishowcase

Inquiry 1: The Impact of Art

Skills & Strategies

Inquiry 2: The Power of Expression

SPACE INVADERS

Inquiry 1: Close Encounters

Skills & Strategies

Inquiry 2: Space Odyssey

WORKSHOP 7

EYEWITNESS *to* HISTORY

Expert Question:
What was it like to be there?

Ⓦ **Writing**
Research Paper 222
FOCUS TRAIT   Sentence Fluency
GRAMMAR   Phrases and Clauses
MECHANICS   Using Commas with Phrases and Clauses

🟥 **Expert Reading**
Remembering 9/11 230
By Juliette Kessler • PERSONAL ESSAY

21 PROJECT RESEARCH
Eyewitness to the Present Day ... 234

DO THE RIGHT THING

Expert Question:
What values do we live by?

Inquiry 1: Classic Questions

Skills & Strategies

Inquiry 2: Dilemmas for Today

[21]Questions

► Answer these questions to get ready for a new [21] Book—
and four more workshops of knowledge for you to explore.

1 **Justify.** Do you think learning about the arts (art, music, drama, dance) is important for everyone? Why or why not?

_____

_____

_____

_____

2 **Evaluate.** Circle one phrase to complete the sentence.

In my opinion, a piece of art should ...

express the artist's views or feelings about life.

make a political statement.

include references to popular culture.

look like a scene from the real world.

3 **Personalize.** Which of the following would you most like to do?

☐ Play a musical instrument in front of an audience.

☐ Write poetry, short stories, or novels.

☐ Take photographs of interesting or important people and places.

☐ Direct or act in plays, movies, or TV shows.

☐ Create artwork such as paintings or sculptures.

4 **Decide.** Do you think writing is a type of art? Why or why not?

_____

_____

_____

_____

5 **Decide.** Some artists earn millions of dollars for selling just one painting or sculpture. Do you think works of art should ever cost this much? Explain your response.

_____

_____

_____

_____

_____

Puppy, 1992 by Jeff Koons

Koons has sold art for as much as $25.7 million.

6 **Consider.** Do you believe in life in outer space?

☐ Yes. If Earth can support life, there must be other planets out there somewhere that support life, too.

☐ Maybe. If there is life, it's probably not as advanced as life on Earth.

☐ No. If we haven't found it by now, it's probably not out there.

Explain your reasoning.

_____

_____

_____

_____

7 **Question.** What are your chances of dying from an asteroid hitting Earth? Check one.

☐ 1 in 100

☐ 1 in 5,000

☐ 1 in 20,000

☐ 1 in 2,518,072

8 **Prioritize.** What do you think our most important space goals should be? Rank each goal from **1** (not important) to **4** (really important).

RATING

_____ stopping asteroids from hitting Earth

_____ finding natural resources we can use on Earth

_____ searching for alien life

_____ setting up human colonies on the moon and Mars

9 **Evaluate.** Space exploration—is it just too expensive, or is it a vital necessity? Put an **X** next to the statement with which you agree the most.

_____ The money spent on space exploration could be used to feed hungry children.

_____ The discoveries we make in space could benefit people on Earth.

_____ The risk of injury or death is too great to justify space exploration.

_____ Space exploration shows other countries that our nation is advanced and powerful.

10 **Imagine.** You are an astronaut on a mission to recover a satellite. Suddenly you lose communication with your space station. Write the thoughts going through your mind.

_____

_____

_____

_____

_____

11 **Decide.** Circle three personality traits that would help a soldier hiding from enemies during a war.

Patience   Courage

Creativity   Intelligence

Sense of humor   Calmness

The fall of the Berlin Wall, 1989

12 **Decide.** Why do you think a wall was built to separate the east and west parts of the German city of Berlin?

_____

_____

_____

_____

_____

13 **Evaluate.** Read the following opinions about national governments. Put an **A** (agree) next to each statement with which you agree. Put a **D** (disagree) next to each statement with which you disagree.

_____ You can help improve your country by getting a job in the government.

_____ It is important for citizens to know when their government does something wrong or unfair.

_____ If the government of your country mistreats people, it is fair to throw them out of office.

_____ Creating a fair government requires sacrifice.

14 **Imagine.** The situation: You and your family must leave your home and report to a prison-like work camp. How would you feel faced with this situation?

_____

_____

_____

_____

_____

_____

15 **Decide.** Which historical event would you most have liked to witness? Check one.

❏ the moon landing

❏ when U.S. troops entered Baghdad in 2003

❏ the inauguration of Nelson Mandela as South Africa's first black president

16 Personalize. What would you be willing to do to help another person? Check ✓ all that apply.

_____ Lend the person money.

_____ Give the person advice, if asked.

_____ Tutor the person for a difficult class.

_____ Other: _____

_____

17 Decide. Do you think it is possible for a criminal to stop committing crimes and lead an honest life? Explain.

_____

_____

_____

_____

18 Evaluate. For each opinion about cheating, put an **A** (agree) next to each opinion you agree with. Put a **D** (disagree) next to each opinion you disagree with.

_____ Students should do their own homework without help from their parents.

_____ Everyone cheats sometimes.

_____ It's okay to buy research papers from the Internet.

_____ Students who are caught cheating should automatically fail the class.

19 Justify. In your opinion, testing drugs on animals is ...
Check one phrase to complete the sentence.

_____ necessary in order to develop important new medicines for people.

_____ a procedure that hurts animals and should be replaced with other kinds of safety tests.

20 Empathize. Imagine a student is harassed for a long time by a bully at school. How should the bullied student deal with the situation? Pick one.

☐ Ask the teacher to punish the bully.

☐ Ask other students for support.

☐ Leave the school.

Explain your answer.

_____

_____

[21] Be an Expert. Look through the Table of Contents on pages IV–VII. Which article or topic looks most interesting to you? Why does it interest you?

_____

_____

_____

_____

_____

After you read the workshops, come back and see if you feel the same way!

21st Century Learning in Action

▶ Rate your 21st Century Skills—and show how you apply these skills to school and life.

Intellectual

C Content Area

Inquiry

expert **21**
™

Personal

Social

Global

Communication and Collaboration

1 I effectively use **note cards, visual aids,** and other **presentation** tools. [**RATING** _____]

2 Three things I can do to help **resolve conflicts** are: _____

_____

_____

_____

_____

Critical Thinking and Problem Solving

3 I'm able to **synthesize information** from a variety of sources when figuring out a problem. [**RATING** _____]

4 If someone else's **reasoning** doesn't make sense, I can usually understand why not. An example of a recent **decision** that someone else (a peer or an adult) made and why I think it was wrong is: _____

_____

_____

_____

Creativity and Innovation

5 I pay attention to **visual design** to make sure my projects look great. [**RATING** _____]

6 An **innovative** idea I'd like to pursue is: _____
_____

One way to make this idea a reality is to: _____
_____
_____
_____

Information and Media Literacy

9 When doing research, I know when to **paraphrase** and when to give a **direct quote** from a source. [**RATING** _____]

10 I am aware of **stereotypes** and how they are used in the **media**. An example of a stereotype that the media often uses is:
_____
_____
_____
_____

College, Workplace, and Life Skills

7 I've interviewed at least a few adults about their **jobs** or **careers**. [**RATING** _____]

8 My **skills** are a good match for these **three** jobs:
_____
_____
_____
_____
_____
_____

ICT Literacy

Information and Communication Technology

11 I use **privacy settings** on social networking sites to make sure my personal information is protected. [**RATING** _____]

12 I use databases, message boards, and other **Web resources** to find the information I need. One Web resource I find especially useful is:

My [21] Page

▶ **Fill in the section for each workshop as you complete it. Keep track of your interests and goals as well.**

Name | ▼

Age | ▼

Hometown | ▼

State | ▼

🌐 My World

Places I'd Like to Explore

• _____
• _____
• _____
• _____

People (Dead or Alive) I'd Like to Meet

• _____
• _____
• _____
• _____

📖 My Media

Media I Like (Books and Movies)

• _____
• _____
• _____

Video Games I'm Playing

• _____
• _____
• _____

Web Sites I'm Visiting

• _____
• _____
• _____

WORKSHOP 5 ☐ Workshop complete Date _____

iShowcase

The artist I enjoyed reading about the most in this workshop is:

_____

Explain your choice:

_____
_____

PROJECT **Self-Portrait: Pick Your Media** What do you want people to learn about you from your self-portrait?

_____
_____
_____
_____

WORKSHOP 6 ☐ Workshop complete Date _____

Space Invaders

Which of these projects do you think should be a space exploration priority?

[ ] explore Mars
[ ] visit an asteroid

[ ] search for extraterrestrials
[ ] drill through the ice on Jupiter's moon

PROJECT **Should We Continue to Explore Space?** Did any of your opponents' arguments change your mind about your original position?

[ ] Yes   [ ] No

Why or why not?

_____
_____
_____

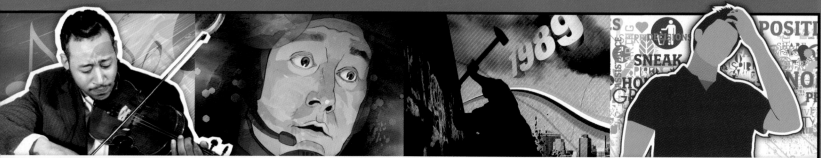

Eyewitness to History

Which historical event presented in this workshop did you find most interesting? Why?

_____

_____

_____

_____

PROJECT **Eyewitness to the Present Day** Which of the items in your time pod do you think is the most interesting? Why?

_____

_____

_____

Do the Right Thing

Would you stop to help a stranger who fell on the sidewalk? Why?

_____

_____

_____

_____

PROJECT **What Would You Do?** What is an ethical dilemma you have faced? What did you do?

_____

_____

_____

☆ My Skills

Topics I'm an Expert In

- _____
- _____
- _____
- _____

Skills I'm an Expert In

- _____
- _____
- _____
- _____

My Goals

Jobs That I Know About

- _____
- _____
- _____

Jobs I Want to Know More About

- _____
- _____
- _____

Skills That I Want to Learn

- _____
- _____
- _____

iShowcase

? Expert Question:
What makes art powerful?

21 Expert Knowledge
What makes art powerful?

A painting can inspire you to look at the world in a new way. A song can bring tears to your eyes. How do artists create art that makes an impact? Start your exploration now.

◉ Anchor Your Knowledge

Watch the Anchor Media, "iShowcase." Meet Savion Glover, who has elevated tap dance to a highly expressive, electrifying art.

◉ Concept Web

Create a concept web of what you know about the power of art.

The Power of Art

WORKSHOP GOALS

To gain expert knowledge about powerful art, you will

- read **informational texts** about people whose lives were changed through art.

- read **literature** by creative people and see **art** from various artists.

- learn **important skills and strategies** to help you understand what you read.

- develop **21st Century Skills** to **set and use criteria** and **analyze images.**

- write a **compare-and-contrast essay** about two works of art or poetry.

- complete an **Expert Project** to create a self-portrait that answers the question "Who Am I?"

▶ Preview the Expert Project

At the end of this workshop, you'll create a self-portrait. Preview the **Expert Project** on pages 76–79.

▶ What will you need to know or do to complete the Expert Project?

_____

_____

_____

_____

▶ Explore Expert Space

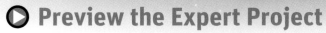 Go to **www.expert21.com/student** to learn more about the topics in this workshop.

DISCOVER ONLINE

• Tap Dancing
• Careers in Art
• Careers in Dance

READ ONLINE

• Surrealism
• Stringed Instruments
• Photojournalism
• Chaim Potok

RESEARCH ONLINE

• American Literature
• Short Story
• Hollywood

▶ Personal Inquiry

Explore the topic of powerful art by asking your own questions. Return to add questions as you continue reading Workshop 5. Plan to revisit your questions.

Savion Glover: Tap Dancer

This dancer inspires and influences people of all ages.

"If I didn't have dance to express myself, I would probably be stealing your car or something else right now.... Tap saved me."

Music runs in **Savion Glover**'s family. "My mom was a singer. The whole family is musically inclined." Glover started drumming lessons when he was four. Two years later, he started tap classes at the Broadway Dance Center in New York City. Glover did not have real tap shoes and had to dance in cowboy boots—but no big deal. He's a natural.

FACTS AND STATS

NAME: Savion Glover

HOMETOWN: Newark, New Jersey

JOB: Dancer on the Broadway stage and in movies; Choreographer; Teacher at dance school he founded

WORKPLACE LITERACIES: Collaborating; setting goals; innovating; understanding the influence of the media; identifying and recording patterns; communicating through dance

EDUCATION: High school diploma

PAY: Dancers can earn from about $21,000 to $54,000 per year.

COOLEST PART OF THE JOB: "I take every opportunity as a chance to learn and share what I know and do. It's cool to see people appreciate what I do."

CAREER CONNECTION
Arts, A/V Technology, and Communications
www.careerclusters.org

Go to 21 ToolKit **Expert File 6.18** to learn more about careers in the arts.

RELATED JOBS: choreographer, set designer, dance therapist, stage manager, artistic director

1985–1988 Broadway and Movie Debuts

One Saturday, ten-year-old Glover auditions for the choreographer of the Broadway show *The Tap Dance Kid*. "A few weeks later, I got a call and was invited to join the production workshop. About a year after that, I started performing professionally." At twelve, he is a star on Broadway. A few years later, Glover makes his movie debut dancing alongside the famous tapper and performer Sammy Davis, Jr., in *Tap*.

1991–1995 *Sesame Street* Regular

When the Public Broadcasting Service (PBS) asks Glover to be a regular on *Sesame Street*, he **decides** to accept—after all, he grew up watching Big Bird and Ernie. "I was happy to be a part of having tap dancing seen every day. I like to do positive things, to be thought of as a **positive role model,** someone kids can relate to."

1992 Hoofing with Hines

While a member of the *Sesame Street* cast, Glover gets a part in the Broadway play *Jelly's Last Jam*. His new co-star is legendary tapper and actor Gregory Hines. "Hines treated me like a younger brother or son. I started to realize that I was part of a tradition and a family of tap dancers."

1995–1998 Bringin' Funk to the People

Glover is asked to create his own show and **collaborates with a team.** His **goal** is to **synthesize** dance, music, and poetry to tell a story. He goes back to the basics of tap to find an innovative way to **express his ideas.** He develops a "funk-like style, doing more rhythmic patterns than steps." Walking in New York, Glover hears two street musicians who play drums on buckets, pans, and household items. He **decides** to make them part of the show to remind the audience that music is everywhere. The **final product:** *Bring in 'Da Noise, Bring in 'Da Funk.* It's a smash Broadway hit, winning four Tony Awards.

2007 A Dancing Penguin

When Glover is asked to choreograph the part of the animated dancing penguin Mumble in *Happy Feet*, he immediately agrees. The director tells Glover to just be himself. But can a penguin dance funk? If Glover's doing the dancing, he sure can.

The Present and the Future

Glover plans to continue teaching at his dance school in Newark and tapping on Broadway and in movies. He has other plans, too, but his number one **goal** is "to get my style out there. Once I see that people all over the world are hip to tap and know it's alive and well, then I'll go on to something else."

ANALYZE WORKPLACE SKILLS

1. Make Decisions
Why did Glover decide to become a regular on *Sesame Street*?

_____

_____

2. Set Goals
Glover's goal is to get his art form out there. How has he worked to achieve that goal?

_____

_____

_____

_____

3. Synthesize Information
Complete the web to show how Glover uses art to express himself and his ideas.

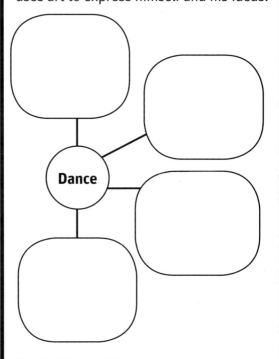

Dance

DISCOVER ONLINE

expert space
Go to **www.expert21.com/student**
to learn more about Tap Dancing; Careers in Art; Careers in Dance.

Fine Art

TEN ARTISTS WHO CHANGED THE WORLD

Who are the great artists of modern times? Why is the art they make so important?

Compare and Contrast COMPREHENSION

To **compare** two subjects, identify what they have in common.

To **contrast** two subjects, identify how they are different.

You can compare and contrast to draw conclusions or make judgments about subjects.

► **Use details from the passage to answer the questions below.**

Vincent van Gogh was a troubled, self-doubting painter who sold just one painting in his lifetime. He should have stuck around. Since his death, he has been hailed as one of the greatest artists of all time—and his paintings are among the priciest.

Pablo Picasso was extremely famous and successful during his life. He was widely seen as the most important painter of his age—and he certainly agreed with that opinion!

What subjects are being compared and contrasted?

_____

What is one similarity between Vincent van Gogh and Pablo Picasso?

_____

What is one difference?

_____

What conclusion can you draw from this comparison and contrast?

_____

Text Features and Visual Features NAVIGATING TEXT

Visual features like illustrations or photographs can show some kinds of information more clearly than words alone can. Text features such as captions and labels often contain information that help readers to understand visuals. A painting's label, for example, usually gives the name of the artist, the title of the painting, when it was painted, its size, what materials it is made from, and who owns the painting.

► **Circle the title of the painting. Underline the painter and information about him. Then answer the question.**

Three Musicians **(1921)**
by Pablo Picasso (1881-1973)

Oil on canvas (204.5 x 188.3 cm/80.5 x 74.1 in), Estate of Pablo Picasso/Artists Rights Society (ARS), New York.

Why do you think many museums put labels such as these next to paintings and other objects they exhibit?

_____

Academic Language VOCABULARY

▶ Rate each word. Then write its meaning and give an example sentence.

Word	Meaning	Example
EXPERT WORDS *Use these words to write and talk about the workshop topic.*		
abstract *ab•stract (adjective)* ① ② ③ ④	showing imagined things rather than what people or objects actually look like	I like realistic art better than abstract art because I like to know what the painting is supposed to be showing.
composition *com•po•si•tion (noun)* ① ② ③ ④		
exhibition *ex•hi•bi•tion (noun)* ① ② ③ ④		
portrait *por•trait (noun)* ① ② ③ ④		
ACADEMIC WORDS *Use these words in all your subject classes.*		
impact *im•pact (noun)* ① ② ③ ④		
reject *re•ject (verb)* ① ② ③ ④	to refuse to accept something	
SELECTION WORDS *Use these words to better understand the selection.*		
depict *de•pict (verb)* ① ② ③ ④		My painting depicts my strong feelings about the ocean.
uproar *up•roar (noun)* ① ② ③ ④		

Rating Scale ① I don't know the word.   ② I've seen it or heard it.   ③ I know its meaning.   ④ I know it and use it.

Noun Suffixes: *-ian, -ist, -tion* WORD ANALYSIS

You have learned that a suffix is a word part added to the end of a base word to change its meaning.

A noun suffix turns the base word into a noun. Sometimes the spelling of the base word changes slightly when a suffix is added.

suffix	meaning	example
-ian, *-ist*	person who does, makes, or believes (something)	music + *-ian* = musician cycle + *-ist* = cyclist
-tion	an act or example (of something)	irritate + *-tion* = irritation

Underline the suffix in each word. Then write the word's meaning.

novelist _____

_____

election _____

Andy WARHOL

Jeff KOONS

Georgia O'KEEFFE

Jackson POLLOCK

Edward HOPPER

TEN ARTISTS
WHO CHANGED
THE WORLD

By Francesca Alta

Alexander CALDER

Vincent VAN GOGH

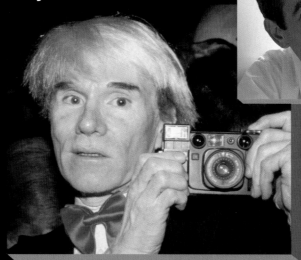

Salvador DALÍ

Pablo PICASSO

Frida KAHLO

Vincent VAN GOGH

Vincent van Gogh was a troubled, self-doubting painter who sold just one painting in his lifetime. He should have stuck around. Since his death, he has been hailed as one of the greatest artists of all time—and his paintings are among the priciest. This painting, one of his most beloved, is an example of post-impressionism, an art movement that used color, shape, and **composition** to make an **impact.** Has the night sky ever looked like this to you?

The Starry Night **(1889)**
by Vincent van Gogh (1853–1890)
Oil on canvas (73 × 92 cm/28¾ 36¼ in).
Museum of Modern Art, New York.

Pablo PICASSO

When Pablo Picasso was 13, his father saw him sketching a pigeon. His father gave up making art himself, saying that his son had surpassed him as an artist. From there it was all up, up, and away for Picasso. Picasso was extremely famous and successful during his life. He was widely seen as the most important painter of his age—and he certainly agreed with that opinion! He painted in many styles but is perhaps best known for his ground-breaking cubist paintings. Cubists made art that was more **abstract** than realistic. See how the musicians are pushed together and shown in a flat plane. Why is that dog under the table?

Three Musicians **(1921)**
by Pablo Picasso (1881–1973)
Oil on canvas (204.5 × 188.3 cm/80.5 × 74.1 in).
Estate of Pablo Picasso/Artists Rights Society (ARS),
New York.

hailed *(v.)* described as being very good
beloved *(adj.)* loved very much by someone

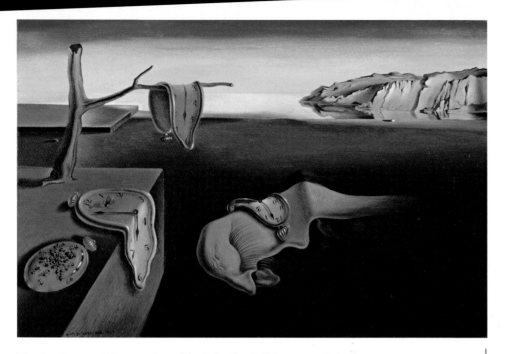

The Persistence of Memory (1921) by Salvador Dalí (1904–1989)
Oil on canvas (24.1 × 33 cm/9.4 × 12.9 in).
Given anonymously. © 2009 Salvador Dalí, Gala-Salvador Dalí Foundation/
Artists Rights Society (ARS), New York.

Salvador DALÍ

From his upturned waxed mustache to the bizarre fashions he wore, Salvador Dalí was anything but ordinary. It's no wonder this Spanish painter came to embrace—and ultimately represent—an unusual artistic movement known as surrealism. Using imaginative, sometimes strange, images, surrealists like Dalí tried to express the workings of the unconscious. They explored dream imagery and recorded memory and fantasy. In this famous work, Dalí **depicts** limp metal watches in an eerie landscape. One watch droops over the sleeping, monster-like head of the painter himself. What do you think the watches represent?

Alexander CALDER

American sculptor Alexander Calder was the son of a sculptor and a painter. Knowing the financial risks of an artist's life, his parents attempted to steer him into a more stable career. Calder earned a degree in mechanical engineering, and worked at several engineering jobs. However, he soon left to apply his skills to his real passion: making art. In 1931, Calder invented the mobile, an abstract sculpture that moves. He would soon become internationally famous for his sheet metal and wire mobiles and stabiles (standing sheet-metal sculptures).

Untitled (1972)
by Alexander Calder (1898–1976)
Private collection. © 2009 Calder Foundation, New York /
Artists Rights Society (ARS), New York.

unconscious *(n.)* the part of the mind that holds thoughts and feelings you did not realize you had

Frida **KAHLO**

"I paint myself because I am the person I know best," said Mexican artist Frida Kahlo, who painted more than 50 bold self-**portraits.** Kahlo began painting at 18, while recovering from a terrible traffic accident. She used art to express the physical pain she endured. After her accident, Kahlo began to use painting to document important events in her very troubled life. In this painting, Kahlo expresses the heartache she experienced after her marriage ended. The artist painted two images of herself, one "loved" and one "**rejected.**" In the "loved" Frida on the right, her heart is whole, but in the "rejected" Frida on the left, her heart is damaged.

The Two Fridas **(1939)**
by Frida Kahlo (1907–1954)
Oil on canvas (170.1 × 170.1 cm/67 × 67 in).
Collection of the Museo de Arte Moderno, Mexico City.

> **Visualize**
> **What visual images would you use to express sadness, happiness, anger, or confusion?**

endured *(v.)* experienced or was subjected to
heartache *(n.)* a strong feeling of great sadness or anxiety

NAVIGATING TEXT

Text Features and Visual Features

🖍 Underline information that tells you when each work of art on pages 12 and 13 was made.

• Circle the information that tells you the size of each work.

• How do the facts in the text features help you better understand the works of art?

_____

_____

_____

_____

_____

_____

_____

COMPREHENSION

Compare and Contrast

The works of Dalí and Kahlo on pages 12 and 13 both contain unusual images. What conclusion does this help you draw about these two artists?

_____

_____

_____

_____

CRITICAL THINKING

Evaluate

Which work of art on these pages do you think is most powerful, and why? Use details about the art in your response.

_____

_____

_____

_____

_____

_____

_____

Georgia O'KEEFFE

When artist Georgia O'Keeffe started spending summers in New Mexico in 1929, she was immediately taken by the state's beautiful landscapes. The shapes and colors of the barren deserts and bare mountains were so inspirational, she once said they made her "feel like flying." O'Keeffe produced many landscape paintings in New Mexico. One of her most famous, shown here, is of Pedernal Peak, a prominent mesa near an area called Ghost Ranch.

***Pedernal* (1941)**
by Georgia O'Keeffe (1887–1986)
Oil on canvas (48.2 × 6.8 cm/19 × 30.25 in).
Gift, The Georgia O'Keeffe Museum.

> **barren** *(adj.)* (of land) too poor to produce any vegetation
> **mesa** *(n.)* a hill with a flat top and steep sides

Jackson POLLOCK

Jackson Pollock was nicknamed "Jack the Dripper" because of his method of "action painting." He would fasten a canvas to the floor and drip or splash paint from all sides, using a stick to spread the paint. Pollock's style caused a critical **uproar,** and his use of painting purely as personal expression spawned a movement known as abstract expressionism, which influenced generations of artists—and still does today.

Convergence (1952)
by Jackson Pollock (1912–1956)
Oil on canvas (237.4 × 393.7 cm/93.4 × 155 in).
Albright-Knox Art Gallery, Buffalo, New York, Gift of Seymour H. Knox, Jr., 1956. © The Pollock-Krasner Foundation/ Artists Rights.

Edward HOPPER

When Edward Hopper was 17, he was greatly influenced by his art teacher, Robert Henri, who claimed that "art could not be separated from life." Henri's teachings inspired Hopper to embrace realism, an art movement that depicted what was "real," or happening in the world. Hopper loved to paint everyday scenes and would peer into shops, homes, and hotels for inspiration. In this painting, he portrays a scene at a city diner late at night. What is the mood of the characters in the painting?

Nighthawks (1942)
by Edward Hopper (1882–1967)
Oil on canvas (84 × 152.4 cm/33.1 × 60 in).
Art Institute of Chicago, Chicago, Illinois.

> **Make Connections**
> **What painting style would you use to make your own masterpiece?**

canvas (*n.*) a strong cloth used as a surface for an oil painting
spawned (*v.*) made a series of things happen

VOCABULARY/WORD ANALYSIS

Noun Suffixes

Review the section on Jackson Pollock, and then complete the following questions:

- Circle the term "abstract expressionism."
- *Expression* is a noun that means "the act of expressing." The suffix *-ism* means "devotion to." Why do you think artists called their movement "abstract expressionism"?

_____

_____

_____

COMPREHENSION

Compare and Contrast

The paintings on pages 14 and 15 are very different from one another. What conclusion can you draw about the artists who created this art?

_____

_____

_____

[21] SMALL GROUPS/INDEPENDENT

COLLABORATE

Debate As a group, choose the painting from pages 10 through 15 that you think shows the most talent and imagination. Debate your selection with a group that has selected a different work.

COMMUNICATE

React and Write Write a letter to one of the artists you have read about so far. Explain what you most admire about his or her work. Include questions you would like to ask this artist.

Andy WARHOL

Whether it was a popular brand of soup or a famous celebrity, Andy Warhol loved to depict well-known, everyday items in his artwork. To create this "pop art," as it was known, Warhol often used a technique called silk screening. This method produced brightly colored prints and allowed Warhol to print multiple copies of each artwork. What do you think Warhol was saying about popular culture by using both celebrities and everyday objects as the subject of his work?

One Hundred Campbell's Soup Cans (1962) **by Andy Warhol (1928–1987)**

Oil on canvas (183 × 132 cm/72 × 52 in). Andy Warhol Foundation.

silk screening (*n.*) making prints by forcing paint or ink onto a surface through a stretched piece of cloth

Puppy (1992)
by Jeff Koons (born 1955)
Stainless steel, soil, geotextile fabric, internal irrigation system, live flowering plants (1,234.4 × 1,234.4 × 650.2 cm/486 × 486 × 256 in). Installations at Arolsen 1992, Sydney 1995–96, Bilbao 1997 (permanent installation), New York Rockefeller Center 2000, private collection (permanent installation) 1992.

Jeff KOONS

The most successful artist during the 1980s was Jeff Koons, whose individual works have sold for over $26 million. Koons belonged to a movement called "neo-pop." Much like pop art in the 1960s, neo-pop incorporated symbols of popular culture. One of Koons's most famous works is a giant topiary called *Puppy*. Created for a temporary **exhibition** in Germany in 1992, this sculpture stood 43 feet high and consisted of stainless steel frames specially designed to hold more than 25 tons of soil and over 70,000 flowering plants. According to Koons, *Puppy* symbolized "love, warmth, and happiness." ∎

> **Question**
> **Why do you think Koons's work has sold for so much money?**

incorporated (v.) included something as part of a group, system, or plan
topiary (n.) trees and bushes cut into the shape of birds, animals, etc.

NAVIGATING TEXT

Text Features and Visual Features

Look at the photographs and the label for Jeff Koons's *Puppy*. What might these features tell you about the type of work the artist likes to create?

_____

_____

_____

_____

_____

_____

VOCABULARY/WORD ANALYSIS

Noun Suffixes

Find the word "artist" in the section on Jeff Koons. Write its base word and suffix below.

_____ + _____
(base word)   (suffix)

An *artist* is a person who makes art. What kind of art do you think a *realist* would make?

_____

_____

_____

COMPREHENSION

Compare and Contrast

Review pages 16 and 17, and complete the following questions:

- <u>Underline</u> details in the text that show how the art of Andy Warhol and Jeff Koons is similar.

- What conclusion can you draw about the way Koons and Warhol felt about popular culture?

_____

_____

_____

_____

_____

WHAT'S the Next BEST THING?
A TASTE of 21ˢᵗ Century Art

The art and artists you've seen so far have each changed the world of art in some way. Here are more artists you should meet—which of them will change the art world next?

Cai GUO-QIANG
Born: 1957 in Quanzhou City, Fujian Province, China
Lives:
New York City, New York

Inopportune: Stage One **(2004)**
Cars, sequenced multichannel light tubes, dimensions variable. Installation view: MASS MoCA, North Adams, Massachusetts. Collection of the artist.

Kara WALKER

Born: 1969 in Stockton, California

Lives: New York City, New York

Detail from Insurrection! (Our Tools Were Rudimentary, Yet We Pressed On) (2002)
Projection, cut paper and adhesive on wall (3.6 × 22.7 m/12 × 74 ½ ft).

Installation view: Solomon R. Guggenheim Museum, New York.

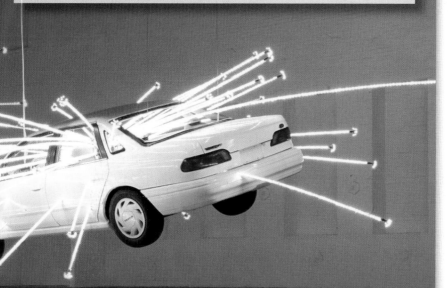

Jessica STOCKHOLDER

Born: 1959 in Seattle, Washington

Lives: New Haven, Connecticut

Sam Ran Over Sand or Sand Ran Over Sam (2004)

Carpet, green waterproof sheet rock, theater lights, yellow and white electrical cords, furniture, lamps, Styrofoam, lumber, freezer, digital projector, acrylic paint, coolers, chicken wire, dimensions variable.

Read and Synthesize

CRITICAL THINKING

Evaluate

Choose one of the works of art on these pages. Which one would be the best choice for a public exhibition in your neighborhood? Explain your answer.

_____

_____

_____

COMPREHENSION

Compare and Contrast

Study the works of art on pages 18 and 19. What is it about each piece that makes it unusual, interesting, or powerful?

_____

_____

Based on this similarity, what conclusion can you draw about the artists who created these works?

_____

_____

_____

NAVIGATING TEXT

Text Features and Visual Features

(Circle) information about the artists on these pages. Box information about the artworks.

- Which artist was not born in the United States? Where was this artist born?

_____

_____

- Which artwork uses some form of paper as a material? What kind of paper is used in the piece?

_____

_____

_____

Louise BOURGEOIS

Born: 1911 in Paris, France

The Nest **(1994)**
Steel (256 × 480 × 401 cm/
101 × 189 × 158 in).
Museum of Modern Art,
San Francisco, California.

Cats and Watermelons **(1992)**
Chromogenic color print (54.6 × 70.5 cm/
21-1/2 × 27-3/4 in).
Courtesy of the artist and Marian
Goodman Gallery, New York.

Gabriel OROZCO

**Born: 1962 in Jalapa,
Mexico**

**Lives: New York
City, Mexico City,
and Paris**

MONUMENTO **(2008)**
Mixed media collage on canvas.
Courtesy of the artist and Sikkema Jenkins & Co.

Mark BRADFORD

**Born: 1961 in Los
Angeles, California**
**Lives: Los Angeles,
California**

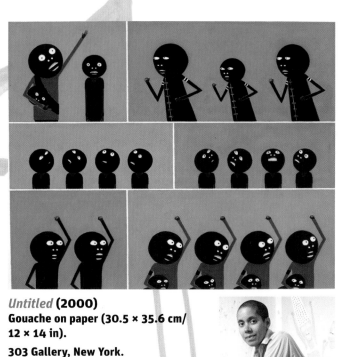

Untitled **(2000)**
Gouache on paper (30.5 × 35.6 cm/
12 × 14 in).
303 Gallery, New York.

Laylah **ALI**

Born: 1968 in Buffalo, New York
Lives: Williamstown, Massachusetts

Bang **(1994)**
Acrylic and collage on canvas
(264 × 305 cm/104 × 120 in).
Collection of Toby Lewis.

Kerry James **MARSHALL**

Born: 1955 in
Birmingham,
Alabama
Lives: Chicago,
Illinois

COMPREHENSION

Compare and Contrast

Choose two artworks on these pages. What is one way in which they are similar?

_____

_____

How are they different?

_____

_____

VOCABULARY/WORD ANALYSIS

Noun Suffixes

Find the word *collection* in the label for *Bang*. Write its base word and suffix below.

_____ + _____
(base word)   (suffix)

What is an art *collection*?

_____

_____

_____

_____

[21] **SMALL GROUPS/INDEPENDENT**

COLLABORATE

Brainstorm Study the works of art on pages 20 and 21. Brainstorm interesting places where each might be displayed.

COMMUNICATE

Respond and Write Write a review of one of the works of art on pages 20 and 21 encouraging people to see or avoid it.

READ ONLINE

expert space
Go to **www.expert21.com/student**
to learn more about Surrealism; Pablo Picasso; Andy Warhol; Frida Kahlo; Edward Hopper; Salvador Dalí.

Profile

Sounds of SuCCESS

Music has inspired and motivated Tourie Escobar, and was a refuge for John Salazar after a family tragedy. Find out how music changed the lives of both these young musicians.

Summarize COMPREHENSION

When you summarize a nonfiction work, you restate its most important ideas and events briefly, in your own words.

Summarizing can help you to identify key points, and to think critically about information by

• analyzing it.

• evaluating it.

▶ **Write two sentences to summarize this passage from "Sounds of Success."**

When Tourie Escobar was in the fourth grade, he took a one-year music class. "I thought I could master the violin," says Tourie. "Then I found out it wasn't easy." When the violin didn't come easily, Tourie lost interest. "I didn't learn anything," he remembers. "At recitals, I'd just fudge."

_____

_____

_____

Do you think Tourie should have stuck with violin class, or given up? Why?

_____

_____

_____

Profiles NAVIGATING TEXT

A profile is a short biography of a person.

Profiles usually

• focus mostly on one aspect of a person's life, and related achievements or events.

• describe how the person became the way he or she is now.

• quote the person and people who know her or him.

▶ **Read this profile. Then underline three actions that led up to Vadim's winning of the Talent Search Award.**

Vadim Conovan, the winner of this year's Talent Search Award, has been training and preparing for this win for a long time. In elementary school, he played three instruments and practiced for hours each day. Focusing on the trumpet in middle school, he studied with a famous teacher and gained experience as a performer. With this award, he has been recognized as one of the most promising young musicians in the country.

Academic Language   VOCABULARY

▶ Rate each word. Then write its meaning and give an example sentence.

Word	Meaning	Example
ACADEMIC WORDS *Use these words in all your subject classes.*		
constructive con·struc·tive (adjective) ① ② ③ ④	useful; helping with improvement	My parents think that playing video games is not a constructive use of my time.
impress im·press (verb) ① ② ③ ④		
CONTENT AREA WORDS *Use these words to talk and write about music and social studies.*		
audition au·di·tion (verb) ① ② ③ ④	to try out for a role or part by giving a performance	
deport de·port (verb) ① ② ③ ④		
forefront fore·front (noun) ① ② ③ ④		
recital re·cit·al (noun) ① ② ③ ④		A number of talented musicians performed at Erin's piano recital.
SELECTION WORDS *Use these words to better understand the selection.*		
excel ex·cel (verb) ① ② ③ ④		
nominate nom·i·nate (verb) ① ② ③ ④		

Rating Scale   ① I don't know the word.   ② I've seen it or heard it.   ③ I know its meaning.   ④ I know it and use it.

Adjective Suffixes: *-al, -ful*   WORD ANALYSIS

An adjective suffix **is a word part added to the end of a base word that turns the base word into an adjective.**

Two common adjective suffixes are *-al* and *-ful*.

  -al means "of; relating to; characterized by."

A *national* problem relates to a nation.

  -ful means "full of; characterized by."

A *cheerful* person is full of cheer.

▶ **Add** *-al* **or** *-ful* **to the words below. Then write the meaning of the new words.**

music_____   _____

color_____   _____

parent_____   _____

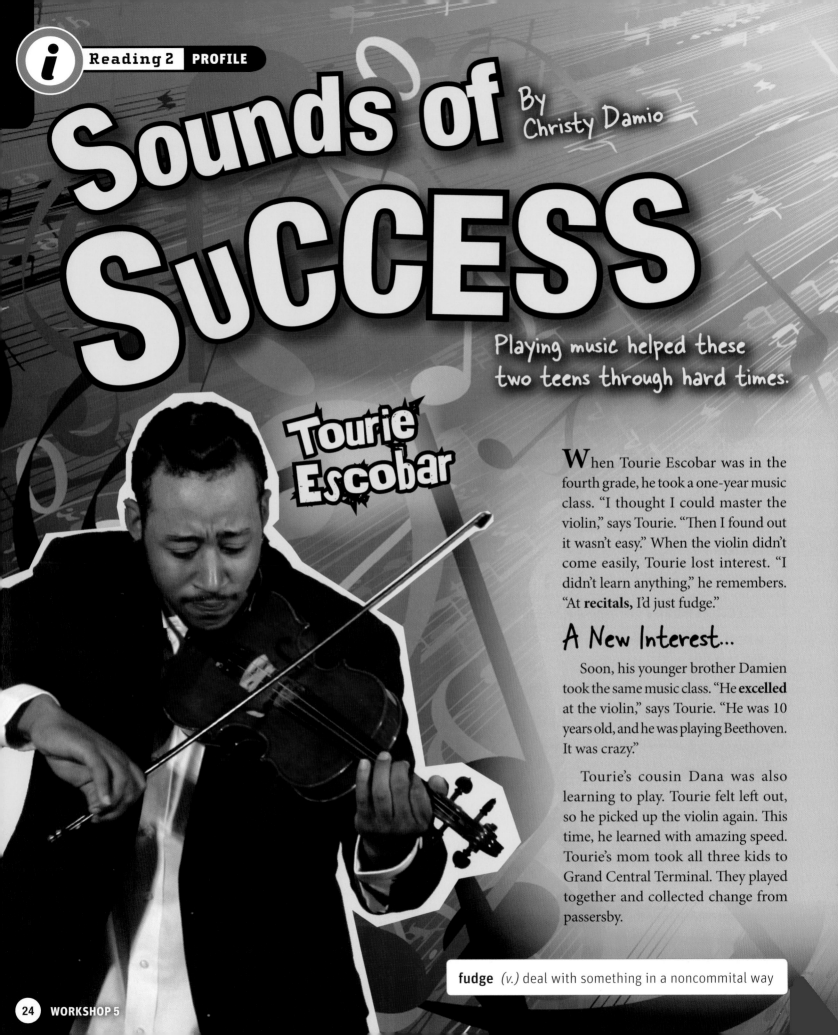

Sounds of SuCCESS

By Christy Damio

Playing music helped these two teens through hard times.

Tourie Escobar

When Tourie Escobar was in the fourth grade, he took a one-year music class. "I thought I could master the violin," says Tourie. "Then I found out it wasn't easy." When the violin didn't come easily, Tourie lost interest. "I didn't learn anything," he remembers. "At **recitals,** I'd just fudge."

A New Interest...

Soon, his younger brother Damien took the same music class. "He **excelled** at the violin," says Tourie. "He was 10 years old, and he was playing Beethoven. It was crazy."

Tourie's cousin Dana was also learning to play. Tourie felt left out, so he picked up the violin again. This time, he learned with amazing speed. Tourie's mom took all three kids to Grand Central Terminal. They played together and collected change from passersby.

---

fudge (v.) deal with something in a noncommittal way

After a year, Tourie **auditioned** for the famous Juilliard School of Music. He couldn't read music, but the teachers were **impressed** with his natural talent. He was accepted.

Tourie attended Juilliard every Saturday, where he learned to read music. After a year, he went back to teaching himself.

Acting Up...

Around age 14, Tourie started playing in New York's subway system. On a good day, Tourie could earn hundreds of dollars in just a few hours. When he realized he was already earning money, Tourie dropped out of school. "I ran with the wrong crowds and got into trouble," he says.

Then Tourie got into a fight and was almost killed. "I thought about the consequences of what I was doing," he says. "So I got together with my brother and talked. We decided it was time to do something **constructive**."

The Birth of a Band...

Before that, the brothers had played separately on the subway. When they started playing together, people loved them even more. Tourie and Damien called themselves Nuttin But Stringz. They played rock, hip-hop, and jazz—all on the violin!

"We played at a private event last year," says Tourie. "I had four days to learn this really fast song. I had people depending on me—the client, my manager, and my brother. I practiced and practiced. In four days, I knew the piece by heart. I felt like I could do anything after that."

A Career to be Proud Of...

Today, Tourie has his GED and a great career. What is he most proud of? "Finishing something," he says. "I didn't even see school through, so I think sticking with the violin is my biggest accomplishment."

Nuttin But Stringz has come a long way. They've played at the White House and on TV. Tourie's favorite moment took place at New York City's famous Carnegie Hall. People come from around the world to hear classical musicians there. "We weren't dressed in the standard suits," says Tourie. "I had on a T-shirt. We performed like rock stars. People got up and started moving!"

Tourie's next big goal is to win a Grammy award. "If we got **nominated**, I'd feel like we finally pushed classical music to the **forefront**," he says. The brothers' hard work has already earned them a place in history.

Damien and Tourie Escobar performing in the White House.

---

classical musicians (*n.*) musicians who play operas and symphonies
standard (*adj.*) accepted as normal or usual

NAVIGATING TEXT

Profiles

 Review "A New Interest" on pages 24 and 25.

- Underline three events that show Tourie's development as a musician.
- What does "A New Interest" tell you about Tourie's musical ability?

_____

_____

COMPREHENSION

Summarize

Summarize "The Birth of a Band" on page 25.

_____

_____

_____

_____

_____

_____

How much did music play a role in the way Tourie turned his life around?

_____

_____

_____

_____

CRITICAL THINKING

Evaluate

Tourie says that "sticking with the violin" is his "biggest accomplishment." Do you agree? Support your response with reasons.

_____

_____

_____

_____

John Salazar can be shy. But when he steps onstage, his shyness disappears. "When I sing, I feel like I could do anything," says John, 17. Looking at this happy, confident teen, it's hard to believe all his success came after the toughest year of his life.

A Hard Year...

When John was 12, his older brother Steve died of cancer. John remembers the night it happened. "We waited in the hospital," he says. "My mom finally told us that he wasn't going to come out of his coma." Soon after, John's dad was **deported** to Mexico. John's mom had to raise four kids alone.

John's mom knew that losing a loved one could lead to depression. She worried that her kids would turn to drugs. To keep them busy, she signed them up to play in a mariachi group at their church. Mariachi is a type of traditional Mexican music. But John was a fan of pop music. "We argued with her," remembers John. "We said, 'No, it's for losers.' She said, 'Too bad.'"

Make Inferences
Why was John's mother looking for things to keep her kids occupied?

A New Talent...

On his first day in the group, John picked up a guitar. "I just totally fell in love with it," he says. "I loved the music."

Playing mariachi music came naturally to John. It felt great to learn something so easily. When John came home from his first practice, he said, "Thank you, Mom, for making me do this."

Soon John learned to play the guitarrón. A guitarrón is a stringed instrument with a humpback. "Right away, I knew I liked it even better than guitar," John remembers. "I knew it was my instrument, and it has been ever since."

John Salazar

A Rich Tradition...

John loves mariachi music because it's part of his heritage. "I was born in the United States, but I'm Mexican," he says. "When I play the songs, I can feel them in me. When you ask anyone what real Mexican music is, they'll say mariachi."

At age 14, John entered Pueblo High School. He got into its advanced mariachi group, Mariachi Aztlán. The group plays at nearby events and travels to competitions. "It's how we show our pride for our tradition and our school," says John.

The group plays each May at the Tucson International Mariachi Conference. The conference includes a show by students, a big concert in which famous musicians play, and a party at a nearby park. "I get to meet famous mariachi players," John says.

"They're really cool people. They love to see us kids keeping up the Mexican tradition."

A Bright Future...

John is a member of Sonidos de Mexico, a professional mariachi group. He plays with the group five times a month. "I'm getting paid for something I love to do," he says. "A lot of people have jobs that they hate. With this job, I get to celebrate my heritage."

John hopes to play in a famous group someday. He also wants to get a college degree in music.

When John looks back on his first day playing music, he can't believe he didn't want to do it. Mariachi music has shaped his life, and he's grateful for it. "When you do what you love and are good at, it'll make you happy," he says. ■

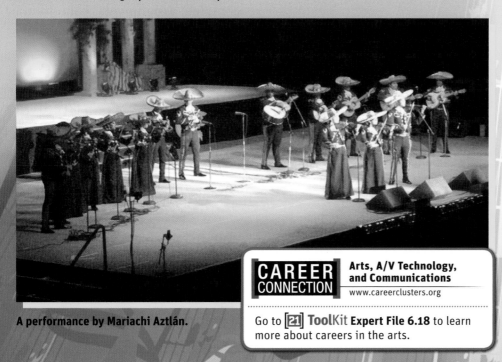

A performance by Mariachi Aztlán.

CAREER CONNECTION

Arts, A/V Technology, and Communications
www.careerclusters.org

Go to **21 ToolKit Expert File 6.18** to learn more about careers in the arts.

advanced *(adj.)* ahead in development
conference *(n.)* a large, formal meeting

VOCABULARY/WORD ANALYSIS

Adjective Suffixes

The word *tradition* means "a custom, idea, or belief that is handed down from one generation to the next." What does *traditional* mean?

_____

Why do you think John first thought that mariachi, a type of traditional Mexican music, was "for losers"?

_____

_____

_____

_____

COMPREHENSION

Summarize

Write one sentence summarizing the last paragraph of the article.

_____

_____

_____

21 SMALL GROUPS/INDEPENDENT

COLLABORATE

 Examine Perspectives Take turns role-playing Tourie or John at a press conference. Answer questions from the rest of the group about your musical career.

COMMUNICATE

Respond and Write Write a paragraph comparing what Tourie and John gained from devoting themselves to music.

W

READ ONLINE

 expert space
Go to **www.expert21.com/ student** to learn more about Stringed Instruments; Grand Central Terminal; Violin; Guitar.

A young photojournalist proves he has what it takes to succeed.

Behind the Lens

Jacob Foko took these photos in Cameroon in 1999. The photos are outtakes from his show, "Cameroon's 100 Faces of Poverty." They show "children of the street" who have no parents and no homes.

"Do not deny your help to others," young Jacob Foko's mother advised him. In Cameroon, the central African country where Foko grew up, those words have special meaning.

Foko, whose father was king of the Baleng tribe in western Cameroon, took his mother's words to heart. Today, he is a photojournalist and the founder of the Global Humanitarian Photojournalists, Inc. (GHP), a non-profit organization based in Santa Barbara, California. The group is dedicated to raising awareness of social injustice. If every king's son became a humanitarian, Foko believes, the world would be a better place.

Jacob first became interested in photography as a high school student in Cameroon. What began as a hobby quickly evolved into a source of income. Bolstered by his early success, Jacob began pursuing photography as a career path, eventually earning the unofficial title of Cameroon's first photojournalist.

As he traveled around Cameroon to complete assignments, Foko found himself welcoming the "opportunity to meet people and see their living conditions, and to develop my sense as a storyteller. I decided to create the Cameroon Association of Humanitarian Photojournalists. [We] focused on telling a different kind of story—a story so commonplace, it was often overlooked."

Foko began to use his camera to capture images of poverty, sacrifice, pain, disease, starvation and oppression. In December 1999, at age 28, he organized a national exhibition titled "Cameroon's 100 Faces of Poverty."

photojournalist (n.) reporter who tells news events through photos

humanitarian (adj.) concerned with improving bad living conditions and preventing unfair treatment of people

These children often have no place to sleep so they make beds using branches.

The Cameroon government did not appreciate Foko's work. "Unfortunately, poverty is not an issue my government wishes to publicly broadcast," Foko says. "It seems the government at the time did not share my vision."

Government agents seized all the photos in Foko's exhibit. "Under despotism, as it was and is in Cameroon, there's no freedom," Foko says. "Freedom of speech is very limited or simply ignored. The government still does not understand the importance of humanitarian photojournalism."

The unwanted government attention did not stop Foko from continuing to cover acts of brutality against political protesters. His work caught the eye of the U.S. Ambassador to Cameroon, who in 2002 invited Foko to give a talk about the challenges of being a photojournalist in Cameroon.

In 2003, the Global Health Council invited Foko to participate in an awards ceremony in the United States. Once in the U.S., Foko decided to stay.

"Due to the growing conflict with the authorities in my country regarding my photographic work, I decided to delay my return [to Cameroon] out of fear for my well-being," he admits. "I have become a permanent resident of the United States and am very happy and grateful to be under the special protection of the U.S. government."

In the U.S., Foko faced just one other obstacle: he spoke virtually no English. "I remember one of my friends telling me that it would be impossible for me to work as a photojournalist in the U.S. because of my poor English.

"I replied, 'Do not deny yourself something before you even take the first step.'" Foko stepped over the barrier by taking English classes, then went to college to study photojournalism.

"My government was not the first and will not be the last to censor and suppress information. Photography is so important to me because it allows me to show the truth of everyday life, however beautiful or ugly it may be." ∎

despotism *(n.)* leadership that uses power in a cruel and unfair way

Read and Synthesize

COMPREHENSION

Compare and Contrast

Review page 28 to help you complete the following:

- Draw a box around the issues Jacob captured with his camera.
- Explain how the government of Cameroon viewed Jacob's work differently than he did.

_____

_____

_____

_____

- What conclusion about the Cameroon government can you draw from this comparison?

_____

_____

_____

NAVIGATING TEXT

Profiles

Review pages 28 and 29. Circle three quotes that give information about how and why Jacob became a photographer.

- What people and experiences do you feel were most important in leading Jacob to this career?

_____

_____

_____

_____

_____

_____

READ ONLINE

 expert space
Go to **www.expert21.com/student** to learn more about Photojournalism; Cameroon.

Think Across Texts

Organize and Synthesize

1. Complete this chart using information from all three selections you have read so far.

What are some of the reasons people become artists? Respond to this question using examples from the selections in "The Impact of Art."	
"Ten Artists Who Changed the World"	
"Sounds of Success"	
"Behind the Lens"	

Compare and Evaluate

2. What is the main message in each selection you have read so far?

"Ten Artists Who Changed the World": _____

_____

_____

"Sounds of Success": _____

_____

_____

"Behind the Lens": _____

_____

_____

3. Which of the three selections did you find most inspiring? Give specific reasons for your choice.

_____

_____

4. Young artists often seek advice from older, more established artists. What advice might each of these artists give to a young artist?

Pablo Picasso: _____

_____

Salvador Dalí: _____

_____

Frida Kahlo: _____

_____

Discuss and Write

5. With a partner, discuss how the three readings in "The Impact of Art" helped you understand how art affects people. Take notes as you talk. Then use your notes to write a response to the question *How can art change lives?*

Apply Word Knowledge

Word Lab

1. **Check them.** Of which might an artist create a **portrait**? Check all correct answers.

- ❏ a car
- ❏ a king
- ❏ a woman
- ❏ a loaf of bread

2. **Complete it.** Complete these sentences with the following words: **audition, forefront, recital, nominate.**

- Tim's performance put him at the _____ of the jazz scene.

- Duane said, "I _____ Leticia for class president."

- I will _____ for the music _____.

3. **Think about it.** Give an example of each.

- when you might hear an **uproar**

  _____

- what might be featured at an **exhibition**

  _____

- a subject at which you **excel**

  _____

4. **Decide.** You want to make a piece of art to **impress** others with something you know about life. Which kind of art would you choose to make: a painting, a film, a poem, or a song . . . and why?

_____

_____

5. **Describe it.** What might be the **impact** of this event?

The star soccer player misses a game.

_____

_____

_____

_____

Word Analysis

6. **Noun Suffixes** Add a suffix from the box to each word below. The new word should have the same meaning as the phrase next to the word. One has been done for you.

-ion	-ence
"act of"	"state of"

concentrate <u>concentration</u> "act of concentrating"

nominate _____ "act of nominating"

depend _____ "state of being dependent on"

7. **Adjective Suffixes** Add a suffix from the box to each word below. The new word should have the same meaning as the phrase next to the word.

-al	-ous or -ious	-ative
"relating to"	"state or quality of"	"inclined to"

medicine _____ "having to do with medicine"

ambition _____ "state of having ambition"

demonstrate _____ "inclined to show"

Set and Use Criteria

You can read—and write—reviews online or in magazines or newspapers. If you write a review, include criteria so readers can understand the reasoning behind your opinions. Criteria are standards you use to judge something.

Criteria for a Film Review

▶ See how this writer used criteria in a movie review.

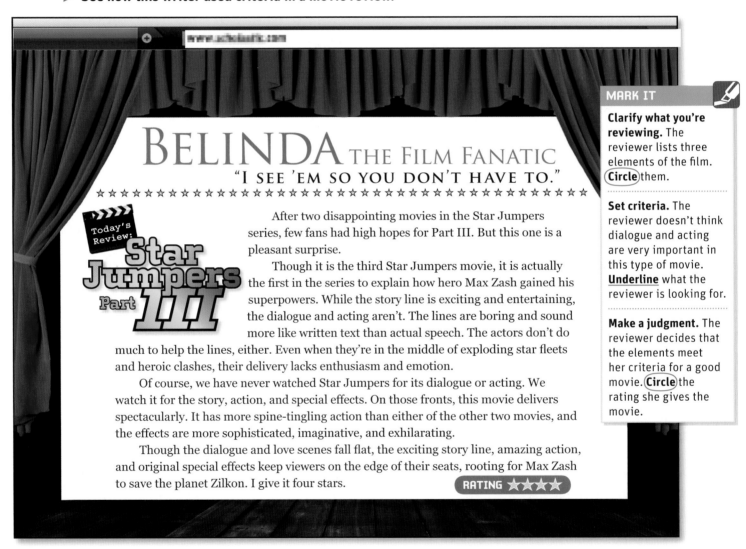

BELINDA THE FILM FANATIC

"I SEE 'EM SO YOU DON'T HAVE TO."

Today's Review: Star Jumpers Part III

After two disappointing movies in the Star Jumpers series, few fans had high hopes for Part III. But this one is a pleasant surprise.

Though it is the third Star Jumpers movie, it is actually the first in the series to explain how hero Max Zash gained his superpowers. While the story line is exciting and entertaining, the dialogue and acting aren't. The lines are boring and sound more like written text than actual speech. The actors don't do much to help the lines, either. Even when they're in the middle of exploding star fleets and heroic clashes, their delivery lacks enthusiasm and emotion.

Of course, we have never watched Star Jumpers for its dialogue or acting. We watch it for the story, action, and special effects. On those fronts, this movie delivers spectacularly. It has more spine-tingling action than either of the other two movies, and the effects are more sophisticated, imaginative, and exhilarating.

Though the dialogue and love scenes fall flat, the exciting story line, amazing action, and original special effects keep viewers on the edge of their seats, rooting for Max Zash to save the planet Zilkon. I give it four stars.

RATING ★★★★

MARK IT

Clarify what you're reviewing. The reviewer lists three elements of the film. Circle them.

Set criteria. The reviewer doesn't think dialogue and acting are very important in this type of movie. <u>Underline</u> what the reviewer is looking for.

Make a judgment. The reviewer decides that the elements meet her criteria for a good movie. Circle the rating she gives the movie.

Here's How ▶ Follow these steps to set and use criteria to review an artistic work:

Step 1 Clarify what you are reviewing. What elements of the work are you evaluating?

Step 2 Set the criteria. Think about the qualities that make each element good or bad. Also decide which criteria are most important and must be met for the work to get a good review.

Step 3 Compare the elements with the criteria. Judge each element against the criteria you set.

Step 4 Make a judgment. Based on your comparison, decide whether enough of the criteria are met to make the work good, or worth recommending.

Apply: Set and Use Criteria

▶ **Read the situation below and follow the steps to create criteria.**

The Situation: You're part of an online music community called Sound Advice. You just bought the latest CD of a hot new band called Seven Roads to Doom. Follow the steps to write an online review of the band's album, *Root Canal*. You can imagine that the music sounds however you like—great or horrible. You can also use this activity to write about a real CD that you have listened to recently.

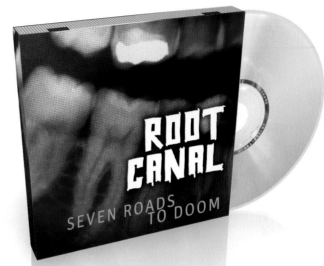

1. **Clarify what you are reviewing.** What elements of the work are you evaluating? Write each element in the first column of the chart.

2. **Set criteria.** What are the ideal characteristics for each element? Write your criteria next to each element in the chart. Circle the criteria that are most important and must be met for you to recommend the work.

3. **Compare the elements and criteria.** How does each element match up against the criteria you set? Write your answers in the chart.

Elements	Criteria	Do the Elements Meet the Criteria?

4. **Make a judgment.** Use the information from your chart to write a brief review stating why you would or would not recommend this work. Give it a star rating (1 to 5) or a thumbs-up or thumbs-down.

_____

_____

_____

Ask a partner to read your review and tell you whether your judgment seemed valid. Based on feedback, revise your criteria if necessary to make your review stronger.

Short Story

Zebra

Can art help heal a person who has been badly injured?
In this story, you will meet a boy who learns the answer
to that question.

QuickWrite

What activity makes you feel calm, peaceful, and engaged? Write a paragraph describing this activity and why you like it.

Character Traits LITERARY ANALYSIS

Like real people, story characters have **traits**, or qualities. Authors reveal a character's traits by describing the character and by describing the character's interactions with others. You can learn about a character's traits by noting what the character says and does and the way others in the story act toward the character.

▶ **What information about character traits do you get from each of these sentences?**

• The man kept looking behind him while walking through the park.

_____

• Sophia refused to apologize for losing his CD, but Anthony invited her to his party anyway.

_____

• Mara scowled and pushed away the dinner her father had cooked for her.

_____

Summarize COMPREHENSION

A summary is a brief restating of the main ideas, steps, or events in a piece of writing.

When you summarize a work of fiction, use your own words and include only the most important characters, ideas, events, and details.

▶ **Write a one- or two-sentence summary of this passage based on part of the story "Zebra."**

As Zebra ran down the steep hill on Franklin Avenue, he felt so light it was as if he had no legs at all, and was flying. He'd start down the hill, feeling as he ran that all it would take would be one little push-off, and he'd be flying. He'd become the soaring bird he had once seen in a movie about Alaska, flying over a river. He'd cruise through the air high over the river, with the wind streaming over him.

Summary:

_____

_____

_____

Academic Language VOCABULARY

▶ Rate each word. Then write its meaning and give an example sentence.

Word	Meaning	Example
EXPERT WORDS *Use these words to write and talk about the workshop topic.*		
sculpture *sculp•ture (noun)* ① ② ③ ④	a three-dimensional work of art made by carving, modeling, or constructing	The artist made a sculpture of a ballet dancer.
CONTENT AREA WORDS *Use these words to talk and write about art.*		
contour *con•tour (noun)* ① ② ③ ④		
intricate *in•tri•cate (adjective)* ① ② ③ ④		
sensation *sen•sa•tion (noun)* ① ② ③ ④		Eric had the strange sensation that the people in the portraits were looking directly at him.
SELECTION WORDS *Use these words to better understand the selection.*		
encrusted *en•crust•ed (verb)* ① ② ③ ④	covered with a hard coating	
laden *lad•en (adjective)* ① ② ③ ④		
rummage *rum•mage (verb)* ① ② ③ ④		
wince *wince (verb)* ① ② ③ ④		

Rating Scale   ① I don't know the word.   ② I've seen it or heard it.   ③ I know its meaning.   ④ I know it and use it.

Roots WORD ANALYSIS

A root is a part of an English word that comes from another language, such as Latin or Greek. The root *manu* comes from the Latin word *manus*, which means "hand." The suffix *-al* means "relating to" or "having to do with." So, *manual* means "relating to hands" or "done by hand."

Circle activities that are usually done manually.

hitting a nail with a hammer   telling someone a funny story   assembling a jigsaw puzzle

Circle another word that has the root *manu*.

mandolin   manufacture   mansion

by Chaim Potok

Zebra

Running meant everything to Zebra. But then he discovered that art can take you places, too.

His name was Adam Martin Zebrin, but everyone in his neighborhood knew him as Zebra.

He couldn't remember when he began to be called by that name. Perhaps they started to call him Zebra when he first began running. Or maybe he began running when they started to call him Zebra.

He loved the name and he loved to run.

When he was very young, his parents took him to a zoo, where he saw zebras for the first time. They were odd-looking creatures, like stubby horses, short-legged, thick-necked, with dark and white stripes.

Then one day he went with his parents to a movie about Africa, and he saw zebras, hundreds of them, thundering across a grassy plain, dust rising in boiling brown clouds.

Was he already running before he saw that movie, or did he begin to run afterward? No one seemed able to remember.

He would go running through the neighborhood for the sheer joy of feeling the wind on his face. People said that when he ran he arched his head up and back, and his face kind of flattened out. One of his teachers told him it was clever to run that way, his balance was better. But the truth was he ran that way, his head thrown back, because he loved to feel the wind rushing across his neck.

Each time, after only a few minutes of running, his legs would begin to feel wondrously light. He would run past the school and the homes on the street beyond the church. All the neighbors knew him and would wave and call out, "Go, Zebra!" And sometimes one or two of their dogs would run with him awhile, barking.

He would imagine himself a zebra on the African plain. Running.

There was a hill on Franklin Avenue, a steep hill. By the time he reached that hill, he would feel his legs so light it was as if he had no legs at all and was flying. He would begin to descend the hill, certain as he ran that he needed only to give himself the slightest push and off he would go, and instead of a zebra he would become the bird he had once seen in a movie about Alaska, he would swiftly change into an eagle, soaring higher and higher, as light as the gentlest breeze, the cool wind caressing his arms and legs and neck.

Then, a year ago, racing down Franklin Avenue, he had given himself that push and had begun to turn into an eagle, when a huge rushing shadow appeared in his line of vision and crashed into him and plunged him into a darkness from which he emerged very, very slowly. . . .

"Never, never, *never* run down that hill so fast that you can't stop at the corner," his mother had warned him again and again.

His schoolmates and friends kept calling him Zebra even after they all knew that the doctors had told him he would never be able to run like that again.

His leg would heal in time, the doctors said, and perhaps in a year or so the brace would come off. But they were not at all certain about his hand. From time to time his injured hand, which he still wore in a sling, would begin to hurt. The doctors said they could find no cause for the pain.

One morning, during Mr. Morgan's geography class, Zebra's hand began to hurt badly. He sat staring out the window at the sky. Mr. Morgan, a stiff-mannered person in his early fifties, given to smart suits and dapper bow ties, called on him to respond to a question. Zebra stumbled about in vain for the answer. Mr. Morgan told him to pay attention to the geography *inside* the classroom and not to the geography outside.

"In this class, young man, you will concentrate your attention upon the earth, not upon the sky," Mr. Morgan said.

Later, in the schoolyard during the midmorning recess, Zebra stood near the tall fence, looking out at the street and listening to the noises behind him.

His schoolmates were racing about, playing exuberantly, shouting and laughing with full voices. Their joyous sounds went ringing through the quiet street.

Most times Zebra would stand alongside the basketball court or behind the wire screen at home plate and watch the games. That day, because his hand hurt so badly, he stood alone behind the chain-link fence of the school yard.

That's how he happened to see the man. And that's how the man happened to see him.

One minute the side street on which the school stood was strangely empty, without people or traffic, without even any of the dogs that often roamed about the neighborhood—vacant and silent, as if it were already in the full heat of summer. The red-brick ranch house that belonged to Mr. Morgan, and the white clapboard two-story house in which Mrs. English lived, and the other homes on the street, with their columned front porches and their back patios, and the tall oaks—all stood curiously still in the warm golden light of the mid-morning sun.

Then a man emerged from wide and busy Franklin Avenue at the far end of the street.

> . . . he asked, in a quiet voice, "What happened to you, Adam?

Zebra saw the man stop at the corner and stand looking at a public trash can. He watched as the man poked his hand into the can and fished about but seemed to find nothing he wanted. He withdrew the hand and, raising it to shield his eyes from the sunlight, glanced at the street sign on the lamppost.

He started to walk up the street in the direction of the school.

He was tall and wiry, and looked to be about forty years old. In his right hand he carried a bulging brown plastic bag. He wore a khaki army jacket, a blue denim shirt, blue jeans, and brown cowboy boots. His gaunt face and muscular neck were reddened by exposure to the sun. Long brown hair spilled out below his dark-blue farmer's cap. On the front of the cap, in large orange letters, were the words LAND ROVER.

He walked with his eyes on the sidewalk and the curb, as if looking for something, and he went right past Zebra without noticing him.

Make Inferences
What can you infer about this man from the description of his appearance?

Zebra's hand hurt very much. He was about to turn away when he saw the man stop and look around and peer up at the red-brick wall of the school. The man set down the bag and took off his cap and stuffed it into a pocket of his jacket. From one of his jeans pockets he removed a handkerchief, with which he then wiped his face. He shoved the handkerchief back into the pocket and put the cap back on his head.

Then he turned and saw Zebra.

He picked up the bag and started down the street to where Zebra was standing. When the man was about ten feet away, Zebra noticed that the left sleeve of his jacket was empty.

The man came up to Zebra and said in a low, friendly, shy voice, "Hello."

> **vacant** *(adj.)* empty
> **wiry** *(adj.)* thin and sinewy

Zebra answered with a cautious "Hello," trying not to look at the empty sleeve, which had been tucked into the man's jacket pocket.

The man asked, with a distinct Southern accent, "What's your name, son?"

Zebra said, "Adam."

"What kind of school is this here school, Adam?"

"It's a good school," Zebra answered.

"How long before you-all begin your summer vacation?"

"Three days," Zebra said.

"Anything special happen here during the summer?"

"During the summer? Nothing goes on here. There are no classes."

"What do you-all do during the summer?"

"Some of us go to camp. Some of us hang around. We find things to do."

Zebra's hand had begun to tingle and throb. Why was the man asking all those questions? Zebra thought maybe he shouldn't be talking to him at all. He seemed vaguely menacing in that army jacket, the dark-blue cap with the words LAND ROVER on it in orange letters, and the empty sleeve. Yet there was kindness in his gray eyes and ruddy features.

The man gazed past Zebra at the students playing in the yard. "Adam, do you think your school would be interested in having someone teach an art class during the summer?"

That took Zebra by surprise. "An *art* class?"

"Drawing, sculpting, things like that."

Zebra was trying *very hard* not to look at the man's empty sleeve. "I don't know. . . ."

"Where's the school office, Adam?"

"On Washington Avenue. Go to the end of the street and turn right."

"Thanks," the man said. He hesitated a moment. Then he asked, in a quiet voice, "What happened to you, Adam?"

"A car hit me," Zebra said. "It was my fault."

The man seemed to **wince.**

For a flash of a second, Zebra thought to ask the man what had happened to *him*. The words were on his tongue. But he kept himself from saying anything.

vaguely *(adv.)* slightly

COMPREHENSION

Summarize

Review page 39. Put a **star** ★ next to two important questions the man asks Zebra.

• <u>Underline</u> Zebra's responses to these questions. Then summarize Zebra and the man's conversation.

_____

_____

_____

_____

_____

_____

_____

LITERARY ANALYSIS

Character Traits

Review the text on the top of page 39. What character traits does Zebra show in his interaction with the man?

_____

_____

_____

_____

_____

_____

VOCABULARY/WORD ANALYSIS

Roots

Circle the word *sculpting* near the end of page 39. It comes from the Latin word *sculpere*, meaning "to carve."

• How does the meaning of the word *sculpere* help explain the meaning of *sculpting*?

_____

_____

_____

_____

_____

_____

The man started back up the street, carrying the brown plastic bag.

Zebra suddenly called, "Hey, mister."

The man stopped and turned. "My name is John Wilson," he said softly.

"Mr. Wilson, when you go into the school office, you'll see signs on two doors. One says 'Dr. Winter,' and the other says 'Mrs. English.' Ask for Mrs. English."

Dr. Winter, the principal, was a disciplinarian and a grump. Mrs. English, the assistant principal, was generous and kind. Dr. Winter would probably tell the man to call his secretary for an appointment. Mrs. English might invite him into her office and offer him a cup of coffee and listen to what he had to say.

The man hesitated, looking at Zebra.

"Appreciate the advice," he said.

Zebra watched him walk to the corner.

Under the lamppost was a trash can. Zebra saw the man set down the plastic bag and stick his hand into the can and haul out a battered umbrella.

The man tried to open the umbrella, but its metal ribs were broken. The black fabric dangled flat and limp from the pole. He put the umbrella into the plastic bag and headed for the entrance to the school.

A moment later, Zebra heard the whistle that signaled the end of recess. He followed his classmates at a distance, careful to avoid anyone's bumping against his hand.

He sat through his algebra class, copying the problems on the blackboard while holding down his notebook with his left elbow. The sling chafed his neck and felt warm and clumsy on his bare arm. There were sharp pains now in the two curled fingers of his hand.

Right after the class he went downstairs to the office of Mrs. Walsh, a cheerful, gray-haired woman in a white nurse's uniform.

She said, "I'm sorry I can't do very much for you, Adam, except give you two Tylenols."

He swallowed the Tylenols down with water.

On his way back up to the second floor, he saw the man with the dark-blue cap emerge from the school office with Mrs. English. He stopped on the stairs and watched as the man and Mrs. English stood talking together. Mrs. English nodded and smiled and shook the man's hand.

The man walked down the corridor, carrying the plastic bag, and left the school building.

> **battered** *(adj.)* old and in bad condition
> **chafed** *(v.)* made sore from rubbing

Zebra went slowly to his next class.

The class was taught by Mrs. English, who came hurrying into the room some minutes after the bell had rung.

"I apologize for being late," she said, sounding a little out of breath. "There was an important matter I had to attend to."

Mrs. English was a tall, gracious woman in her forties. It was common knowledge that early in her life she had been a journalist on a Chicago newspaper and had written short stories, which she could not get published. Soon after her marriage to a doctor, she had become a teacher.

This was the only class Mrs. English taught.

Ten students from the upper school—seventh and eighth grades—were chosen every year for this class. They met for an hour three times a week and told one another stories. Each story would be discussed and analyzed by Mrs. English and the class.

Mrs. English called it a class in the *imagination*.

Zebra was grateful he did not have to take notes in this class. He had only to listen to the stories.

That day, Andrea, the freckle-faced, redheaded girl with very thick glasses who sat next to Zebra, told about a woman scientist who discovered a method of healing trees that had been blasted apart by lightning.

Mark, who had something wrong with his upper lip, told in his quavery voice about a selfish space cadet who stepped into a time machine and met his future self, who turned out to be a hateful person, and how the cadet then returned to the present and changed himself.

Kevin talked in blurred, high-pitched tones and often related parts of his stories with his hands. Mrs. English would quietly repeat many of his sentences. Today he told about an explorer who set out on a journey through a valley filled with yellow stones and surrounded by red mountains, where he encountered an army of green shadows that had been at war for hundreds of years with an army of purple shadows. The explorer showed them how to make peace.

When it was Zebra's turn, he told a story about a bird that one day crashed against a closed windowpane and broke a wing. A boy tried to heal the wing but couldn't. The bird died, and the boy buried it under a tree on his lawn.

> **Make Inferences**
> **What do you think Adam's story reveals about himself?**

When he had finished, there was silence. Everyone in the class was looking at him.

"You always tell such sad stories," Andrea said.

> **quavery** *(adj.)* in a shaking manner

COMPREHENSION

Summarize
Review page 40. Summarize the events of Zebra's day between recess and the start of English class.

_____

_____

_____

_____

CRITICAL THINKING

Evaluate
• What do the students' stories in Mrs. English's class tell you about them?

_____

_____

_____

• What does Zebra's story tell you about his state of mind?

_____

_____

_____

_____

LITERARY ANALYSIS

Character Traits
Look back at Andrea's comment to Zebra at the bottom of page 41. What does Andrea's comment to Zebra reveal about her character? Explain your response.

_____

_____

_____

_____

_____

The bell rang. Mrs. English dismissed the class.

In the hallway, Andrea said to Zebra, "You know, you are a very gloomy life form."

"Andrea, get off my case," Zebra said.

He went out to the schoolyard for the mid afternoon recess. On the other side of the chain-link fence was the man in the dark-blue cap.

Zebra went over to him.

"Hello again, Adam," the man said. "I've been waiting for you."

"Hello," said Zebra.

"Thanks much for suggesting I talk to Mrs. English."

"You're welcome."

"Adam, you at all interested in art?"

"No."

"You ever try your hand at it?"

"I've made drawings for class. I don't like it."

"Well, just in case you change your mind, I'm giving an art class in your school during the summer."

"I'm going to camp in August," Zebra said.

"There's the big long month of July."

"I don't think so," Zebra said.

"Well, okay, suit yourself. I'd like to give you something, a little thank-you gift."

He reached into an inside pocket and drew out a small pad and a pen. He placed the pad against the fence.

"Adam, you want to help me out a little bit here? Put your fingers through the fence and grab hold of the pad."

Extending the fingers of his right hand, Zebra held the pad to the fence and watched as the man began to work with the pen. He felt the pad move slightly.

> **Predict**
> Do you think Adam will change his mind about the art class?

"I need you to hold it real still," the man said.

He was standing bent over, very close to Zebra. The words LAND ROVER on his cap shone in the afternoon sunlight. As he worked, he glanced often at Zebra. His tongue kept pushing up against the insides of his cheeks, making tiny hills rise and fall on his face. Wrinkles formed **intricate** spidery webs in the skin below his gray eyes. On his smooth forehead, in the blue and purple shadows beneath the peak of his cap, lay glistening beads of sweat. And his hand—how dirty it was, the fingers and palm smudged with black ink and **encrusted** with colors.

Then Zebra glanced down and noticed the plastic bag near the man's feet. It lay partly open. Zebra was able to see a large pink armless doll, a dull metallic object that looked like a dented frying pan, old newspapers, strings of cord, crumpled pieces of red and blue cloth, and the broken umbrella.

"One more minute is all I need," the man said.

He stepped back, looked at the pad, and nodded slowly. He put the pen back into his pocket and tore the top page from the pad. He rolled up the page and pushed it through the fence. Then he took the pad from Zebra.

"See you around, Adam," the man said, picking up the plastic bag.

Zebra unrolled the sheet of paper and saw a line drawing, a perfect image of his face.

He was looking at himself as if in a mirror. His long straight nose and thin lips and sad eyes and gaunt face; his dark hair and smallish ears and the scar on his forehead where he had hurt himself years before while roller skating.

In the lower right-hand corner of the page the man had written: "To ADAM, with thanks. John Wilson."

Zebra raised his eyes from the drawing. The man was walking away.

Zebra called out, "Mr. Wilson, all my friends call me Zebra."

> **extending** *(v.)* stretching out
> **metallic** *(adj.)* made of or containing metal

The man turned, looking surprised.

"From my last name," Adam said. "Zebrin. Adam Martin Zebrin. They call me Zebra."

"Is that right?" the man said, starting back toward the fence. "Well, in that case you want to give me back that piece of paper."

He took the pad and pen from his pocket, placed the page on the pad, and, with Zebra holding the pad to the fence, did something to the page and then handed it back.

"You take real good care of yourself, Zebra," the man said.

He went off toward Franklin Avenue.

Zebra looked at the drawing. The man had crossed out ADAM and over it had drawn an animal with a stubby neck and short legs and a striped body.

A zebra!

Its legs were in full gallop. It seemed as if it would gallop right off the page.

They call me Zebra.

A strong breeze rippled across the drawing, causing it to flutter like a flag in Zebra's hand. He looked out at the street.

The man was walking slowly in the shadows of the tall oaks. Zebra had the odd **sensation** that all the houses on the street had turned toward the man and were watching him as he walked along. How strange that was: the windows and porches and columns and front doors following intently the slow walk of that tall, one-armed man—until he turned into Franklin Avenue and was gone.

The whistle blew, and Zebra went inside. Seated at his desk, he slipped the drawing carefully into one of his notebooks.

From time to time he glanced at it.

Just before the bell signaled the end of the school day, he looked at it again.

Now *that* was strange!

He thought he remembered that the zebra had been drawn directly over his name: the head over the A and the tail over the M. Didn't it seem now to have moved a little beyond A?

---

rippled *(v.)* to move in a way resembling small waves
intently *(adv.)* in a determined manner

COMPREHENSION

Draw Conclusions
Why do you think Zebra tells John Wilson his nickname? Use the questions below to help you.
• What I know about nicknames:

_____

_____

_____

• Conclusion I can draw:

_____

_____

_____

_____

_____

VOCABULARY/WORD ANALYSIS

Roots
Find the word *signaled* near the end of page 43. It comes from the Latin word *signare*, which means "to sign."
• What does the bell signal?

_____

_____

21 SMALL GROUPS/INDEPENDENT

COLLABORATE

Investigate With your group, discuss the things Mr. Wilson might do with the everyday objects he collects from the trash. Present your ideas to the class.

COMMUNICATE

Reflect and Write Adam calls himself Zebra because he loves zebras, and he loves running. If you could take the name of one animal, what would it be? Write a paragraph explaining your choice.

Probably he was running a fever again. He would run mysterious fevers off and on for about three weeks after each operation on his hand. Fevers sometimes did that to him: excited his imagination.

He lived four blocks from the school. The school bus dropped him off at his corner. In his schoolbag he carried his books and the notebook with the drawing.

His mother offered him a snack, but he said he wasn't hungry. Up in his room, he looked again at the drawing and was astonished to discover that the zebra had reached the edge of his name and appeared poised to leap off.

It *had* to be a fever that was causing him to see the zebra that way. And sure enough, when his mother took his temperature, the thermometer registered 102.6 degrees.

She gave him his medicine, but it didn't seem to have much effect, because when he woke at night and switched on his desk light and peered at the drawing, he saw the little zebra galloping across the page, along the **contours** of his face, over the hills and valleys of his eyes and nose and mouth, and he heard the tiny clickings of its hooves as cloudlets of dust rose in its wake.

He knew he was asleep. He knew it was the fever working upon his imagination.

But it was so real.

The little zebra running . . .

When he woke in the morning the fever was gone, and the zebra was quietly in its place over ADAM.

> **Visualize**
> **How do these details about the drawing help you understand what Adam is going through?**

Later, as he entered the school, he noticed a large sign on the bulletin board in the hallway:

SUMMER ART CLASS

The well-known American artist Mr. John Wilson will conduct an art class during the summer for students in 7th and 8th grades. For details, speak to Mrs. English. There will be no tuition fee for this class.

During the morning, between classes, Zebra ran into Mrs. English in the second-floor hallway.

"Mrs. English, about the summer art class . . . is it okay to ask where—um—where Mr. Wilson is from?"

"He is from a small town in Virginia. Are you thinking of signing up for his class?"

"I can't draw," Zebra said.

"Drawing is something you can learn."

"Mrs. English, is it okay to ask how did Mr. Wilson—um—get hurt?"

The school corridors were always crowded between classes. Zebra and Mrs. English formed a little island in the bustling, student-jammed hallway.

"Mr. Wilson was wounded in the war in Vietnam," Mrs. English said. "I would urge you to join his class. You will get to use your imagination."

For the next hour, Zebra sat impatiently through Mr. Morgan's geography class, and afterward he went up to the teacher.

"Mr. Morgan, could I—um—ask where is Vietnam?"

Mr. Morgan smoothed down the jacket of his beige summer suit, touched his bow tie, rolled down a wall map, picked up his pointer, and cleared his throat.

"Vietnam is this long, narrow country in southeast Asia, bordered by China, Laos, and Cambodia. It is a land of valleys in the north, coastal plains in the center, and marshes in the south. There are barren mountains and tropical rain forests. Its chief crops are rice, rubber, fruits, and vegetables. The population numbers close to seventy million people. Between 1962 and 1973, America fought a terrible war there to prevent the south from falling into the hands of the communist north. We lost the war."

"Thank you."

---

registered *(v.)* gave a specific reading	
bustling *(adj.)* very busy	

Roots

Circle the word *imagination* in the middle of column 2 on page 44. It comes from the Latin word *imago*, meaning "image."

• Why does Mrs. English say that students will need their imagination in Mr. Wilson's class?

_____

_____

_____

• Circle two other words that have the root *imago* and have to do with creativity.

imagery   immaculate

immature   imaginary

Analyze

Underline the questions Zebra asks about Mr. Wilson.

• Why do you think Zebra decides to take the summer art class even though he doesn't like to draw?

_____

_____

_____

Character Traits

Review page 45.

• How do Zebra's parents respond when he tells them he wants to take the summer art class?

_____

_____

• What do the responses tell you about each of these characters?

_____

_____

_____

"I am impressed by your suddenly awakened interest in geography, young man, though I must remind you that your class is studying the Mediterranean," said Mr. Morgan.

During the afternoon recess, Zebra was watching a heated basketball game, when he looked across the yard and saw John Wilson walk by, carrying a **laden** plastic bag. Some while later, he came back along the street, empty-handed.

Over supper that evening, Zebra told his parents he was thinking of taking a summer art class offered by the school.

His father said, "Well, I think that's a fine idea."

"Wait a minute. I'm not so sure," his mother said.

"It'll get him off the streets," his father said. "He'll become a Matisse instead of a lawyer like his dad. Right, Adam?"

"Just you be very careful," his mother said to Adam. "Don't do anything that might injure your hand."

"How can drawing hurt his left hand, for heaven's sake?" said his father.

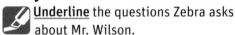

awakened *(adj.)* gave rise to an emotion

That night, Zebra lay in bed looking at his hand. It was a dread and a mystery to him, his own hand. The fingers were all there, but like dead leaves that never fell, the ring and little fingers were rigid and curled, the others barely moved. The doctors said it would take time to bring them back to life. So many broken bones. So many torn muscles and tendons. So many injured nerves. The dark shadow had sprung upon him so suddenly. How stupid, stupid, *stupid* he had been!

He couldn't sleep. He went over to his desk and looked at John Wilson's drawing. The galloping little zebra stood very still over ADAM.

How stupid, stupid, *stupid* he had been!

Early the following afternoon, on the last day of school, Zebra went to Mrs. English's office and signed up for John Wilson's summer art class.

"The class will meet every weekday from ten in the morning until one," said Mrs. English. "Starting Monday."

Zebra noticed the three plastic bags in a corner of the office.

"Mrs. English, is it okay to ask what Mr. Wilson—um—did in Vietnam?"

"He told me he was a helicopter pilot," Mrs. English said. "Oh, I neglected to mention that you are to bring an unlined notebook and a pencil to the class."

"That's all? A notebook and a pencil?"

Mrs. English smiled. "And your imagination."

When Zebra entered the art class the next Monday morning, he found about fifteen students there—including Andrea from his class with Mrs. English.

The walls of the room were bare. Everything had been removed for the summer. Zebra noticed two plastic bags on the floor beneath the blackboard.

He sat down at the desk next to Andrea's.

She wore blue jeans and a yellow summer blouse with blue stripes. Her long red hair was tied behind her head with a dark-blue ribbon. She gazed at Zebra through her thick glasses, leaned over, and said, "Are you going to make gloomy drawings, too?"

Just then John Wilson walked in, carrying a plastic bag, which he put down on the floor next to the two others.

He stood alongside the front desk, wearing a light-blue long-sleeved shirt and jeans. The left shirtsleeve had been folded back and pinned to the shirt. The dark-blue cap with the words LAND ROVER sat jauntily on his head.

"Good morning to you-all," he said with a shy smile. "Mighty glad you're here. We're going to do two things this summer. We're going to make paper into faces and garbage into people. I can see by your expressions that you don't know what I'm talking about, right? Well, I'm about to show you."

He asked everyone to draw the face of someone sitting nearby.

Zebra hesitated, looked around, then made a drawing of Andrea. Andrea carefully drew Zebra.

He showed Andrea his drawing.

"It's awful." She grimaced. "I look like a mouse."

Her drawing of him was good. But was his face really so sad?

John Wilson went from desk to desk, peering intently at the drawings. He paused a long moment over Zebra's drawing. Then he spent more than an hour demonstrating with chalk on the blackboard how they should not be thinking *eyes* or *lips* or *hands* while drawing, but should think only *lines* and *curves* and *shapes*; how they should be looking at where everything was situated in relation to the edge of the paper; and how they should not be looking *directly* at the edges of what they were drawing but at the space *outside* the edges.

---

jauntily *(adv.)* in a lively or cheerful manner
grimaced *(v.)* made an ugly, twisted expression

Zebra stared in wonder at how fast John Wilson's hand raced across the blackboard, and at the empty sleeve rising and falling lightly against the shirt.

"You-all are going to learn how to *see* in a new way," John Wilson said.

They made another drawing of the same face.

"Now I look like a horse," Andrea said. "Are you going to add stripes?"

"You are one big pain, Andrea," Zebra said.

Shortly before noon, John Wilson laid out on his desk the contents of the plastic bags: a clutter of junked broken objects, including the doll and the umbrella.

Using strips of cloth, some lengths of string, crumpled newspaper, his pen, and his one hand, he swiftly transformed the battered doll into a red-nosed, umbrella-carrying clown, with baggy pants, a tattered coat, a derby hat, and a somber smile. Turning over the battered frying pan, he made it into a pedestal, on which he placed the clown.

"That's a **sculpture**," John Wilson said, with his shy smile. "Garbage into people."

The class burst into applause. The clown on the frying pan looked as if it might take a bow.

"You-all will be doing that, too, before we're done," John Wilson said. "Now I would like you to sign and date your drawings and give them to me."

When they returned the next morning the drawings were on a wall.

Gradually, in the days that followed, the walls began to fill with drawings. Sculptures made by the students were looked at with care, discussed by John Wilson and the class, and then placed on shelves along the walls: a miniature bicycle made of wire; a parrot made of an old sofa cushion; a cowboy made of rope and string; a fat lady made of a dented metal pitcher; a zebra made of glued-together scraps of cardboard.

"I like your zebra," Andrea said.

"Thanks," Zebra said. "I like your parrot."

One morning John Wilson asked the class members to make a contour drawing of their right or left hand. Zebra felt himself sweating and trembling as he worked.

> **Question**
> **Why do you think Adam is having this reaction?**

"That's real nice," John Wilson said, when he saw Andrea's drawing.

He gazed at the drawing made by Zebra.

---

miniature *(adj.)* much smaller than normal

COMPREHENSION

Summarize

✎ **Box** the paragraph on page 46 in which Mr. Wilson demonstrates how he wants the students to draw.

• Summarize Mr. Wilson's advice here.

_____

_____

_____

_____

_____

LITERARY ANALYSIS

Character Traits

Review the text in column 2 on page 46 that describes Zebra's reaction to Andrea's drawing of him. What does Zebra's reaction say about him?

_____

_____

_____

_____

CRITICAL THINKING

Analyze

✎ <u>Underline</u> the paragraph near the end of page 47 that describes what the students make in class.

• How do these works of art relate to John Wilson's method of drawing?

_____

_____

_____

_____

_____

_____

"You-all were looking at your hand," he said. "You ought to have been looking at the edge of your hand and at the space outside."

Zebra drew his hand again. Strange and ugly, the two fingers lay rigid and curled. But astonishingly, it looked like a hand this time.

One day, a few minutes before the end of class, John Wilson gave everyone an assignment: draw or make something at home, something very special that each person *felt deeply* about. And bring it to class.

Zebra remembered seeing a book titled *Incredible Cross-Sections* on a shelf in the family room at home. He found the book and took it into his room.

There was a color drawing of a rescue helicopter on one of the Contents pages. On pages 30 and 31, the helicopter was shown in pieces, its complicated insides displayed in detailed drawings. Rotor blades, control rods, electronics equipment, radar scanner, tail rotor, engine, lifeline, winch—all its many parts.

Zebra sat at his desk, gazing intently at the space outside the edges of the helicopter on the Contents page.

He made an outline drawing and brought it to class the next morning.

John Wilson looked at it. Was there a stiffening of his muscular neck, a sudden tensing of the hand that held the drawing?

He took the drawing and tacked it to the wall.

The next day he gave them all the same home assignment: draw or make something they *felt very deeply* about.

That afternoon, Zebra went **rummaging** through the trash bin in his kitchen and the garbage cans that stood near the back door of his home. He found some sardine cans, a broken eggbeater, pieces of cardboard, chipped buttons, bent bobby pins, and other odds and ends.

With the help of epoxy glue, he began to make of those bits of garbage a kind of helicopter. For support, he used

his desktop, the floor, his knees, the elbow of his left arm, at one point even his chin. Struggling with the last piece— a button he wanted to position as a wheel—he realized that without thinking he had been using his left hand, and the two curled fingers had straightened slightly to his needs.

> **Question**
> Why do you think Adam has strong feelings about the helicopter?

His heart beat thunderously. There had been so many hope-filled moments before, all of them ending in bitter disappointment. He would say nothing. Let the therapist or the doctors tell him. . . .

The following morning, he brought the helicopter to the class.

"Eeewwww, what is *that*?" Andrea grimaced.

"Something to eat you with," Zebra said.

"Get human, Zebra. Mr. Wilson will have a laughing fit over that."

But John Wilson didn't laugh. He held the helicopter in his hand a long moment, turning it this way and that, nodded at Zebra, and placed it on a windowsill, where it shimmered in the summer sunlight.

The next day, John Wilson informed everyone that three students would be leaving the class at the end of July. He asked each of those students to make a drawing for him that he would get to keep. Something to remember them by. All their other drawings and sculptures they could take home.

Zebra lay awake a long time that night, staring into the darkness of his room. He could think of nothing to draw for John Wilson.

In the morning, he sat gazing out the classroom window at the sky and at the helicopter on the sill.

"What are you going to draw for him?" Andrea asked.

Zebra shrugged and said he didn't know.

"Use your imagination," she said. Then she said, "Wait, what am I seeing here? Are you able to move those fingers?"

---

thunderously (*adv.*) in a very loud manner

"I think so."

"You *think* so?"

"The doctors said there was some improvement."

Her eyes glistened behind the thick lenses. She seemed genuinely happy.

He sat looking out the window. Dark birds wheeled and soared. There was the sound of traffic. The helicopter sat on the windowsill, its eggbeater rotor blades ready to move to full throttle.

Later that day, Zebra sat at his desk at home, working on a drawing. He held the large sheet of paper in place by pressing down on it with the palm and fingers of his left hand. He drew a landscape: hills and valleys, forests and flatlands, rivers and plateaus. Oddly, it all seemed to resemble a face.

Racing together over that landscape were a helicopter and a zebra.

It was all he could think to draw. It was not a very good drawing. He signed it: "To JOHN WILSON, with thanks. Zebra."

The next morning, John Wilson looked at the drawing and asked Zebra to write on top of the name "John Wilson" the name "Leon."

"He was an old buddy of mine, an artist. We were in Vietnam together. Would've been a much better artist than I'll ever be."

Zebra wrote in the new name.

"Thank you kindly," John Wilson said, taking the drawing. "Zebra, you have yourself a good time in camp and a good life. It was real nice knowing you."

He shook Zebra's hand. How strong his fingers felt!

"I think I'm going to miss you a little," Andrea said to Zebra after the class.

"I'll only be away a month."

"Can I help you carry some of those drawings?"

"Sure. I'll carry the helicopter."

Zebra went off to a camp in the Adirondack Mountains. He hiked and read and watched others playing ball. In the arts and crafts program he made some good drawings and even got to learn a little bit about watercolors. He put together clowns and airplanes and helicopters out of discarded cardboard and wood and clothing. From time to time his hand hurt, but the fingers seemed slowly to be coming back to life.

"Patience, young man," the doctors told him when he returned to the city. "You're getting there."

---

plateaus *(n.)* areas of high, flat land

LITERARY ANALYSIS

Character Traits

How does Zebra react when he discovers that his fingers have straightened slightly? What does this tell you about him?

_____

_____

_____

_____

VOCABULARY/WORD ANALYSIS

Roots

Circle the word *rotor* near the top of page 49. The word *rotor* comes from the Latin word *rota*, meaning "wheel." How does that information help you figure out the meaning of the word *rotor*?

_____

_____

_____

_____

_____

_____

CRITICAL THINKING

Synthesize

Think about how people form friendships. Then draw a conclusion about Andrea and Zebra's friendship. Support your answer by referring to the story.

_____

_____

_____

_____

_____

_____

_____

One or two additional operations were still necessary. But there was no urgency. And he no longer needed the leg brace.

On the first day of school, one of the secretaries found him in the hallway and told him to report to Mrs. English.

"Did you have a good summer?" Mrs. English asked.

"It was okay," Zebra said.

"This came for you in the mail."

She handed him a large brown envelope. It was addressed to Adam Zebrin, Eighth Grade, at the school. The sender was John Wilson, with a return address in Virginia.

"Adam, I admit I'm very curious to see what's inside," Mrs. English said.

She helped Zebra open the envelope.

Between two pieces of cardboard were a letter and a large color photograph.

The photograph showed John Wilson down on his right knee before a glistening dark wall. He wore his army jacket and blue jeans and boots, and the cap with the words LAND ROVER. Leaning against the wall to his right was Zebra's drawing of the helicopter and the zebra racing together across a facelike landscape. The drawing was enclosed in a narrow frame.

The wall behind John Wilson seemed to glitter with a strange black light.

Zebra read the letter and showed it to Mrs. English.

Chaim Potok

BORN February 17, 1929, in New York

DIED July 23, 2002, in Pennsylvania

AUTHOR FILE

MAJOR WORKS Potok's most famous work is the novel *The Chosen* (1967), which was the first book depicting Orthodox Judaism published by a major publisher.

WHAT INFLUENCED HIM Potok cited James Joyce, Thomas Mann, Fyodor Dostoevsky, Ernest Hemingway, and S.Y. Agnon as his chief literary influences.

OTHER JOBS In addition to being an award-winning novelist, Potok was a historian, a religious scholar, an artist, and an editor.

ON WRITING "If I had a plot that was all set in advance, why would I want to go through the agony of writing the novel? A novel is a kind of exploration and discovery, for me at any rate."

Dear Zebra,

One of the people whose names are on this wall was among my very closest friends. He was an artist named Leon Kellner. Each year I visit him and leave a gift—something very special that someone creates and gives me. I leave it near his name for a few hours, and then I take it to my studio in Virginia, where I keep a collection of those gifts. All year long I work in my studio, but come summer I go looking for another gift to give him.

Thank you for your gift.

Your friend,
John Wilson

P.S. I hope your hand is healing.

Question
Why do you think Mr. Wilson considers Adam's drawing special?

urgency (n.) a matter requiring immediate action
leafed (v.) turned the pages of a book quickly

Mrs. English stood staring awhile at the letter. She turned away and touched her eyes. Then she went to a shelf on the wall behind her, took down a large book, leafed through it quickly, found what she was searching for, and held it out for Zebra to see.

Zebra found himself looking at the glistening black wall of the Vietnam Memorial in Washington, D.C. And at the names on it, the thousands of names. . . .

Later, in the school yard during recess, Zebra stood alone at the chain-link fence and gazed down the street toward Franklin Avenue. He thought how strange it was that all the houses on this street had seemed to turn toward John Wilson that day, the windows and porches and columns and doors, as if saluting him.

Had that been only his imagination?

Maybe, Zebra thought, just maybe he could go for a walk to Franklin Avenue on Saturday or Sunday. He had not walked along Franklin Avenue since the accident; had not gone down that steep hill. Yes, he would walk carefully down that hill to the corner and walk back up and past the school and then the four blocks home.

Andrea came over to him.

"We didn't get picked for the story class with Mrs. English," she said. "I won't have to listen to any more of your gloomy stories."

Zebra said nothing.

"You know, I think I'll walk home today instead of taking the school bus," Andrea said.

"Actually, I think I'll walk, too," Zebra said. "I was thinking maybe I could pick up some really neat stuff in the street."

"You are becoming a pleasant life form," Andrea said. ■

COMPREHENSION

Summarize
Summarize how Zebra has changed since the beginning of the story.

_____

_____

_____

_____

CRITICAL THINKING

Synthesize
What do you think Franklin Avenue symbolizes to Zebra at the end of the story?

_____

_____

_____

_____

21 | **SMALL GROUPS/INDEPENDENT**

COLLABORATE

Investigate John Wilson teaches his art students to draw by looking at the space outside the objects they are drawing. With your group, try drawing a simple object with this technique. Does it seem to work?

COMMUNICATE

React and Write Make a word web about Zebra's recovery from his injuries. Then write a paragraph explaining how Zebra recovered.

READ ONLINE

Go to **www.expert21.com/student** to learn more about Chaim Potok; Vietnam War; Zebra.

Letters

Letters to a Young Artist

How does a person get to be a successful artist?
Is talent all it takes?

QuickWrite

What do you think it takes to become a success in the arts? List four or five qualities you think a successful artist needs to have.

Author's Style LITERARY ANALYSIS

An **author's style** is his or her manner of writing. It involves how something is said rather than what is said. For example, one writer may use informal language and straightforward sentences. Another may prefer complex sentences and poetic language.

Authors have different **purposes** for writing: to express thoughts or feelings, to persuade, to entertain, to inform, or to explain. The style an author chooses is directly related to his or her purpose for writing.

▶ **Read the passage. Then answer the questions.**

So you say you want to become an artist. What next? Should you go to art school? What kind of art do you want to pursue? There are many questions to ask yourself if you decide to take the journey toward a life in the arts. And once you answer those questions, you need to create a plan to achieve your goals. The following steps should help you create this plan.

What is the author's purpose?

_____

_____

What style does the author use to achieve her purpose?

_____

_____

_____

Compare and Contrast COMPREHENSION

To **compare** two things is to tell how they are alike. Words such as *like, also,* and *similarly* help you to recognize a comparison.

Authors use many strategies to compare one thing to another. Sometimes, an author will give an example or describe a personal experience to get an idea across.

▶ **Read this passage from "Letters to a Young Artist." Then answer the questions.**

Being "in it, and out of it, at the same time," is a sort of fundamental first exercise one should do as one develops as an artist. Did you take ballet when you were younger, or do you now? You know how in the beginning of the class you go through all the positions in the warm-up, and the positions become the foundation or the basis of ballet? It's a basic vocabulary. Like when you bake, you need flour, butter, sugar, some kind of liquid, etc. The fundamental ingredients.

Circle a word in the next-to-last sentence that tells you the author is making a comparison.

What does the author compare to a developing artist's learning of a fundamental exercise?

_____

_____

Academic Language VOCABULARY

▶ **Rate each word. Then write its meaning and give an example sentence.**

Word	Meaning	Example
ACADEMIC WORDS *Use these words in all your subject classes.*		
concentration con•cen•tra•tion *(noun)* ① ② ③ ④	focusing your thoughts and attention on something	Loud music disturbs my concentration when I'm reading.
foundation foun•da•tion *(noun)* ① ② ③ ④		
fundamental fun•da•men•tal *(adjective)* ① ② ③ ④		
suspend sus•pend *(verb)* ① ② ③ ④	to stop something for a short time	
SELECTION WORDS *Use these words to better understand the selection.*		
compassion com•pas•sion *(noun)* ① ② ③ ④		
devoid de•void *(adjective)* ① ② ③ ④		
intellectual in•tel•lec•tu•al *(adjective)* ① ② ③ ④		
rigor rig•or *(noun)* ① ② ③ ④		I don't have the rigor it takes to be a long-distance runner.

Rating Scale ① I don't know the word. ② I've seen it or heard it. ③ I know its meaning. ④ I know it and use it.

Roots WORD ANALYSIS

A root is part of a word that comes from another language, such as Latin or Greek. Knowing the meanings of common roots can help you figure out the meanings of unfamiliar English words. For example, the root *act,* which means "to act," can give you a hint about the meaning of action.

Underline the words that contain the Latin root *act*.

activity   proactive   acquire

actress   attention   inactivity

Letters to a Young Artist

Anna Deavere Smith, a famed actor and writer, advises teenagers about skills needed to succeed in the arts. She wrote a series of letters between herself and a fictional teen artist called BZ. BZ stands in for any young person who is considering life as an artist.

"Developing an Artist's Eye, Ear, and Heart"

Dear BZ:

Being "in it, and out of it, at the same time," is a sort of **fundamental** first exercise one should do as one develops as an artist.

Did you take ballet when you were younger, or do you now? You know how in the beginning of the class you go through all the positions in the warm-up, and the positions become the **foundation,** or the basis of ballet? It's a basic vocabulary. Like when you bake, you need flour, butter, sugar, some kind of liquid, etc. The fundamental ingredients.

Well, I believe that fundamental to becoming an artist is understanding the position of an artist, rehearsing that position, and practicing that position. It is from that position that you will develop an eye, an ear, and a heart. These three organs are essential. Yes, as a painter you will need a hand, and as an actor I need a voice and a body—but before getting to those, we need to develop the eye, the ear, the heart.

We do that by learning how to step outside of given situations to watch, to listen, and to feel, and to feel as others as much as to feel things about others. Feeling as others is empathy. Feeling for others is sympathy. Empathy is more useful and more important. It requires more **rigor**. That rigor will make you stronger of heart and spirit. Empathy requires a very highly developed imagination. It is more active than sympathy. It requires more **intellectual** development. Sympathy, to me, is just tears. Empathy is potentially very productive.

---

rehearsing *(v.)* practicing to prepare for a performance
essential *(adj.)* absolutely necessary
sympathy *(n.)* feeling of sorrow for someone else's misfortune

Stepping outside gives you the space to watch, listen, feel. To step outside, you must **suspend** opinions and judgments. It doesn't mean that you are **devoid** of them. It means that you can control them long enough to watch, listen, and feel. You store what you have learned, and then you do what you will with what you have gathered. You may even try to influence how others watch, listen, and feel. But first and foremost you must be able to step outside.

Read an essay by Bertolt Brecht, the mid-twentieth-century German playwright, called "Street Scene." In it he describes an accident scene, where people come out into the street and describe an accident. They all give their version. He calls the telling—the storytelling that happens—a kind of "natural theater." It will remind you that you have to be available to watch and listen and feel for all scenes.

To me, artists are students of the human condition, potentially. Being outside does not mean being without **compassion**. But it does mean that you may sometimes become clinical.

Years ago I interviewed the head of pediatric surgery at Sloan-Kettering Hospital in New York. I asked him what had moved him to become a cancer surgeon for children. I thought he would tell me a moving story about having seen a child suffering, but instead he replied, "I wanted to do bigger operations."

What was driving him was his desire to be a very good surgeon, and to discover things. I think as artists we too should want to do "bigger operations."

Standing in and out at the same time is a structural matter. It is a way of bringing order to the otherwise chaotic situation of life. I say chaotic because as an artist you are both in life and commenting on life. That's your position.

ADS
New York City
February 2000

clinical *(adj.)* unemotional

LITERARY ANALYSIS

Author's Style

Review the third and fourth paragraphs on page 54. What is the purpose of these paragraphs?

_____

_____

_____

_____

Check ✓ the box next to the style the author uses to achieve this purpose.

☐ She uses complete sentences and language that offers examples to the reader.

☐ She uses sentence fragments and poetic language, writing as a poet might.

COMPREHENSION

Compare and Contrast

On page 55, draw a box around the paragraphs in which the author compares artists to surgeons.

• What phrase in this section helps you see that the author is making a comparison?

_____

_____

CRITICAL THINKING

Analyze

What do you think about the author's advice to be "in it, and out of it, at the same time"? Does she provide enough examples to support her belief?

_____

_____

_____

_____

_____

_____

_____

Dear B2:

Jealousy? Hmmm. Jealousy links up with competition. It's hard to compete, really compete, in the art world. That's why award ceremonies are a little suspect. Athletes can compete; businesses can compete. I don't know how much you can really compete as an artist. You can compete with yourself.

"Competition and Jealousy"

You are an explorer. You understand that every time you go into the studio, you are after something that does not yet exist. Maybe it's the same for a runner. I don't know. But with running or swimming or gymnastics or tennis, the achievement is measurable. Forget about competition. Rather, commit yourself to find out the true nature of your art. How does it really work; what's the essence of it? Go for that thing that no one can teach you. Go for that communion, that real communion with your soul, and the discipline of expressing that communion to others. That doesn't come from competition. That comes from being one with what you are doing. It comes from **concentration** and from your own ability to be fascinated endlessly with the story, the song, the jump, the color you are working with.

I know this sounds a little monkish or even sort of "holier than thou," but I really do believe it. And that said, jealousy is a human sentiment. Few of us are above it. John Lahr, a writer, told me that the major emotion in Los Angeles is envy. I have to say, he's probably right. And a lot of it has to do with how close to or how far from an Academy Award one is. And L.A., the capital of smoke and mirrors, would have some believe that the award is just a step away. When you drive down Hollywood Boulevard, some of those dreamers look as though the dream ate them alive.

Keep it real. Even jealousy is based on fantasies: a fantasy that someone else has what belongs to you.

ADS
Los Angeles

Make Connections
Has being jealous of someone ever affected the choices you made? How?

communion (n.) a special relationship with someone or something

Dear B2:

Your question "How did you find your mentors?" is a good one. I sought them out on my own, and they came from all sorts of backgrounds. Many of them were unexpected. They are not all actors, or writers, or artists, for that matter. Tonight I had dinner with someone I consider a mentor: Studs Terkel. More on that in a moment.

Mentors are different from teachers in general because you pick them. You seek them out, or sometimes they declare themselves as your mentor. I suppose in the strict sense of the word, a mentor is someone who takes the responsibility of "schooling you," showing you the ropes, bringing you through the system. I think of them also as inspirational people who have broken ground or lit a path.

And now Studs. I consider Studs Terkel, the great radio man, a mentor. I don't know very many people who are as truly learned as he is. He is now ninety years old. He has interviewed thousands of people, from regular working people to Martin Luther King. One of his best friends was the great gospel singer Mahalia Jackson. When I visit him in Chicago, all kinds of people approach him—he's a part of the community. Just the fact that he's out there puts me on a path and lights the way.

Although it's important to make communities with like-minded people—people who are your age, your generation, who are working on projects that have resonance with yours—I am a firm believer in crossing generations to find mentorship and inspiration and a sense of furthering the craft. So I'd say that as you begin to seek mentorship, be creative about where you look. Look in unlikely places. It will enrich your work. It will broaden your work and make it more likely that you will cross boundaries and reach a wider, more culturally and intellectually diverse audience.

ADS
Chicago
February 2002

declare *(v.)* announce with authority
resonance *(n.)* special meaning something has for a person

Read and Synthesize

LITERARY ANALYSIS

Author's Style

Review the author's letter on competition and jealousy. Why do you think the author chooses to include language such as "Hmmm" and "Keep it real"?

_____

_____

_____

VOCABULARY/WORD ANALYSIS

In the first paragraph on page 57, the Latin root *ment* means "mind." **Underline** a word that has this root.

- Explain how the meaning of this word is related to *mentor*.

_____

_____

_____

[21] SMALL GROUPS/INDEPENDENT

COLLABORATE

Make Decisions Talk about career paths you might want to follow once you are out of school. Who would make a good mentor for you? Discuss the qualities of a good mentor and how you would go about choosing one.

COMMUNICATE

React and Write Write a letter in response to one of the letters in this section. Comment on the author's ideas, and ask her any questions you still have.

READ ONLINE

expert space
Go to **www.expert21.com/student** to learn more about Anna Deavere Smith; Mahalia Jackson; Studs Terkel.

What is the power of poetry? Here are some thoughts from poets who are inspired by poetry.

I Want to Write

By Margaret Walker

I want to write

I want to write the songs of my people.

I want to hear them singing melodies in the dark.

I want to catch the last floating strains from their sob-torn throats.

I want to frame their dreams into words; their souls into notes.

I want to catch their sunshine laughter in a bowl;

fling dark hands to a darker sky

and fill them full of stars

then crush and mix such lights till they become

a mirrored pool of brilliance in the dawn.

strains *(n.)* sounds of music

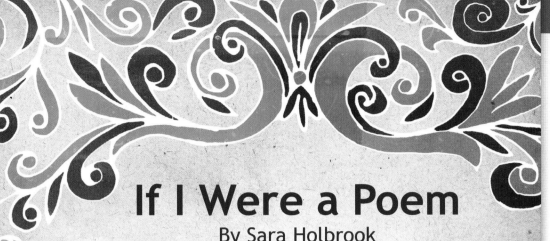

If I Were a Poem
By Sara Holbrook

If I were a poem,

I would grab you by the ankles

and rustle you up to
    your every leaf.

I would gather your branches

in the power of my winds
    and pull you skyward,

if I were a poem.

If I were a poem,

I would walk you down
    beside the rushing stream,

swollen with spring,
    put thunder in your heart,

then lay you down, a new lamb
    to sing you to softly sleep,

if I were a poem.

If I were a poem,

I wouldn't just talk to you of
    politics, society and change,

I would be a raging bonfire to
    strip you of your outer wrap,

and then I would reach
    within and with one touch

ignite the song in our own soul.

If I were a poem,

I would hold my lips one
    breath away from yours

and then I would move the
    breadth of one bee closer,
    not to sting,

but to brush you with
    my wings as I retreat,

to leave you holding
    nothing but a hungry,
    solitary sigh,

if I were a poem.

If I were a poem,

my thoughts would
    finally be put to words

through your own poetry,
    I would push you that far.

if I were a poem.

breadth (n.) distance from side to side of something
retreat (v.) to move away from someone or something

LITERARY ANALYSIS

Author's Style

What purpose do you think Margaret Walker had for writing the poem on page 58?

_____

_____

_____

_____

What style does the author use to achieve her purpose?

_____

_____

COMPREHENSION

Compare and Contrast

Sometimes writers use figurative language, or language that does not literally mean what it says, to compare two things. What is the author of "If I Were a Poem" comparing throughout her poem?

_____

What is the poet's purpose for making this comparison?

_____

_____

_____

CRITICAL THINKING

Evaluate

Compare the styles of the two poems. Which author do you think did a better job of expressing her love of writing? Use specific language from the poems to explain your view.

_____

_____

_____

READ ONLINE

expert space
Go to **www.expert21.com/student** to learn more about Versification: The Art of Making Poetry; Margaret Walker.

Think Across Texts

Organize and Synthesize

1. What role do you think art plays in different people's lives? Answer this question using information, examples, and ideas from the following selections:

What role can art play in people's lives?	
"Zebra"	
"Letters to a Young Artist"	
"I Want to Write" and "If I Were a Poem"	

Compare and Evaluate

2. Sum up in one or two sentences what the writer of "Letters to a Young Artist" says about mentors.

_____

_____

_____

_____

_____

_____

3. What do you think each person listed below would say about the purpose of making art?

• The speaker in "I Want to Write":

_____

_____

• The speaker in "If I Were a Poem":

_____

_____

• Mr. Wilson in "Zebra":

_____

_____

4. The author of "Letters to a Young Artist" says that artists should feel empathy, or feel *as* others feel. Do you think Mr. Wilson felt empathy for Zebra in the story "Zebra"? Explain your answer.

_____

_____

_____

_____

_____

_____

_____

_____

Discuss and Write

5. With a partner, discuss how the three readings in "The Power of Expression" helped you understand why people make art. Take notes as you talk. Then use your notes to write a response to the question *How do works of art affect us?*

Apply Word Knowledge

Word Lab

1. **Think about it.** What are the **foundation** skills for playing a certain sport? Name the sport, and list three foundation skills.

_____

_____

_____

2. **Check it.** What things might you **rummage** through? Check two.

❏ a doorway

❏ a trash can

❏ a sock drawer

❏ a window

3. **Finish it.** Complete the sentences below with the words **contour, intricate,** and **devoid.**

I began my drawing by tracing the

_____ of the fish in the

photo. I noticed that my drawing was

_____ of details. So I drew

_____ designs resembling

scales on the inside of the fish shape.

4. **Think about it.** What might make you **wince**?

_____

_____

_____

5. **Think about it.** What helps your **concentration**? What disturbs your **concentration**?

This helps me: _____

This doesn't help me: _____

6. **Complete it.** Use **encrusted** or **laden** in your answer to these questions.

What weighs many students down as they walk to school and back?

_____

What might cause a person's hands to be covered with mud, dirt, and sand?

_____

_____

Word Analysis

7. The word _reject_ comes from Latin _re_ (meaning "back") and _jacere_ (meaning "to throw"). Based on this knowledge, draw a line to match each word below to its meaning.

project (v.)   to force into

projectile (n.)   to throw forward

inject (v.)   something that is thrown
                                  with force

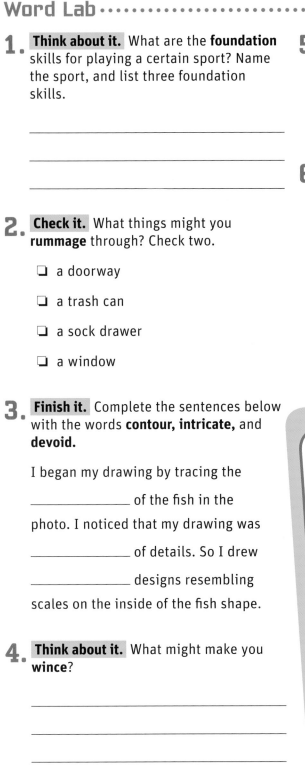

Analyze Images

CAREER CONNECTION

Arts, A/V Technology, and Communications
www.careerclusters.org

Go to **21 Tool**Kit **Expert File 6.18** to learn more about careers in the visual arts.

Artists use many different styles, methods, and materials to express themselves. Learning how to view and think about a work of art will help you to enjoy it more and understand it better.

View a Painting

▶ Look at the painting below and analyze what the artist is trying to say. Pay close attention to the title, use of color and shapes, and the caption.

MARK IT

Preview the image. <u>Underline</u> the information in the caption that tells what inner mood this painting might be about.

Analyze the elements. The artist uses elements such as color and shape to draw your attention to certain parts of the painting. Put a **star** ★ next to the part of the painting that first got your attention.

Einsamkeit — loneliness by Alexej Jawlensky, 1912

Alexej Jawlensky is a Russian-born painter. His work is part of the expressionist movement. Expressionism is a style in which the artist does not reproduce a subject accurately, but instead expresses an inner mood.

[Here's How] ▶ Follow these steps to analyze images:

Step 1 Preview the image. What is your first impression? What captures your attention or creates a strong feeling? Now read the title and caption. What does the title tell you about the work? What information does the caption provide?

Step 2 Analyze the elements. Notice the lines, colors, composition, lighting, and perspective. What do you notice first? Does the artist use lighting and/or color to create a certain mood or feeling? Are the shapes of people or objects symbolic?

Step 3 Interpret what you see. Why do you think the artist created this image? To create a certain feeling or emotion? To make you think about a subject in a new way? To share an experience?

Apply: Visuals in Graphic Novels

▶ **Study the image below, and follow the steps to analyze the cover of this graphic novel.**

1. **Preview the image.** What is your first impression of the image?

_____

_____

What does the title tell you?

_____

_____

2. **Analyze the elements.** What do the lines or shapes first draw your attention to?

_____

_____

Describe the colors.

_____

_____

What mood or feeling do they create?

_____

_____

3. **Interpret what you see.** How does the image make you feel?

_____

_____

What do you think the artist is trying to say?

_____

_____

_____

Compare-and-Contrast Essay

A compare-and-contrast essay shows how two subjects are the same (comparison) and different (contrast). Comparing and contrasting is a kind of analysis, breaking down a subject to explain it. It can be used in movie reviews, consumer guides for things like electronics, and in many other places.

In this writing workshop, you will write a compare-and-contrast essay about two paintings, the worldview each portrays, and which one you relate to more.

Example: In a court case, a judge has to decide if two songs are similar enough for one to be considered a copy of the other.

The judge heard the prosecutor's case stating the song "My Sweet Lord" was plagiarizing, or copying, "He's So Fine." Experts gave their opinions. They compared the pattern of notes in both songs and said that they were alike. The only differences they could find were places where extra notes were added to fit with the lyrics. The judge ruled that it was plagiarized, even though it might have happened accidentally or unconsciously.

▶ **Analyze Features** A strong compare-and-contrast essay has the following features:

FEATURE	🖍 MARK IT
Look for these features in the Student Model on the next page.	Mark the features as you read the Student Model.
1. An **introduction** introduces the subjects being compared and contrasted. (Organization)	<u>Underline</u> the two subjects that are going to be compared and contrasted.
2. Comparison, or ways that each subject is alike. (Ideas)	(Circle) the comparison (what the two subjects have in common).
3. Contrast, or ways that each subject is different. (Ideas)	Check ✓ the contrast (what is different about the two subjects).
4. Focus Trait: Word Choice Use specific and accurate words that communicate meaning clearly.	Star ★ specific, accurate words.
5. A strong **conclusion** that sums up why one is better or preferred. (Organization)	Draw a box around the statement in the conclusion that sums up why the writer prefers one painting to the other.

Traits of Writing

Traits of Writing is a model for assessing and teaching. The traits work within the writing process to support revision and editing.

Each puzzle piece below represents one of the **traits** that define good writing.

Each trait is made up of four **key qualities.** The trait you will focus on in this lesson is **Word Choice.**

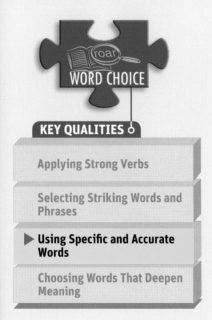

KEY QUALITIES ⚬

Applying Strong Verbs

Selecting Striking Words and Phrases

▶ **Using Specific and Accurate Words**

Choosing Words That Deepen Meaning

▶ **Read Jamie Hernandez's compare-and-contrast essay about two works of art.**

STUDENT MODEL

Two Paintings, One Empty Wall
by Jamie Hernandez

Have you ever wanted to take home a famous work of art? I like to imagine how pieces of art would look if hanging on my wall. In this case, I am considering *Three Musicians* by Pablo Picasso and *Nighthawks* by Edward Hopper. It should be easy to choose between them, because these paintings are different in almost every way.

Picasso paints in a style called Cubism, which jumbles the appearance of ordinary things. The objects and people are barely recognizable. Although you can see three figures, two instruments, and sheet music, the unnatural shapes overlap each other and the background in unexpected ways.

On the other hand, Hopper paints in a style called Realism. The image portrayed is as clear as a movie scene. A couple and a single man sit at the counter, drinking coffee, while another man reaches for something behind the counter. You can see them through a glass window. You can also see the dark, barren street outside.

The colors in both paintings are similar. The Picasso painting uses blue with brown, yellow, orange, and tan. The Hopper painting uses green with the same colors. However, the mood created with these colors is nearly opposite. In the Picasso painting, these colors jostle each other and make the painting seem like it's moving. They crowd together and draw your eyes to the center of the painting. In the Hopper painting, the colors remain aloof. There is a feeling of quiet isolation.

Normally, I prefer the realistic style, where I recognize what I'm looking at. However, I feel happy when I look at *Three Musicians*. I can imagine them jamming and having a blast. *Nighthawks* makes me feel sad. The couple doesn't look happy to be there. The other customer is sitting alone, with his shoulders hunched. I imagine the coffee in their mugs growing cold. The guy behind the counter is working the late shift. I can imagine his sore feet. So if I could have one of these paintings, I would want the one that lifts my mood as I look at it every day in my room.

▶ **Read Jamie's notes about how she worked on her compare-and-contrast essay.**

ORGANIZATION

I started out stating the paintings I was going to compare and contrast. Then I decided to make the lead more personal by considering which one I'd want in my room.

WORD CHOICE

When I revised my essay, I used the electronic thesaurus on my computer to find "barren" instead of "empty" and "jostle" instead of "bump."

▶ **Analyze how Jamie developed and organized her ideas. Fill in the missing parts of the diagram.**

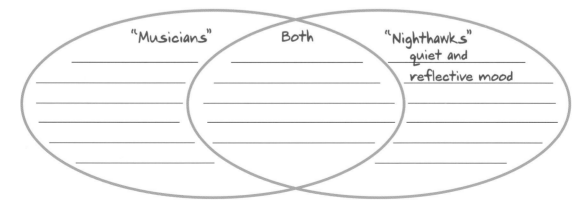

"Musicians" Both "Nighthawks"
quiet and
reflective mood

How Do I Get Started?

Your Topic:

Assignment: Compare-and-Contrast Essay

Purpose: to compare and contrast two paintings and say which one you can relate to more

Audience: your choice

Ideas: Finding a Topic

Finding a topic you care about makes writing easier and more fun. Use these Think-Abouts as you work on your ideas.

- Have I chosen a topic that I really like? *The author likes art enough to imagine that she could get to keep the painting she liked the best.*
- Do I have something new to say about this topic?
- Am I writing about what I know and care about?
- Have I gathered enough information so that I'm ready to write?

◊ KEY QUALITIES

▶ Finding a Topic

Focusing the Topic

Developing the Topic

Using Details

▶ **Model** Look at Reading 5, "Letters to a Young Artist," in this workshop. Review Anna Deavere Smith's letter on the first two pages. What does she include that shows she has something new to say on this topic?

▶ **Practice** One way to find a topic that interests you is to think about how you relate to it.

Painting 1: What I relate to most about it is_____

_____

Painting 2: What I relate to most about it is_____

_____

▶ **Plan Your Essay** Use the diagram below to plan your essay. Revise as necessary.

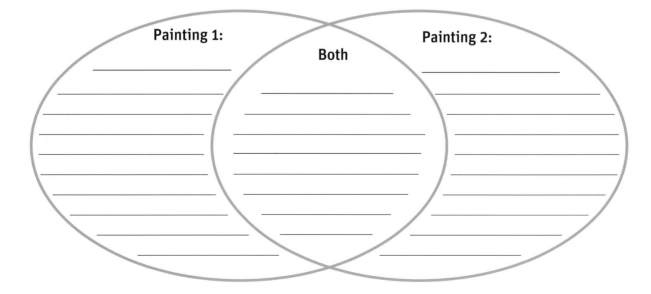

Painting 1:

Both

Painting 2:

How Do I Get Organized?

Organization: Creating the Lead

Good writers think about how to order and chunk their ideas. Ask yourself these Think-Abouts as you work on your organization.

- Did I give the reader something interesting to think about right from the start?
- Will the reader want to keep reading?
- Have I tried to get the reader's attention? *For example, the writer of the Student Model states that she wants to keep one of the paintings.*
- Did I let the reader know what is coming?

ORGANIZATION

○ KEY QUALITIES

▶ **Creating the Lead**

Using Sequence Words and Transition Words

Structuring the Body

Ending With a Sense of Resolution

▶ **Model** Go back to Reading 2, "Sounds of Success." Review John Salazar's story, which starts on page 26. What in the first paragraph makes you want to read the rest of the piece?

▶ **Practice** Think up a new opening for the Student Model on page 65. Remember to be sure your opening makes sense with the rest of the story.

_____

_____

_____

_____

_____

▶ **Write a Paragraph** Practice what you learned about writing an exciting lead for your compare-and-contrast essay here.

_____

_____

_____

_____

_____

_____

▶ **Draft Your Essay** Write a first draft.

Quick Check

▶ **Check how well you created the lead for your compare-and-contrast essay. Have a writing partner rate it, too.**

6 = Expert   **3** = Making Strides

5 = Well Done   **2** = On the Way

4 = Almost There   **1** = Getting Started

Organization

1. Did I give the reader something interesting to think about right from the start?
Self   ① ② ③ ④ ⑤ ⑥
Partner   ① ② ③ ④ ⑤ ⑥

2. Will the reader want to keep reading?
Self   ① ② ③ ④ ⑤ ⑥
Partner   ① ② ③ ④ ⑤ ⑥

3. Have I tried to get the reader's attention?
Self   ① ② ③ ④ ⑤ ⑥
Partner   ① ② ③ ④ ⑤ ⑥

4. Did I let the reader know what is coming?
Self   ① ② ③ ④ ⑤ ⑥
Partner   ① ② ③ ④ ⑤ ⑥

How Do I Use Specific, Accurate Words to Improve My Word Choice?

FOCUS TRAIT

Word Choice: Using Specific and Accurate Words

Good writers choose words that communicate precisely. Use these Think-Abouts as you choose specific and accurate words.

- Have I used nouns and modifiers that help the reader see a picture? *For example, the author writes "quiet isolation" to help the reader understand the mood of the Hopper painting.*

- Did I avoid using words that might confuse the reader?

- If I tried a new word, did I check to make sure I used it correctly?

- Are these the best words that can be used?

○ KEY QUALITIES

Applying Strong Verbs

Selecting Striking Words and Phrases

▶ Using Specific and Accurate Words

Choosing Words That Deepen Meaning

▶ **Model** Go back to Reading 1, "Ten Artists Who Changed the World." Look at the section on Frida Kahlo and underline the nouns and modifiers that you think are specific and accurate.

▶ Read Ruth Culham's writing blog below to get advice on improving your writing.

Ask the Expert: Ruth Culham

Ruth Culham, an award-winning teacher, is the author of *6+1 Traits of Writing: The Complete Guide for Middle School* and other books on writing.

Q & A: Word Choice: Using Specific and Accurate Words

Uri Unclear **Writes:**

> Sometimes I wonder what to write about. There's a lot of stuff, and most of it is interesting and fun, but I'm just not sure. I'd like to write a fastidious paper and get a superior score. Can you help me?

Dear Uri Unclear: Write about something you are passionate about; it will make choosing the words easier. Try for words and phrases that help the reader see what you are writing about. Stay away from *stuff* and *fun* because they are boring! It looks like you used the thesaurus to find *fastidious* and *superior*. Can you replace those words so they sound more natural? Reach and stretch, but don't go too far! You want your words to sound *just right*!

Posted by: Ruth Culham | November 2 at 01:31 PM

▶ **Practice** Read the sample paragraphs, and think about which sentences use specific and accurate words.

<u>Underline</u> the general words.

(Circle) the words that are specific and accurate.

Star ★ the sample that shows the best use of specific and accurate words.

Sample 1: The Scream

This famous painting shows a bald man holding his hands to his head. His mouth is hanging open like a capital letter O. He is standing on a bridge. The sky is yellow and orange. It could be that a terrible explosion is lighting the sky, but other people walking in the background do not appear panicked. So it seems to be a personal tragedy.

Sample 2: The Scream

The famous painting shows some guy with a funny face. He is standing around, and maybe something really bad has happened. The sky is different colors. There are other people there, too. So maybe it's just this person's problem.

▶ **Revise** Now use specific, accurate words to improve your compare-and-contrast essay. Choose a paragraph from your first draft, and revise it below. Remember to stretch for new words, but be sure they are natural sounding and that you know what they mean.

_____

_____

_____

_____

_____

_____

_____

_____

_____

Quick Check

▶ **Check your essay for how well you chose specific and accurate words. Then have a writing partner rate it, too.**

6 = Expert   **3** = Making Strides

5 = Well Done   **2** = On the Way

4 = Almost There   **1** = Getting Started

Word Choice

1. Have I used nouns and modifiers that help the reader see a picture?
Self ① ② ③ ④ ⑤ ⑥
Partner ① ② ③ ④ ⑤ ⑥

2. Did I avoid using words that might confuse the reader?
Self ① ② ③ ④ ⑤ ⑥
Partner ① ② ③ ④ ⑤ ⑥

3. If I tried a new word, did I check to make sure I used it correctly?
Self ① ② ③ ④ ⑤ ⑥
Partner ① ② ③ ④ ⑤ ⑥

4. Are these the best words that can be used?
Self ① ② ③ ④ ⑤ ⑥
Partner ① ② ③ ④ ⑤ ⑥

Revise with Technology Use the dictionary feature in your word processing program to help you check the meaning of any new words you want to use.

How Can I Finish a Great Paper?

Grammar: Using Pronouns Correctly

CONVENTIONS

- Reflexive pronouns are used to refer back to the subject of a sentence. They can also be used to emphasize the subject.

Example: The painting sold <u>itself</u>. (*itself* shows that the object of the verb *sold* is the same as the subject of the sentence, *painting*)

I <u>myself</u> would not buy that painting. (*myself* emphasizes the subject *I*)

- Indefinite pronouns replace nouns without specifying the exact noun they replace.

Example: <u>One</u> of the paintings hangs in a museum.

▶ **Practice** Rewrite this paragraph correctly.

I ourselves would have no problem comparing and contrasting two works of art. It's interesting to think about how the artists are expressing yourself.

_____

_____

Mechanics: Using Quotation Marks

CONVENTIONS

Use quotation marks when writing dialogue or quoting someone's exact words. Quotation marks also are used around the title of a poem or song.

1. Put periods or commas before the closing quotation marks. Put semicolons (;) and colons (:) after the closing quotation marks.

2. Put the question mark inside the quotation marks if the quotation is a question. Put the question mark outside the quotation if the quotation is not a question.

Example: Did you enjoy the production of "Annie"?

▶ **Practice** Rewrite this paragraph correctly.

My favorite poem is "If I Were a Poem". What do you think Margaret Walker means when she says "A mirrored pool of brilliance in the dawn?"

_____

_____

▶ **Proofread** Find and correct any errors in your essay. Put a check beside the types of errors you find. Then write three corrected sentences below.

❑ pronouns used correctly ❑ contractions used correctly

❑ quotation marks used correctly ❑ spelling

❑ subject/verb agreement ❑ other: _____

1. _____

_____

2. _____

_____

3. _____

_____

PRESENTATION

PUBLISH/PRESENT

▶ **Write Your Final Draft** Now, using your edited draft, begin creating a final draft for presentation.

🖥 Use word processing software to type your final draft. Make sure to format your margins and spacing according to your teacher's request.

Check your final draft against the Traits of Writing Scoring Guide on pages 336–339 and correct any errors before you present it.

▶ **Beyond the Classroom** Extend your finished compare-and-contrast essay.

List two ideas for photos that could illustrate your compare-and-contrast essay:

_____

_____

Look online for a blog, message board, magazine, or newspaper where you could publish your compare-and-contrast essay.

List two places you could upload or share your essay for publication.

_____

Quick Check

▶ **Check your essay for how well you used conventions. Then have a writing partner rate it, too.**

6 = Expert	**3** = Making Strides
5 = Well Done	**2** = On the Way
4 = Almost There	**1** = Getting Started

Conventions

1. Did I use pronouns correctly?
Self ① ② ③ ④ ⑤ ⑥
Partner ① ② ③ ④ ⑤ ⑥

2. Did I use quotation marks correctly?
Self ① ② ③ ④ ⑤ ⑥
Partner ① ② ③ ④ ⑤ ⑥

3. Did I use correct subject/verb agreement?
Self ① ② ③ ④ ⑤ ⑥
Partner ① ② ③ ④ ⑤ ⑥

4. Is the spelling in the essay correct?
Self ① ② ③ ④ ⑤ ⑥
Partner ① ② ③ ④ ⑤ ⑥

READ ONLINE

expert space
Go to **www.expert21.com/ student** to find photographs and other visuals to illustrate your compare-and-contrast essay.

You have learned about the importance of art to individuals and society. Now apply your expert reading strategies to the following memoir about the impact reading had on one famous writer. ▶

Introduction to SHELF LIFE

By Gary Paulsen

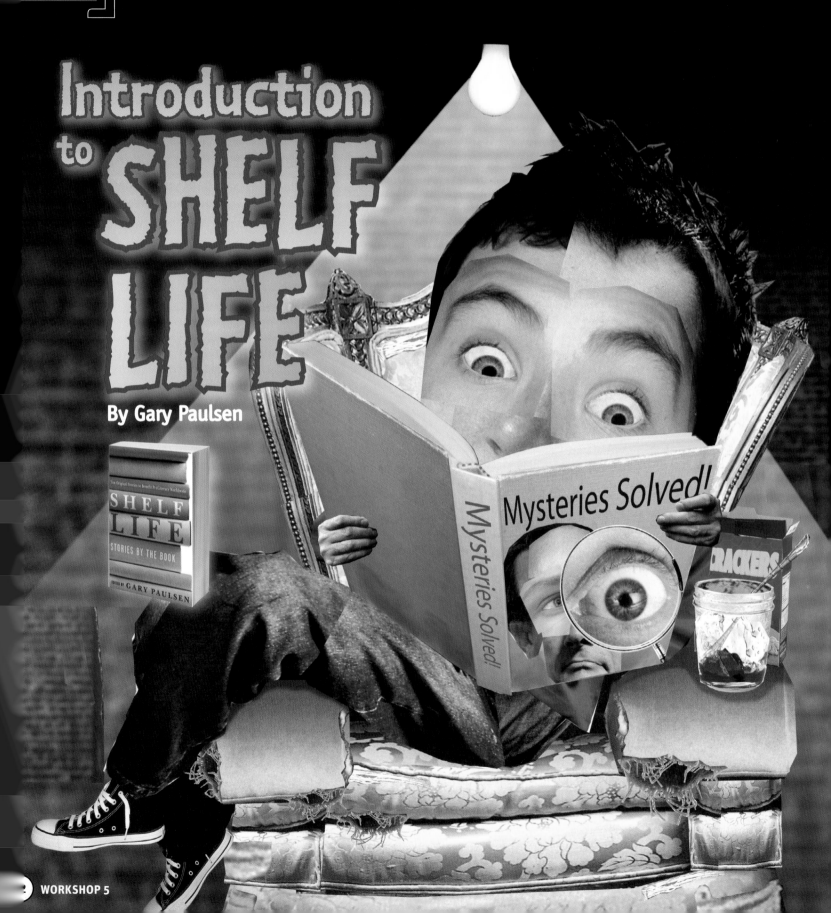

Books saved my life.

First reading them, then writing them.

As surely as my lead dog Cookie pulled me from the bottom of a lake after I fell through the ice, books are the reason I survived my miserable childhood. As certainly as my sloop *Scallywag* has safely taken me through storms and huge seas, books have sustained me as an adult.

The awfulness of my childhood has been well covered. But I remember two women who took the time to help me when I was a boy and both women, not so coincidentally, helped me with books.

Because I lived from the age of seven to when I was nearly ten in the Philippine Islands and had a private military tutor, I had never been to a public school.

We came back to the States when I was just short of ten and moved to Washington, D.C., so my father, who was in the army, could work at the Pentagon. My mother promptly enrolled me in public school, took me there the first morning, handed me over to a teacher, and left.

I was painfully shy, terrified at the mob of kids and could not go into the room. It was an old school and at the back of the classroom, there was a cloakroom, a shallow closet the width of the room but closed in except for one door. I went in the closet and took my coat off with the rest of the children but then I could not leave, simply could not make my legs move to walk out into the classroom. I was too frightened.

There were many things the teacher could have done wrong. She could have forced me out, dragged me into the classroom, could have made me leave. Instead she did everything right.

She looked into the closet, saw me sitting back in the corner and disappeared for a moment and said something to the children. Then she came back into the closet and sat down next to me in the corner and put her arm around me.

She had a book, a picture book. I cannot recall the contents of the book except that it had a horse's head on the cover and she sat next to me quietly for a time and read to me softly and let me turn the pages. I was lost in the quiet of the cloakroom, lost in the book so deeply that everything else fell away.

After a time, it could have been ten minutes or an hour or my whole life, she asked me if I thought I could come out into the room and take my seat at a desk. I nodded and she stood and took my hand and led me into the classroom.

A few years later, when I was thirteen, another woman, a librarian, gave me another book and I consider every good thing that has ever happened to me since then a result of that woman handing me that book.

I'd been wandering the streets of the small Minnesota town we lived in one bitter winter evening. I sold newspapers, trying to scrape together a little money so that I could buy better clothes, believing, as kids do, that the right clothes might somehow lift me from my wretchedly unpopular social life.

I stopped in the library to warm up. The librarian noticed me, called me over, and asked if I wanted a library card. Then she handed me a card with my name on it and gave me a book.

Later that night back at home, or what passed for home—a crummy apartment in the bad part of town—I took the book, a box of crackers, and a jar of grape jelly down to the basement, to a hideaway I'd created behind the furnace where someone had abandoned a creaky old armchair under a bare light bulb.

> **Books have sustained me as an adult.**

sloop *(n.)* a small ship with one central mast
crummy *(adj.)* of bad quality

I sat in the corner, eating jelly-smeared crackers, plodding through the book. It took me forever to read. I was such a poor reader that, by the time I'd finished a page, I'd have forgotten what I'd read on the page before and I'd have to go back. That first book must have taken me over a month to finish, hunched over the pages late at night.

I wish I could remember the name of that first book—I can't even remember what it was about. What I do remember about that evening at the library was that it marked the first of many nights the librarian would give me a book. "Here," she'd say, handing me a few battered volumes. "I think you'll like these." She would hand select books that she thought would interest me—Westerns, mysteries, survival tales, science fiction, Edgar Rice Burroughs. I would take them home to hide in the basement and read; I'd bring them back and we'd talk about them, and she'd give me more books.

But she wasn't just giving me books, she was giving me . . . everything. She gave me the first hint I'd ever had in my entire life that there was something other than my parents screaming at each other in the kitchen. She handed me a world where I wasn't going to get beaten up by the school bullies. She showed me places where it didn't hurt all the time.

I read terribly at first but as I did more of it, the books became more a part of me and within a short time they gave me a life, a look at life outside myself that made me look forward instead of backward.

Years later, after I'd graduated from high school, joined the army, gotten married, had children, and made a career as an electronics engineer working in satellite tracking, books once again changed the course of my life. This time, though, I wrote them.

I was sitting in a satellite tracking station at about nine o'clock at night when suddenly I knew that I had to be a writer. In that instant, I gave up or lost everything that had made up my life until that point—my work, my family, certainly my earning potential.

Writing had suddenly become everything . . . everything . . . to me.

I stood up from the console, handed in my security badge, and headed for Hollywood. I had to go to a place where I knew writers were; I had to be near them, had to learn from them. I got a job as a proofreader of a men's magazine, going from earning $500 a week to $400 a month, and apprenticed myself to a couple of editors.

These two men gave me writing assignments, and in order to continue receiving their help, I had to write an article, a chapter of a book, or a short story every night, every single night, no exceptions, no excuses, for them to critique. If I missed a single day, they would no longer help me.

I have been writing for over thirty years, spent most of it starving, trying to make it work for me, in my mind; trying to make words come together in the right patterns, movements, what some have called the loops and whorls of the story dance, and it has always been hard. It is, sometimes, still difficult. But I love writing more now, I think, than I ever have. The way the stories dance, the rhythms and movements of them, is grandly exciting to me.

I remember the first acceptance letter, the first

> **"I want to write, and I want as many young readers as possible to see what I write. That's it."**

---

console (n.) a flat board that contains the controls of a machine

whorls (n.) spiral patterns

time a publisher told me my writing was worthy of publication, the first after many, many rejections. There will never be another first like this one; not first love nor first hope nor first time never, no never like this.

Dear author: We have decided to publish your book.

Can you imagine? Your life, your work, your hopes and thoughts and songs and breath, we have decided to publish your book. We have decided to publish you. Such words thunder, burn into your mind, your soul.

Since then I have written every day and I have told many stories. Stories of love and death and cold and heat and ice and flame, stories sad and stories happy and stories of laughter and tears and places soft and hard, of dogs and the white-blink of arctic ice, stories of great men and beautiful women and souls and devils and gods, stories of lost dreams and found joys and aches and torture and great rolling hills and towering storms and things quick and hot and slow and dull, stories of graves and horses, pigs and kings, war and the times between wars, stories of children's cheeks and the soft hair at a woman's temple when it is moist, stories of rage and spirit and spit and blood and bodies on fences and hay so sweet you could eat the grass.

I write from my life, from what I see and hear and smell and feel, from personal inspection at zero altitude and I write because it is, simply, all that I am, because in the end I do not want to do any other thing as much as I want to write. But the force behind it, the thing that pushes me to write, that wakes me at night with story ideas, that makes the hair on the back of my neck go up when a story works, that causes my breath to stop and hold with a sentence that comes right, and that makes coming to the computer or the pad of paper every morning with a cup of tea and a feeling of wonderful newness and expectations, the engine that drives me to write is, surely, love.

I personally want just two things. I want to write, and I want as many young readers as possible to see what I write. That's it. To write and to have readers.

I work all the time. I get up at four thirty in the morning, meditate for half an hour, then start working. Not always writing, but working. If I'm not writing, I read and study and write until I fall asleep at night.

I owe everything I am and everything that I will ever be to books.

It was and still is a wonder for me, what books are and how they become part of a reader's mind and soul. I thank all of the writers I've read and all of the readers who've read my books for allowing me the unending thrill of being a part of this crazy dance of words. And I wish the same kind of joy for everyone who holds a copy of this book in their hands. ■

Reflect

1. Circle all the expert strategies you used while reading this article.

   A. Visualizing   **B.** Clarifying

   C. Other: _____

2. Use the letters above to label where in the article you applied the expert strategies.

3. Select one expert strategy you used. Explain why you applied that strategy where you did.

   _____
   _____
   _____
   _____

READ ONLINE

expert space
Go to **www.expert21.com/student** to learn more about American Literature; Short Story; Hollywood.

---

temple (*n.*) the flat area on each side of the forehead
meditate (*v.*) relax and think about one thing or idea

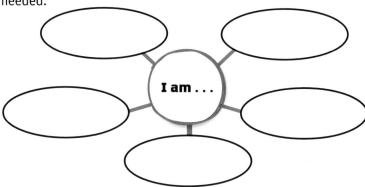

Self-portrait
Pick Your Media

THE SITUATION

Every artist has his or her own perspective on the world. What's yours?

Your school is holding an art exhibition with "Identity" as its theme. To enter the show, each student must make a collage that uses a variety of materials to answer the question "Who Am I?"

YOUR CHALLENGE

With materials you find in your home or at school, you will create a self-portrait in a medium of your choice.

As you plan and create your self-portrait, you will

- Brainstorm descriptive words.
- Answer questions about yourself.
- See how other artists express their identities.
- Choose symbols to represent your personality and interests.
- Gather materials.
- Create your self-portrait.

CAREER CONNECTION
Arts, A/V Technology, and Communications
www.careerclusters.org

Go to **21** ToolKit **Expert File 6.18** to learn more about careers in art.

1 Brainstorm words that describe you.

First, think about what makes you *you*. For 90 seconds, list every word or phrase you can think of to describe yourself. Use the web below to note your descriptive words. Add more bubbles as needed.

I am . . .

2 Answer questions.

Now it's time to think like an artist. Answer the questions below to begin thinking visually.

- What are your favorite colors? Which color best matches your personality?

_____

- What kind of fabric represents your personal style (e.g., denim, satin, batik)?

_____

- What texture describes you? For example, is your hair curly? Are your hands rough? Is your personality prickly?

_____

_____

- What three objects hold meaning for you?

_____

_____

3 See how others express their identity.

Review the selections you've read in this workshop to recall how people use art to express themselves. Look at the **Resource Bank** on the following pages and resources from **Expert Space** to see how artists communicate their identities in a variety of media. On the lines below, tell what ideas or techniques from these artworks you might use.

_____

_____

_____

_____

4 Choose symbols.

When people look at your self-portrait, you want them to see who you are. For that to happen, you need to choose pictures, objects, and words that symbolize different aspects of your personality. In the chart below, list things you might use to visually represent yourself. A sample has been included for you.

My Appearance:
old shoelaces from sneakers that I love to wear

My Values/Beliefs/Hopes:

My Personality:

My Interests/Hobbies:

5 Choose your media and collect your materials.

How do you want to express your self-portrait? Think about the media you need. If you decide to do a collage, collect the items you want to include. Use the list below as a starting point. If you prefer, you can compile your collage electronically, collecting your materials online. Doing so will allow you to include music or video clips as well as text and images.

- Photos, maps, postcards
- Magazine, newspaper, and Internet clippings (text or pictures)
- Fabric scraps
- Wallpaper
- Foil
- Ribbon
- Beads
- Buttons
- Feathers
- Stamps, tickets, tags
- Song lyrics

6 Create your self-portrait.

Use the tip sheet below to help you as you put together your self-portrait. Plus, use the **[21] Tool**Kit **Expert File 2.10** on Visual Design Basics for more guidance. When your self-portrait is ready, complete the sentence starter below.

My self-portrait shows that I am _____

_____.

Tips for Creating a Cool Collage

1. Choose your base. You may use poster board, colored paper, a shoebox lid—anything that will be easy to affix your materials to.

2. Consider using unusual materials. What might sandpaper represent? A piece of window screen?

3. Your collage does not have to be flat; a string of beads or crumpled paper can give the piece life.

4. Pay attention to colors and textures. What are you trying to say? Each piece you add to the collage must reflect you—what you like, what you believe, who you are.

5. As you work, remove any pieces that distract from your message. Rearrange until you are happy with what the collage says about you.

PROJECT
RESOURCE BANK

SCULPTURE
Artist: Nare Setyan
Media: Mixed Media Sculpture

POEM
Poet: Julio Noboa
Form: Poetry

Identity
by Julio Noboa

Let them be as flowers,
always watered, fed, guarded, admired,
but harnessed to a pot of dirt.

I'd rather be a tall, ugly weed,
clinging on cliffs, like an eagle
wind-wavering above high, jagged rocks.

To have broken through the surface of stone
to live, to feel exposed to the madness
of the vast, eternal sky.
To be swayed by the breezes of an ancient sea,
carrying my soul, my seed beyond
the mountains of time
or into the abyss of the bizarre.

> This poem explores the theme of identity. Circle the words that are used to describe the speaker. Why does the speaker prefer to be a weed rather than a flower?

_____

_____

_____

> Nare Setyan has Sticklers Syndrome, a condition that causes retinal detachment, so, by 12, she had become completely blind. She created this self-portrait sculpture, and won an art and writing award for it as a teenager. What parts of her personality is she emphasizing?

_____

_____

COLLAGE

Artist: Romare Bearden

Media: Mixed Media

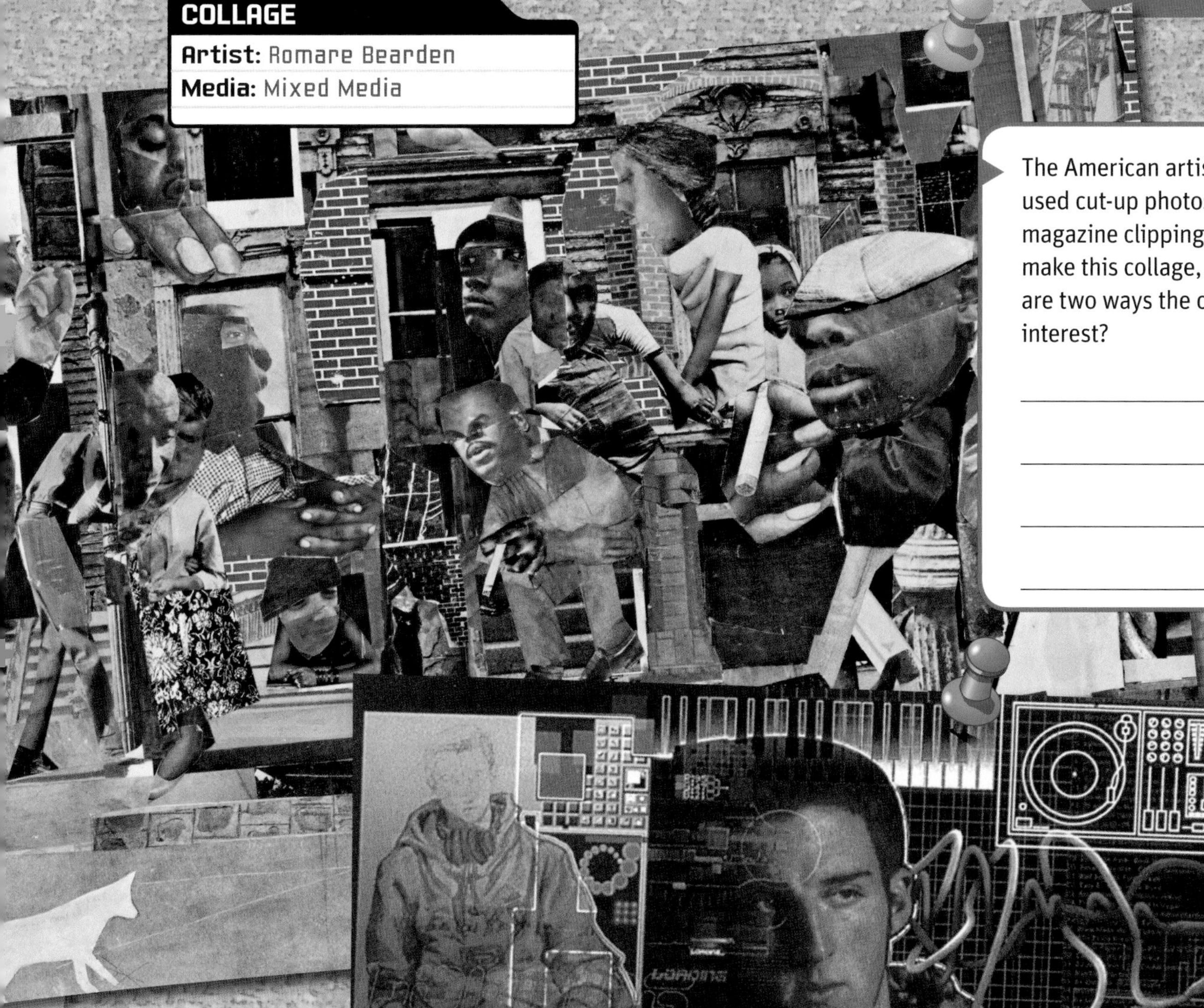

The American artist Romare Bearden used cut-up photos, newspaper and magazine clippings, and colored paper to make this collage, called *The Dove*. What are two ways the collage creates visual interest?

_____

_____

_____

_____

In this self-portrait by a teenager, which image catches your eye first?

_____

_____

_____

COMPUTER ART

Artist: Tim Dunigan

Media: Photo and Computer Graphics

Strategy Check

Use your knowledge and strategies from the workshop to answer these questions.

COMPREHENSION

Compare and Contrast

1. Select two forms of art that you read about in this workshop: painting, sculpture, music, photography, or writing. In the Venn diagram below, compare and contrast how each type of art can communicate power.

Art Form: _____   Art Form: _____

Summarize

2. Summarize one piece of advice that the author gives in "Letters to a Young Artist."

_____

_____

_____

LITERARY ANALYSIS

Character Traits

3. Describe the relationship between Zebra and Andrea in "Zebra." How does it change and why? Include evidence from the story.

_____

_____

_____

_____

_____

Author's Style

4. An author's **style** is sometimes determined by his or her **purpose** in writing. Read the following three descriptions of writing styles. Then match each style to a purpose. Read the three purposes described below the styles. Write *a, b,* or *c* on the blank next to each purpose to show which style best suits it.

a. formal, precise language

b. colorful descriptions; simple words

c. conversational and friendly

1. Explain to a teacher why you didn't do well on the last quiz. _____

2. Give advice to a good friend. _____

3. Describe an amusing character in a story for children. _____

NAVIGATING TEXT

Text Features and Visual Features

5. What information can you get from captions or labels for works of art that you cannot get from the art alone?

_____

_____

_____

VOCABULARY/WORD ANALYSIS

Multiple-Meaning Words

6. Suffixes can change a word's meaning and part of speech. Add the suffix *-ion* or *-al* to the words below. Then list the meaning of each new word.

Word	With Suffix	Meaning
concentrate (verb)		
clinic (noun)		
exhibit (verb)		
music (noun)		

Roots

7. Which of the following words contains the root *struct*, which means "to build"? Fill in the circle next to the correct answer.

- Ⓐ struck
- Ⓑ contraption
- Ⓒ struggle
- Ⓓ construction

Set and Use Criteria

8. First, select a type of art—writing, sculpture, or painting. Then decide on four criteria people might use when evaluating works of art.

Criteria

1. _____

2. _____

3. _____

4. _____

Analyze

9. What makes a person successful in the arts? Use examples from the selections in this workshop, as well as examples from your own life, to support your analysis.

_____

_____

_____

_____

_____

_____

_____

_____

What makes art powerful?

10. Use what you learned in this workshop to respond to the Expert Question.
Jot down some notes here. Then use a separate sheet of paper to write your response.

_____

_____

SPACE INVADERS

Expert Question:
Should we explore outer space?

21 Should we explore outer space?

As we study and explore space, we learn more about what wonders we can find out there—and what kinds of space events might affect us on planet Earth.

▶ Anchor Your Knowledge

Watch the Anchor Media, "Space Invaders," and meet Barbara Morgan, a teacher who is also an astronaut.

0:00/ 2:30

WORKSHOP GOALS

To gain expert knowledge about values, you will

- study **informational texts** about the search for life on other planets, and the dangers we face from space.

- read a **graphic story** about an alien invasion.

- learn **important skills and strategies** to help you understand what you read.

- develop **21st Century Skills** to **evaluate sources** and **deliver speeches**.

- write a **science fiction story** about a topic that interests you.

- complete an **Expert Project** by holding a debate about space.

▶ Opinionaire

Before reading this workshop, put a check mark to the left of each statement you agree with. Then, come back **after** the workshop is completed to see if you changed your mind.

BEFORE		TOPIC: **Exploring Space**	AFTER	
Y	N		Y	N
		Humans are the only intelligent form of life in the universe.		
		Space really is the final frontier—and that is good enough reason to explore it.		
		Lucky for us, asteroids never get too close to Earth.		
		Riding on a space shuttle is a pretty safe, routine event.		
		If an asteroid is on a collision course for Earth, there is nothing we can do about it.		
		We started exploring space so the military could get a technological edge on our enemies.		
		We might discover things on other planets that can have a major effect on our lives.		
		Space exploration is a waste of resources that could be spent solving Earth's problems.		

⊙ Preview the Expert Project

Preview the Expert Project on pages 152–155. At the end of this workshop, you'll hold a debate about the wisdom of investing in space exploration.

Asteroids are a potential source of valuable raw materials. A single asteroid could provide millions of tons of nickel, iron, magnesium, and other metals and minerals—and there are about one million asteroids in the solar system. One day, mining operations on asteroids could supply these resources to Earth and our colonies in space. It is estimated that the mineral wealth in the asteroid belt between Mars and Jupiter would be equivalent to about $100 billion for every person on Earth.

Asteroid Ida, and its satellite Dactyl, is located in the asteroid belt between Mars and Jupiter.

▶ What will you need to know or do to complete the Expert Project?

_____

_____

_____

_____

⊙ Explore Expert Space

Go to **www.expert21.com/student** to learn more about the topics in this workshop.

DISCOVER ONLINE

- Careers in Astronomy
- Time Line of Space Exploration
- Science Fiction

READ ONLINE

- Mars
- Asteroid
- Search for Extraterrestrial Life
- Space Stations

RESEARCH ONLINE

- Space Tourism
- Unidentified Flying Objects
- The Future of the Space Program

⊙ Personal Inquiry

Explore the topic of space exploration by asking your own questions. Return to add questions as you continue reading Workshop 6. Plan to revisit your questions.

Barbara Morgan: Astronaut/Teacher

"I am an ordinary person, who had an extraordinary experience."

FACTS AND STATS

NAME: Barbara Morgan

HOMETOWN: Boise, Idaho

JOB: Former NASA astronaut for the Teacher in Space Program; Distinguished Educator in Residence, Boise State University

EDUCATION: Bachelor of Arts, Biology, Teaching Credential

WORKPLACE: Space Shuttle *Endeavour*; NASA Johnson Space Center; Boise State University

WORKPLACE LITERACIES: Collaborate; communicate; make decisions; solve problems; analyze risk

PAY: Astronaut candidates can earn $59,493 to $130,257 per year.

CAREER CONNECTION Science, Technology, Engineering, and Mathematics
www.careerclusters.org

Go to **21** ToolKit Expert File 6.30 to learn more about careers in space research.

RELATED JOBS: Engineer, researcher, lab assistant, teacher, shuttle parts manufacturer

Meet a teacher and astronaut who served aboard the Space Shuttle *Endeavour*.

On August 8, 2007, the Space Shuttle *Endeavour* STS-118 lifted off from the Kennedy Space Center in Florida. On board was Barbara Morgan, Mission Specialist and Teacher in Space. Her destination: the International Space Station. Her mission: to help with its construction. Here is what a day in space was like for her.

STEP 1 — Rise and Shine

Like everyone else, astronauts begin the day with breakfast. But for them, eating is a bit more challenging. At first, Morgan found it hard to swallow her food. "It felt like it stayed up near your throat." But it got easier and can even be fun—like when you catch floating M&M's with your mouth.

STEP 2 — What's the Plan?

Next, Morgan read the latest flight plan and examined it for changes. Mission Control oversees every mission detail from the ground and creates the plans—one for each day. Throughout the flight, crew members stayed in **frequent contact** with Mission Control and reported their activities and any changes.

STEP 3 — Workload

Next, Morgan began her day's work. Working with a **partner,** she used the robotic arm to carefully lift 7,000 pounds of equipment to hand off to the space station's robotic arm. Using a robotic arm might sound simple, but it's far from it. Morgan spent countless hours in training at the Johnson Space Center in Houston learning how to use the arm. "It was a little like learning to drive a car, with many things going on and knowing what to pay attention to. It's also a lot of fun. It's math in action." Next, she and her **crewmates** transferred tons of used equipment back to the shuttle through a tunnel that connected the shuttle with the space station.

STEP 4 — Teamwork

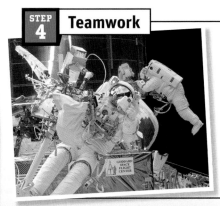

In space, teamwork is crucial. Crewmates are almost always paired up when they're working. "One person might be controlling the robotic arm while another is watching to make sure it's done right." Spacewalkers are always sent out two at a time.

STEP 5 — Decisions About Safety

During their liftoff, chunks of foam struck the shuttle and damaged some tile. In orbit, Morgan and her crewmates used a camera on the robotic arm to take photos of the damaged tiles and send them to NASA. NASA managers examined the data and **analyzed risk.** They **decided** that the tiles are safe enough and that trying to fix them might cause more damage.

STEP 6 — Downtime?

The crew was "almost always working, studying, and reviewing their tasks." Even with all the demands, they made time for some fun. They communicated with students on Earth and answered their questions about the mission. They even celebrated a teammate's birthday—using a flashlight bulb for a candle.

STEP 7 — Day's End

Before bed, crew members prepared for the next day, reviewed flight plans and made necessary changes, and checked e-mail. Finally, they zipped themselves up in "flimsy sleeping bags." To keep from floating around bumping into equipment during the night, they clipped their bags to the wall.

ANALYZE WORKPLACE SKILLS

1. Communicate
Why is it important for the astronauts to stay in contact with the ground team?

_____

_____

_____

2. Collaborate
Give two examples of ways that astronauts collaborate.

_____

_____

_____

Why is teamwork so important in space?

_____

_____

_____

_____

3. Analyze Risk and Make Decisions
What problem did the crew face on liftoff?

_____

_____

How did NASA decide what to do about the problem?

_____

_____

_____

_____

_____

DISCOVER ONLINE

 expert space
Go to **www.expert21.com/student**
to learn more about Careers in Astronomy;
Time Line of Space Exploration.

Graphic Novel

THE ZERO HOUR

All of the young children in Mink's neighborhood are playing an alien invasion game. At first Mink's mother smiles at the children's harmless fun. What makes her come to believe that the game may not be harmless after all?

QuickWrite

What kinds of games did you play when you were little? Did any of the games involve using your imagination? Describe one game that required imagining things.

Graphic Stories: Text and Visuals LITERARY ANALYSIS

Graphic stories **combine text and visuals.** The events in a story are told through illustrations, which appear in **panels.** The characters' words are shown in **speech bubbles.** Other information may appear in **captions.**

When you read a graphic story

• look at the illustrations.

• read the text in captions and speech bubbles.

• use visuals to track story events and changes in setting.

• look at characters' facial expressions for clues to what they think and feel.

▶ **Read the following panels. Then complete the sentences below.**

• This story is set in _____.

• The characters are _____.

Draw Conclusions COMPREHENSION

When you draw a conclusion, you figure out things an author has not directly stated.

To draw a conclusion, take details from what you are reading and use them as evidence to build an interpretation of the story that makes sense of the plot and characters' actions.

▶ **Using the panels from the previous exercise, complete the chart below.**

Detail 1		Detail 2		Detail 2
	+		**=**	Mary is worried.

Academic Language VOCABULARY

▶ Rate your knowledge of each word. Then write its meaning and an example sentence.

Word	Meaning	Example
CONTENT AREA WORDS *Use these words to talk and write about social studies.*		
dimension di•men•sion (noun) ① ② ③ ④	a measurement of space; in science fiction, a universe	I read a science fiction story about aliens from another dimension.
futuristic fu•tur•is•tic (adjective) ① ② ③ ④		
SELECTION WORDS *These words are key to understanding this selection.*		
cluttered clut•tered (adjective) ① ② ③ ④		
deceptively de•cep•tive•ly (adverb) ① ② ③ ④		
disdain dis•dain (verb) ① ② ③ ④		Delia is a fashion snob and disdains any clothes she thinks are beneath her standards.
evoke e•voke (verb) ① ② ③ ④	to call to mind a certain feeling or idea	
suspenseful sus•pense•ful (adjective) ① ② ③ ④		
underfoot un•der•foot (adverb) ① ② ③ ④		

Rating Scale ① I don't know the word. ② I've seen it or heard it. ③ I know its meaning. ④ I know it and use it.

Context Clues WORD ANALYSIS

Context clues are words and phrases that help you puzzle together the meaning of a new or unfamiliar word.

Clues might be contrasting or supporting terms. In other cases, the clues might rephrase the meaning of the unfamiliar word or provide illustrative examples.

▶ Read this sentence. Underline the context clues that help you understand what *futuristic* means.

I love imagining <u>futuristic</u> inventions such as cars that fly and personal robots!

What does *futuristic* mean?

_____

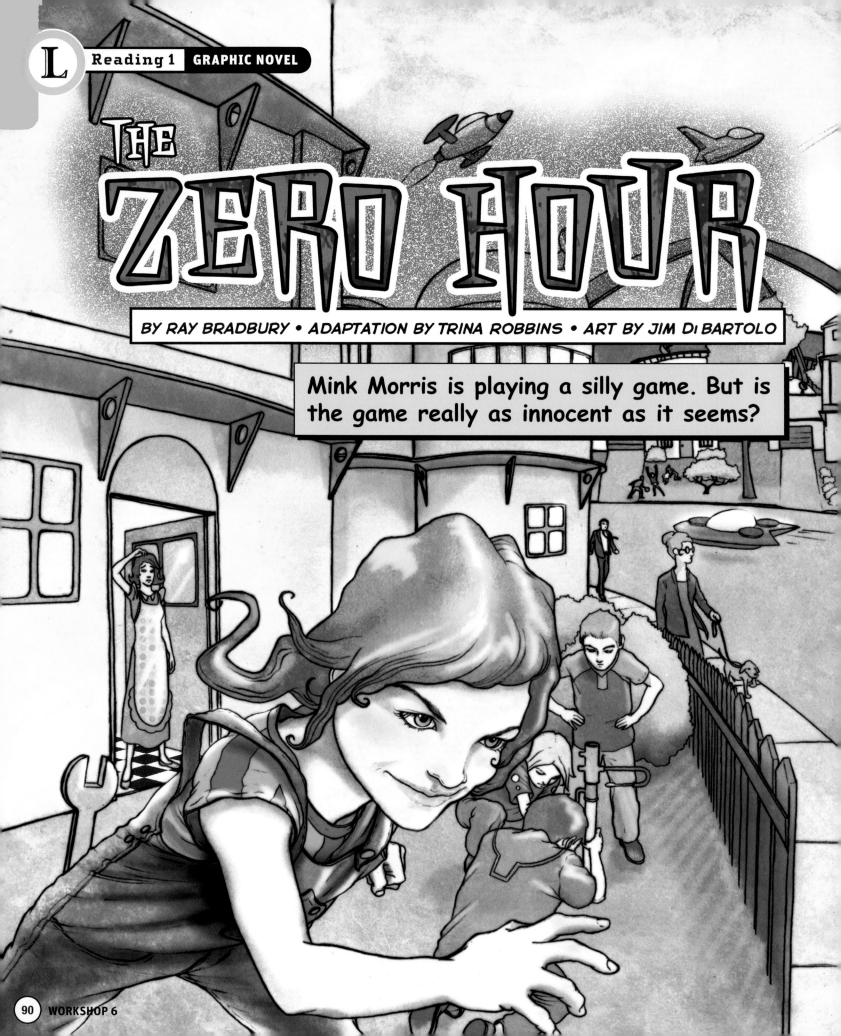

THE ZERO HOUR

BY RAY BRADBURY • ADAPTATION BY TRINA ROBBINS • ART BY JIM DI BARTOLO

Mink Morris is playing a silly game. But is the game really as innocent as it seems?

In 1947, webcams, videoconferencing, and the Internet hadn't been invented. In fact, human beings had yet to walk on the moon. Because people knew so little about space and technology, writers would often imagine what the future would look like. It was at this time in history that Ray Bradbury wrote his **suspenseful** science fiction story "The Zero Hour."

Bradbury's story takes place in a **futuristic** American neighborhood. People travel in jet-fueled cars, speak to each other over specialized television sets, and order lunch from ultramodern vending machines. Although none of this technology existed when Bradbury wrote the story, some of it actually exists today.

The world Ray Bradbury created in "The Zero Hour" is filled with neat little houses and lawns. Bradbury's setting is meant to **evoke** feelings of peace and happiness. Everything is perfect ... until one day, when a **deceptively** innocent girl makes a mysterious new friend named Drill.

videoconferencing (n.) using telephones and televisions to speak to people in other locations

hearty (*adj.*) vigorous
bustle (*n.*) energetic activity

Make Predictions
What do you think the children are doing?

Read and Synthesize

COMPREHENSION

Draw Conclusions

Review page 92. Who is shown leading the children in their game?

_____

_____

_____

• Why might this contribute to the older children disdaining the invasion game?

_____

_____

_____

_____

LITERARY ANALYSIS

Graphic Stories: Text and Visuals

Put a **check** ✓ next to visual details in the pictures on pages 92–93 that show that this story takes place in the future.

VOCABULARY/WORD ANALYSIS

Context Clues: Examples

Review the second caption on page 92. <u>Underline</u> the context clues that would help you find the meaning of the term *affair* as it is used here.

• What does affair mean?

_____

_____

• Describe the difference between how the younger children play and how the older children play.

_____

_____

_____

_____

_____

_____

_____

_____

The comic panels

They couldn't figure a way to attack.

Drill says in order to make a good fight you got to have a new way of surprising people. And they couldn't figure a way to surprise Earth.

Until, one day, they thought of children!

Make Connections
If you heard Mink's story, would you believe her?

COMPREHENSION

Draw Conclusions

Review the following details from the story. Write whether the detail supports the conclusion that the invasion is imaginary or real.

1. Adults have seen the children playing, but have not been worried by them.

_____

_____

2. The children seem to have a very strict schedule for the invasion.

_____

_____

3. The invasion only involves young children.

_____

_____

LITERARY ANALYSIS

Graphic Stories: Text and Visuals

Review the last panel on page 95. What does Mink's expression tell you about her feelings toward the invasion game.

_____

_____

_____

21 SMALL GROUPS/INDEPENDENT

COLLABORATE

Create Stories Imagine that you and your group are space aliens about to invade Earth. Discuss your plans for conquering the world.

COMMUNICATE

Respond and Write Write a short dialogue between Drill and an Earth child in which Drill describes the invasion. Begin by jotting down notes, and then write them in dialogue form.

Question
What questions do you have about the way Mink is behaving?

AT FOUR O'CLOCK THE AUDIO-VISOR BUZZED.

Hello, Mary. How are things in New York?

Fine. How are things in Scranton? You look tired.

The children. **Underfoot.**

My Mink, too. The super-Invasion.

Are your kids playing that game too?

Oh, yes. Were we this bad when we were kids?

Worse. Don't know how my parents put up with me.

Parents learn to shut their ears.

Hmm . . . shut their ears?

What's wrong, Mary?

Oh, nothing. Just thought . . . never mind.

My boy Tim worships some guy named— Drill, I think it was.

Josephine in Boston says her kids are wild on this new game, too. It's sweeping the country.

COMPREHENSION

Draw Conclusions

From Mink's discussion of the invasion on page 96, explain why Drill would choose younger children to help in the invasion instead of older children or adults. Use details from the story to support your conclusion.

_____

_____

_____

_____

_____

_____

_____

_____

_____

_____

_____

_____

LITERARY ANALYSIS

Graphic Stories: Text and Visuals

Review page 97. (Circle) the images and underline the text that shows Mink's mother's changing attitude toward the invasion game.

• Describe Mink's mother's new attitude.

_____

_____

_____

_____

_____

CRITICAL THINKING

Evaluate

Assuming the invasion is real, are Mink's reasons for helping Drill reasonable? Discuss the wisdom of Mink's motives with a partner.

Five o'clock—five o'clock. Time's a-wasting. Five o'clock.

Ha! Zero hour.

A BEETLE CAR HUMMED INTO THE DRIVEWAY. MR. MORRIS.

Hello, darling.

Hello, Henry.

Swell day. Makes you glad to be alive.

OUTSIDE, THE CHILDREN WERE SILENT. TOO SILENT.

BZZZZT!

What's that?

I don't know. Those children haven't anything dangerous out there, have they? Nothing electrical?

Heck, no. I looked.

Just the same, you'd better go tell them to quit. It's after five. Tell them—ha, ha—to put off their invasion until tomorrow.

THE BUZZING GREW LOUDER.

Make Inferences
What does *zero hour* mean?

COMPREHENSION

Summarize
Summarize what happens at zero hour.

_____

_____

_____

_____

_____

_____

_____

_____

LITERARY ANALYSIS

Graphic Stories: Text and Visuals
Review pages 98–99. (Circle) the images and underline the dialogue that prove the invasion game is more than just pretend.

• Do you think Mrs. Morris's reaction on page 98 is realistic?

_____

_____

_____

_____

_____

_____

_____

_____

_____

_____

VOCABULARY/WORD ANALYSIS

Context Clues
The slang term *swell* was used often in Ray Bradbury's time. Find the panel in which the word *swell* is used, and underline the sentence that helps explain its meaning.

• What is another word for *swell*?

_____

_____

THE EXPLOSION!

KA-
-KRAKA
FA-

-BOOOOM!

THERE WERE OTHER EXPLOSIONS IN OTHER YARDS ON OTHER STREETS.

Up this way! In the attic! That's where it is!

It's not in the attic! It's outside!

ANOTHER EXPLOSION OUTSIDE. THE CHILDREN SCREAMED WITH DELIGHT.

No, no! I'll show you. Hurry! I'll show you!

THERE WAS NO TIME TO ARGUE WITH HENRY TO CONVINCE HIM. LET HIM THINK HER INSANE.

THEY TUMBLED INTO THE ATTIC. SHE SLAMMED THE DOOR, LOCKED IT, THREW THE KEY INTO A FAR, **CLUTTERED** CORNER.

There, there. We're safe until tonight. Maybe we can sneak out. Maybe we can escape!

Are you crazy? Why'd you throw the key away, honey?

Quiet. They'll hear us. Oh, gosh, they'll find us soon enough—

Clarify
Why are the children happy about what's happening?

Read and Synthesize

COMPREHENSION

Draw Conclusion

On page 101, <u>underline</u> the text that explains why Mrs. Morris lies about where the explosion noises are coming from.

• Is hiding in the attic a good idea?

_____

• Provide two pieces of evidence from the story that support your conclusion.

1. _____

_____

_____

2. _____

_____

_____

LITERARY ANALYSIS

Graphic Stories: Text and Visuals

What mood do the illustrations on pages 100–101 convey?

_____

_____

_____

CRITICAL THINKING

Synthesize

How does the author drop clues about the invasion throughout the story?

_____

_____

_____

_____

_____

_____

_____

_____

_____

_____

Ray Bradbury

AUTHOR FILE

BORN August 22, 1920, in Waukegan, Illinois

CLAIM TO FAME Bradbury is one of the most successful science fiction writers of our time. He has published hundreds of short stories and classic books, such as *Martian Chronicles*, *Something Wicked This Way Comes*, *Dandelion Wine*, and *The Illustrated Man*.

OTHER CREDITS Bradbury wrote episodes of *The Twilight Zone*, *Alfred Hitchcock Presents*, and the screenplay of *Moby Dick*. He also helped design EPCOT Center and the 1964 World's Fair.

A LIFETIME OF SUCCESS Bradbury has received a lifetime achievement award from the National Books Foundation and a special award from the Pulitzer Prize committee. He also has a star on the Hollywood walk of fame, a crater on the moon named "Dandelion Crater" after his novel *Dandelion Wine,* and a comet named after him (9766 Bradbury).

FAVORITE AUTHORS H.G. Wells, Jules Verne, Emily Dickinson, Robert Frost

Peekaboo.

Question
What questions are you left with at the end of the story?

LITERARY ANALYSIS

Graphic Stories: Text and Visuals

Compare Mrs. Morris's emotions on page 102 with Mr. Morris's reaction.

Mrs. Morris: _____

_____

Mr. Morris: _____

_____

• Complete the table by writing in the dialogue and visual clues that reveal how each character feels?

Mr. Morris	Mrs. Morris

21 SMALL GROUPS/INDEPENDENT

COLLABORATE

Represent Imagine you are going to turn this story into a radio play. Pick any one page from the story. Create a list of the number of speaking parts you will need. Then create a list of sound effects you will need to make the story work.

COMMUNICATE

Discuss and Write With a partner, discuss what might happen to the kids who helped Drill. Write a paragraph explaining your ideas.

READ ONLINE

expert space
Go to **www.expert21.com/student** to learn more about Mars; Ray Bradbury; Technology and Society.

Science Feature

CRASH COURSE

W **QuickWrite**

When you think of outer space, what comes to mind? Does outer space make you feel curious, fearful, or indifferent? Why?

Do you have any idea what would happen if a giant asteroid crashed into Earth? It could be a disaster of unprecedented size! Fortunately, scientists are working on ways to protect the planet in case a monster asteroid heads our way.

Cause and Effect COMPREHENSION

A cause is the reason that something happens. An effect is the result of a cause.

To find an effect, ask yourself "What happened?" To find a cause, ask yourself "Why did it happen?"

A series of causes and effects is called a **causal chain.**

▶ **Read the sentences below. Then complete the chart to show a causal chain.**

When the asteroid hit Earth, massive amounts of soil and debris were thrown into the sky. This material combined with the smoke of wildfires that burned worldwide. Together they darkened the sky until the light of the sun was dimmed. As a result, the temperature dropped on the surface of the planet and regular rainfalls were toxic.

An asteroid impacts Earth.

↓

↓

↓

The temperature on the surface of the planet drops.

Graphic Aid: Diagrams NAVIGATING TEXT

Many nonfiction texts include graphic aids such as maps, photographs, and diagrams.

Diagrams are illustrations that show the parts of an object or explain a process.

▶ **Look at the parts of the diagram.**

• Underline the title.

• Circle the word that describes what the moon is doing when it becomes *more* visible from Earth.

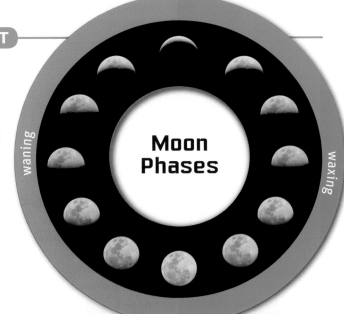

waning   **Moon Phases**   waxing

Academic Language VOCABULARY

▶ **Rate your knowledge of each word. Then write its meaning and an example sentence.**

Word	Meaning	Example
EXPERT WORDS *Use these words to write and talk about the workshop topic.*		
asteroid as•ter•oid *(noun)* ① ② ③ ④	a piece of space rock that orbits the sun	A large asteroid can have a devastating effect if it hits a planet.
comet com•et *(noun)* ① ② ③ ④		
meteor me•te•or *(noun)* ① ② ③ ④	a bright streak caused by a space rock entering Earth's atmosphere	
ACADEMIC WORDS *Use these words in all your subject classes.*		
detect de•tect *(verb)* ① ② ③ ④		
device de•vice *(noun)* ① ② ③ ④		
scope scope *(verb)* ① ② ③ ④		
CONTENT AREA WORDS *Use these words to talk and write about social studies.*		
friction fric•tion *(noun)* ① ② ③ ④		The friction that results when two rocks collide can sometimes cause sparks to fly.
propel pro•pel *(verb)* ① ② ③ ④		

Rating Scale ① I don't know the word. ② I've seen it or heard it. ③ I know its meaning. ④ I know it and use it.

Context Clues: Definition WORD ANALYSIS

Sometimes authors include **definitions** of words with which readers may be unfamiliar. As you read, look for definitions that explain unfamiliar terms. Sometimes, a definition appears in parentheses after the unfamiliar term.

▶ **Read this sentence. Circle the definition that explains what asteroids are.**

Comets and <u>asteroids</u> are chunks of space rock. Scientists think they may be bits of matter left over from the formation of planets.

CRASH COURSE

BY NANCY HONOVICH

A massive asteroid crashing into Earth seems like the stuff of movies, but the truth is, it could happen. Fortunately for people on Earth today, it probably won't happen for hundreds of thousands of years. Still, scientists are scrambling to spot potential threats and are making plans to avert disaster.

On July 16, 1994, astronomers around the world turned their telescopes toward Jupiter. They were about to watch an amazing event. A group of icy space rocks known as the Shoemaker-Levy 9 **comet** sped toward the giant planet at 60 kilometers (37 miles) per second.

As the comet hit the gaseous planet, it caused shock waves (powerful blasts of air). Great bursts of gas shot into Jupiter's upper atmosphere. When the blasts finally stopped, scientists discovered that Jupiter had been deeply scarred. Great clouds of gas and dust had formed in the planet's atmosphere. The clouds stayed there for several months. And the scientists who had observed the event were left wondering: Could this happen to Earth?

After seeing Shoemaker-Levy 9's collision with Jupiter, scientists reacted by paying closer attention to space rocks that could pose a threat to Earth. Comets and large **asteroids** are chunks of space rock that often measure hundreds of meters in diameter. Usually they orbit the sun in paths millions of miles away from Earth. But sometimes they come within 100,000 miles of our planet. That may seem like a huge distance. But for many scientists, it's too close for comfort.

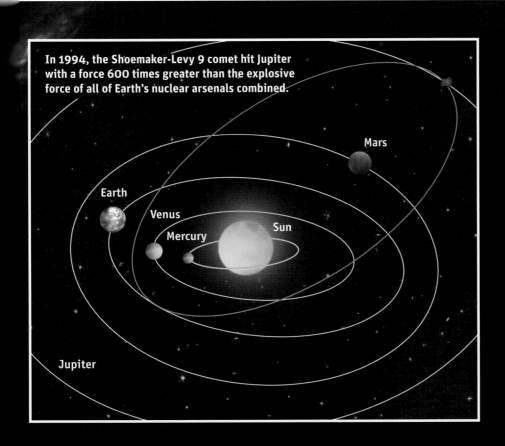

In 1994, the Shoemaker-Levy 9 comet hit Jupiter with a force 600 times greater than the explosive force of all of Earth's nuclear arsenals combined.

Mars

Earth

Venus

Sun

Mercury

Jupiter

orbit *(v.)* travel around something

COMPREHENSION

Cause and Effect

List two effects of the impact of the Shoemaker-Levy 9 comet on the planet Jupiter.

1. _____

_____

_____

_____

2. _____

_____

_____

_____

NAVIGATING TEXT

Graphic Aids: Diagrams

Review the diagram on page 107. What do the large rings in the diagram represent?

_____

_____

_____

_____

_____

Why might the diagram maker include objects, like Earth and the sun, that were not directly involved in the impact?

_____

_____

_____

_____

_____

_____

_____

_____

_____

_____

DINO KILLER

Could a giant rock really destroy all life on Earth? About 65 million years ago, one asteroid may have nearly accomplished that feat.

According to the prevailing theory, the 6-mile-wide asteroid sped toward Earth at up to 67,000 miles per hour. When it hit, it created a nearly 120 mile-wide hole called the Chicxulub (CHEEK-zhu-loob) crater. The crater now lies on the seafloor just north of Mexico's Yucatán Peninsula. It is buried under millions of years worth of mud.

Scientists hypothesize what happened. Seconds after impact, a shock wave buckled Earth's crust (surface). The shock wave killed every living thing within a several thousand-mile-wide radius and triggered faraway earthquakes. Some Chicxulub quakes would overwhelm today's Richter scale—a scale that measures an earthquake's energy, from 1 to 10—and score a 12. (Compare that

to a 1999 quake which hit Izmet, Turkey, and measured 7.4 on the Richter scale. It leveled the city and claimed more than 30,000 human lives.) Underwater earthquakes resulted in tsunamis. The monster waves buried entire coastlines and toppled mountains into oceans.

On impact, the Chicxulub crater spit 25 trillion tons of earth across the planet and into space. "Some debris was thrown halfway to the Moon," Dan Durda, an asteroid scientist at the Southwest Research Institute in Colorado, says. Within an hour, debris rained back toward Earth. Traveling at high speeds, the debris tore through the atmosphere. **Friction** caused much of it to catch fire in the air, igniting wildfires worldwide.

As Durda explains, "It was every ecological disaster you can think of happening at the same time."

Dark Days

In the fiery aftermath, soot blocked out sunlight for years. The lack of sun caused the planet to suffer a long cold spell. Chemical reactions from the fires increased the amounts of toxic chemicals like nitric acid in the atmosphere. The toxic chemicals caused destructive acid rain.

In the end, only one-quarter of all life on Earth survived. Fortunately, says Durda, "large impacts of this size happen once in hundreds of millions of years."

Small Packages, Big Surprises

Smaller impacts happen with surprising frequency. There are 170 known impact craters on Earth. Many more are hidden by built-up mud, new bodies of water, or erosion. However, if we look at the Moon, whose landscape isn't affected by these Earth processes, we can count 300,000 craters. One 0.03-inch-wide meteorite hits Earth about once every thirty seconds, with little effect. Fortunately, the larger the meteorite, the less likely it is to strike.

Unlikely as they are, even medium-sized objects with the potential to strike us are worthy of study. In 1908, a massive explosion occurred over a remote area of Russia. The blast, called the Tunguska event after the nearby Tunguska River, leveled trees across an area larger than Washington, D.C. Scientists believe it was caused by a large asteroid or comet exploding upon entering the atmosphere, though they never found meteorite debris, nor did they determine the exact cause of the blast. (Of course, unfounded theories about alien attacks persist.) However, the devastation people observed helped start the discussion about whether and how humans could prevent such a collision, considering that the event could have happened over a populated city.

> **Question**
> **What questions do you have after reading this section?**

> **debris** *(n.)* scattered pieces of something that has been destroyed
> **aftermath** *(n.)* consequences of a disaster

SPACE ROCKS: WHAT'S THE DIFFERENCE?

ASTEROIDS

Millions of these large rocks orbit the inner solar system. They come in three main types: rock, metal (iron and nickel), and both rock and metal. Some asteroids, like Ceres, measure nearly 600 miles across. Most asteroids are found orbiting in a ring between the planets Mars and Jupiter.

COMETS

These "dirty snowballs" consist of snow and dust grains. They orbit nearly one light-year (9.5 trillion km) from the sun. Some comets swing near the sun, where they are vaporized by the sun's heat. Humans have been observing comets throughout recorded history. The famous philosopher Aristotle wrote about them and a comet is depicted in the Bayeux Tapestry, which records the Norman conquest of England in the year 1066.

METEOROIDS

These bits of dust and rock are debris from comets or asteroids. Thousands enter the atmosphere daily. Friction burns them up—you see a streak of light, or a **meteor**. If a piece of the meteoroid manages to survive the high heat and hits the ground, it is called a meteorite. The largest meteorite ever discovered in the United States weighs more than 15 tons. It is currently on display in the American Museum of Natural History in New York.

vaporized *(v.)* turns to dust

COMPREHENSION

Cause and Effect

Review the first section of "Dino Killer." Find a causal chain in the story of the Chicxulub crater. **Number** the first three steps in the chain.

WORD ANALYSIS

Context Clues: Definition

Review page 108. <u>Underline</u> the definition of "Richter scale."

- What is the difference between a standard earthquake and an asteroid strike like the one that happened in Chicxulub, Mexico, millions of years ago?

_____

_____

_____

_____

_____

_____

_____

_____

_____

21 SMALL GROUPS/INDEPENDENT

COLLABORATE

Represent Your group has been given the job of making the cover of a nonfiction book about the "Dino Killer" asteroid. Decide what details will appear on your book cover.

COMMUNICATE

Respond and Write Write a brief introduction to a science television program on asteroids. Begin by jotting down notes. Then turn them into a brief script. Read your introduction aloud to the class.

W

WHAT ARE ASTEROIDS?

Asteroids range in size from a grain of sand to several hundred miles wide. Scientists think asteroids may be leftover "bits" of space matter that didn't clump together to form a planet when the solar system formed 4.6 billion years ago.

Some asteroids are made of crumbly, granite-like rocks. This type of asteroid easily breaks apart when entering Earth's atmosphere. Other asteroids are metallic. Metallic asteroids are made mostly of nickel and iron. They are less likely to break apart in Earth's atmosphere. Fortunately, open spaces or oceans cover most of Earth. It's more likely that a small metallic asteroid will splash down in the ocean than strike human-populated areas.

Today, 90 percent of all known asteroids reside in the asteroid belt. The asteroid belt is the region of space between the orbits of Jupiter and Mars. Others, called Trojan asteroids, form a cloud beside Jupiter. The Trojan asteroids are held captive by the planet's and the sun's gravity (attracting force).

Spotting a Killer Asteroid

Today, astronomers regularly survey space to **scope** out and chart the course of asteroids on a collision course with Earth. By 2010, astronomers hope to have pinpointed 90 percent of near-Earth asteroids (NEAs) with a width larger than 1 kilometer. The impact of a space rock that size or larger could devastate the planet. Approximately 1,000 NEAs larger than 1 kilometer orbit

near Earth, according to the National Optical Astronomy Observatory.

To search for asteroids, astronomers take a picture of the sky. A few minutes later, they take another picture. Astronomers look at both pictures to see which objects have moved. The objects that have moved might be asteroids. David Tholen of the University of Hawaii's Institute for Astronomy studies asteroids. He uses computer-controlled telescopes and CCD (charge-coupled **device**) cameras. CCD cameras are twenty times more sensitive than film to faint starlight. "The astronomer divides the sky into a grid," says Tholen, "and the telescope repeatedly searches the grid."

Asteroids that orbit near Earth move a lot in the images. Faraway stars don't seem to move at all. Astronomers use an asteroid's changing position in each image to calculate its orbit. If an asteroid looks like it may travel close to Earth and is wider than a half kilometer (the length of five football fields), astronomers track it carefully.

Known Near-Earth Asteroids

Until recently, whenever astronomers discovered an NEA, news headlines declared that the end of the Earth was near. Not anymore. "Scientists now realize that thousands of small asteroids have the potential to hit Earth," says Richard Binzel. Binzel is a planetary astronomer at the Massachusetts Institute

of Technology. Binzel and his colleagues created an asteroid danger scale to calm the public. The scale is called the Torino Impact Hazard Scale. The scale rates NEAs from 0 to 10. Zero means there is no hazard from the NEA. "Ten means we're certain to be hit, and it'll be as bad as the dinosaurs," says Binzel. For years, no asteroid has been rated above 2.

Asteroids' orbits vary, but most take between three and six years to circle the sun one time. Scientists can predict the path such an asteroid will take, and can **detect** many potentially dangerous asteroids years or decades before their orbits swing them too close. But some asteroids take hundreds of years to orbit the sun. These long-orbiting asteroids are easy to miss, and their paths are very difficult to predict. Scientists fear these asteroids most. In August 2002, a 2,500-foot asteroid strayed 330,000 miles from Earth. The asteroid—called "2002 NY40"—had been spotted only a month before.

> **Make Inferences**
> **What is the significance of asteroid "2002 NY40"?**

Impending Doom?

One asteroid is especially worrisome to astronomers. In 2004, scientists discovered an asteroid they named Apophis, after the ancient Egyptian mythological demon that sought to plunge the world into eternal darkness. This rock measures about 300 meters (984 feet) across. That's tiny compared

> **devastate** *(v.)* to destroy
> **calculate** *(v.)* to figure out using mathematics

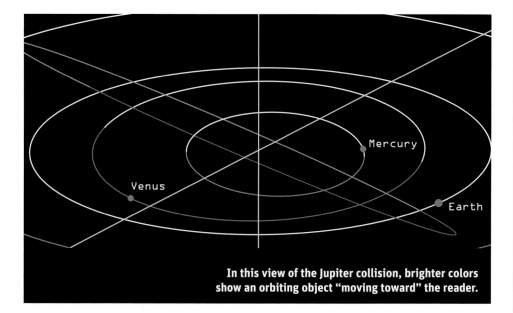

In this view of the Jupiter collision, brighter colors show an orbiting object "moving toward" the reader.

to the asteroid that destroyed the dinosaurs, but it still could cause tremendous destruction.

Scientists have mapped Apophis's entire 233-day orbit around the sun. They have been calculating its whereabouts in relation to Earth for decades from now. On April 13, 2029, Apophis will swing within approximately 35,400 kilometers (21,997 mi) of Earth. That's ten times closer to Earth than the Moon. During that near miss, Earth's gravity could pull Apophis onto a new course. Seven years later, in 2036, there is a slim (1 in 45,000) but real chance that Apophis could strike Earth. An impact of this size would have catastrophic consequences.

How Bad Would It Be?

If an asteroid the size of Apophis were to strike Earth, it wouldn't mean the end of life on the planet. But it would still be terrible. The Barringer Crater, a 1-mile-wide hole in the Arizona desert, was carved out when a meteorite crashed into Earth 49,000 years ago. Apophis is approximately ten times bigger than that meteorite. It has roughly one thousand times as much mass. So it would release a thousand times as much energy during impact.

A blast of heat would be the first effect. It would set off forest fires for hundreds of miles around the impact. The fires would then propel huge amounts of ash and soot into the atmosphere. These clouds of ash, in turn, would block sunlight, causing temperatures to drop. In addition, billions of tons of rock and dust would be blown sky-high during the impact. All this material would then fall back to pummel the Earth over the next few days. That's if the asteroid were to strike land. If it crashed in the ocean, there would be massive tsunamis. The best-case scenario for an impact would be if the asteroid landed in the Pacific Ocean, the deeper of the two oceans. But even then, a giant tsunami would wash ashore along western North and South America, and eastern Asia. Cities along the coastlines would be destroyed.

---

whereabouts *(n.)* location

CRITICAL THINKING

Evaluate
Do you think asteroids pose a serious threat to life on Earth? Why or why not? Provide evidence from the text to support your opinion.

_____

_____

_____

_____

_____

NAVIGATING TEXT

Graphic Aids: Diagrams
Review the diagram on page 111. What problem does showing the orbits in two colors solve?

_____

_____

_____

COMPREHENSION

Cause and Effect
Review the text under the heading *How Bad Would It Be?* on page 111. <u>Underline</u> the effects an asteroid the size of Apophis would have if it hit an ocean.

• Write the effects in the cause-and-effect chain below.

PLANETARY DEFENSE

Scientists are coming up with some far-out ideas for diverting a killer asteroid. One strategy: Send a spacecraft to knock it off its path. The spacecraft would be equipped with powerful engines. By bumping the asteroid, it would nudge it into a different orbit. "It wouldn't take much," says Binzel. Think of balls on a pool table. A tiny tap will cause a billiard ball to veer and miss a pool-table pocket. An asteroid could be nudged in the same way. A tiny tap could create a huge difference in its orbit, Binzel says. Another option: set off a bomb on the asteroid. This would reduce its size. However, a bomb would blow the asteroid into many smaller pieces, giving astronomers many smaller, but still-dangerous, objects to worry about.

Some scientists believe a bucket of paint could solve the problem. While asteroids vary in shape and color, most are dark rock. The rock heats up by absorbing sunlight. (Think about wearing a black shirt during summer—it gets hot.) Heat radiating off the sunlit sides of large asteroids actually acts as a weak "rocket engine" that **propels** the asteroid.

Scientists think this principle, called the Yarkovsky effect, could be altered. How? By painting an asteroid a less-heat-absorbing color. A white paint job could alter the asteroid's orbit. This

Barringer Crater, in Arizona, measures nearly 1 mile wide and 570 feet deep. It is the site of an impact that occurred 49,000 years ago.

would be a good method for dealing with regularly orbiting asteroids. We could paint them far in advance of any impact. With twenty or thirty years' warning of a potential killer, "it's a case where time is on our side," says Binzel.

Gravity, the same force that could pull an asteroid toward Earth, could also be used to defend against a collision. Scientists could launch a massive object into space and park it within a few football field–lengths of the asteroid. The massive gravity from this object would tug on the asteroid. Over time, that object's gravitational pull would slowly deflect the asteroid away from Earth's path.

Scientists also think "mirror bees" have a good chance of success. A group of small satellites with mirrors 30 to 100 feet wide would swarm around an asteroid. The mirrors would reflect sunlight onto the asteroid, heating one spot to the point that it starts to release a stream of gas. The gas would work like a rocket engine, blowing the asteroid onto a new course. Still, the best chance Earth has is the odds against a strike.

Consider this talk of cosmic collisions a source of wonder rather than worry. Look both ways before you cross the road, and look to the stars for inspiration. ∎

Summarize
Summarize three different asteroid collision solutions scientists are investigating.

diverting *(v.)* moving onto a different path
veer *(v.)* to change direction suddenly

ASTEROIDS: THREAT AND RISK

THREAT

An asteroid the size of...		Enters Earth's atmosphere...	Potentially causing...
	Dust, and Small Rocks	Continually	Shooting stars
	A Car	Twice a Month	An aerial explosion with the force of an atomic bomb
	A Blue Whale	Every few centuries	A powerful shockwave traveling 100 miles
	The Titanic	Every few hundred centuries	A tsunami, if it hit an ocean.
0.5 miles	Half Mile	A few times per million years	A regional calamity
1.0 miles	One Mile	Every million years	A world-wide calamity
3.0 miles	Three Miles	Every ten million years	Human extinction; such an impact may have killed the dinosaurs

RISK

How likely is death by an asteroid impact? Before you panic, check out the chart below, which compares the odds and causes of dying in the United States.

Cause of Death	Chances
Motor vehicle accident	1 in 100
Fire	1 in 800
Electrocution	1 in 5,000
Asteroid/Comet impact	1 in 20,000
Passenger aircraft crash	1 in 20,000
Flood	1 in 30,000
Tornado	1 in 60,000

Source: C.R. Chapman and D. Morrison, 1994, *Nature* 367z, 33–40.

odds (*n.*) chances

COMPREHENSION

Cause and Effect

If an asteroid the size of a car were to enter Earth's atmosphere, what effect would it have?

_____

_____

_____

_____

_____

_____

The destructive force of an asteroid is determined by what feature?

_____

_____

_____

_____

_____

_____

_____

21 SMALL GROUPS/INDEPENDENT

COLLABORATE

Debate In a group, debate whether or not you feel it's worth spending millions of dollars to defend Earth from asteroid collisions. Use evidence from the text to support your view.

COMMUNICATE

React and Write Write a scene from a movie about an asteroid that is headed for Earth. Begin by listing ideas, then write the scene.

READ ONLINE

 expert space
Go to **www.expert21.com/student** to learn more about Asteroids; History of Earth; Meteor and Meteorite.

BIZARRE BEINGS FROM BEYOND

Creatures From Science Fiction

What would creatures from other worlds look like? Here are five extraterrestrials (ETs) as imagined by science fiction writers. Read about the special powers and unique qualities that allow these fictional creatures to thrive in their places in the universe.

All images come from *Barlowe's Guide to Extraterrestrials* by Wayne Douglas Barlowe, Ian Summers, and Beth Meacham.

Cinrusskin 1

From *Hospital Station*
by James White

Cinrusskin are insectlike creatures about 1.5 meters tall. They have small wings and six legs, four of which have sucker-tipped "hands." These hands are capable of doing extremely delicate work. This ability, combined with their sensitivity and caring nature, leads many Cinrusskin to become doctors or surgeons specializing in interspecies medicine.

Athshean 2

From *The Word for World Is Forest*
by Ursula K. Le Guin

Athsheans are about 1 meter tall and are covered with fur that can be deep green or brown. This helps them blend in with the dense forests on the planet Athshe, in which they live. The Athsheans live in small groups inside tunnels dug under tree roots. They are pacifists. Athsheans substitute competitive singing for physical combat.

Ixchel 3

From *A Wrinkle in Time*
by Madeleine L'Engle

The Ixchel are gentle, giant creatures measuring nearly 3.2 meters tall. Because their home planet has an opaque atmosphere, they evolved without eyes. The tentacles on their arms function as both fingers and speech organs. The tentacles on their heads act like ears. They are compassionate, strong, and very good at math.

---

interspecies *(adj.)* occurring between species
opaque *(adj.)* completely blocks out light

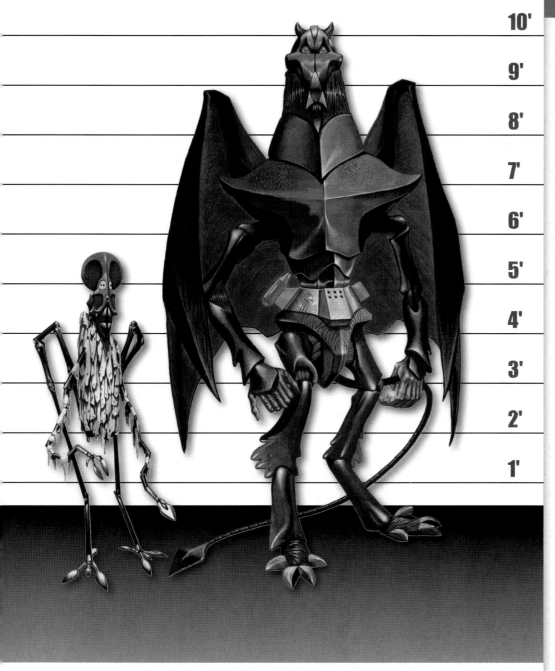

| 10' |
| 9' |
| 8' |
| 7' |
| 6' |
| 5' |
| 4' |
| 3' |
| 2' |
| 1' |

Cygnostik

From *A Little Knowledge*
by Michael Bishop

4

Cygnostiks come from Cygnostikoi, a cold and dark planet that revolves around a two-star system. These creatures are about 2 meters tall and have two sets of eyes; each set is sensitive to the light given off by one of the two stars. Having two sets of eyes also allows them to see a spiritual realm that humans cannot. Cygnostiks speak a musical language that humans can't reproduce without electronics.

realm *(n.)* region

Overlord

From *Childhood's End*
by Arthur C. Clarke

5

Overlords are 3.6-meter-tall creatures that have huge wings. Their homeworld's thick atmosphere and low gravity made flying the best way to get around. Overlords are highly intelligent and have developed an advanced scientific culture. They explore the galaxy, collecting and studying other life forms. ■

Read and Synthesize

NAVIGATING TEXT

Text Features

 (Circle) the illustration of the alien you would most like to read about.

- Draw a box around the name of that alien in the caption.
- Underline the author and title of the book in which the alien is found.
- List three details that describe the alien.

1. _____

_____

_____

_____

2. _____

_____

_____

_____

3. _____

_____

_____

_____

VOCABULARY/WORD ANALYSIS

Context Clues: Example

Review the description of the Athsheans. Star ★ the word that means "peaceful."

- What behavior from the description is an example of the peaceful nature of the Athsheans?

_____

_____

_____

_____

READ ONLINE

 expert space
Go to **www.expert21.com/ student** to learn more about Search for Extraterrestrial Life; Ursula Le Guin; Madeleine L'Engle.

Think Across Texts

Organize and Synthesize ·······························

1. Complete this web using information from "Zero Hour," "Crash Course," and "Bizarre Beings From Beyond."

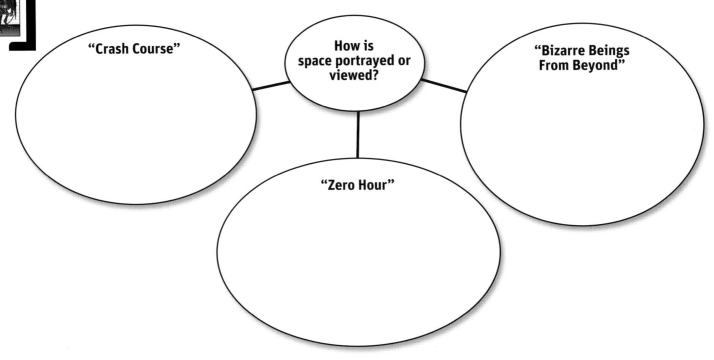

"Crash Course"

How is space portrayed or viewed?

"Bizarre Beings From Beyond"

"Zero Hour"

Compare and Evaluate ··························

2. How is the art on the title page of "Crash Course" similar to the art in "Bizarre Beings from Beyond"? How is it different. Explain.

_____

_____

_____

_____

3. Choose a type of alien from "Bizarre Beings From Beyond." Would those aliens invade Earth like the aliens in "Zero Hour"? Explain your response.

_____

_____

_____

4. Most of the aliens from these readings are described as noble, intelligent, and peaceful creatures. Why do you think so many authors create aliens that are described as peaceful, gentle, and intelligent?

_____

_____

_____

_____

_____

_____

Discuss and Write ··················

5. With a group, discuss how the readings in "Close Encounters" help imagine life beyond Earth. Then write a response to the question *What would an invasion from space be like?*

Apply Word Knowledge

Word Lab

1. **Finish it.** Complete the sentence below with the words **asteroid** and **meteor.**

I learned that a(n) _____ is a chunk of space rock that orbits the sun, while a(n) _____ is the trail of light caused by a piece of space rock entering our atmosphere.

2. **Tell.** What is an example of a movie that is **suspenseful**?

_____

_____

3. **Choose.** Which word fits in the sentence below?

evoke   **detect**

I don't _____ any problem with my cell phone, but it still won't turn on.

4. **Check.** What might be **underfoot**?

☐ horses
☐ puppies
☐ cars and trucks
☐ children's toys

5. **Think about it.** What task seemed deceptively simple before you actually tried to do it?

_____

_____

_____

_____

_____

_____

_____

_____

Word Analysis

6. Read each sentence below. Underline the context clue that helps reveal the meaning of the word in dark type.

• As the comet hit, it caused **shock waves** (powerful blasts of air).

• Metallic asteroids are made mostly of **metals** such as iron and nickel.

• **Athsheans** are covered with fur and live in forests on the planet Athshe.

7. Look at the underlined context clues in the sentences below. Write *example* or *definition* on the line to tell what kind of context clue the sentence contains.

Catastrophes such as floods, fires, and tsunamis are a fact of life.	_____
A **tsunami,** or monster wave, can cause widespread destruction.	_____
Rain and wind can cause earth to wash away in a process known as **erosion.**	_____

Evaluate Sources

Finding a Web site on any topic is easy. But finding a reliable site is a little harder. You need to check out how trustworthy its information is to judge if the site is worth your time.

Use a NASA Web site

▶ The NASA (National Aeronautics and Space Administration) Web site is a great source for information on space. Examine the features of a trustworthy and useful Web site.

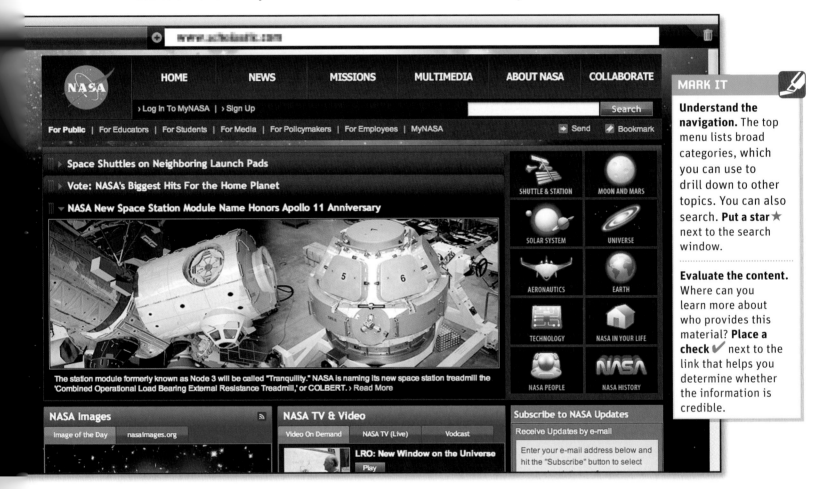

MARK IT

Understand the navigation. The top menu lists broad categories, which you can use to drill down to other topics. You can also search. **Put a star** ★ next to the search window.

Evaluate the content. Where can you learn more about who provides this material? **Place a check** ✔ next to the link that helps you determine whether the information is credible.

Here's How ▶ Follow these steps to evaluate sources:

Step 1 Determine who is publishing the site. Official sites published by schools or the government should be reliable. See if you can find the author of the site's content. Are the authors experts? How can you tell?

Step 2 Determine the site's purpose. Ask yourself why the site was created. Is it trying to inform, persuade, or sell? Is it biased? Look for personal opinions and point of view. Does the purpose of the site match your purpose?

Step 3 Evaluate whether the information is useful. Look for a bibliography or Web links. A good site refers you to other sources. Where else could you check to validate the information? Is the information current? A site may tell when it was last updated or have a copyright date. Is it easy to find information?

Apply: Evaluating a Web site about UFOs

▶ **Evaluate this Web site to decide whether it is a source you want to trust.**

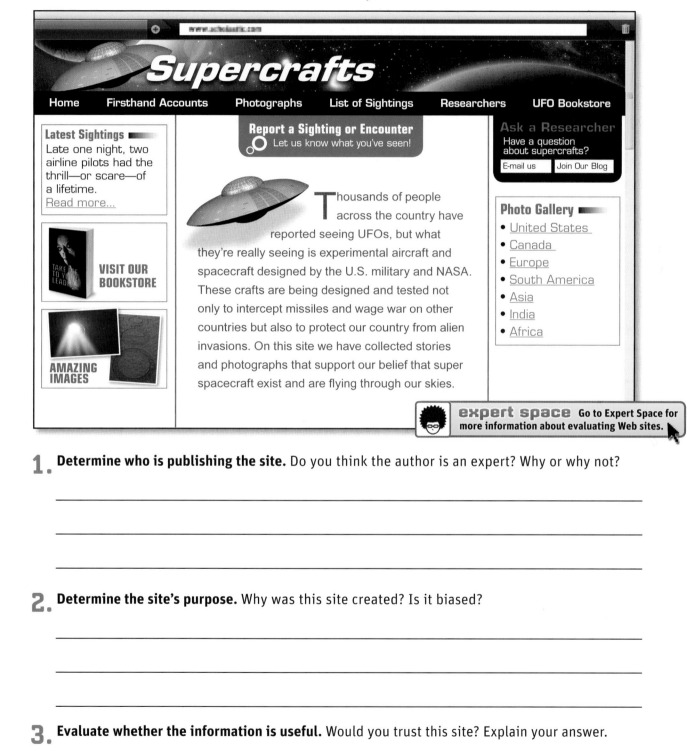

1. **Determine who is publishing the site.** Do you think the author is an expert? Why or why not?

   _____

   _____

   _____

2. **Determine the site's purpose.** Why was this site created? Is it biased?

   _____

   _____

   _____

3. **Evaluate whether the information is useful.** Would you trust this site? Explain your answer.

   _____

   _____

Short Story

WHO'S THERE?

Working in outer space is every astronaut's dream, but no one can be totally sure what will happen thousands of miles above Earth. When the astronaut in this story encounters a surprise during a mission, his mind takes him to some pretty strange places.

QuickWrite

If you could have a job based in outer space, what would you like it to be? What challenges would you face, being so far from home? Write a paragraph describing how you think you would feel about your work.

Suspense LITERARY ANALYSIS

Suspense is a feeling of growing tension and excitement felt by a reader.

A writer creates suspense by raising questions in the reader's mind.

The use of foreshadowing is one way that writers create suspense. Foreshadowing occurs when a writer provides hints about what will happen in a story. Foreshadowing makes readers eager to find out what will happen next.

▶ **Underline examples of foreshadowing used to create suspense in the passage below.**

> When I climbed into the spacecraft, all I could think about was what I would find when I reached the Space Station. Would my coworkers still be alive, or would they all have perished when the giant meteor hit the station? I was so anxious to get going, I didn't bother to check the emergency supplies. I just strapped in and hit the launch switch.

List two questions that this passage raises.

1. _____

2. _____

Draw Conclusions COMPREHENSION

A **conclusion** is an interpretation of events within a story that a reader must create because the author does not state it directly.

To draw conclusions, take the details in a story and use them as evidence to create an interpretation that adds meaning to the story.

The more evidence that supports a conclusion, the stronger the conclusion is.

▶ **Read the following passage, and use details from the story to complete the chart.**

> I pulled out my binoculars and searched the sky near Jupiter. My radar screen indicated that an enemy spacecraft was just miles to my right, but I couldn't see anything. Was something wrong with my radar? Or was it possible that the enemy had figured out a way to make its crafts invisible? Captain Ramirez had told me the enemy was clever and had highly advanced technology. I started to sweat. If the spacecraft was out there somewhere, I had very little time to get to the safety of the space station before they captured my space pod—or worse!

Detail #1	Detail #2	Conclusion
		The narrator is a soldier during war time.

Academic Language   VOCABULARY

▶ **Rate your knowledge of each word. Then write its meaning and an example sentence.**

Word	Meaning	Example
ACADEMIC WORDS *Use these words in all your subject classes.*		
acquire ac·quire *(verb)* ① ② ③ ④	to obtain or get something	When I save up enough money, I'm going to acquire a new cell phone.
exclusive ex·clu·sive *(adjective)* ① ② ③ ④		
CONTENT AREA WORDS *Use these words to talk and write about science.*		
cylinder cyl·in·der *(noun)* ① ② ③ ④	a shape like a tube or can	
mechanism mech·a·nism *(noun)* ① ② ③ ④		The flash mechanism inside my camera broke, so I must take it to be repaired.
SELECTION WORDS *These words are key to understanding this selection.*		
intermittent in·ter·mit·tent *(adjective)* ① ② ③ ④		
intolerable in·tol·er·a·ble *(adjective)* ① ② ③ ④		
salvage sal·vage *(noun)* ① ② ③ ④		
stationary sta·tion·a·ry *(adjective)* ① ② ③ ④		

Rating Scale   ① I don't know the word.   ② I've seen it or heard it.   ③ I know its meaning.   ④ I know it and use it.

Context Clues: Synonyms and Antonyms   WORD ANALYSIS

Synonyms are words that have almost the same meaning, such as *acquire* and *get*.

Antonyms are words that have opposite meanings, such as *stationary* and *mobile*.

You can sometimes use synonyms and antonyms as context clues. Sometimes definitions appear in parentheses.

▶ **Read the sentence below. Circle an antonym for** *intermittent*.

At first the sound was <u>intermittent</u>*, but after a while it became continuous.*

What is a synonym for *intermittent*?

_____

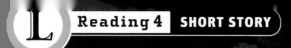
WHO'S THERE?

By Arthur C. Clarke

It's business as usual for an astronaut on a mission to recover a wayward satellite—until he hears a strange sound coming from an unexpected place.

When Satellite Control called me, I was writing up the day's progress report in the Observation Bubble—the glass-domed office that juts out from the axis of the Space Station like the hubcap of a wheel. It was not really a good place to work, for the view was too overwhelming. Only a few yards away I could see the construction teams performing their slow-motion ballet as they put the station together like a giant jigsaw puzzle. And beyond them, twenty thousand miles below, was the blue-green glory of the full Earth, floating against the raveled star clouds of the Milky Way.

"Station Supervisor here," I answered. "What's the trouble?"

"Our radar's showing a small echo two miles away, almost **stationary,** about five degrees west of Sirius. Can you give us a visual report on it?"

Anything matching our orbit so precisely could hardly be a meteor; it would have to be something we'd dropped—perhaps an inadequately secured piece of equipment that had drifted away from the station. So I assumed but when I pulled out my binoculars and searched the sky around Orion, I soon found my mistake. Though this space traveler was man-made, it had nothing to do with us.

"I've found it," I told Control. "It's someone's test satellite—cone-shaped, four antennas, and what looks like a lens system in its base. Probably US Air Force, early nineteen-sixties, judging by the design. I know they lost track of several when their transmitters failed. There were quite a few attempts to hit this orbit before they finally made it."

After a brief search through the files, Control was able to confirm my guess. It took a little longer to find out that Washington wasn't in the least bit interested in our discovery of a twenty-year-old stray satellite, and would be just as happy if we lost it again.

"Well, we can't do that," said Control. "Even if nobody wants it, the thing is a menace to navigation. Someone had better go out and haul it aboard."

---

raveled *(adj.)* tangled up
secured *(v.)* attached

LITERARY ANALYSIS

Suspense

How does the title of this story create suspense?

_____

_____

_____

How does the introduction to the story use foreshadowing?

_____

_____

_____

_____

COMPREHENSION

Draw Conclusions

Why does Control want the Station Supervisor to haul in the satellite? What problems could the satellite cause if it is left to drift?

_____

_____

_____

_____

_____

_____

CRITICAL THINKING

Evaluate

How does Arthur C. Clarke reveal his opinion of astronomy and space exploration to the reader?

_____

_____

_____

_____

_____

_____

That someone, I realized, would have to be me. I dared not detach a man from the closely knit construction teams, for we were already behind schedule—and a single day's delay on this job cost a million dollars. All the radio and TV networks on Earth were waiting impatiently for the moment when they could route their programs through us, and thus provide the first truly global service, spanning the world from Pole to Pole.

"I'll go out and get it," I answered, snapping an elastic band over my papers so that the air currents from the ventilators wouldn't set them wandering around the room. Though I tried to sound as if I was doing everyone a great favor, I was secretly not at all displeased. It had been at least two weeks since I'd been outside; I was getting a little tired of stores schedules, maintenance reports, and all the glamorous ingredients of a Space Station Supervisor's life.

The only member of the staff I passed on my way to the air lock was Tommy, our recently **acquired** cat. Pets mean a great deal to men thousands of miles from Earth, but there are not many animals that can adapt themselves to a weightless environment. Tommy mewed plaintively at me as I clambered into my spacesuit, but I was in too much of a hurry to play with him.

At this point, perhaps I should remind you that the suits we use on the station are completely different from the flexible affairs men wear when they want to walk around on the moon. Ours are really baby spaceships, just big enough to hold one man. They are stubby cylinders, about seven feet long, fitted with low-powered propulsion jets, and have a pair of accordion-like sleeves at the upper end for the operator's arms. Normally, however, you keep your hands drawn inside the suit, working the manual controls in front of your chest.

As soon as I'd settled down inside my very **exclusive** spacecraft, I switched on the power and checked the gauges on the tiny instrument panel. There's a magic word, "FORB," that you'll often hear spacemen mutter as they

> ## In space, the great enemy is the sun, which can blast you to blindness in seconds.

climb into their suits; it reminds them to test fuel, oxygen, radio, and batteries. All my needles were well in the safety zone, so I lowered the transparent hemisphere over my head and sealed myself in. For a short trip like this, I did not bother to check the suit's internal lockers, which were used to carry food and special equipment for extended missions.

As the conveyor belt decanted me into the air lock, I felt like a baby being carried along on its mother's back. Then the pumps brought the pressure down to zero, the outer door opened, and the last traces of air swept me out into the stars, turning very slowly head over heels.

The station was only a dozen feet away, yet I was now an independent planet—a little world of my own. I was sealed up in a tiny, mobile **cylinder,** with a superb view of the entire universe, but I had practically no freedom of movement inside the suit. The padded seat and safety belts prevented me from turning around, though I could reach all the controls and lockers with my hands or feet.

In space, the great enemy is the sun, which can blast you to blindness in seconds. Very cautiously, I opened up the dark filters on the "night" side of my suit, and I turned my head to look out at the stars. At the same time, I switched the helmet's external sunshade to automatic, so that whichever way the suit gyrated, my eyes would be shielded from that **intolerable** glare.

Presently, I found my target—a bright fleck of silver whose metallic glint distinguished it clearly from the surrounding stars. I stamped on the jet-control pedal and felt the mild surge of acceleration as the low-powered rockets set me moving away from the station. After ten seconds of steady thrust, I estimated that my speed was great enough, and cut off the drive. It would take me five minutes to coast the rest of the way, and not much longer to return with my **salvage.**

> **plaintively** *(adv.)* sadly
> **decanted** *(v.)* transferred

And it was at that moment, as I launched myself out into the abyss, that I knew that something was horribly wrong.

It is never completely silent inside a spacesuit; you can always hear the gentle hiss of oxygen, the faint whirr of fans and motors, the susurration of your own breathing—even, if you listen carefully enough, the rhythmic thump that is the pounding of your heart. These sounds reverberate through the suit, unable to escape into the surrounding void; they are the unnoticed background of life in space, for you are aware of them only when they change.

Make Predictions
What do you think the sound is?

They had changed now; to them had been added a sound which I could not identify. It was an **intermittent**, muffled thudding, sometimes accompanied by a scraping noise, as of metal upon metal.

I froze instantly, holding my breath and trying to locate the alien sound with my ears. The meters on the control board gave me no clues; all the needles were rock-steady on their scales, and there were none of the flickering red lights that would warn of impending disaster. That was some comfort, but not much. I had long ago learned to trust my instincts in such matters; their alarm signals were flashing now, telling me to return to the station before it was too late . . .

Even now, I do not like to recall those next few minutes, as panic slowly flooded into my mind like a rising tide, overwhelming the dams of reason and logic which every person must erect against the mystery of the universe. I knew then what it was like to face insanity; no other explanation fitted the facts.

For it was no longer possible to pretend that the noise disturbing me was that of some faulty **mechanism.** Though I was in utter isolation, far from any other human being or indeed any material object, I was not alone. The soundless void was bringing to my ears the faint but unmistakable stirrings of life.

In that first, heart-freezing moment it seemed that something was trying to get into my suit—something invisible, seeking shelter from the cruel and pitiless vacuum of space. I whirled madly in my harness, scanning the entire sphere of vision around me except the blazing, forbidden cone toward the sun. There was nothing there, of course. There could not be—yet that purposeful scrabbling was clearer than ever.

abyss (n.) an immeasurably huge space
susurration (n.) murmur

COMPREHENSION

Compare and Contrast

Review page 124. Circle two examples of the author using comparisons and contrasts in his description.

LITERARY ANALYSIS

Suspense

Review page 125. Underline the sentences that foreshadow potential trouble for the main character.

• How do these sentences foreshadow the action to come?

_____

_____

_____

_____

_____

_____

_____

_____

_____

_____

_____

VOCABULARY/WORD ANALYSIS

Synonyms and Antonyms

Review the last sentence in the eighth paragraph on page 124. Draw a box around a phrase that helps you understand the word *gyrated*.

• What is a synonym for *gyrate*?

_____

_____

LITERARY ANALYSIS

Suspense

Review the last paragraph on page 125. Circle descriptive words and phrases that the author uses to help create suspense.

Despite the nonsense that has been written about us, it is not true that spacemen are superstitious. But can you blame me if, as I came to the end of logic's resources, I suddenly remembered how Bernie Summers had died, no farther from the station than I was at this very moment?

It was one of those "impossible" accidents; it always is. Three things had gone wrong at once. Bernie's oxygen regulator had run wild and sent the pressure soaring, the safety valve had failed to blow—and a faulty joint had given way instead. In a fraction of a second, his suit was open to space.

I had never known Bernie, but suddenly his fate became of overwhelming importance to me—for a horrible idea had come into my mind. One does not talk

about these things, but a damaged spacesuit is too valuable to be thrown away, even if it has killed its wearer. It is repaired, renumbered—and issued to someone else . . .

What happens to the soul of a man who dies between the stars, far from his native world? Are you still here, Bernie, clinging to the last object that linked you to your lost and distant home?

As I fought the nightmares that were swirling around me—for now it seemed that the scratchings and soft fumblings were coming from all directions—there was one last hope to which I clung. For the sake of my sanity, I had to prove that this wasn't Bernie's suit—that the metal walls so closely wrapped around me had never been another man's coffin.

It took me several tries before I could press the right button and switch my transmitter to the emergency wavelength. "Station?" I gasped. "I'm in trouble! Get records to check my suit history and—"

I never finished; they say my yell wrecked the microphone. But what man alone in the absolute isolation of a spacesuit would not have yelled when something patted him softly on the back of the neck?

I must have lunged forward, despite the safety harness, and smashed against the upper edge of the control panel. When the rescue squad reached me a few minutes later, I was still unconscious, with an angry bruise across my forehead.

Clarify
What caused the sound that the astronaut heard?

And so I was the last person in the whole satellite relay system to know what had happened. When I came to my senses an hour later, all our medical staff was gathered around my bed, but it was quite a while before the doctors bothered to look at me. They were much too busy playing with the three cute little kittens our badly misnamed Tommy had been rearing in the seclusion of my spacesuit's Number Five Storage Locker. ■

Arthur C. Clarke

AUTHOR FILE

BORN December 16, 1917, Minehead, England

A FAMOUS ODYSSEY In 1968, famed director Stanley Kubrick adapted one of Clarke's novels, *2001: A Space Odyssey,* for the big screen. The movie was nominated for four Academy Awards and is still considered one of the greatest movies ever made.

FINDING INSPIRATION IN THE STARS As a boy, Clarke loved reading American science fiction magazines and gazing at the stars. He later served in the air force during World War II and earned degrees in math and physics.

IT'S NEVER TOO LATE Although Clarke published a few stories in magazines while in his twenties, he didn't decide to become a serious writer until he was thirty-four. He continued writing science fiction until the day he died, in 2008.

rearing (v.) caring for
seclusion (n.) a place where it is easy to be alone

LITERARY ANALYSIS

Suspense
Think back on the whole of the story. Identify a detail that foreshadowed the conclusion of the story.

_____

_____

_____

_____

_____

_____

_____

_____

_____

_____

_____

_____

_____

21 **SMALL GROUPS/INDEPENDENT**

COLLABORATE

Create Stories What if the noise had been made by something dangerous? Write a paragraph summarizing how the story would have ended if it were a horror story.

COMMUNICATE

Respond and Write Take notes about the challenges the astronaut in the story faces. Then write a paragraph about how you would have responded to the same situation.

READ ONLINE

expert space
Go to **www.expert21.com/student** to learn more about Space Stations; Arthur C. Clarke; Dressing for Space.

Editorial

THE CASE FOR SPACE

In 2003, the space shuttle Columbia *exploded upon its return to Earth. All eight crew members lost their lives. Disasters such as this lead some people to ask whether the space program is really worth the risk and cost. Find out why one scientist says it is.*

QuickWrite

Do you think space exploration is worth the billions of dollars we spend on it? Explain your views.

Cause and Effect   COMPREHENSION

A **cause** is the reason something happens.

An **effect** is the result of a cause.

In a **causal chain,** an effect becomes the cause of the next event.

A causal chain is different from a **sequence,** in which events happen one after the other, but one event is not necessarily the cause of the next event.

▶ **Read this passage. Then complete the cause-and-effect chart below.**

Space exploration was once an international competition. Every major world power wanted to get ahead in the "race for space." Now, exploring space is so expensive that individual countries can not afford it. Future projects are likely to be joint ventures between countries. This will encourage cooperation rather than competition among nations.

Cause	Effect/Cause	Effect
Individual countries can not afford space exploration.	_____	_____

Structure of an Argument   NAVIGATING TEXT

The **structure of an argument** is the way an author organizes the parts of his or her argument.

Those parts include a statement of the author's position and support for that position.

Often, an author also includes an opposing view and argues against it. One way to structure an argument is to begin with an opposing position.

▶ **Read the following passage. Underline the author's position, and box the opponent's view. Then complete the chart.**

Many teachers feel that their most important tool for teaching science is a textbook. While it's true that textbooks explain complex science concepts in a clear way, students lose interest if they only read about science and never get a chance to apply it. Students learn more when they are actively engaged. More of their time should be spent working with others to conduct experiments.

Opponent's View	Author's View
Opinion:	Opinion:
Reason:	Reason:

Academic Language VOCABULARY

▶ Rate your knowledge of each word. Then write its meaning and an example sentence.

Word	Meaning	Example
EXPERT WORDS *Use these words to write and talk about the workshop topic.*		
deflect de•flect (verb) ① ② ③ ④	To make something go in a different direction	One way to deflect an asteroid headed for Earth is to hit it with a spacecraft.
justify jus•ti•fy (verb) ① ② ③ ④		
ACADEMIC WORDS *Use these words in all your subject classes.*		
inherently in•her•ent•ly (adjective) ① ② ③ ④	basically; by nature	
seep seep (verb) ① ② ③ ④		
SELECTION WORDS *These words are key to understanding this selection.*		
awry a•wry (adverb) ① ② ③ ④		
juxtapose jux•ta•pose (verb) ① ② ③ ④		Photographers sometimes juxtapose before-and-after photos to make a point.
traverse tra•verse (verb) ① ② ③ ④		
vulnerable vul•ner•a•ble (adjective) ① ② ③ ④		

Rating Scale   ① I don't know the word.   ② I've seen it or heard it.   ③ I know its meaning.   ④ I know it and use it.

Synonyms and Antonyms WORD ANALYSIS

Synonyms are words that have almost the same meaning.

Antonyms are words that have opposite meanings.

Sometimes synonyms and antonyms can serve as context clues.

▶ Read each sentence below. Then complete the item below it.

This lever causes the plane to <u>accelerate</u>, and that one causes it to <u>slow</u>.

Accelerate and **slow** are _____

Accelerate means _____

The scientist made a passionate <u>appeal</u> to Congress, and they listened to her <u>request</u>.

Appeal and **request** are _____

An appeal is a _____

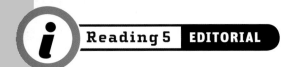
Adapted
from

THE
CASE
FOR
SPACE

By Neil deGrasse Tyson

On February 1, 2003, the space shuttle *Columbia* was returning from a two-week-long mission in space. The shuttle accelerated as gravity pulled it toward Earth. NASA's Mission Control tracked *Columbia's* progress with a large radar screen that blinked its trajectory across a map. The red light blinked over California, then Nevada, then New Mexico. Suddenly, over northern Texas, the blinking stopped. Mission Control lost contact with the crew.

As *Columbia* streaked across the sky at more than 16,000 miles per hour, heat **seeped** though a damaged protective tile on the shuttle's outer shell. The shuttle instantly caught fire and disintegrated. Pieces fell to the ground like dozens of fiery meteorites. All seven crew members lost their lives.

After the *Columbia* disaster, many critics questioned whether space exploration was worth the financial cost and human sacrifice. Tyson wrote this passionate appeal for the value of the space program. This editorial ran in *Natural History*, the magazine published by the American Museum of Natural History.

The *Columbia* crew included six American astronauts and Ilan Ramon, the first Israeli astronaut (pictured here on the far right).

appeal *(n.)* a defense of a person or idea

COMPREHENSION

Cause and Effect

Review page 131. <u>Underline</u> the sentence that explains what damaged the *Columbia* on reentry.

- (Circle) the effects of this event.

NAVIGATING TEXT

Structure of an Argument

Using what you know from the introduction, draw a box around the goal of the author's argument?

- Identify two arguments against space exploration the author will have to overcome in order to successfully make his case.

1. _____

_____

_____

_____

_____

_____

2. _____

_____

_____

_____

_____

_____

VOCABULARY/WORD ANALYSIS

Synonyms and Antonyms

Review the first paragraph of the introduction. What word provides a clue as to the meaning of *trajectory*?

_____

_____

_____

Are *trajectory* and the word you chose synonyms or antonyms?

_____

April, 2003

In the months since the space shuttle *Columbia*'s fatal reentry through Earth's atmosphere, it seems that everyone has become a NASA critic.

In the 1960s, space was an exotic frontier. Space was **traversed** by the few, the brave, and the lucky. In 1961, the Soviet cosmonaut Yuri Gagarin became the first person to orbit Earth. A few weeks later, President John F. Kennedy had a message for Congress. He said, "I believe that this nation should commit itself to achieving the goal, before this decade is out, of landing a man on the moon and returning him safely to the earth."

But most people have forgotten the rest of his speech. Kennedy never suggested the moon landing be accomplished for its own sake. He was issuing a powerful appeal to beat Communism. Clearly the president knew that although bravery may win battles, science and technology can win wars.

But what about discovery for its own sake? Are the scientific returns on a manned mission to Mars **inherently** important enough to **justify** its costs? After all, any future mission to Mars will be long and expensive. But the United States is a wealthy nation. It has the money. And the technology is imaginable. Those aren't the issues.

Expensive projects are **vulnerable** because they take a long time. They must be sustained across changeovers in political leadership. They must survive downturns in the economy. Photographs of homeless children and unemployed factory workers **juxtaposed** with images of astronauts frolicking on Mars make a powerful case against the continued funding of space missions.

Actually, there may be a way to keep going places. But it involves a slight shift in what the government usually calls national defense. Science and technology can win wars, as the history of military conflict suggests. Therefore, instead of counting our smart bombs, perhaps we should be counting our smart scientists and engineers. And there is no shortage of seductive projects for them to work on:

- We should search Mars. We should look for fossils and find out why liquid water no longer runs on its surface.
- We should visit an asteroid or two. We should learn how to **deflect** them. What if one is discovered heading our way? How embarrassing it would be for us big-brained, opposable-thumbed humans to meet the same fate as the proverbially pea-brained dinosaurs.
- We should drill through the kilometers of ice on Jupiter's moon Europa. We should explore the liquid ocean below for living organisms.
- We should explore Pluto. We should look at its newly discovered family of icy bodies in the outer solar system. These bodies hold clues to our planetary origins.
- We should probe Venus's thick atmosphere. We need to understand why its greenhouse effect has gone **awry,** causing a surface temperature of 900 degrees Fahrenheit.

Communism *(n.)* the political order of the Soviet Union, chief military rival of the United States from the 1950s to the 1990s

With missions and projects such as those, the United States can guarantee itself an academic pipeline bursting with the best and the brightest astrophysicists, biologists, chemists, engineers, geologists, and physicists. And they will collectively form a new kind of "missile silo." The silo will be filled with great minds ready to come forward whenever they are called.

The U.S. space program shouldn't die along with the crew of the space shuttle *Columbia* because nobody is willing to write the check to keep it going. That would be to move backward just by standing still. ∎

> **Clarify**
> What are some reasons people think we should stop funding space missions?

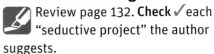
Dr. Neil deGrasse Tyson

BORN October 5, 1958, New York City

AMONG THE STARS In 2007, *Time* magazine included Dr. Tyson on its list of 100 most influential people in the world. In 2000, the asteroid "13123 Tyson" was named after him.

AUTHOR FILE

NO LIMITS Dr. Neil deGrasse Tyson is one of the top astrophysicists in the United States. He has obsessed over astronomy since he was a teenager. However, he was not single-minded in his pursuits: he also captained his high school's wrestling team and won a gold medal in a national dance competition while in college. He completed his Ph.D. at Columbia University in 1991, and in 1996, he became the director of the Hayden Planetarium of the American Museum of Natural History in New York City. He has written *The Sky Is Not the Limit: Adventures of an Urban Astrophysicist*, *Death by Black Hole: and Other Cosmic Quandaries*, and other books.

silo (n.) underground shelter for a missile

Read and Synthesize

COMPREHENSION

Cause and Effect

Review page 132. List two changes that can have a negative effect on projects such as space exploration.

1. _____

_____

_____

2. _____

_____

_____

NAVIGATING TEXT

Structure of an Argument

Review page 132. **Check** ✓ each "seductive project" the author suggests.

- **Circle** the project you find the most interesting.

[21] SMALL GROUPS/INDEPENDENT

COLLABORATE

Debate Select one of five projects mentioned in this reading. Present three reasons why the project you selected would be the best project to pursue. Present your argument to the group.

COMMUNICATE

React and Write Was the author persuasive? In a diary entry, summarize the author's arguments, and then write a paragraph expressing your own opinion.

READ ONLINE

expert space
Go to **www.expert21.com/student** to learn more about Space Shuttle; John F. Kennedy; Pluto.

ELEGY FOR CHALLENGER

BY DIANE ACKERMAN

A poet responds to an unexpected tragedy.

Christa McAuliffe, the first teacher to travel into space, was one of seven astronauts to board the *Challenger* space shuttle on January 28, 1986. She had been selected from over 11,000 candidates to be the first astronaut in NASA's Teacher in Space Project. Schools tuned in their classroom televisions for the live broadcast. Students watched as *Challenger* left its launchpad. But 73 seconds after liftoff, a seal on the booster rocket cracked. Flames ignited the fuel tank. The shuttle broke free from the booster rocket. Momentum carried the crew cabin 65,000 feet into the air, until it arched back down to Earth. It finally crashed into the ocean 2 minutes, 45 seconds after the breakup.

It was the shuttle program's first fatal accident. The tragedy forced NASA to review its safety standards. It also reminded everyone of the losses humans will endure in the name of progress and exploration.

An elegy is a mournful poem dedicated to the dead. Here, poet Diane Ackerman recognizes the bravery of the *Challenger* astronauts and the lessons to be learned from their deaths.

Wind-walkers,
how we envied you
riding a golden plume
on a glitter-mad trajectory
to watch Earth roll
her blooming hips below
and scout the shores
of still unnamed seas.

You were the Balboas
we longed to be,
all star-spangled grin,
upbeat and eager,
a nation's cameo.

When the sun went out
and you blew into your shadow,
horrors clanged
like falling bells.

You orbit our thoughts now
as last we saw you:
boarding a shuttle bound
out of this world,
quivering with thrill,
deadset, but tingling
to pitch an outpost
in our wilderness of doubt,
and climb that old ladder
whose rungs lead only higher.

We still dream your dreams,
though we taste your fire. ■

Balboa (n.) Vasco Núñez de Balboa, a Spanish explorer

LITERARY ANALYSIS

Figurative Language

A metaphor compares two people or things without using the word *like* or *as*. **Underline** a metaphor that compares the *Challenger* crew to other notable explorers.

COMPREHENSION

Main Ideas and Details

Does the poet believe that space exploration is worth the cost of tragedies like the *Challenger* disaster?

• (Circle) one stanza that you feel supports your conclusion.
• Explain how the stanza you selected supports your conclusion.

_____

_____

_____

_____

_____

_____

_____

_____

_____

_____

_____

_____

_____

_____

_____

_____

_____

_____

READ ONLINE

expert space
Go to **www.expert21.com/student** to learn more about Reagan Speech after *Challenger* Disaster; NASA; Manned Space Programs.

Think Across Texts

Organize and Synthesize

1. Complete this web using information from "Who's There?," "The Case for Space," and "Elegy for *Challenger*."

What feelings and opinions about space exploration are presented?

"Who's There?"

"Elegy for *Challenger*"

"The Case for Space"

Compare and Evaluate

2. Would you rather read science fiction stories, such as "Who's There?" or do you prefer nonfiction selections about real space missions, such as "The Case for Space"? Give at least two reasons for your preference.

_____

_____

_____

_____

3. "The Case for Space" describes several things that got Americans excited about space exploration in the 1960s. What is one thing that you believe could get Americans excited about space again?

_____

_____

_____

_____

_____

4. Imagine a conversation between Diane Ackerman and Neil deGrasse Tyson. What would each writer say about why we should study space?

Diane Ackerman: _____

_____

_____

_____

_____

Neil deGrasse Tyson: _____

_____

_____

_____

_____

_____

Discuss and Write

5. With a partner, discuss how the readings in "Space Odyssey" depict space exploration. Then write a response to the question *What's out there?*

Apply Word Knowledge

Word Lab

1. **Pick one.** Which of these words fits in the sentence below? Write that word on the line.

seep   **deflect**

By focusing on his opponent's faults, the politician hoped to

_____ attention from his own shortcomings.

2. **Decide.** Which things below might someone **yearn** for? Write *would* or *wouldn't* next to each possibility below.

• a trip to the dentist _____

• a favorite meal   _____

3. **Describe.** Describe something you would find **intolerable**?

_____

_____

_____

4. **Finish it.** Complete the sentence below with the words **reminiscent** and **vulnerable**.

That book is _____ of a time when people were much more

_____ to disease than they are today.

5. **Think about it.** What event would **justify** missing your best friend's birthday?

_____

_____

_____

6. **Choose.** Which area of land would you rather **traverse**? Circle one, and then tell why.

• the mountains of Montana   • a sandy beach
• the desert of Arizona   • the moon's surface

Why?

_____

_____

_____

Word Analysis

7. Select a synonym and an antonym from this list and place it next to the appropriate word in the table.

still   wrong
O.K.   strong
receive   lose
delicate   moving

	SYNONYM	ANTONYM
stationary		
awry		
vulnerable		
acquire		

8. Read each pair of sentences below. Circle the synonyms. Draw a box around the antonyms.

• I justified my actions. Jen defended her opinions.

• I find neckties to be intolerable. Mark thinks bowties are acceptable.

Deliver Speeches

Does speaking in front of a group make you panic? It needn't. If you know how to prepare and practice, you can make your point, support it, and be proud of it.

A Speech About Space

▶ Read a speech delivered by a girl who wants to be the first kid in space.

It's time to send a kid into space. I propose that we send a kid into space soon—me! There are three reasons why we should do this. First of all, according to NASA, over 33 nations have sent people into space since the first person went there in 1961. Plus, NASA has had 150 manned missions so far. Not one included a kid. Lastly, kids are the ones who have the most to learn and benefit from space travel. Why else would they send Barbara Morgan—a teacher—into space? I volunteer for the trip. I have high grades in science, I'm healthy, and I've wanted to be an astronaut my whole life. Who else is better qualified?

MARK IT

Circle the "signpost" words that help the listener keep track of when a new point is being made.

Underline the ideas that weren't in the notes. These are examples of extemporaneous speaking.

I want to be first kid in space.
Three reasons:
- 33 nations have sent people into space (nasa.gov)
- NASA: 150 manned missions (nasa.gov)
- teacher has already been sent to space, like Barbara Morgan (E21 book and Expert Space)

Future astronaut?:
Jenny Soto, age 13,
Phoenix, Arizona

Here's How ▶ **To deliver speeches, follow these steps:**

Step 1 Build your knowledge. Speeches sound best when you have data and information to back up your point of view.

Step 2 Write notes, not the whole speech. Write the ideas and facts that you want to include using bullets or numbers to help organize.

Step 3 Practice using the notes while speaking extemporaneously (while thinking on-the-spot). Use "signpost" words and phrases to help listeners follow your ideas.

Step 4 Address your audience. Use eye contact. Add any information you think would appeal to them. Plus, be sure to speak at a good volume and speed.

Apply: Speak Out!

▶ **Use this writing frame to get started, then deliver a speech.**

1. **Build your knowledge.** Here are some ideas for a short speech. Pick one, or write your own idea.

_____ It's not my parents' business if my room is messy.

_____ The voting age should be lowered to 15 years old.

_____ Students should (or should not) get rewarded with cash to get good grades.

_____ **Your Idea:** _____

Find two facts that support your point of view:

_____

_____

_____

2. **Write your notes.** Use this space to list your two main points. List them in a few words—don't write a whole sentence.

3. **Practice.** With a partner, present and listen to each other's speeches. Give helpful feedback about presentation skills, especially about speed and volume.

4. **Address your audience.** What is something you could add that would make your idea more appealing to your audience?

Your audience: _____

_____

Appealing idea: _____

_____

Traits of Writing

Traits of Writing is a model for assessing and teaching. The traits work within the writing process to support revision and editing.

Each puzzle piece below represents one of the **traits** that define good writing.

Each trait is made up of four **key qualities.** The trait that you will focus on in this lesson is Voice.

KEY QUALITIES

▶ **Establishing a Tone**

Conveying the Purpose

Creating a Connection to the Audience

Taking Risks to Create Voice

Fictional Narrative

A fictional narrative tells what happens to a character during a series of imagined events. A fictional narrative is usually written to entertain. Fictional narratives are used in stories on all topics, long jokes, novels, graphic novels, scripts for plays, movies, and television shows, and in many other places.

In this writing workshop, you will write a fictional narrative set in the future.

Example: This excerpt from the short story "The Lani People" by J.F. Bone takes place in the future when people have left Earth to live on other planets.

> There were over six thousand planets in the Brotherhood of Man. At two months per planet, not figuring transit time, it would take more than a thousand Galactic Standard years to visit them all, and a man could look forward to scarcely more than five hundred at best. The habitat of Man had become too large. There wasn't time to explore every possibility.

▶ **Analyze Features** A strong fictional narrative has the following features:

FEATURE	🖊 MARK IT
Look for these features in the Student Model on the next page.	Mark the features as you read the Student Model.
1. A **setting** that helps the reader know where and when the fictional narrative takes place. (Ideas)	Draw a box around information that helps the reader "see" the setting.
2. Sensory details that help the reader picture the experience. (Ideas)	Circle the details that help the reader imagine the experience.
3. Well-developed **characters** and natural **dialogue.** (Ideas)	Check ✓ information that gives insight about the characters.
4. Plot events told in a way that is easy to follow. (Organization)	Star ★ each event in the fictional narrative.
5. Focus Trait: Voice A tone that fits the content of the fictional narrative.	Underline words or phrases in the fictional narrative that show the tone.

▶ Read Derek Miyake's fictional narrative set in the future.

STUDENT MODEL

Bang, Zoom to the Moon
by Derek Miyake

Last year, in 2542, we went on vacation to the moon. When my parents first told us where we'd be going, the reaction was pretty bad. "Not the stupid moon again!" Zyphir whined. She had a point. We had been to the moon before at least a dozen times. "What about Saturn? Ring-boarding is supposed to be so cool!" she said. "You know we can't afford a trip to the outer planets," Apollo said. I guess the first-born tends to take that practical approach. "Fine!" said Zyphir in a way that is not at all fine. But she is the baby of the family, and she just wants what she wants.

The first day of the school break, we packed up our moonsuits and our lunar lungs, and left for the liftoff pad. It wasn't very exciting, like a fire drill we had practiced a lot. But that changed once we were nearly through the atmosphere. Bang! The entire ship shuddered and started to go into a freefall. "We're going to die!" Zyphir screamed. Apollo put his arm around her shoulder to comfort her. He turned to look at me and muttered quietly, "That can't be good. Go check it out." I headed for the adult sector of the ship to see what my parents had to say. My mother was an airbus pilot and my father was an airbus mechanic, so I figured they would know.

I finally found my parents up near the cockpit. They were trying to help the crew get control of the ship. We had hit some space junk, and the impact had knocked the pilot and co-pilot unconscious. The radio was out, too. My mom was staring hard at it. It didn't look like the airbus controls. "It kind of looks like the control screen of Lunar Longshot, that virtual reality game I used to play all the time," I said. "Show me the altitude adjustment," said mom. I pointed to an icon. She touched it and a grid appeared. She smiled and said, "Okay, I got it." We continued like this together until we got the ship back on course. Meanwhile, my dad worked on getting the radio back online. If the rest of the vacation is anything like that, boredom will be the least of our worries!

▶ Analyze how Derek developed his ideas.

▶ Read Derek's notes about how he worked on his fictional narrative.

IDEAS

I started to write about a future family's vacation to the moon, but then I went back and focused on the trip getting there instead of trying to write about the whole vacation.

VOICE

At first I took a humorous tone to the narrative, but then I realized that being too humorous made it less suspenseful, so I deleted the jokes and asides when the characters were in danger.

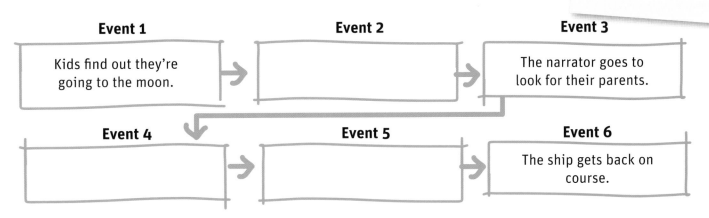

Event 1	**Event 2**	**Event 3**
Kids find out they're going to the moon.		The narrator goes to look for their parents.

Event 4	**Event 5**	**Event 6**
		The ship gets back on course.

How Do I Get Started?

Your Topic:

Assignment: Fictional narrative

Purpose: To tell a fictional narrative set in the future

Audience: Your choice

Ideas: Focusing the Topic

Focus your topic to cover what is important to say. Use these Think-Abouts as you work on your ideas:

- Have I zeroed in on one small part of a bigger idea?
- Can I tell you my idea in a simple sentence?
- Have I chosen the information that captures my idea best? *For example, the Student Model doesn't tell every aspect of the trip, just the parts that are important to the fictional narrative.*
- Have I thought deeply about what the reader will need to know?

IDEAS

KEY QUALITIES

Finding a Topic

▶ Focusing the Topic

Developing the Topic

Using Details

▶ **Model** Go back to Reading 1, "Zero Hour," in this workshop. Underline at least five details that help to capture the idea the author is focusing on.

▶ **Practice** Focus your topic by zeroing in on a smaller part of a bigger idea.

Big Idea: _____

_____

What smaller part of this big idea can I focus on? _____

_____

▶ **Plan Your Fictional Narrative** Use the organizer below to jot down ideas for your fictional narrative.

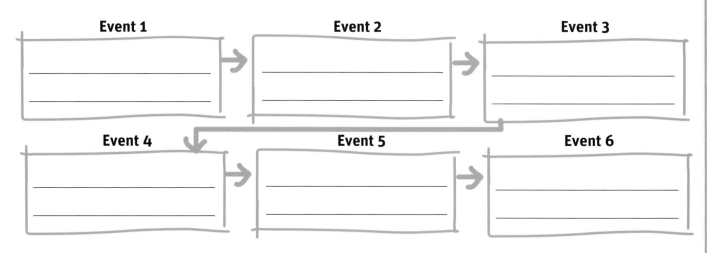

Event 1	Event 2	Event 3

Event 4	Event 5	Event 6

How Do I Get Organized?

Organization: Using Sequence Words and Transition Words

ORGANIZATION

Good writers use sequence words and transition words in their work to help readers understand how ideas connect. Ask yourself these Think-Abouts as you work on your organization.

- Have I used sequence words such as *later, then,* and *meanwhile*?

- Did I use a variety of transition words such as *however, because, also,* and *for instance*?

- Have I shown how ideas connect from sentence to sentence?

- Does my organization make sense from paragraph to paragraph? *Notice the beginning of each paragraph in the Student Model.*

KEY QUALITIES

Creating the Lead

▶ Using Sequence Words and Transition Words

Structuring the Body

Ending With a Sense of Resolution

▶ **Model** Go back to Reading 2, "Crash Course," and highlight examples of sequence words and transition words.

▶ **Practice** Use sequence words and transition words as you rewrite a section from the Student Model in your Expert Journal. You can use different transition and sequence words to express the same ideas.

_____

_____

_____

_____

_____

▶ **Write a Paragraph** Practice using sequence and transition words as you write a first draft of one of your paragraphs here.

_____

_____

_____

_____

▶ **Draft Your Fictional Narrative** Write a first draft.

Quick Check

▶ Check how well you focused the topic for your fictional narrative. Have a writing partner rate it, too.

6 = Expert   **3** = Making Strides

5 = Well Done   **2** = On The Way

4 = Almost There **1** = Getting Started

Ideas

1. Have I zeroed in on one small part of a bigger idea?
   Self   ① ② ③ ④ ⑤ ⑥
   Partner   ① ② ③ ④ ⑤ ⑥

2. Can I tell you my idea in a simple sentence?
   Self   ① ② ③ ④ ⑤ ⑥
   Partner   ① ② ③ ④ ⑤ ⑥

3. Have I chosen the information that captures my idea best?
   Self   ① ② ③ ④ ⑤ ⑥
   Partner   ① ② ③ ④ ⑤ ⑥

4. Have I thought deeply about what the reader will need to know?
   Self   ① ② ③ ④ ⑤ ⑥
   Partner   ① ② ③ ④ ⑤ ⑥

How Do I Establish a Tone?

FOCUS TRAIT

Voice: **Establishing a Tone**

Good writers make sure their tone is well-established in their final drafts. Use these Think-Abouts to make sure you establish a tone in your fictional narrative.

- Can I name the primary voice of my writing (for example, happy, frustrated, knowledgeable, scared, convincing)?
- Have I varied the tone from the beginning to the end? *The tone of the Student Model is slightly humorous but it becomes more serious when the action becomes more dangerous.*
- Have I been expressive?
- Did I show that I care about this topic?

VOICE

KEY QUALITIES

▶ **Establishing a Tone**

Conveying the Purpose

Creating a Connection to the Audience

Taking Risks to Create Voice

▶ **Model** Go back to Reading 6, "Elegy for *Challenger*," and see if you can name the primary voice of the writing. Highlight words and phrases that emphasize the tone.

▶ Read Ruth Culham's writing blog below to get advice on improving your writing.

Ask the Expert: Ruth Culham

Ruth Culham, an award-winning teacher, is the author of *6+1 Traits of Writing: The Complete Guide for Middle School* and other books on writing.

Q & A: Establishing a Tone

 Vera Various **Writes:**

> It was a hilarious, crazy day at the mall. Suddenly, I remembered I had to go to swim practice in the morning. Meanwhile, my sister started screaming and fighting with her best friend. Later, my parents went out for their anniversary dinner. All this happened in one day. How will I figure out what tone to use in my writing?

 Vera Various, what a busy day! It will be hard to write about it all in a short piece since the tones would vary so much: funny, serious, scary, and romantic. Why don't you focus on one of these events and establish the right tone for it? Then, if you want to add more, you can transition to that idea and tone next.

Posted by: Ruth Culham | December 22 at 04:30 P.M.

▶ **Practice** Read the sample paragraphs and think about how each establishes a tone.

Underline expressive language.

Circle the passage that best establishes a strong tone.

> ### Sample 1: Broken Bubble
> People are anxious and fearful. A crack has appeared in the bubble that protects our city's atmosphere. The bubble has existed for longer than anyone can remember, so we're terrified of what's out there. Now that our perfect, seamless sky is broken, we live in fear. Are there some mutant germs that will destroy us? All we can do is watch and wait.

> ### Sample 2: Broken Bubble
> Well, there is a crack in the sky now and soon the sky might be falling. Or not. The bubble could hold up or we might figure out how to fix it. We've been living in this bubble so long, we have no idea what is outside. It's possible the planet has healed. We'll have to learn more about the situation. In the meantime, all we can do is try to relax.

▶ **Revise** Now use tone to establish the voice of your writing. Choose a paragraph from your first draft and revise it below. Remember to use expressive language. Vary the tone if a situation or mood in your fictional narrative changes.

_____

_____

_____

_____

_____

_____

_____

_____

_____

Quick Check

▶ **Check how well you established a tone for your fictional narrative. Then have a writing partner rate it, too.**

6 = Expert   **3** = Making Strides

5 = Well Done   **2** = On The Way

4 = Almost There **1** = Getting Started

Voice

1. Can I name the primary voice of my writing (for example, happy, frustrated, knowledgeable, scared, convincing)?
Self   ① ② ③ ④ ⑤ ⑥
Partner   ① ② ③ ④ ⑤ ⑥

2. Have I varied the tone from the beginning to the end?
Self   ① ② ③ ④ ⑤ ⑥
Partner   ① ② ③ ④ ⑤ ⑥

3. Have I been expressive?
Self   ① ② ③ ④ ⑤ ⑥
Partner   ① ② ③ ④ ⑤ ⑥

4. Did I show that I care about this topic?
Self   ① ② ③ ④ ⑤ ⑥
Partner   ① ② ③ ④ ⑤ ⑥

Revise With Technology Use the thesaurus feature in your word processing program to be sure that you have found words that help you to be expressive.

How Can I Finish a Great Paper?

Grammar: Using Modifiers

Adjectives and adverbs are modifiers, or describing words. Adjectives modify nouns, and adverbs modify verbs.

- *Good* is an adjective that describes a noun or pronoun. *Well* is an adverb that describes a verb.

Example: It was a **good,** sturdy spaceship. We traveled **well** in it.

- The words *farther* and *further* can be used as adjectives or adverbs. *Farther* refers only to physical distance traveled. *Further* means "more," "a greater amount," or "in addition."

Example: The **farther** we traveled from Earth, the **further** we got in our research.

▶ **Practice Rewrite this paragraph correctly below.**

We had to drive six miles further to get to the runway. Then we were ready for takeoff. It went good, for the most part. All systems were well.

_____

_____

Mechanics: Using Colons, Semicolons, and Parentheses

- Use colons before a list.
- Use a semicolon to separate parts of a complex list.
- Use parentheses to separate additional information.

Example: NASA (National Aeronautics and Space Administration) sent these animals into space: Baker, a squirrel monkey; Able, a rhesus monkey; and Ham, a chimpanzee.

▶ **Practice Rewrite this paragraph correctly below.**

The shuttles that have been sent into space are *Columbia* lost in 2003, *Challenger* lost in 1986, *Discovery*, *Atlantis* and *Endeavour* all still operational as of 2008.

_____

_____

_____

_____

▶ **Proofread** Find and correct any errors in your story. Put a check beside the types of errors you find. Then write three corrected sentences below.

❏ using modifiers

❏ using colons, semicolons, and parentheses

❏ using pronouns

❏ using quotation marks

❏ misspellings

❏ other: _____

1. _____

_____

2. _____

_____

3. _____

_____

PUBLISH/PRESENT

PRESENTATION

▶ **Write Your Final Draft** Now, using your edited draft, begin creating a final draft for presentation.

🖥 Use word processing software to type your final draft. Make sure to format your margins and spacing according to your teacher's request.

Check your final draft against the Traits of Writing Scoring Guide on page 336–339 and correct any errors before you present it.

▶ **Beyond the Classroom** Extend your finished fictional narrative.

List two ideas for photos that could illustrate your fictional narrative:

_____

_____

Look online for a blog, message board, magazine, or newspaper where you could publish your fictional narrative.

List two places you could upload or share your fictional narrative for publication.

_____

Quick Check

▶ Check how well you used conventions in your fictional narrative. Then have a writing partner rate it, too.

6 = Expert   **3** = Making Strides

5 = Well Done   **2** = On The Way

4 = Almost There **1** = Getting Started

Conventions

1. Did I use modifiers correctly?
Self   ① ② ③ ④ ⑤ ⑥
Partner   ① ② ③ ④ ⑤ ⑥

2. Did I use colons, semicolons, and parentheses correctly?
Self   ① ② ③ ④ ⑤ ⑥
Partner   ① ② ③ ④ ⑤ ⑥

3. Did I use pronouns correctly?
Self   ① ② ③ ④ ⑤ ⑥
Partner   ① ② ③ ④ ⑤ ⑥

4. Did I use quotation marks correctly?
Self   ① ② ③ ④ ⑤ ⑥
Partner   ① ② ③ ④ ⑤ ⑥

READ ONLINE
expert space
Go to **www.expert21.com/ student** to find photographs and other visuals to illustrate your fictional narrative.

21

Expert Reading

You have learned about the benefits and problems of space exploration. Now apply your expert reading strategies to the following article about space tourism. ▶

Postcards from SPACE

TRUE STORIES from SPACE TOURISTS

By Adam Fisher

DENNIS TITO

GREG OLSEN

MARK SHUTTLEWORTH

ANOUSHEH ANSARI

CHARLES SIMONYI

RICHARD GARRIOTT

In 1995, Peter Diamandis co-founded Space Adventures Ltd. with an audacious idea: space tourism. But, in 2001, former NASA engineer Dennis Tito became the first "space tourist" when he flew to the International Space Station and back in a Soyuz capsule's third seat, next to the commander and engineer. Because of Tito and Space Adventures, the stars are now open to anyone who can pay the fare.

Since Tito, five have followed. First was Mark Shuttleworth, a young South African Internet tycoon. The second was Greg Olsen, a scientist. The first female space tourist, Anousheh Ansari, an Iranian-American telecommunications entrepreneur, flew third. Fourth was computer scientist Charles Simonyi. Finally, there was Richard Garriott, the son of a NASA astronaut and the inventor of Ultima online. So far, Space Adventures claims to have sold $200 million worth of space travel.

Technology Review Magazine asked each of the five travelers to describe the trip. Most have never met, but they all told essentially the same story of blastoff, weightlessness, re-entry, and revelation. Overall, their words tell the story of what a space vacation is like.

Olsen: It was June 18, 2003. I was sitting in Starbucks reading the *New York Times,* with a great big coffee. There was a story about Space Adventures. And I said, "Wow. This sounds like something I'd like to do!"

Simonyi: The way you get there is very simple. You call Space Adventures. The price is $35 million. It used to be $25, and now it's $35.

All those who decide to go to the International Space Station must learn Russian and train at Star City, near Moscow, for at least three months.

Ansari: When you go to Star City, it's down to basics, and sometimes not even basics. The first day I came, there was no hot water. The next day, there was no hot water. I was going to the gym and taking showers over there. Finally I went down, and it's like, "Do you know when the hot water will come back?"

They said, "Yeah, in about a month." When you turn on the faucet, brown rusty water comes out. If you let it run for 10 or 15 minutes, it starts getting clear, and you can take a decent clean shower. It is a military base. It taught me that you don't need a lot of things to live happily.

Garriott: On the space station everybody speaks English, so it is no big deal. But on the Soyuz all the commands are in Russian, and all the instruments are labeled in Russian. So you want to get some fundamental mastery of Russian.

Simonyi: Learning about the docking, communication, and re-entry systems was interesting.

The trip to the International Space Station begins with a bus ride to the launchpad and an elevator ride to a Soyuz capsule atop a Russian rocket the height of a 16-story building.

Ansari: Before the flight I was worried I would be a nervous wreck. I had told my flight surgeon, "If you see my blood pressure or my heart rate is high, don't let them stop the flight!"

Simonyi: Being in the Soyuz before launch is the greatest. You feel so centered, so comfortable. There's this nice humming noise. It smells fantastic. And you have plenty of time. The whole point, I think, is that there's no hurry. There's no pressure.

Ansari: You sit there and you're like, "I'm finally here!" It's a surreal situation. You're like, "I'm actually sitting on top of a rocket. In a few minutes it will ignite, and I will be sent off with these amazing speeds into space." For someone who is a civilian, it's, like, unbelievable.

Olsen: At launch, we got to about three and a half G's (G forces). I tried to raise my arm, and it felt like I had a 10-pound weight on it. After about eight minutes the G forces go away and you know you're going close to 17,000 miles an hour.

Ansari: The next thing I knew, this pen that was attached to a string started floating. It was just so crazy in my head. I was like, "I'm in space!" It took another while before they allowed us to take off the belts and be able to float in the cabin. You have to take it really easy, move slowly, move your head slowly or don't move your head at all if possible.

surreal *(adj.)* dreamlike
G forces *(n.)* forces exerted on the body from acceleration

I felt great during the launch. I felt great right after the launch. Then it was time to sleep, and we set our sleeping bags. After I woke up, I was like, "Oh, it's my first day in space, first morning in space." I was so excited. I started flying out of my sleeping bag. Flying around, looking out the window. Going from one window to the other window.

Garriott: Just being able to flip and spin like an incredible professional gymnast and land with your face next to a window looking out at a big gorgeous sunrise is really fantastic.

Ansari: That's when the whole Soyuz started spinning around my head. I knew that I just did something I wasn't supposed to—and I got really ill.

Olsen: About 40 percent of all people who go into space do. It has nothing to do with being macho.

After two days of travel, the Soyuz capsule reaches low Earth orbit and begins to dock with the International Space Station.

Olsen: When we drifted into the ISS, the first thing I did was hit my head on the ceiling. This was on Moscow television.

For the space tourists, there's not much to do aboard the ISS. They generally occupy themselves by taking snapshots, checking e-mail, and phoning home. Richard Garriott shot a sci-fi film starring his fellow astronauts and cosmonauts. And everyone on board spends a surprising amount of time simply looking for things.

Olsen: After we docked, shook hands, and said hello, there was about an hour when we could just sort of wander around. [Being at the ISS is] a lot like camping. Backpacking, actually.

Ansari: Cleaning yourself is an ordeal. There is no shower aboard the space station. You have these wet towels and dry towels that you use every day to wipe yourself, and a package with your personal toiletries up there—basically, your comb, your toothbrush, and whatever else they allow you to take up there. I was always losing things. I would write something, then put the pen down, forgetting that the pen would float off the table. I lost my lipstick, my lip gloss.

Simonyi: When something goes drifting, it's very difficult to find. On Earth, when you lose something, you look on the floor. Here, you can't. You are looking at everything, and there is just stuff everywhere. It could be anywhere. Behind anything.

Shuttleworth: You'd often come across someone looking for something, and it would be floating just behind their head.

For working astronauts and cosmonauts, every minute of every day on the ISS is scheduled, so mealtimes are the one chance that the space tourists get to really interact with the natives.

Garriott: The galley table is covered with spoons that are standing up like trees, because they put double-sided tape on the table. You can just tap the bottom end of your spoon handle on the table and it sticks there.

Ansari: [Dinner] was my favorite time on board the station, because during the day, everyone is busy. This is the only chance you get to sit—of course, not sit, because there are no chairs to sit on—to float around the table and talk.

The flight back to Earth takes three and a half hours from undocking to landing, and on the way down, the Soyuz sheds two of its three sections. Both the service module, with its solar panels and communication equipment, and the habitation module (or "living room") burn up in the atmosphere. The heat-shielded re-entry module, containing the cosmonauts, deploys a succession of parachutes and retro-rockets to slow the spacecraft before impact.

Shuttleworth: I thought the flight down was the best bit of the whole thing. The launch is kind of [boring]: you're 15 meters away from the engines, which is

habitation *(n.)* a place to live

where all the action is. On the return, by contrast, the vehicle blows itself up and separates into all these pieces. And then this tiny little piece that has you in it comes straight back into the atmosphere with fireworks going off all around it. So you're in the thick of it.

Ansari: There was this orange glow, with sparks and things.

Simonyi: It looks like Pepto-Bismol. It's this solid pink plasma.

Ansari: Looking out the window, I blurted out, "It feels like I'm riding a shooting star!"

Olsen: All of a sudden things start vibrating, and you can feel the deceleration. We get about four and a half G's, and it becomes hard to breathe. The capsule is being tossed around. There's no radio contact. You just kind of have to go through it.

Shuttleworth: You're on your back, spinning around, and the G force is building up, and your vehicle is [breaking down]. It's intense. You've got to focus on the G forces building up.

Garriott: The next big event is the opening of the drag chute, which can get a bit rough and tumble. Then when the main parachute opens, it's kind of like being at the end of a whip that has been cracked. Debris begins to scatter through the capsule even if it is really

held down. Lots of projectiles. We were all in space suits with helmets closed, so we were all quite well protected.

Ansari: I thought it was going to be hard, but I never thought it was going to be this hard. The impact was shocking. You hit the ground so hard that the impact stops the blood flow. It felt like thousands of needles ran through my back.

Olsen: We bounced, we rolled a bit, we made some radio contact. We were instructed to wait for the search-and-rescue people. The next thing I know, I hear some banging on the capsule. They're just letting us know, "Hey, we're here."

Shuttleworth: The three of us were kind of staring out with our eyes wide open, smiling and looking at the hatch. In the impact, a whole spadeful of dirt had basically gone onto the hatch. And as they opened the hatch, we all got a face full of dirt. Sort of, "Welcome back to Earth." It was very funny.

Garriott: Even just 10 days in space and you really do lose the ability to really even stand up properly.

Olsen: It was like when you graduate from college. You have this wonderful feeling of accomplishment. I really felt good about myself in a serene, secure way, not in an egotistical or bragging way, but just, "Wow." ∎

Reflect

1. Circle all the expert strategies you used while reading this article.

   A. Visualizing

   B. Clarifying

   C. Other: _____

   D. Other: _____

   E. Other: _____

2. Use the letters above to label where in the essay you applied the expert strategies.

3. Select one expert strategy you used. Explain why you applied that strategy where you did.

   _____

   _____

   _____

   _____

RESEARCH ONLINE

expert space
Go to **www.expert21.com/student** to learn more about Space Tourism; The Future of the Space Program.

---

projectiles *(n.)* objects flying through space
serene *(adj.)* peaceful and calm

PROJECT
DEBATE

SHOULD WE CONTINUE TO Explore Space?

THE EVENTS

The Facts: The U.S. government funds NASA (National Aeronautics and Space Administration), an agency dedicated to exploring space. NASA's 2010 budget was $18.7 billion. Is space exploration worth it?

The Pros: Space exploration brings scientific advances and increased knowledge of planets and the universe.

The Cons: Space exploration is too dangerous, and money spent on it should be used to solve problems on Earth.

YOUR CHALLENGE

Your team will debate this issue: Should we continue to explore space?

To prepare for your debate, you will

- ask questions about space exploration.
- study information to answer questions.
- choose a position.
- synthesize information.
- prepare responses to opposing team's arguments.
- practice for the debate.

CAREER CONNECTION Science, Technology, Engineering, and Mathematics
www.careerclusters.org

Go to **21** **Tool**Kit **Expert File 6.30** to learn more about careers in aerospace engineering.

1 Ask Questions

Ask questions on the notepad below about the pros and cons of space exploration. The answers should help you choose a position in the debate.

Space Exploration Questions

2 Study the Data

List some of the answers to your questions here. Look at the articles in this workshop, as well as these resources:
- the **Fact File** on the following pages.
- **Expert Space** for more information.

3 Choose a Position

Discuss with your partner the information you have gathered. Then choose a position to take in the debate, and write a sentence that clearly states it.

_____

_____

Go back to the **Fact File** and **Expert Space** to gather more information to support your point of view and prepare for opposing arguments.

4 Synthesize Information

Make a chart like the one below. List support for your team's opinion. Also list support for the opposing team's position. This will help you prepare for any challenges.

Our Team's Position	Our Opposing Team's Position

5 Plan Your Response

Discuss with your partner how to respond to your opponents' arguments.

If they say_____

_____

_____

we will say_____

_____

_____

6 Learn the Form and Practice the Debate

There are many different types of debate formats. The type you will take part in is called a Lincoln-Douglas debate, named after a series of debates held by Abraham Lincoln and Stephen A. Douglas in 1858. Use **21 Tool**Kit **Expert File 1.13** to learn all about Lincoln-Douglas debates.

- With your partner, plan and practice your debate.

- Assign a role to you and your partner: One person will be the first speaker and will answer the cross-examiner, the other will be the cross-examiner and will give the rebuttal.

- Write note cards with facts and reasons to support your arguments and to answer those of your opponents.

- Listen respectfully to your opponents and speak clearly when it's your turn.

BUDGET STATISTICS
Source: U.S. Office of Management and Budget Report
Date Accessed: January 22, 2009

NASA FISCAL YEAR (FY) 2009 BUDGET REQUEST SUMMARY
(Budget Authority, Dollar amounts in millions)

	FY 2009	FY 2010	FY 2011	FY 2012	FY 2013
Science	4,441.5	4,482.0	4,534.9	4,643.4	4,761.6
Exploration	3,500.5	3,737.7	7,048.2	7,116.8	7,666.8
Space Operations	5,774.7	5,872.8	2,900.1	3,089.9	2,788.5

U.S. BUDGET FOR FISCAL YEAR 2009
Discretionary Funding by Major Agency
(Dollar amounts in millions)

Corps of Engineers—Civil Works	
• Construction	1,402
• Operation and Maintenance	2,475
• Flood Control and Coastal Emergencies	40
Environmental Protection Agency	
• Clean Water State Revolving Fund	555
• Clean Diesel Grants	49
Department of Health and Human Services	
• Food and Drug Administration	1,771
• Centers for Disease Control and Prevention	5,691

> Compare the data presented in the two charts. **Circle** the amount of money budgeted for space exploration for Fiscal Year 2009. Draw a **box** around the amount budgeted for flood control and coastal emergencies that same year.

NEWS REPORT
Source: Texas Newspaper
Date: February 1, 2003

Circle the words that tell what happened to the *Columbia*. Do you think space exploration is worth the risk? Explain.

_____

_____

_____

_____

A U.S. Army helicopter video captured the debris from the space shuttle Columbia.

Saturday, Houston, TX—The space shuttle Columbia broke apart soon after entering Earth's atmosphere, killing all seven astronauts on board. The shuttle appeared to disintegrate over Texas, scattering debris across hundreds of miles of land. Crew members Rick Husband, William McCool, Kalpana Chawla, Laurel Clark, Ilan Ramon, David Brown, and Michael Anderson were returning to Earth after a successful 16-day mission.

NASA WEB SITE

Source: NASA Orbital Debris Web site
Date Accessed: February 5, 2009

| About Us | FAQs | Photo Gallery | Contact Us | Other Links |

Near-Earth Objects as Future Resources Program

Asteroids are a potential source of valuable raw materials. A single asteroid could provide millions of tons of nickel, iron, magnesium, and other metals and minerals—and there are about one million asteroids in the solar system. One day, mining operations on asteroids could supply these resources to Earth and our colonies in space. It is estimated that the mineral wealth in the asteroid belt between Mars and Jupiter would be equivalent to about $100 billion for every person on Earth.

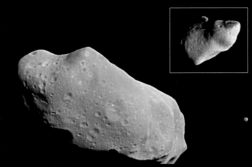

Asteroid Ida, and its satellite Dactyl, is located in the asteroid belt between Mars and Jupiter.

> What does this article tell you about the rewards of mining asteroids? What doesn't it tell you?
>
> _____
>
> _____
>
> _____

PRESIDENT'S SPEECH

Source: White House Press Release
Date: January 14, 2004

President Bush Announces New Vision for Space Exploration Program

NASA Headquarters, Washington, D.C.
3:25 P.M. EST

> Former President George W. Bush gives several reasons for continuing space exploration. **Circle** two. Do you agree with these reasons? Explain.
>
> _____
>
> _____

THE PRESIDENT: We have undertaken space travel because the desire to explore and understand is part of our character. And that quest has led to advances in weather forecasting, in communications, in computing, search and rescue technology, robotics, and electronics. [It has] helped to create our satellite telecommunications network and the Global Positioning System. Medical technologies that help prolong life—such as the imaging processing used in CAT scanners and MRI machines—trace their origins to technology engineered for the use in space . . . .

Today I announce a new plan to return to the moon by 2020 . . . . the moon is home to abundant resources . . . .With the experience and knowledge gained on the moon, we will then be ready to take the next steps of space exploration: human missions to Mars and to worlds beyond . . . .

President Bush speaks out on space travel.

Strategy Check

Use your knowledge and strategies from the workshop to answer these questions.

Draw Conclusions

1. Author Neil deGrasse Tyson suggests that NASA should start a number of new and exciting space projects in order to attract top-notch scientists. What conclusion has the author drawn about scientists?

_____

_____

_____

_____

What do you know about people in real life that support this conclusion?

_____

_____

_____

Cause and Effect

2. Complete the cause-and-effect charts to show what happened and why in the story "Who's There?"

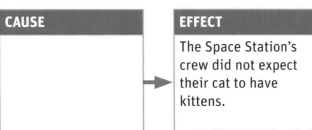

CAUSE	EFFECT
	The Space Station's crew did not expect their cat to have kittens.

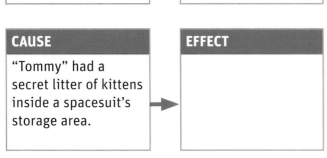

CAUSE	EFFECT
"Tommy" had a secret litter of kittens inside a spacesuit's storage area.	

Suspense

3. In the story "The Zero Hour," which event is most suspenseful? Summarize the event and explain what makes it suspenseful.

_____

_____

_____

Structure of an Argument

4. Reread the last paragraph of Neil deGrasse Tyson's editorial "The Case for Space." What is the purpose of this paragraph?

_____

_____

Graphic Aids: Diagrams

5. What is the purpose of this diagram?

_____

_____

_____

_____

Context Clues

6. Read the sentences below. Use context clues to figure out the meaning of the term *acid rain*.

Chemical reactions from fires increased the amounts of toxic chemicals like nitric acid in the atmosphere. The chemicals caused destructive <u>acid rain</u>, which harmed many plants and animals.

What is **acid rain**? Fill in the bubble next to the correct answer.

(A) a dangerous biological weapon

(B) rain polluted by chemicals in the air

(C) toxic chemicals in the atmosphere

(D) chemical reactions from fires

Synonyms and Antonyms

7. Which word below is an antonym for *futuristic*? Fill in the bubble next to the correct answer.

(A) antagonistic

(B) inherently

(C) old-fashioned

(D) forward-thinking

Evaluate Sources

8. If you had to write a research paper about the U.S. space program, where would you look for information?

Rate each source with a number from 1 (low score) to 3 (high score). If you're not sure of the answer, put a question mark in the box.

	accurate	in-depth	up-to-date
encyclopedia			
an expert's			
official NASA			

Analyze/Synthesize

9. What kinds of emotions and ideals are inspired by the notion of outer space? Use examples from the selections in Workshop 6 to answer this question.

_____

_____

_____

_____

_____

_____

_____

_____

❓ EXPERT QUESTION

Should we explore outer space?

10. Use what you learned in this workshop to respond to the Expert Question. Jot down some notes here. Then use a separate sheet of paper to write your response.

_____

_____

EYEWITNESS *to* HISTORY

Expert Question:
What was it like to be there?

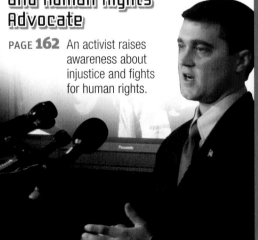
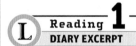

Inquiry 2 Lessons from History

Reading 4
PERSONAL NARRATIVE

No More Strangers Now

By Bandile Mashinini and Mark Abrahamson

Two South African teens—one black, one white—reflect on their homeland's history from opposite sides of a country once divided by racial lines.

PAGE **194**

Reading 5
MEMOIR

A Refugee in Her Own Country

By Loung Ung

A young girl experiences the brutality of General Pol Pot's Khmer Rouge regime—and survives to tell her family's gripping story.

PAGE **204**

Reading 6
PERSONAL NARRATIVE

One Giant Leap for Humankind

By Andrés Eloy Mendoza Rodriguez

When astronauts Buzz Aldrin and Neil Armstrong first landed on the moon in 1969, an estimated 600 million people—one-fifth of the world's population at the time—witnessed it.

PAGE **216**

Write and Communicate

Expository Writing

Research Paper

Imagine yourself present at a major historic event. Research and write a paper about this historic event as if you were an eyewitness.

PAGE **222**

Apply Expert Skills

[21] Expert Reading

PERSONAL ESSAY

Remembering 9/11

By Juliette Kessler

A teen reporter is assigned to write about the September 11, 2001 attacks on the United States. 9/11 is an event this writer will never forget. She was there.

PAGE **230**

expert 21 PROJECT RESEARCH

Eyewitness to the Present Day

PAGE **234**

✓ Strategy Check

PAGE **238**

[21] 21st Century Skills

Play a Role
PAGE **220**

So, tell me, what were your impressions of what happened to our country these last few days?

I always thought the wall would be permanent. I never imagined it would be torn down by people in the street.

American visitor

What was it like to be there?

Revisit tragic and triumphant times in history through the accounts of young people who were there.

▶ Anchor Your Knowledge

Watch the Anchor Media, "Eyewitness to History," and meet Brian Steidle, a former marine who works to prevent violence and killing in Sudan, West Africa.

WORKSHOP GOALS

To gain expert knowledge about significant historical events, you will

- study **informational texts** about the Berlin Wall, the Iraq War, apartheid in South Africa, and the 1969 moon landing.

- read **literature** about the Holocaust and a brutal political regime in Cambodia.

- learn **important skills and strategies** to help you understand what you read.

- develop **21st Century Skills** to **ask questions** and **interpret primary sources.**

- write a **research paper** about a historical event that interests you.

- complete an **Expert Project** to create a time capsule that represents your era.

▶ Anticipation Guide

Before reading this workshop, respond to each statement below in the column on the left. Check **Y (yes)** if you agree with the statement. Check **N (no)** if you disagree. Then, **after** you complete the workshop, return here to evaluate these statements again in the column at the right. Compare your responses. Have any of your ideas changed?

BEFORE		TOPIC: **Witnessing History**	AFTER	
Y	N		Y	N
		People who suffer oppression always remain hostile to their former oppressors.		
		Space travel is a universal achievement that many countries still hold as a goal.		
		Governments often separate people when political or racial tensions rise.		
		Many young children were intentionally killed during the Holocaust.		
		People are capable of enduring great challenge and rising above much adversity.		
		It is important to protect and display artifacts from 9/11 and other events of historical significance.		
		Communications from war zones should be censored by the military to protect citizens from the violence.		
		People, by nature, are inherently good and willing to help one another.		

◉ Preview the Expert Project

At the end of this workshop, you'll create a time capsule to represent your era. Preview the **Expert Project** on pages 234–237.

▶ What will you need to know or do to complete the Expert Project?

_____

_____

_____

_____

◉ Explore Expert Space

 Go to **www.expert21.com/student** to learn more about the topics in this workshop.

DISCOVER ONLINE

- Careers in Documentary Filmmaking
- Darfur
- Genocide

READ ONLINE

- The Holocaust
- The Fall of the Berlin Wall
- Apartheid
- Khmer Rouge

RESEARCH ONLINE

- 21st Century News Stories
- September 11, 2001
- The Global Financial Crisis

◉ Personal Inquiry

Explore the topic of each person's experience of history by asking your own questions. Return to add questions as you continue reading Workshop 7. Plan to revisit your questions.

Brian Steidle: U.S. Marine and Human Rights Advocate

> "If I can speak to an audience and one person leaves that room with some action points, something they can do...then I feel like I've done my part."

FACTS AND STATS

NAME: Brian Steidle

CURRENT JOBS: Founder, Executive Director of HOPE (Help Other People Everywhere); Writer; Activist

MILITARY CAREER: United States Marine Corps Captain, 1999–2003

EDUCATION: B.A. in Foreign Affairs; M.B.A.

WORKPLACE LITERACIES: Examining perspectives; asking questions; solving problems; making decisions; communicating and collaborating

PAY: New Marines make about $23,500 a year; very experienced Marines earn up to $72,800 a year; Nonprofit Directors make, on average, about $50,000 a year.

CAREER CONNECTION
Government and Public Administration
www.careerclusters.org

Go to 21 ToolKit **Expert File 6.22** to learn more about public service careers.

RELATED JOBS: Marine, aid worker, nonprofit administrator, reporter, writer, filmmaker, journalist.

This eyewitness to killing and brutality fights for peace.

After finishing his service with the U.S. Marines, Brian Steidle volunteered to monitor a cease-fire in the Darfur region of Sudan, West Africa. In April 2004, the government of Sudan and rebels from Darfur agreed to stop fighting, but the violence, as Steidle learned, continued. Six months in Darfur changed his life forever.

MONTH 1 — A New Mission

When Steidle's helicopter landed in Darfur, he was greeted by representatives from the African Union and volunteers. This international team was on a peacekeeping mission to stop genocide—murder with the intention of eradicating an entire race.

MONTH 2 — Monitoring a Cease-Fire

There was ongoing fighting as militias destroyed villages and killed civilians—and the villagers fought back. As an unarmed observer, Steidle was "to make recommendations, not intervene." The team's job: investigate attacks, talk to both sides, and report ideas for ending the violence. Steidle **studied** maps and **read** reports.

MONTH 3 — Investigating Attacks

When the team learned of an attack, they first traveled to the village and **interviewed** people. Each time, Steidle witnessed murder, torture, looting, and destruction. "People said they knew they would be attacked, but they had no way to defend themselves and nowhere to go." Steidle spent hours **taking pictures** and **collecting evidence.**

MONTH 4 — Meeting with the Enemy

Almost daily villages were burned, people were killed and tortured, and families were torn apart. After documenting the attacks in each village, the team traveled across Darfur in search of the militia men accused of attacks—to get their side of the story. These groups moved from area to area, so Steidle's team had to track them down. The men in the militias usually denied any involvement.

MONTH 5 — Trying to Resolve Conflict

The team **analyzed the evidence** and **wrote reports.** Then the team **collaborated** to **make recommendations** to the African Union about what should be done. However, the team rarely had **consensus.** Representatives from the Sudanese government on the team always believed that the militias were not responsible.

MONTH 6 — Leaving the Mission

"At first I thought our reports were useful—that the world governments would do something to stop the attacks." He lost faith as the killing went on and on. Finally, the U.S. government declared that the attacks in Darfur were acts of genocide. Genocide is an international crime that the United Nations is committed to preventing. This gave Steidle hope that help would come. However, the genocide continued. At that point, Steidle decided to work on a different kind of report.

AFTER SUDAN — Steidle's Mission

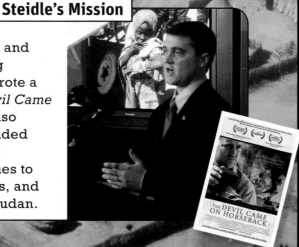

Steidle returned to the U.S. and dedicated his life to ending genocide worldwide. He wrote a book about Sudan, *The Devil Came on Horseback*, which was also made into a movie. He founded HOPE, an organization that supports peace. He continues to speak at events, raise funds, and investigate war crimes in Sudan.

ANALYZE WORKPLACE SKILLS

1. Examine Perspectives

What information did Steidle gather and organize from the two groups?

_____

_____

_____

2. Ask Questions

What kinds of questions do you think Steidle asked the villagers in order to find out the information he needed?

_____

_____

_____

3. Collaborate

What steps did the team take to prepare a report?

DISCOVER ONLINE

expert space
Go to **www.expert21.com/student** to learn more about Careers in Documentary Filmmaking; Darfur; Genocide.

Diary Excerpt

The Diary of a Young Girl

Anne Frank was a thirteen-year-old German Jewish girl who lived in hiding with her family at the end of World War II. This suspenseful excerpt from her diary gives some insight into how ordinary people coped with unbelievable tragedy.

W QuickWrite

What would you do if you experienced discrimination so severe that you had to go into hiding to stay safe? Write a paragraph describing how you would feel and react.

Author's Voice   LITERARY ANALYSIS

The term author's voice refers to a writer's unique use of language, which allows a reader to "hear" an author's personality.

To express his or her voice, an author considers:

- audience (*Who are my readers?*)
- word choice (*Should my words be formal or casual?*)
- syntax (*How long or short should my sentences be?*)
- tone (*What is my attitude toward this subject?*)

▶ Circle the word that best describes the author's voice in each sentence.

- I really wanted to just hang out and chill, but my mother was on my case about homework.

  Author's voice: informal   formal

- A warm breeze stirred the long fronds of the stately palm trees above me.

  Author's voice: descriptive   plain

- I'm not gonna go anywhere ever again, and you can't make me!

  Author's voice: mature   childish

Make Inferences   COMPREHENSION

When you make an inference, you form ideas about things that are not directly stated in the text.

You can make an inference about an author's purpose, perspective, or point of view.

The author's choice of words and details can help you infer how the author feels about his or her subject.

▶ Underline words and details in this passage from "The Diary of a Young Girl" that reveal how Anne Frank feels about the Nazi capture of Jews.

It is terrible outside. Day and night more of those poor miserable people are being dragged off, with nothing but a rucksack and a little money. On the way they are deprived even of these possessions. Families are torn apart, the men, women, and children all being separated. Children coming home from school find that their parents have disappeared. Women return from shopping to find their homes shut up and their families gone.

Anne feels _____

_____

_____

Academic Language `VOCABULARY`

▶ Rate your knowledge of each word. Then write its meaning and an example sentence.

Word	Meaning	Example
EXPERT WORDS *Use these words to write and talk about the workshop topic.*		
succession suc•ces•sion (noun) ① ② ③ ④	a series of events that happen one after the other	The point guard made a succession of brilliant moves during the game and was named most valuable player.
ACADEMIC WORDS *Use these words in all your subject classes.*		
prohibited pro•hib•it•ed (adj.) ① ② ③ ④	forbidden by law or by authority	
restriction re•stric•tion (noun) ① ② ③ ④		In the U.S., people convicted of crimes have restrictions placed on their voting rights.
SELECTION WORDS *These words are key to understanding this selection.*		
appoint ap•point (verb) ① ② ③ ④	to choose someone for a position or job	
dejected de•ject•ed (adj.) ① ② ③ ④		
deprive de•prive (verb) ① ② ③ ④		
peculiar pe•cu•liar (adj.) ① ② ③ ④		
wretched wretch•ed (adj.) ① ② ③ ④		

Rating Scale ① I don't know the word. ② I've seen it or heard it. ③ I know its meaning. ④ I know it and use it.

Base Words `WORD ANALYSIS`

A base word is a complete word that can stand alone. New words can be made from base words by adding beginnings (prefixes) and endings (suffixes).

New words can also be made when two base words are joined together. A compound word is two words joined together to form a new word.

What two base words make up the word *grandmother*?

_____

What two base words make up the word *throughout*?

_____

from
The Diary of a Young Girl
By Anne Frank

RESTRICTIONS

SECRET ANNEXE

YOURS, ANNE

AMSTERDAM IN HOLLAND

DEAR KITTY,

MARGOT

THE GESTAPO

DADDY AND MUMMY

How does a young girl's diary become a classic record of one of history's most tragic chapters?

In 1921, Adolf Hitler was elected leader of the National Socialist German Workers'—also known as the Nazi—Party, and later he established a totalitarian state that he ruled through brute force. He blamed Germany's economic problems on Jewish people and declared white, blond, and blue-eyed Germans "the Aryan master race." Hitler and the Nazis believed that the Aryans should rule the world, so they launched a systematic attack on Jews and other minority groups whom they considered racially "inferior." Jews lost their jobs. Their children could not attend schools with Aryan children. They lived in total segregation in all aspects of life.

In the early 1940s, as World War II raged throughout Europe, Hitler adopted "the final solution" to what he called "the Jewish question." He called for the extermination, or killing, of all Jews. Special S.S.[1] forces rounded up and tortured hundreds of thousands of Jews from Germany, Poland, and surrounding European nations. During the Holocaust, innocent men, women, and children were stripped of their rights and sent to death. These prisoners were taken from their homes and forced to live in horrible, **wretched** conditions in concentration camps—prisons where people were tortured, **deprived** of basic necessities like food and water, and killed. By the end of the war, an estimated six million Jews and others who were not part of Hitler's "master race" were exterminated. More than one million were under the age of sixteen.

Thirteen-year-old Anne Frank and her family, who were Jewish, tried to escape the Nazis by going into hiding in Holland in 1942. An excerpt from her diary follows.

---

[1] The S.S., or the Schutzstaffel in German, were members of a police force who worked for Adolf Hitler. S.S. guards ran the Nazi concentration camps where millions of people lost their lives throughout Europe.

---

totalitarian *(adj.)* exercising control over the freedom, will, or thought of others
Aryan *(adj.)* of Northern European ancestry, especially someone with blond hair and blue eyes

Saturday, 20 June, 1942

I don't want to set down a series of bald facts in a diary like most people do, but I want this diary itself to be my friend, and I shall call my friend Kitty. No one will grasp what I'm talking about if I begin my letters to Kitty just out of the blue, so, albeit unwillingly, I will start by sketching in brief the story of my life.

My father was thirty-six when he married my mother, who was then twenty-five. My sister Margot was born in 1926 in Frankfort-on-Main, I followed on June 12, 1929, and, as we are Jewish, we emigrated to Holland in 1933, where my father was **appointed** Managing Director of Travies N.V. This firm is in close relationship with the firm of Kolen & Co. in the same building of which my father is a partner.

The rest of our family, however, felt the full impact of Hitler's anti-Jewish laws, so life was filled with anxiety. In 1938 after the pogroms, my two uncles (my mother's brothers) escaped to the U.S.A. My old grandmother came to us, she was then seventy-three. After May 1940 good times rapidly fled: first the war, then the capitulation [surrender], followed by the arrival of the Germans, which is when the sufferings of us Jews really began. Anti-Jewish decrees followed each other in quick **succession**. Jews must wear a yellow star, Jews must hand in their bicycles, Jews are banned from trams and are forbidden to drive. Jews are only allowed to do their shopping between three and five o'clock and then only in shops which bear the placard "Jewish shop." Jews must be indoors by eight o'clock and cannot even sit in their own gardens after that hour. Jews are forbidden to visit theaters, cinemas, and other places of entertainment. Jews may not take part in public sports. Swimming baths, tennis courts, hockey fields, and other sports grounds are all **prohibited** to them. Jews may not visit Christians. Jews must go to Jewish schools, and many more **restrictions** of a similar kind.

So we could not do this and were forbidden to do that. But life went on in spite of it all.

> **Make Inferences**
> What does the final line of this first entry reveal about the author?

Yours, Anne

Sunday morning, 5 July, 1942

Dear Kitty,

Daddy has been at home a lot lately, as there is nothing for him to do at business; it must be rotten to feel so superfluous. Mr. Koophuis has taken over Travies and Mr. Kraler the firm Kolen & Co. When we talked across our little square together a few days ago, Daddy began to talk of us going into hiding. I asked him why on earth he was beginning to talk of that already. "Yes, Anne," he said. "You know that we have been taking food, clothes, furniture to other people for more than a year now. We don't want our belongings to be seized by the Germans, but we certainly don't want to fall into their clutches ourselves. So we shall disappear of our own accord and not wait until they come and fetch us."

Yours, Anne

Wednesday, 8 July, 1942

Dear Kitty,

Years seem to have passed between Sunday and now. So much has happened, it is just as if the whole world had turned upside down. But I am still alive, Kitty, and that is the main thing, Daddy says.

Yes, I'm still alive, indeed, but don't ask where or how. You wouldn't understand a word, so I will begin by telling you what happened on Sunday afternoon.

At three o'clock someone rang the front doorbell. I was lying lazily reading a book on the veranda in the sunshine, so I didn't hear it. A bit later, Margot appeared at the kitchen door looking very excited. "The S.S. have sent a call-up notice for Daddy," she whispered. "Mummy has gone to see Mr. Van Daan already." (Van Daan is a friend who works with Daddy in the business.) It was a great shock to me, a call-up; everyone knows what that means. I picture concentration camps and lonely cells—should we allow him to be doomed to this? "Of course he won't go," declared Margot, while we waited together. "Mummy

> **pogroms** (n.) an organized massacre of people
> **superfluous** (adj.) more than is required

has gone to the Van Daans to discuss whether we should move into our hiding place tomorrow. The Van Daans are going with us, so we shall be seven in all."

Margot and I were sent out of the room. Van Daan wanted to talk to Mummy alone. When we were alone together in our bedroom, Margot told me that the call-up was not for Daddy, but for her. I was more frightened than ever and began to cry. Margot is sixteen; would they really take girls of that age away alone? But thank goodness she won't go, Mummy said so herself; that must be what Daddy meant when he talked about us going into hiding.

Into hiding—where would we go, in a town or the country, in a house or a cottage, when, how, where . . . ?

These were questions I was not allowed to ask, but I couldn't get them out of my mind. Margot and I began to pack some of our most vital belongings into a school satchel. The first thing I put in was this diary, then hair curlers, handkerchiefs, schoolbooks, a comb, old letters; I put in the craziest things with the idea that we were going into hiding. But I'm not sorry, memories mean more to me than dresses.

Luckily it was not so hot as Sunday; warm rain fell steadily all day. We put on heaps of clothes as if we were going to the North Pole, the sole reason being to take clothes with us. No Jew in our situation would have dreamed of going out with a suitcase full of clothing.

I had on two vests, three pairs of pants, a dress, on top of that a skirt, jacket, summer coat, two pairs of stockings, lace-up shoes, woolly cap, scarf, and still more, I was nearly stifled before we started, but no one inquired about that.

Margot filled her satchel with schoolbooks, fetched her bicycle, and rode off behind Miep [a family friend] into the unknown, as far as I was concerned. You see I still didn't know where our secret hiding place was to be. At seven-thirty the door closed behind us. Moortje, my little cat, was the only creature to whom I said farewell.

Yours, Anne

---

sole *(adj.)* only
fetched *(v.)* went to get something

Read and Synthesize

LITERARY ANALYSIS ▸

Author's Voice

Review the entry for Sunday morning, 5 July, 1942, and consider the author's voice.

- How would you describe the author's voice in this entry?

Ⓐ bored and impatient

Ⓑ worried and introspective

Ⓒ cheerful and hopeful

Ⓓ entertaining and funny

- <u>Underline</u> words or details in this entry that show you Anne's voice.

COMPREHENSION ▸

Make Inferences

Review the entry for Wednesday, 8 July, 1942. Why do you think Anne is not allowed to ask questions about where her family will be hiding?

_____

_____

_____

_____

_____

_____

_____

CRITICAL THINKING ▸

Evaluate

When Anne is packing to go into hiding, why do you think she says, "memories mean more to me than dresses"? Explain.

_____

_____

_____

_____

_____

_____

_____

_____

A view of the attic and Anne Frank's desk in the Secret Annex.

Thursday, 9 July, 1942

Dear Kitty,

Only when we were on the road did Mummy and Daddy begin to tell me bits and pieces about the plan. For months as many of our goods and chattels and necessities of life as possible had been sent away and they were sufficiently ready for us to have gone into hiding of our own accord on July 16. The plan had had to be speeded up ten days because of the call-up, so our quarters would not be so well organized, but we had to make the best of it. The hiding place itself would be in the building where Daddy has his office. Daddy didn't have many people working for him: Mr. Kraler, Koophuis, Miep, and Elli Vossen, a twenty-three-year-old typist who all knew of our arrival. Mr. Vossen, Elli's father, and two boys worked in the warehouse; they had not been told.

---

chattels *(n.)* personal properties that can be moved
sufficiently *(adv.)* in a way that is adequate or enough

I will describe the building: there is a large warehouse on the ground floor, which is used as a store. The front door to the house is next to the warehouse door, and inside the front door is a second doorway, which leads to a staircase. There is another door at the top of the stairs, with a frosted glass window in it, which has "Office" written in black letters across it. That is the large main office. A small dark room containing the safe, a wardrobe, and a large cupboard leads to a small somewhat dark second office. Mr. Kraler and Mr. Van Daan used to sit here, now it is only Mr. Kraler.

From Kraler's office a long passage goes past the coal store, up four steps and leads to the showroom of the whole building: the private office. Dark, dignified furniture, linoleum and carpets on the floor, radio, smart lamp, everything first-class. Next door there is a roomy kitchen with a hot-water faucet and a gas stove. Next door the W.C. [toilet and washroom]. That is the first floor.

A wooden staircase leads from the downstairs passage to the next floor. There is a small landing at the top. There is a door at each end of the landing, the left one leading to a storeroom at the front of the house and to the attics. The right-hand door leads to our "Secret Annexe."

There is a steep staircase immediately opposite the entrance. On the left a tiny passage brings you into a room which was to become the Frank family's bed-sitting-room, next door a smaller room, study and bedroom for the two young ladies of the family. On the right a little room without windows containing the washbasin and a small W.C. compartment, with another door leading to Margot's and my room. If you go up the next flight of stairs and open the door, you are simply amazed that there could be such a big light room in such an old house by the canal. There is a gas stove in this room (thanks to the fact that it was used as a laboratory) and a sink. This is now the kitchen for the Van Daan couple, besides being general living room, dining room, and scullery.

A tiny little corridor room will become Peter Van Daan's apartment. Then, just as on the lower landing, there is a large attic. So there you are, I've introduced you to the whole of our beautiful "Secret Annexe."

Yours, Anne

> **Make Inferences**
> **Why do you think the author refers to the hiding place as "beautiful"?**

---

scullery (n.) a small room off the kitchen where food is prepared and utensils are cleaned and stored

LITERARY ANALYSIS

Author's Voice
Review the entry for Thursday, 9 July, 1942. The author's voice in this entry can best be described as
Ⓐ casual and choppy
Ⓑ short and concise
Ⓒ descriptive and conversational
Ⓓ wordy and complicated

VOCABULARY/WORD ANALYSIS

Base Words
Review the second paragraph on page 171.
- Circle the compound word *showroom*.
- What two base words make up *showroom*? _____ and _____
- Based on these two words, how would you define *showroom*?

_____

_____

_____

_____

_____

_____

21 SMALL GROUPS/INDEPENDENT

COLLABORATE

Examine Perspectives Imagine what it would be like for two families to share a tiny living space. Discuss some of the challenges that might arise.

COMMUNICATE

React and Write Pick a member of the Frank family other than Anne, and write a journal entry for Thursday, 9 July, 1942, from that person's perspective.

Saturday, 11 July, 1942

Dear Kitty,

I expect you will be interested to hear what it feels like to "disappear"; well, all I can say is that I don't know myself yet. I don't think I shall ever feel really at home in this house, but that does not mean that I loathe it here, it is more like being on vacation in a very **peculiar** boardinghouse. Rather a mad idea, perhaps, but that is how it strikes me. The "Secret Annexe" is an ideal hiding place. Although it leans to one side and is damp, you'd never find such a comfortable hiding place anywhere in Amsterdam, no, perhaps not even in the whole of Holland.

Yours, Anne

Friday, 14 August, 1942

Dear Kitty,

The Van Daans arrived on July 13. We thought they were coming on the fourteenth, but between the thirteenth and sixteenth of July the Germans called up people right and left which created more and more unrest, so they played for safety, better a day too early than a day too late. At nine-thirty in the morning (we were still having breakfast) Peter arrived, the Van Daans' son, not sixteen yet, a rather soft, shy, gawky youth; can't expect much from his company. He brought his cat (Mouschi) with him. Mr. and Mrs. Van Daan arrived half an hour later, and to our great amusement she had a large pottie in her hat box. "I don't feel at home anywhere without my chamber," she declared.

Yours, Anne

> **Clarify**
> How many people are now living in the "Secret Annexe"?

Westerbork was a "transit camp" where Dutch and German Jews were detained before being transported to extermination camps such as Auschwitz.

> **gawky** *(adj.)* tall and not graceful

Friday, 9 October, 1942

Dear Kitty,

I've only got dismal and depressing news for you today. Our many Jewish friends are being taken away by the dozen. These people are treated by the Gestapo without a shred of decency, being loaded into cattle trucks and sent to Westerbork, the big Jewish camp in Drente. Westerbork sounds terrible: only one washing cubicle for a hundred people and not nearly enough lavatories. There is no separate accommodation. Men, women, and children all sleep together.

If it is as bad as this in Holland, whatever will it be like in the distant and barbarous regions they are sent to? We assume that most of them are murdered. The English radio speaks of their being gassed.

Yours, Anne

Anne Frank died in Auschwitz, in Nazi German occupied Poland. It was the largest of the Nazi concentration camps.

---

barbarous *(adj.)* savagely cruel or harsh

Read and Synthesize

COMPREHENSION

Make Inferences
Review the entry for Saturday, 11 July, 1942. Even though she says she will never really feel at home there, why do you think Anne does not hate the hiding place?

_____

_____

_____

_____

_____

CRITICAL THINKING

Evaluate
How do you think Anne Frank's diary has impacted our understanding of the Holocaust? How does it compare to reading academic texts in a history book?

_____

_____

_____

_____

_____

_____

LITERARY ANALYSIS

Author's Voice
Review the entry for Friday, 14 August, 1942.

• What does the narrator's voice tell you about her personality?

_____

_____

_____

_____

_____

• <u>Underline</u> phrases in the text that support your response.

Tuesday, 20 October, 1942

Dear Kitty,

My hand still shakes, although it's two hours since we had the shock. I should explain that there are five fire extinguishers in the house. We knew that someone was coming to fill them, but no one had warned us when the carpenter, or whatever you call him, was coming.

The result was that we weren't making any attempt to keep quiet, until I heard hammering outside on the landing opposite our cupboard door. I thought of the carpenter at once and warned Elli, who was having a meal with us, that she shouldn't go downstairs. Daddy and I posted ourselves at the door so as to hear when the man left. After he'd been working for a quarter of an hour, he laid his hammer and tools down on top of our cupboard (as we thought) and knocked at our door. We turned absolutely white. Perhaps he had heard something after all and wanted to investigate our secret den. It seemed like it. The knocking, pulling, pushing, and wrenching went on. I nearly fainted at the thought that this utter stranger might discover our beautiful secret hiding place.

And just as I thought my last hour was at hand, I heard Mr. Koophuis say, "Open the door, it's only me." We opened it immediately. The hook that holds the cupboard, which can be undone by people who know the secret, had got jammed. That was why no one had been able to warn us about the carpenter. The man had now gone downstairs and Koophuis wanted to fetch Elli, but couldn't open the cupboard again. It was a great relief to me, I can tell you. In my imagination the man who I thought was trying to get in had been growing and growing in size until in the end he appeared to be a giant and the greatest fascist that ever walked the earth.

Well! Well! Luckily everything was okay this time!

Yours, Anne

Wednesday, 13 January, 1943

Dear Kitty,

It is terrible outside. Day and night more of those poor miserable people are being dragged off, with nothing but a rucksack and a little money. On the way they are deprived even of these possessions. Families are torn apart, the men, women, and children all being separated. Children coming home from school find that their parents have disappeared. Women return from shopping to find their homes shut up and their families gone.

The Dutch people are anxious too, their sons are being sent to Germany. Everyone is afraid.

And every night hundreds of planes fly over Holland and go to German towns, where the earth is plowed up by their bombs, and every hour hundreds and thousands of people are killed in Russia and Africa. No one is able to keep out of it, the whole globe is waging war and although it is going better for the Allies, the end is not yet in sight.

And as for us, we are fortunate. Yes, we are luckier than millions of people. It is quiet and safe here, and we are, so to speak, living on capital. We are even so selfish as to talk about "after the war," brighten up at the thought of having new clothes and new shoes, whereas we really ought to save every penny, to help other people, and save what is left from the wreckage after the war.

Jewish families were stripped of their belongings and taken to concentration camps.

---

fascist *(n.)* a person who believes in a totalitarian system of government ruled by a dictator
rucksack *(n.)* a type of knapsack carried by hikers and bicyclists

The children here run about in just a thin blouse and clogs; no coat, no hat, no stockings, and no one helps them. Their tummies are empty; they chew an old carrot to stay the pangs, go from their cold homes out into the cold street and, when they get to school, find themselves in an even colder classroom. Yes, it has even got so bad in Holland that countless children stop the passers-by and beg for a piece of bread. I could go on for hours about all the suffering the war has brought, but then I would only make myself more **dejected**. There is nothing we can do but wait as calmly as we can till the misery comes to an end. Jews and Christians wait, the whole earth waits; and there are many who wait for death.

Yours, Anne

> **Clarify**
> What is going on in the outside world beyond the "Secret Annexe"?

Epilogue

For two years, the Franks and the Van Daans followed the events of World War II over their illegal radio. On August 4, 1944, after information about them was provided by an informer, the Nazi police discovered the secret annex and arrested its inhabitants. All were sent to concentration camps, where everyone, except Anne's father Otto Frank, perished. ■

 Annelies Marie Frank

BORN June 12, 1929 in Frankfurt, Germany

FAMILY Anne grew up with her parents, Otto and Edith Frank, and her older sister, Margot.

AUTHOR FILE

ACTIVITIES While in hiding, Anne could not move or make noise during the day. However, at night, she was free to pursue her love of ballet. She wrote, "I have a craze for dancing and ballet . . . and practice dance steps every evening diligently." The Franks along with Otto's coworker, Hermann Van Pels (Mr. Van Daan in the diary), and his family spent their evenings in the secret annex listening to the radio, reading books, and playing board games.

REMEMBERED On May 3, 1960, The Anne Frank House opened in Amsterdam. This museum, dedicated to Anne and the victims of the Holocaust, is located in the building where Anne and her family hid from the Nazis.

CELEBRATED Anne was named one of *Time* magazine's 100 Heroes & Icons of the 20th Century.

Read and Synthesize

LITERARY ANALYSIS ▸

Author's Voice

Review the last two paragraphs from Tuesday, 20 October, 1942, and the first paragraph from Wednesday, 13 January, 1943. How does the narrator's voice change between these two entries?

_____

_____

_____

_____

COMPREHENSION ▸

Make Inferences

Review Anne's entry for Wednesday, 13 January, 1943.

- **Underline** the figurative language in the third paragraph.
- What can you infer about Anne's statement "there are many who wait for death"?

_____

_____

_____

_____

CRITICAL THINKING ▸

Synthesize

How is Anne's experience similar to something you have heard about in the news or read about in a history book? How are Anne's responses the same as or different from the responses of other people who have experienced great tragedy?

_____

_____

_____

_____

READ ONLINE ▸

 expert space
Go to **www.expert21.com/student** to learn more about The Holocaust; Anne Frank; World War II.

The FALL of the WALL

BY GILLIAN COX WITH PHOTOS BY TIME.COM

Through pictures and words, eyewitnesses capture the end of an era in the long-

At the end of World War II, the United States and the Soviet Union emerged as "superpowers." These two nations had worked together to defeat Germany, Italy, and Japan, but after the war, an intense rivalry began between them. Each new superpower had its own set of allies and supporters, and the two sides held opposing views about how the world should be governed in the post-WWII era. The tension and suspicion between the superpowers was known as the Cold War. It was the main influence affecting world politics for more than 40 years.

The city of Berlin, Germany, was a stage where Cold War tensions were acted out. After World War II, West Berlin was controlled by the United States, France, and Britain. The Soviet Union controlled East Berlin. It was a very tense setup for all. In 1961, Soviet-controlled East Germany sealed off East Berlin by building a 96-mile-long wall to separate it from the West.

The heavily policed Berlin Wall divided families and friends in the city. It also symbolically divided the world for more than two generations—until 1989, when Cold War tensions thawed, and one day the wall came tumbling down.

The Berlin Wall

B E R L I N

West Berlin

East Berlin

rivalry *(n.)* competition

allies *(n.)* persons, groups, or states that have joined for mutual help and support

Read and Synthesize

NAVIGATING TEXT

Text Features and Visual Features

 Read the text and look at the map on page 177.

- (Circle) information about the Berlin Wall in both the text and the map.

- What are two important facts about the Berlin Wall that you can learn only from reading the text?

_____

_____

_____

_____

- What are two important facts about the wall that you can learn only from looking at the map?

_____

_____

_____

_____

COMPREHENSION

Make Inferences

The text says that the wall divided families and friends in Berlin. What inference can you draw from this?

_____

_____

_____

VOCABULARY/WORD ANALYSIS

- Circle the two base words in the compound word below.

  superpowers

- Use the meaning of the base words and the context of the text on page 177 to write a definition of the word *superpowers*.

_____

_____

_____

▼ Building Up the Wall > May 1962. An East German police officer stands guard as repairs are made to part of the wall damaged by overnight explosions. The Wall evolved into a complex system of concrete barricades, military blockades, watchtowers, and gun posts. Hundreds died while attempting to cross from East to West Berlin.

▲ Waving Across the Wall > December 1962. Shadows of West Berliners on the wall as they wave to relatives in East Berlin. The physical barrier not only separated the city along political lines but also separated families and friends from one another.

▲ Tearing Down the Wall > November 9, 1989. At midnight, Germany's Communist rulers gave permission for gates along the wall to be opened. East and West Berliners took part in chipping away mortar, collecting "pieces of history."

Crossing the Wall > Crowds clambered on top of the Wall and finally crossed safely over the barrier that had separated them for almost 30 years. ▷

Gillian: An American in Berlin

The evening started out ordinarily enough for my friends and me. We were a mixed group of students—a few native Berliners, two or three English kids, and myself, an American student on an exchange program.

We were eating dinner at my friend's loft when the news came that the Berlin Wall was coming down. None of us believed what we had heard, as we had grown up in the shadow of the Wall and all the stories surrounding it. We had learned about the Cuban Missile Crisis and the Berlin Blockade. We had listened to President Ronald Reagan say that the USSR [Soviet Union] was an "evil empire." For us, the Berlin Wall was another item, which was to be taken for granted. Its fall was not to be believed.

Because none of us believed our ears, we walked outside into the crisp, windy evening. Once outside, we saw throngs of people rushing toward the Wall with hammers and chisels in their hands. I ran back to my friend's loft and grabbed my camera; I had to document this event. Upon my return, we fell into the crowd and found ourselves at the new border crossing and started to chip away at the Wall. As I banged away at the graffiti-laden concrete, I realized I had pieces of history in my hands. Tears of joy streamed down my cheeks. I placed the pieces of the Wall into my pockets, knowing that what I had was an artifact that was to be passed to future generations. The entire night and into the dawning of the next day, we walked along the border.

Wherever there were places that concrete panels had been moved by the authorities, East Berliners walked in. We found ourselves welcoming the new arrivals with bananas, Coca-Cola, flowers, and anything else that smacked of Western consumerism. We were overjoyed that East Berliners, who for so long had stared at the West with wanting in their eyes, could finally experience the abundance we had always taken for granted. We, as Westerners, could not imagine growing up without Coca-Cola, an ATM card, and brand names on everything we saw and bought. As Western students, we wanted to share all that we had at that moment with the new arrivals from the East, so we did.

On the morning of November 12, 1989, the border was opened at Potsdamer Platz. Historically, Potsdamer Platz had been a very smart, elegant street in Berlin. During the years of Berlin's division, it was nothing more than a field overgrown with weeds. The morning of November 12, the stage was set to re-create the Potsdamer Platz of old. At the border crossing that morning, I saw two old women, who had presumably not seen each other in 28 years, hug in the middle of what had been no-man's-land.

At that moment, I realized that not only was a country reunifying, but families were reunifying as well. ∎

---

consumerism *(n.)* the belief that it is good to buy and use a lot of goods and services

presumably *(adv.)* likely to be true, although not certain

COMPREHENSION

Make Inferences
Review the third paragraph on page 179. What inference can you make about the author's feelings about history?

_____

_____

_____

_____

_____

_____

_____

_____

21 SMALL GROUPS/INDEPENDENT

COLLABORATE

Debate Gillian says that she and the others wanted to share all the things that "smacked of Western consumerism" with the people from East Berlin. Do you think that material things really represent "the good life"? Choose a side and hold a debate.

COMMUNICATE

React and Write Imagine you were one of the people who moved from East to West Berlin when the Berlin Wall came down. Write a letter to a friend explaining how your life has changed.

W

READ ONLINE

expert space
Go to **www.expert21.com/student** to learn more about The Fall of the Berlin Wall; Germany; Cold War.

Correspondence

From Iraq With Love

How does the experience of war affect those whose job it is to fight? In this selection, two young American soldiers describe the brutal realities of their situations.

W **QuickWrite**

Under what circumstance is war justified? What are some reasons nations go to war? Discuss your thoughts on armed conflict.

Make Inferences   COMPREHENSION

When you make an **inference**, you form ideas about things that are not directly stated in the text.

An author's choice of words and details can help you infer how he or she feels about a topic.

Sometimes an author experiences conflicting emotions. You can make inferences to figure out why.

▶ **Read the passage from "From Iraq With Love," and answer the questions.**

> [The soldiers] died standing with their friends, doing their jobs, fulfilling some far-flung nearly non-existent notion called duty. . . they would never shirk their duties, never call in sick, never give in to fear, never let down.

What does the writer say about duty?

_____

_____

What inference can you make about the writer's feelings about duty?

_____

_____

Primary Sources   NAVIGATING TEXT

Primary sources are original accounts or records created by a person who directly experienced the events. Primary sources can include

• letters and journals.

• interviews.

• photographs.

Primary sources may reflect emotions or opinions.

▶ **Underline the vivid, eyewitness details in this passage from "From Iraq With Love." Then answer the questions.**

> What do you say to your men after you've scraped up an entire Iraqi family off the road, right next to the shattered bodies of your soldiers, held together only by their shoelaces, body armor, or helmets? "We're fighting the good fight"? I don't think so. We're just fighting. And now we're dying.

What does the soldier's opinion of the war seem to be? _____

_____

How would a news report about the same event differ from this personal account?

_____

_____

Academic Language VOCABULARY

▶ Rate each word. Then write its meaning and an example sentence.

Word	Meaning	Example
ACADEMIC WORDS *Use these words in all your subject classes.*		
impending im•pend•ing (adj.) ① ② ③ ④		
objective ob•jec•tive (noun) ① ② ③ ④	a goal one plans to achieve; the job at hand	My objective is to paint a mural in my room over the weekend.
CONTENT AREA WORDS *Use these words to talk and write about social studies.*		
casualty cas•u•al•ty (noun) ① ② ③ ④		
demise de•mise (noun) ① ② ③ ④		
shun shun (verb) ① ② ③ ④		
trauma trau•ma (noun) ① ② ③ ④		
SELECTION WORDS *These words are key to understanding this selection.*		
discreet dis•creet (adj.) ① ② ③ ④	showing good judgment in the way information is shared	
irrevocable ir•rev•o•ca•ble (adj.) ① ② ③ ④		I told Jake that our breakup was irrevocable and that he should look for a new girlfriend.

Rating Scale   ① I don't know the word.   ② I've seen it or heard it.   ③ I know its meaning.   ④ I know it and use it.

Base Words WORD ANALYSIS

A base word is a complete word that can stand alone. Prefixes and suffixes can be added to base words to form new words.

Sometimes the spelling of a base word changes when a suffix is added.

▶ To revoke something means "to take something back." Circle the prefix and underline the suffix in *irrevocable*.

> *irrevocable*

Notice the *k* in *revoke* changes to a *c* when the suffix *-able* is added to the base word. Give an example of something that a parent might revoke from a child who fails a class at school.

_____

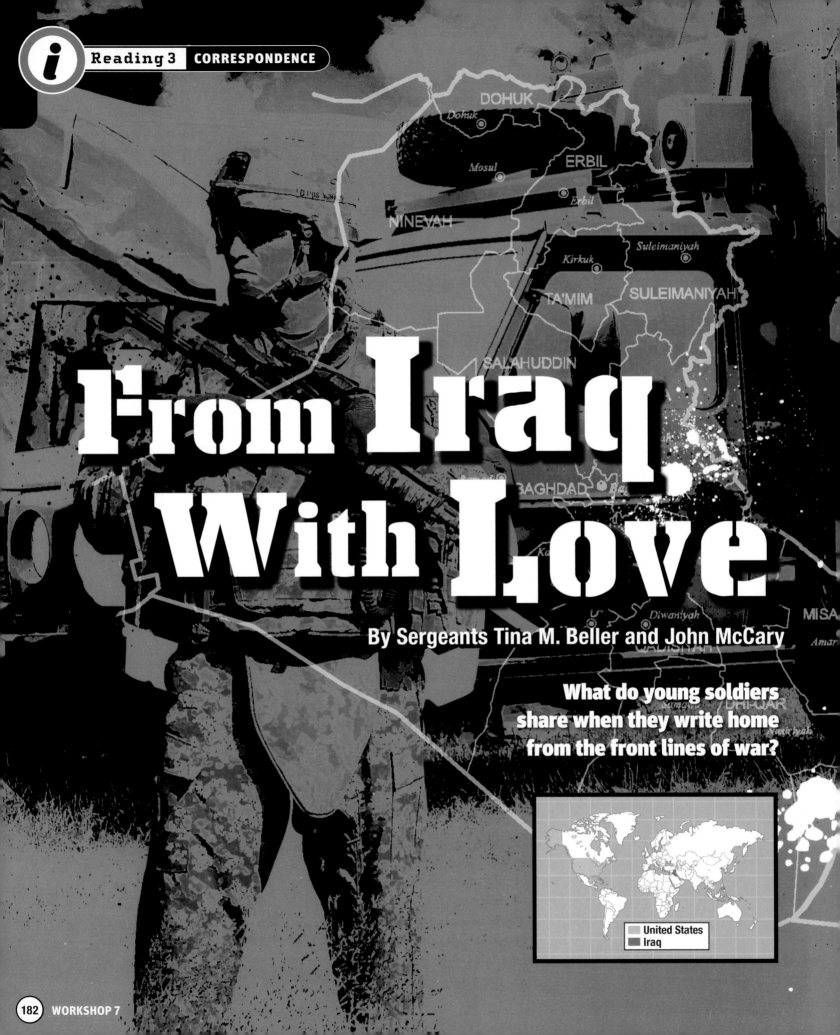

From Iraq With Love

By Sergeants Tina M. Beller and John McCary

What do young soldiers share when they write home from the front lines of war?

United States
Iraq

How do we know what really happens in a war zone? How do young soldiers bear witness to the history they experience in the midst of brutality and loss?

In previous conflicts, U.S. troops rarely described the true nature of warfare in their letters home because strict censorship rules did not allow it. During the Iraq War, which began in 2002, soldiers had access to high-tech communication tools. In an age of 24-hour cable media, the Internet, and email, many Americans at home heard breaking news from the war zone almost instantly.

The following excerpts are from emails by two young U.S. sergeants deployed in Iraq.

The Smell of Fresh Paint

Tina Beller was stationed near an abandoned Iraqi palace that was being remodeled for use as an embassy. Iraqi insurgents, or armed rebels, launched a deadly rocket strike one morning.

From: Tina Beller
Date: September 2004
Subject: The Smell of Fresh Paint

Dear Mom and Dad,

I am sure by now you can read the news and know that we were severely attacked with a barrage of rockets yesterday morning, your night time. At any rate, I am just writing to let you know that physically I remain unharmed. Emotionally and mentally is a different story. I never thought my day would start out this way.

I was the first responder to a building within our compound that was hit by a rocket. I was driving back into the compound around 6:30 A.M. from my usual early morning routine when the hair on my arms stood up. I suspected something was up, but couldn't identify what it was.

I saw smoke in the distance and a man waving his arms above him in the universal distress signal. I thought maybe something was on fire from an explosion. Where I live, in the well-padded palace, I thought we were safe. And for certain, I never thought we would have **casualties**: Iraqi workers, civilians—three of them.

The first Iraqi I saw came briskly walking down the street toward me. He seemed very alarmed, sort of crazy. I could tell he was in shock. He reminded me of a Ping-Pong ball walking back and forth, talking, mumbling, although I had no idea who he was speaking to. His mandible was completely shattered inside the structure of his mouth. He made zero sense when he spoke. He just kept giving me sign language over his belly. I thought he was trying to tell me someone was pregnant. Was that someone in the building?

---

deployed *(v.)* sent to another country for combat or service in war
mandible *(n.)* the bone of the lower jaw

Read and Synthesize

VOCABULARY/WORD ANALYSIS

Connotation and Denotation

Review the second paragraph of the introduction on page 183.

- Circle the word *censorship*.
- What is the connotation of this word? Explain.

_____

_____

_____

_____

_____

_____

_____

COMPREHENSION

Make Inferences

Review paragraph 3 of Tina's email on page 183. What inference can you make about the palace where Tina is staying and where the attack took place?

The text says...	
I know that...	
My inference	

NAVIGATING TEXT

Primary Sources

Underline the writer's personal thoughts and feelings in paragraphs 1–3 of this eyewitness account.

- Circle the factual information in the same paragraphs of this primary source.

I was kind of worried. His head was abnormally larger than the rest of his slender body. The mixture of blood and spit that poured from his mouth looked really weird, like a fountain, a bright red gurgling fountain. I later discovered he died as well . . . **trauma** to his head.

His buddy, who sat cross-legged with his back to me in the now demolished living room, was chanting and rocking. I couldn't figure out why he didn't hear me calling for him. I kept saying it to myself, and then I remember speaking out loud, as I scratched and pounded, through a door that I couldn't budge: "Why isn't he listening to me? Why isn't he getting up?" The others explained that the rocket blew his eardrum out and the poor guy couldn't hear me. The three workers were probably honoring their first call to prayer at the time when the rocket struck.

I still wonder: why didn't I just go in through the front window since it was all blown out? But they tell me not to second-guess my actions or myself. Had I gone through the window, maybe then I would have seen the dead guy, the third casualty, camouflaged with soot and debris, and the remnant of the rocket blocking the door.

Since the attack, I have gone back once to see the area. Partial remains were still on the cement floor from the deceased. Somebody tried to be **discreet** but did a poor job covering it up. They had cheap yellow police tape around the place. Yeah, as if that's going to keep people out.

I found several pairs of men's sandals that were blown about like they were nothing. And of course, pools of blood, some dark and brown, some still red and fresh, reminded me of the tragedy that occurred earlier that morning. I saw cans of fresh paint stacked outside the building. Some Koreans had hired the three dead Iraqis to fix up the place for the Korean Embassy.

The veterans I spoke to last night told me I will probably smell paint sometime in the future, and it will remind me of this day, this horrible event. They also told me it wasn't my fault, and I couldn't have saved the workers since their injuries were far too great for my little hands. From what they had heard, I had done the right thing, the honorable thing. "Geez Beller, you didn't run back to your room and hide like a lot of them did," said one of our senior sergeants, a Vietnam veteran. "Just remember this, next time somebody comes up to you asking you about your story in disbelief, you look at them and ask them with a stone cold face, 'Were you there? Then how would you really know what happened?'"

Keep well,

Tina

> **Make Inferences**
> **Why do you think Beller spoke to the veterans about what she witnessed during the rocket attack?**

remnant *(n.)* small part of something that remains after the rest has been destroyed

embassy *(n.)* office building for officials who represent their government in a foreign country

To the Fallen

John McCary lost several friends from his unit in a series of insurgent attacks.

From: John McCary
Date: January 2004
Subject: To the Fallen

Dear All,

We are dying. Not in a philosophical, chronological, "the end comes for all of us sooner or later" sense. Just dying. Sure, it's an occupational hazard. Yeah, you can get killed walking down the street in Anytown, USA. But not like this. Not car bombs that leave craters in the road, not jeering crowds that celebrate your **demise.** It's never been a fair fight. We haven't always played nice.

But not like this. No one leaves the gate looking to kill, or die. No one wakes up in the morning and says, "I sure hope blowing up a whole group of Iraqis goes well today." You may be worn out, hounded by hours on end of brutal work, but you never wake up thinking, "Today we'll kill a whole bunch of 'em."

They killed my friends. And not in some heroic fight to defend sovereign territory, not on some suicide mission to extract a prisoner or save a family in distress. Just standing out directing traffic. Just driving downtown to a meeting. Just going to work.

It's nothing new, not really. I know what that look is now, the one on the faces of WWII soldiers coming back from a patrol, Vietnam vets standing at the Wall. But now it's us. You know the little blurb from Connie Chung that says "Two Coalition Soldiers were killed at a checkpoint today after a car bomb exploded while waiting in line"? And you think, "Ah, just two. At least it wasn't like thirty. At least it wasn't in a movie theatre, or the town square."

> **Clarify**
> What "look" is the author talking about, and why does he refer to soldiers from past wars?

Yeah . . . I changed my mind about that one. When you sit at the memorial service, gazing down at the display: a pair of laced tan combat boots, a hastily printed 8" x 10" photo, their service rifle, barrel down, their Kevlar helmet set on top of the buttstock, and you hear their friends say, "He talked about his son every night. He's two. He can hardly talk, but his dad just knew he would be a great linebacker." Or someone says, "his wife is currently commanding a platoon elsewhere in Iraq. She will accompany the body home but has chosen to return to her own flock, to see them home safely though her husband will not join her. Our thoughts go out to their families."

---

philosophical *(adj.)* relating to beliefs about the nature and meaning of life
hounded *(v.)* to be followed by someone and questioned in a threatening way

Primary Sources

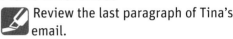 In the fifth paragraph on page 184, Tina includes details such as the men's sandals. Specific details like these help readers realize what Tina's experience was really like.

- **Underline** other details on page 184 that help readers visualize the events.

COMPREHENSION

Make Inferences

Review the last paragraph of Tina's email.

- Draw a box around the Vietnam veteran's advice to Tina.
- What inference can you make about the way soldiers are often treated by people who weren't present during a battle?

_____

_____

_____

_____

_____

_____

CRITICAL THINKING

Analyze

Review John McCary's email on page 185. Which words below describe how he seems to feel about the war? Circle them.

accepting   confused

angry   confident

Why do you think he feels this way?

_____

_____

_____

_____

_____

_____

WHAT THOUGHTS?! What do you think? What will you do knowing this? What help will you be, blubbering in the stands, snot drizzling from your nose, wishing you could have known beforehand, wishing you could have stopped it, pleading to God you could have taken their place, taken the suffering for them? What do you say to the fathers of the men responsible, when you find them relaxing in their homes the next day, preparing for a meal?

You feel . . . compelled, to respond. To what? On whom? Why? Will your children say, "I'm sure glad Dad died to make Iraq safer"? No. They died standing with their friends, doing their jobs, fulfilling some far-flung nearly nonexistent notion called duty. They died because their friends could've died just as easily, and knowing that they would never shirk their duties, never call in sick, never give in to fear, never let down. When you've held a conversation with a man, briefed him on his mission, his **objective**, and reminded him of the potential consequences during the actioning of it, only to hear he never returned, you do not breathe the same ever after. Breath is sweet. Sleep is sweeter. Friends are priceless. And you cry. There's no point, no gain, no benefit, but you are human and you must mourn. It is your nature.

It is also now undeniable, **irrevocable,** that you will see your mission through. You will strive every day, you will live, though you are not ever again sure why. Ideals . . . are so . . . far, far away from the burnt stink of charred metal. I, we, must see it through to the end. They have seen every instant, every mission, every chore, every day through, not to its end but to theirs. How can you ever deny, degrade, desecrate their sacrifice and loss with anything less than all you have?

I'm OK, Mom. I'm just a little . . . shaken, a little sad. I know this isn't any Divine mission. This is Man's doing. This is Man's War. And War it is. It is not fair, nor right, nor simple . . . nor is it over. I wish the presence of those responsible only to dissipate, to transform into average citizens, fathers, sons, and brothers. I don't care about bloodlust, justice, or revenge. But they will not rest until our souls are wiped from this plane of existence, until we no longer exist in their world. Nothing less suffices. And so we will fight. And we will not give up. We cannot. Our lives are forever tied to those lost, and we cannot leave them now, as we might have were they still living.

We have . . . so little time . . . to mourn, so little time to sigh, to breathe, to laugh, to remember. To forget. Every day awaits us, impatient, **impending.** So now we rise, **shunning** tears, biting back trembling lips and stifling sobs of grief . . . and we walk, shoulder . . . to shoulder to the Call of Duty, in tribute to the Fallen.

John ■

CAREER CONNECTION

Government and Public Administration
www.careerclusters.org

Go to [21] ToolKit **Expert File 6.22** to learn more about careers in national security.

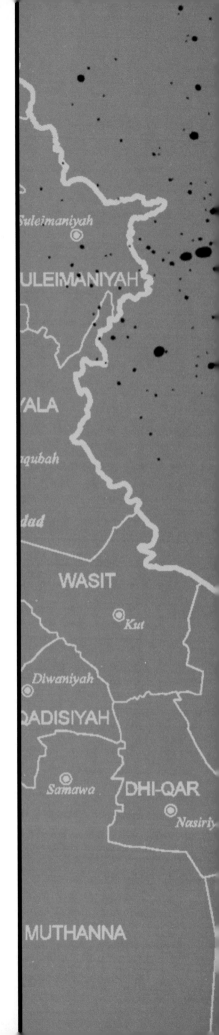

---

desecrate *(v.)* to damage something respected
dissipate *(v.)* to gradually get weaker and then disappear completely

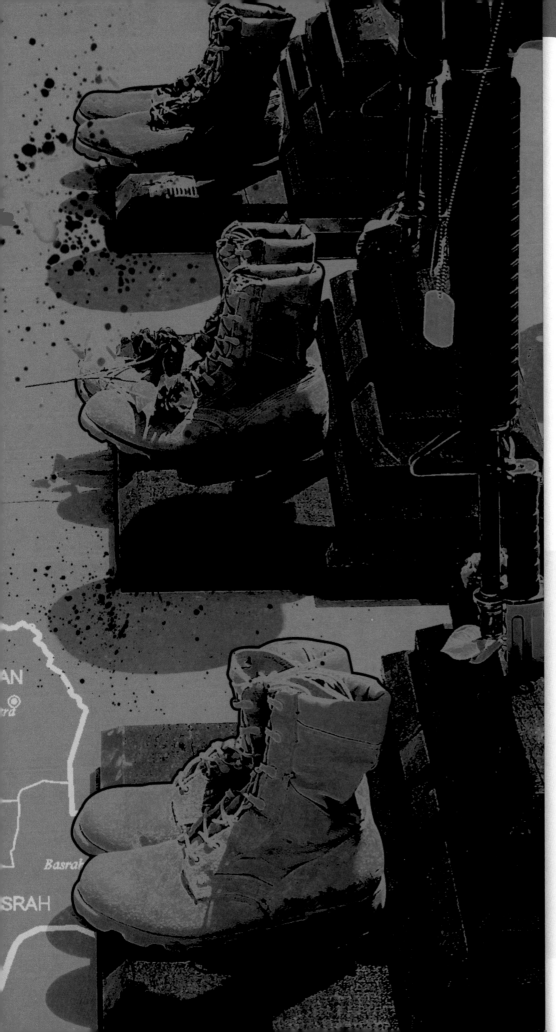

COMPREHENSION

Make Inferences

Review the third paragraph on page 186. What does John mean when he says, "Ideals are so far, far away from the burnt stink of charred metal"?

_____

_____

_____

_____

_____

_____

VOCABULARY/WORD ANALYSIS

Base Words

Review the third paragraph to help you complete the following:

• (Circle) the word *undeniable*.

• Write its prefix, base word, and suffix below.

_____ + _____ + _____

  prefix   base word   suffix

21 SMALL GROUPS/INDEPENDENT

COLLABORATE

Examine Perspectives How do these emails affect your perspective on war? What do Tina's and John's experiences have in common? How are they different? Discuss these questions.

COMMUNICATE

React and Write Write an email responding to either Tina or John. (Imagine you're a close friend or family member.) What would you say?

READ ONLINE

expert space
Go to **www.expert21.com/student** to learn more about The Iraq War; Military Occupation; War Correspondence.

Think Across Texts

Organize and Synthesize ··

1. You read four eyewitness accounts. How might they differ if someone else wrote them? Tell about something each person below might focus on in his or her version of the events you read about.

Anne Frank's mother	
A native Berliner on the day the wall came down	
A veteran soldier from Tina Beller's or John McCary's military unit	

Compare and Evaluate ··

2. How has modern technology changed the way in which people view war? Support your opinion with examples from the selections.

_____

_____

_____

_____

3. How does the format of each account—a diary, photographs, and email—affect the kind of information presented in it? Explain.

_____

_____

_____

_____

_____

_____

_____

4. Can war ever bring out the good in people? State your opinion and support it using examples from at least two readings.

_____

_____

_____

_____

_____

_____

_____

_____

_____

_____

Discuss and Write ··················

5. With a partner, discuss how the three readings in "We Were There" helped you understand the different ways people experience war. Take notes as you talk. Then use your notes to write a response to the question: *How do young people keep a record of history?*

Apply Word Knowledge

Word Lab

1. **Connect them.** Draw a line connecting each word in the left column with the phrase on the right that provides an example of the word's meaning.

succession	a new president is elected
trauma	workers bombed in a war
casualty	distress after a car accident

2. **Name them.** Give an example of each.

- an **objective** of a sports team

_____

_____

- an **impending** event at your school

_____

_____

3. **Describe them.** Describe things that would make you feel each of the following feelings:

- **wretched:** _____

_____

- **deprived:** _____

_____

- **dejected:** _____

_____

- **peculiar:** _____

_____

4. **Complete it.** Complete each of the following sentences.

If something is **irrevocable,** _____

_____ .

If someone is **discreet,** _____

_____ .

If you wanted to shun **someone,** _____

_____ .

If something is **prohibited,** _____

_____ .

If you place a **restriction** on someone's behavior, _____

_____ .

Word Analysis

5. Draw a line between the two base words in each compound word below.

- indoors
- upside
- sunshine

- bedroom
- schoolbooks
- doorway

6. Complete each sentence by adding the correct suffix from the box to the base word in parentheses.

-ly	-ate
-ness	-ment

- Toya makes physical _____ a priority. (fit)
- She jogs _____ around the park each day. (brisk)
- She finds _____ in playing many sports. (enjoy)
- Her friends think she is _____ to be in such good shape, but she really works at it. (fortune)

21

Ask Questions

CAREER CONNECTION Arts, A/V Technology, and Communications
www.careerclusters.org

Go to **21 ToolKit Expert File 6.18** to learn more about careers in communications.

Would you rather watch an event, read about an event, or talk to someone who experienced it? Learn how to ask the right questions to get firsthand knowledge of a subject.

Learn to Conduct an Interview

▶ **Read this interview a student, Robert, conducted with an American soldier who served in Iraq.**

ROBERT: Sgt. Smith, I understand you completed two tours of duty in Baghdad and Basra beginning in December 2005. What was it like when you first returned to your home in Tucson in January 2007?

SGT. SMITH: I was thrilled to be home, but soon I felt isolated and didn't know how to fit back into my life. No one understood what I went through. And I couldn't get the images of war out of my head.

ROBERT: It must have been challenging to cope with your feelings and to adjust to life back home.

SGT. SMITH: I joined an Iraqi veterans' group so I have a place to go to talk things out. It helps me sort out my feelings about the war, too.

ROBERT: How has the group helped you?

SGT. SMITH: It has helped me understand that other veterans feel the same way. It also made me realize that even though I witnessed so much death and destruction, serving my country was the right thing to do.

ROBERT: Despite your feelings about war, you enlisted for a second tour of duty. Why?

SGT. SMITH: I felt ready to go back. My country and my buddies needed me. I couldn't do anything to help people at home and didn't feel right being there. I felt I had to finish the job I started.

ROBERT: Thanks for your time, Sgt. Smith. Your story will help others understand what it's like to serve in Iraq.

MARK IT

Do your homework. <u>Underline</u> the information that shows Robert did research before conducting his interview.

Put a check ✔ next to two open-ended questions that allow the person to respond with more than "yes" or "no."

Use question words such as Who, What, When, Where, or How. (Circle) question words used by the interviewer.

[Here's How] **To ask questions, follow these steps:**

Step 1 **Research the person's background.** Use written or online sources. Take notes on what you want to focus on. This allows you to ask questions that ask for more than basic information.

Step 2 **Prepare your questions.** Ask questions that draw out interesting details. Avoid questions that can be answered with a yes or no.

Step 3 **Conduct the interview.** Be polite, speak clearly, and listen carefully. Ask if you can record the interview but also take notes. Ask follow-up questions to get more information. Thank your subject in person and with a note.

Step 4 **Transcribe, or write out, the interview** and your notes. Highlight the most important quotes and those that provide the information you need.

Apply: Prepare Interview Questions

▶ **If you had a chance to interview one of the soldiers in Reading 3, "From Iraq with Love," what would you ask? Follow the steps to prepare your interview.**

1. **Research the person's background.** Look back in this workshop at Reading 3, "From Iraq with Love," to gather more information about one of the soldiers.

Person to interview: _____

Topics to cover: _____

2. **Prepare your questions.** Ask questions that bring forth interesting, detailed responses. Avoid questions that can have a yes or no reply. Write your questions in the chart.

My Questions

3. **Conduct the interview.** Take turns role-playing with a partner, where one of you pretends to be the soldier and the other is the interviewer. Be courteous, speak clearly, and listen to the subject's answers. If you are the interviewer, don't just stick to your prepared questions: Ask follow-up questions to get more information. Thank your subject at the end of the interview.

4. **Write out the interview and your notes.** Underline or highlight the most valuable quotes and those that give the most relevant information.

Personal Narrative

NO MORE STRANGERS NOW

For decades the black citizens of South Africa suffered under the oppression of the minority white rulers. How did people get along when the racial oppression was finally lifted?

W QuickWrite

Imagine that two South African young people, one white and one black, meet one another just after the oppressive government regime has ended. What might they say? Write a brief conversation between them.

Fact and Opinion COMPREHENSION

A **fact** is a statement that can be proven objectively.

An **opinion** is a statement of belief. An opinion cannot be proven, but it may be supported by **evidence**, such as examples and statistics.

As you read, evaluate how well an author supports opinions. This can help you decide if the author's viewpoint is valid, or reasonable.

▶ Read the passage below from "No More Strangers Now." Circle the opinion. Underline evidence that supports that opinion.

> In school, too, we weren't being told the real picture of South Africa. In the private school I attended, the government told the teachers what textbook to work from and what to teach. Certain books, like African literature, were just not allowed, and if teachers were caught teaching them in a class, they would be fined or put in prison.

Do you think the author's opinions about the limits of his education are valid? Explain.

_____

_____

_____

Author's Perspective NAVIGATING TEXT

An **author's perspective** is his or her way of looking at a topic. To figure out an author's perspective, ask yourself:

- What was the author's role in the situation he or she is describing?

- What is the author's unique viewpoint? How might someone else see the situation differently?

▶ Answer the following questions about the passage above.

- When the author was a student, did he experience the hardships of black South Africans as an insider or as an outsider?

_____

- How do you think the author's perspective about leadership in South Africa might have changed as he discovered the realities of his education?

_____

_____

Academic Language   VOCABULARY

▶ Rate each word. Then write its meaning and an example sentence.

Word	Meaning	Example
EXPERT WORDS *Use these words to write and talk about the workshop topic.*		
atrocity a·troc·i·ty *(noun)* ① ② ③ ④	a terrible cruelty done to a person or group	Soldiers witnessed shocking atrocities committed during attacks on villages in Darfur.
CONTENT AREA WORDS *Use these words to talk and write about social studies.*		
assess as·sess *(verb)* ① ② ③ ④		
subsequent sub·se·quent *(adj.)* ① ② ③ ④		At our subsequent meetings, we're going to choose the new class officers.
SELECTION WORDS *These words are key to understanding this selection.*		
fugitive fu·gi·tive *(noun)* ① ② ③ ④		
incriminating in·crim·i·nat·ing *(adj.)* ① ② ③ ④	evidence that makes someone look guilty	
paranoid par·a·noid *(adj.)* ① ② ③ ④		
propaganda prop·a·gan·da *(noun)* ① ② ③ ④		
solitary sol·i·ta·ry *(adj.)* ① ② ③ ④		

Rating Scale   ① I don't know the word.   ② I've seen it or heard it.   ③ I know its meaning.   ④ I know it and use it.

Denotation and Connotation   WORD ANALYSIS

A word's denotation is its meaning. Its connotation is the positive, neutral, or negative feeling that is associated with the word. Authors use words with certain connotations to communicate how they feel or what they want readers to know about a topic.

Write *positive*, *negative*, or *neutral* under each word to show its connotation.

    inspire   *influence*   *corrupt*

    _____   _____   _____

NO MORE STRANGERS NOW

By Bandile Mashinini and Mark Abrahamson

From 1948-1994, South Africa was a nation divided into black and white. Apartheid ("apartness") was a system of racial segregation that gave privilege, power, and freedom to the country's white minority population while denying the black majority basic human rights. All black South Africans were separated into townships and forced to comply with harsh and limiting "race laws." Those who protested apartheid were tortured, sentenced to death, banished, or imprisoned for life.

Soweto, the country's largest African township, became a focal point of black resistance on June 16, 1976, when the apartheid government tried to introduce Afrikaans[1] as the language of instruction in African schools. Students in Soweto, infuriated by the thought of learning in the language

townships *(n.)* separate living areas for non-whites

of apartheid, organized a march. When the students reached a police roadblock, officers opened fire and killed marchers.

The march and **subsequent** deaths sparked the Soweto Uprisings, which spread throughout the country and resulted in seven hundred deaths by October of 1977. Ninety percent of those who died were under the age of twenty-three.

After decades of resistance, Nelson Mandela's historic 1994 election as a black president of South Africa ended apartheid. What follows are different perspectives about the end of apartheid from two South African teens—one black, one white.

---

[1] Afrikaans is a language derived from Dutch and used today as one of the official languages of South Africa. Under apartheid, Afrikaans was associated with the white minority population in power.

resistance (n.) movement to fight against oppression

STRUGGLE IN THE BLOOD

For eighteen-year-old Bandile Mashinini, political activism is a family affair. His older brother was one of the main organizers of the June 16 march that sparked the Soweto Uprisings.

REDISCOVERING THE NATION

Sixteen-year-old Mark Abrahamson grew up in an affluent, all-white suburb of Cape Town—more than 800 miles and a world away from Soweto.

STRUGGLE IN THE BLOOD by Bandile Mashinini

I'm the last born of thirteen children. Several of my older brothers were very involved with the anti-apartheid movement, and three of them ended up going into exile.

No one really knows exactly when my brothers left. It's not like they wanted it to be a mystery; they did it for safety reasons. If they'd announced when they were leaving and where they were going, I have no doubt it would have reached the police station in a second. You just didn't know who to trust in those days.

My brother Tsietsi was the police's number one **fugitive.** He had been one of those responsible for arranging the June 16 march. The way things were, you couldn't start a series of events like the Soweto Uprisings and still live a normal life. Once the authorities knew you were capable of stirring up the whole township in one day like that, once your name was shouted out as a hero a few times, either you left the country or faced imprisonment.

That's when the police started busting down the doors of our house, looking for Tsietsi, like three times a day. I remember one time I was playing outside and I saw three police vans pull up. I ran between the cops, and by the time I found my mom to tell her, four guns were pointed at both of our heads—rifles, shotguns, pistols, the works. Other times you'd hear noise outside, then boom, they were in the house, shaking you up on the bed. "Get up, kaffir, let's see who you are." They'd have this big flashlight in your face, guns pointing at you. They'd search under everything, on top of everything, behind everything; they'd ransack the whole place.

Because my brothers were political, we had ANC (African National Congress) T-shirts and documents in our house that in the eyes of the law were **incriminating.**

> Once the authorities knew you were capable of stirring up the whole township in one day like that . . .

We'd put them inside the coal stove and cover them up. But sometimes we'd sleep in those shirts, and a few nights when the cops came, it was like, "Wake up! Here's another terrorist wearing Mandela. In the van, buddy." They'd take people in my house to prison for a whole night's interrogation on why they were wearing a political T-shirt.

My mother was also arrested and spent seven months in **solitary** confinement. One of my brothers in exile tried to make contact with her, and somehow the police found out about it. The charge was aiding terrorists, helping them escape, which she did, but one has to ask—who were the terrorists, really?

Clarify
Why did the police see the family's political ties as incriminating?

This kind of harassment went on from when I was born until the late eighties. At first it was very scary; I'd be shaken up by the whole thing. But later I got used to it and saw it as part of our life. In fact, I'd even think, *Once in a while we ought to give those fools tea, they visit us so often.* I mean, they would kick down the door in 1984 and ask where Tsietsi was, even though he'd left in the seventies. It was like, you know he's not in the country, so why are you looking for him here?

As a kid I didn't really understand the deep meaning of the politics that my family was following. I knew there were good guys and bad guys. The ANC were the good guys; cops, the bad guys. I was a noisy little character, yelling, "Amandla!" ["Power to us!"] and that kind of thing because I could sense that if I belonged to this family, it was in the blood to view things politically. That's what we're known for.

---

kaffir (n.) racist term used to address black South Africans
ransack (v.) to search a place very thoroughly, often stealing things and causing damage

Now that I'm older, I realize that my brothers, filling the better part of their days with ANC training camps and the cause, lost a part of their lives that is associated with just being young. When we celebrated holidays at home, when everyone was sharing and having a good time, my brothers were in the field somewhere, forced out of their own country by white people and living like some sort of creatures on the run, never able to settle down.

Two of my brothers finally came home in the early nineties, but Tsietsi never came back. He died in 1990 while still living as an exile in Guinea. There's a lot of controversy and suspicion surrounding his death. There was a story that he died of a nervous breakdown, and I know he had a disease of some sort that affected his nerves and led to violent episodes. But we also know he died with bruises all over his face and very fresh injuries. I don't think there was ever a postmortem performed on him, so no one really knows what happened.

Bandile has a lot of friends in Pimville, the section of Soweto where the Mashininis live. He likes to chat about politics with his friends. "The Mashininis have political blood."

---

episodes *(n.)* incidents in a person's life or experience

postmortem *(n.)* autopsy, or examination of a dead body to discover the cause of death

CRITICAL THINKING

Evaluate

Underline details on page 196 that describe the actions of the South African police.

• What judgment can you make about police behavior during apartheid?

_____

_____

_____

_____

_____

_____

NAVIGATING TEXT

Author's Perspective

As a child, what was the author's perspective on his family's politics?

What he knew: _____

_____

_____

What he didn't know: _____

_____

_____

• Draw a box around the paragraph that supports your answer.

COMPREHENSION

Fact and Opinion

In the first paragraph on page 197, Bandile says his brothers lost part of their lives that is associated with being young. Is this a fact or an opinion?

_____

What evidence does Bandile give to support his opinion?

_____

_____

_____

_____

_____

We brought Tsietsi's body back to South Africa and buried him in a cemetery outside Soweto. Later there was a special memorial tombstone built at his grave, and there was a big unveiling. You see, people still identify Tsietsi as a hero. If a person recognizes me as a Mashinini, even now they make a lot of noise, like, "I used to go to school with your brother!" His name still carries a lot of power, and some Africanist organizations even shout it in their slogans today.

Tsietsi, together with my other brothers and the rest of their generation, helped achieve the society we have now. Unfortunately Tsietsi did not get to enjoy the new South Africa like the rest of us. Now that it's here, we ought to make the most of it; we ought to be a generation of South Africans who live their lives to the fullest and have

> Tsietsi, together with my other brothers and the rest of their generation, helped achieve the society we have now.

fun. But just because the "big struggle" is seen to be over doesn't mean we should party the rest of our lives; we should take off from where the previous generation left us.

To me that means getting a job in the new government so that I can be part of the actual improvement of our nation. We have a new constitution, and it's a great foundation, but it's still only ink on paper. I want to make sure we build well on top of it. This is going to be hard work, but then I'd be a dreamer if I thought I'd never have to make any sacrifices. I can never imagine there's an end to the struggle.

Clarify
What does the author mean by the phrase "only ink on paper"?

Bandile sometimes visits the grave of his brother Tsietsi. "Tsietsi contributed to making the new South Africa possible. Now we must take it from here."

unveiling (n.) the removal of a cover from

REDISCOVERING THE NATION
by Mark Abrahamson

I often think to myself, I'm just so lucky to have been on this end of the whole apartheid system, lucky to have been brought into the world which I was born into. Around here we've got television, we've got two cars in the garage, we're linked to the Internet, we've got the hi-fi system. What would have happened if I had been on the other side? Would I still be the same kind of guy?

The majority of South Africans were oppressed during the time of my upbringing, but I was in a very protected environment and was kept away from the violence and the **atrocities** that were being committed. I think a lot of people outside South Africa have this perception that it was so violent that someone was getting shot around every corner, but it wasn't like that in my area. I've never seen a man killed before, even though just twenty kilometers away in the townships, kids were being subjected to some *oke* [guy] walking into their house and gunning their parents down.

There were just such strong barriers between our two environments. As a kid I remember being at parks in our area and thinking to myself, *Now why is that black person there? He shouldn't be there.* It wasn't because I had anything against that person; that was just the normal way it was. If you look at Cape Town, it's quite remarkable: You've got a relatively affluent core center, and right next to it, really right over here, you've got a lot of poverty and unhappiness in the townships. But it didn't seem like these problems were right here in Cape Town; it seemed very distant, almost as if it was in another African country somewhere.

We weren't just sheltered; there was also an active hiding of the truth, **propaganda,** by the apartheid government. They knew that if we were able to analyze the true situation, sooner or later we would have come to the conclusion that it was wrong. The government controlled the television stations, for example, and the news became a joke after a while because it was so propagandist. If there was any violence in the townships, it was blamed on African forces fighting each other and not on white government intervention, which is what it was.

oppressed *(adj.)* treated unfairly or cruelly
affluent *(adj.)* wealthy, having lots of money

COMPREHENSION

Fact and Opinion

Underline the evidence in the story that Bandile uses to express his opinions about his generation.

- Based on evidence in this story, do you think Bandile's opinions are valid? Why or why not?

_____

_____

_____

_____

_____

_____

NAVIGATING TEXT

Author's Perspective

How do Bandile's and Mark's experiences of apartheid differ?

_____

_____

_____

_____

_____

VOCABULARY/WORD ANALYSIS

Denotation and Connotation

In the last paragraph on page 199, Mark writes that the apartheid government used *propaganda*. How does his word choice affect your understanding of the government?

_____

_____

_____

_____

_____

_____

You also didn't really hear about the ANC. Whenever you did, it was through the news, "these people are messing up our land" kind of thing. And I hadn't seen pictures of Mandela, because you weren't allowed to have a picture of him anywhere around. He was made out to be scary, violent. "If he ever comes out," the government told us, "it will be the end of South Africa; we'll be thrown into civil war." I remember when I finally saw him released from prison on TV, it consciously came to mind: *Why'd they put that funny old man in prison for so long? What could he have done?*

In school, too, we weren't being told the real picture of South Africa. In the private school I attended, the government told the teachers what textbook to work from and what to teach. Certain books, like African literature, were just not allowed, and if teachers were caught teaching them in a class, they would be fined or put in prison. I remember reading Rudyard Kipling's books about African animals, but that's not really African literature, is it? It was almost like we could've been at a school in England.

> You can see things on television, but to actually be there and meet the people, reality kind of hits you.

Clarify
How might the school's action be an example of propaganda?

I think I picked up on the racial situation quite young, but the whole process of **assessing** the situation and then feeling guilty is something which I've had to come to terms with much more recently. I don't know what I would've done if I was in my twenties at the height of apartheid. I don't know if I would've actually stood up and said, "I think it's completely wrong, and this is what I'm going to do about it."

But things have changed. We weren't told the truth for so long, but now we're hearing it all. We're starting to hear about the brutal attacks on people, to see pictures like the one of three policemen with their feet on a black man that they killed like it's a trophy. I've been shocked by what's come out, but I think it's necessary to hear it. What happened in our past is a wound. If we don't first put antiseptic on the wound, if we don't dig up our skeletons, literally and figuratively, it's never going to heal properly.

There's an age of rediscovery in South Africa at the moment, of finding out what's really out there, of getting to know everyone who is living here and consciously trying to live in harmony. We're the generation that's the bridge from the previous South Africa to a new one. Therefore I think it's crucial to become involved in this transformation, so that you have the sense of actually making a difference.

At my school I'm very involved in an organization called Interact, which focuses on community work. On Freedom Day [a national holiday commemorating the country's first democratic elections] this year there was a walk organized through all the townships, just to make us more aware of the city. Interact made it public to our school. I was very interested because I hadn't spent a long stretch of time in a township or really seen what was going on there. You can see things on television, but to actually be there and meet the people, reality kind of hits you.

So I went on the walk, and I got to see at close quarters what you normally just see from the road. We had to walk through a lot of really bad conditions. We even saw this one squatter community built over a rubbish dump. It was eye-opening because where we live around here, it's fairly clean. Walking through these places, I thought to myself, *The only reason I'm not here is because of my skin color, which I didn't even choose.* I also noticed that most of the people in the townships were quite friendly, happy people. I was expecting a lot more anger and irritation, like, "Why are you walking here?" But they actually wanted to show us around.

antiseptic *(n.)* a chemical substance that prevents a wound from becoming infected
squatter *(adj.)* having to do with people who occupy property without permission or paying rent

Mark Abrahamson, like many white South Africans, has had to come to terms with what happened during apartheid.

There's a fear now, especially among the more **paranoid** whites, that we're moving from a white supremacy to a black one, that black people are going to come knocking on our door, saying, "We're gonna divide your house in two." But that isn't what's happening. It seems there's this incredible feeling of forgiveness on the part of black people. It's like, "You know these white people have been terrible to us, but we're just going to show them that we're not made of the same stuff." I think we must be quite thankful for this atmosphere because as far as I'm concerned, black people have every right to turn the whole thing around and say, "Three hundred years we've been under this oppression, now it's your turn for the next three hundred."

Some white people are leaving South Africa, but I have no intention of doing so. I think if I was to be scooped up and put in Europe or America, I would be able to survive, but I would be very homesick for South Africa. Not many people have the privilege to be living in a country that is changing so rapidly, and I feel quite proud of my land, and I know that I belong here. I see our future being a positive one. I would like to be able to look back on my youth and say to myself, I was, even in a small way, somehow part of this success. ■

supremacy *(n.)* a situation in which a group or idea is more powerful than anything else

CRITICAL THINKING

Analyze
What does Mark mean when he describes his generation as "the bridge from the previous South Africa to the new one"? How does this compare with Bandile's opinion about their generation?

_____

_____

_____

COMPREHENSION

Fact and Opinion
Mark sees the future of South Africa as a positive one. What evidence has he given to support his opinion?

_____

_____

_____

_____

_____

21 **SMALL GROUPS/INDEPENDENT**

COLLABORATE

Mind Map Create a chart comparing and contrasting the details of Bandile's and Mark's experiences growing up in South Africa and their perspectives on their country today.

COMMUNICATE

React and Write What lessons can you learn from Mark and Bandile about resolving conflicts? Make some notes. Then write a paragraph expressing your view.

READ ONLINE

expert space
Go to **www.expert21.com/student** to learn more about Apartheid; South Africa; Nelson Mandela.

Memoir

A Refugee in Her Own Country

Some people have experienced unimaginable horrors at the hands of governments. If they survive, the experience changes them forever. This memoir relates events from the author's childhood.

QuickWrite

Imagine that you were suddenly forced to leave your home and all your possessions. What would you do to maintain your courage?

Description: Sensory Detail   LITERARY ANALYSIS

Description is writing that helps a reader to picture events, objects, and characters.

To create vivid descriptions, writers often use sensory details—words and phrases that appeal to the reader's senses of sight, hearing, touch, smell, and taste.

▶ **Read this passage related to "A Refugee in Her Own Country." Underline sensory details.**

Seven months after the Khmer Rouge forcefully evacuated us from our home in Phnom Penh, we arrive in the village of Ro Leap. It is late in the afternoon. The clouds separate in the sky and the sun shines beams of white light on our new home. Ro Leap looks like all the other villages we passed through on our travels. Surrounded by the jungle, it is green and lush during the rainy season and dusty and flammable during the dry season. Looking up at the sky, I smile, thankful for a safe arrival. This is our third relocation in seven months. I hope we will stay for a while.

Fact and Opinion   COMPREHENSION

A **fact** is a statement that can be proven true. An **opinion** is a belief. You can evaluate a writer's opinion by reading and thinking about evidence the writer gives to support the opinion. As you read, ask yourself:

• Is what I am reading a fact or an opinion?

• How well does the writer support opinions with examples and other evidence?

▶ **Read this passage about the author of "A Refugee in Her Own Country." Circle an opinion in the passage. Underline evidence that supports the opinion.**

Until she was five, Loung Ung lived in the Cambodian city of Phnom Penh. She was the daughter of a high-ranking government official. When an army invaded the city in the spring of 1975, Loung and her family fled. The family moved from village to village, struggling to survive. Loung and her family met challenges bravely. Instead of giving up, they fought to survive.

Think about the evidence the writer presents to support the opinion you circled. Do you agree with the opinion? Why or why not?

_____

_____

_____

_____

Academic Language   VOCABULARY

▶ **Rate each word. Then write its meaning and an example sentence.**

Word	Meaning	Example
EXPERT WORDS *Use these words to write and talk about the workshop topic.*		
century cen•tu•ry (noun) ① ② ③ ④	a period of 100 years	I was five years old when the world celebrated the end of the 20th century, on December 31, 1999.
revolution rev•o•lu•tion (noun) ① ② ③ ④		
ACADEMIC WORDS *Use these words in all your subject classes.*		
comprise com•prise (verb) ① ② ③ ④		
regulation reg•u•la•tion (noun) ① ② ③ ④		
CONTENT AREA WORDS *Use these words to talk and write about social studies.*		
allegiance al•le•giance (noun) ① ② ③ ④		
capitalist cap•i•tal•ist (noun) ① ② ③ ④	a person who favors a society in which most goods and property are owned by individuals, not the government	
ration ra•tion (verb) ① ② ③ ④		During World War II, the government rationed food to make sure there was enough for the troops.
relocation re•lo•ca•tion (noun) ① ② ③ ④		

Rating Scale   ① I don't know the word.   ② I've seen it or heard it.   ③ I know its meaning.   ④ I know it and use it.

Denotation and Connotation   WORD ANALYSIS

A word's denotation is its dictionary definition. A connotation is the positive, neutral, or negative feeling a word carries.

For example, *thin* has a neutral connotation, *scrawny* has a negative connotation, and *lean* has a positive connotation.

▶ **Read the sentence below. The word *walked* in this sentence has a neutral connotation.**

  They <u>walked</u> across the street.

Circle a word to replace *walked* to give the sentence a positive connotation.

  They _____ across the street.   *strolled*   *lurched*

A Refugee in Her Own Country

From *First They Killed My Father* By Loung Ung

General Pol Pot and his Khmer Rouge army took over the capital city seven months ago. The Khmer Rouge soldiers terrorize the cities and countryside, forcing people out of their homes and into work camps. By the end of their brutal reign, nearly two million will be dead of execution, starvation, forced labor, or disease.

AUTHOR'S NOTE:

What follows is a story of survival: my own and my family's. Though these events constitute my experience, my story mirrors that of millions of Cambodians. If you had been living in Cambodia during this period, this would be your story, too.

I don't understand why they are looking at me as if I am a strange animal, when in reality, we look very much the same.

An unidentified young girl stands next to a man with an artificial leg. The Khmer Rouge used land mines to terrorize civilian populations. Unexploded mines are still a problem in Cambodia. More than 40,000 Cambodians have lost limbs to land mines since 1979.

The town square is situated forty feet from the road and consists of nothing more than a dried up piece of land and a few trees. The town square is a place where people gather to hear announcements, instructions, work assignments, or, in our case, wait for the village chief. Behind the town square, villagers live in the same kind of thatched-roof huts that sit on raised stilts, all lined up in neat rows about fifty feet from each other at the edge of the forest.

The truck driver orders the new arrivals to get out and wait for instructions from the village chief. My family quickly jumps off the truck, leaving me behind. Standing at the edge of the truck, I fight the impulse to run and hide in the far corner. All around the truck, villagers have gathered to take their first look at us new people. These villagers are all dressed in the familiar loose-fitting black pajama pants and shirts with a red-and-white checkered scarf wrapped across their shoulders or around their head. They look like an older version of the Khmer Rouge soldiers that stormed into our city, except they do not carry guns.

"**Capitalists** should be shot and killed," someone yells from the crowd, glaring at us. Another villager walks over and spits at Pa's feet. Pa's shoulders droop low as he holds his palms together in a gesture of greeting. I cower at the edge of the truck, my heart beating wildly, afraid to get off. Fearing that they might spit at me, I avoid their eyes.

They look very mean, like hungry tigers ready to pounce on us. Their black eyes stare at me, full of contempt. I don't understand why they are looking at me as if I am a strange animal, when in reality, we look very much the same.

"Come, you have to get off the truck," Pa says gently to me. My feet drag my body cautiously toward his open arms. As Pa lifts me in his arms, I whisper in his ear, "Pa, what are capitalists and why should they be killed?" Saying nothing, Pa puts me down.

There are five hundred base people already living in Ro Leap. They are called "base people" because they have lived in the village since before the revolution. Most of them are illiterate farmers and peasants who supported the **revolution.** The Angkar[1] says they are model citizens because many have never ventured out of their village and have not been corrupted by the West. We are the new people, those who have migrated from the city.

Peasants who have lived in the countryside since before the revolution

---

[1] The "Angkar," literally "the organization," was the government of Cambodia under the Khmer Rouge.

impulse *(n.)* a sudden, strong desire to do something
contempt *(n.)* disrespect

are rewarded by being allowed to stay in their villages. All others are forced to pick up and move when the soldiers say so. The base people will train us to be hard workers and teach us to have pride in our country. Only then will we be worthy to call ourselves Khmer. I cannot comprehend why they hate me or why capitalists must be killed, but this will have to wait. I walk over and take hold of [my older sister] Chou's hand, and together we follow Ma to the gathering at the town square.

When I ask my ten-year-old brother, Kim, what a capitalist is, he tells me it is someone who is from the city. He says the Khmer Rouge government views science, technology, and anything mechanical as evil and therefore it must be destroyed. The Angkar says the ownership of cars and electronics such as watches, clocks, and televisions created a deep class division between the rich and the poor. This allowed the urban rich to flaunt their wealth while the rural poor struggled to feed and clothe their families. These devices have been imported from foreign countries and thus are contaminated. Imports are defined as evil because they allowed foreign countries a way to invade Cambodia, not just physically but also culturally. So now these goods are abolished. Only trucks are allowed to operate, to **relocate** people and carry weapons to silence any voices of dissent against the Angkar.

> **Question**
> **What questions do you have about capitalism?**

Shuddering at Kim's explanation, I nestle closer to Chou and lean my head on her shoulder. While we wait for the chief, other trucks full of migrants continue to arrive. By the end of the day, approximately sixty families, about five hundred new people, now fill the town square. As the sun lowers itself behind the tree line, the chief finally makes his appearance to the crowd of new people. He is as tall as Pa, with an angular body and cropped gray hair that sits straight on his head like dense jungle bushes. Where his eyes should be are two dark pieces of coal separated by a sharp, thin nose, below which are thin lips that spit out saliva. The chief walks in a slow, casual stride, hands and legs moving precisely, deliberately. The black pajama pants hang looser on his body than those on the two soldiers who follow behind him. There is nothing remarkable about him, except that he is able to command the two men who wear rifles slung across their backs.

"In this village, we live by strict rules and **regulations** set for us by the Angkar. We expect you to follow every rule. One of our rules applies to how we dress. As you see, we wear the same clothes. Everyone wears his or her hair in the same style. By wearing the same thing, we rid ourselves of the corrupt Western creation of vanity." He speaks in the heavy accent of the jungle people, which is hard for me to understand.

> **flaunt** (v.) to show something off
> **angular** (adj.) lean and bony

LITERARY ANALYSIS

Description: Sensory Details

Underline sensory details used to describe the village on page 206.

- What do these details tell you about what life will be like under the Khmer Rouge?

_____

_____

_____

_____

_____

VOCABULARY/WORD ANALYSIS

Denotation and Connotation

Near the bottom of page 206, the Angkar says that the farmers have not been *corrupted* by the West. Why do you think the Angkar used the word *corrupted*?

_____

_____

_____

_____

_____

COMPREHENSION

Fact and Opinion

Check ✓ the opinions in the first full paragraph on page 207.

- How do these opinions help you understand the way the author is feeling at this point in the story?

_____

_____

_____

_____

_____

_____

"Lying on top of the pile is a pink silk shirt, a blue jean jacket, and brown corduroy pants—all remnants of past lives to be destroyed."

With a flick of the chief's wrist, one soldier walks up to a family. He reaches out and takes a bag from a woman. She lowers her eyes as the bag slides off her shoulder. He rummages through the bag and looks in disgust at the colorful clothes inside. He dumps the contents of the bag in the middle of the circle of people. One by one this is repeated. Bags upon bags of clothes belonging to all the families in the square are dumped into a pile. Lying on top of the pile is a pink silk shirt, a blue jean jacket, and brown corduroy pants—all remnants of past lives to be destroyed.

Before the soldier even approaches, Ma has gathered all our bags and put them in a small pile in front of our family. The soldier picks up our bags and begins to throw our clothes onto the pile. His hand reaches into one bag and pulls out something red—my breath quickens. A little girl's dress. He scowls as if the sight of such a thing turns his stomach, then balls up the dress in his hand and throws it on top of the pile. I follow the dress with my eyes, focusing all my energy on it, wanting desperately to rescue it from the pile. My first red dress, the one Ma made for me for the New Year's celebration. I remember Ma taking my measurements, holding the soft chiffon cloth against my body, and asking me if I liked it. "The color looks so pretty on you," she said, "and the chiffon material will keep you cool." Ma made three identical dresses for Chou, Geak, and me. All had puffy sleeves and skirts that flared above the knee.

I do not know when the soldier finishes dumping all the clothes onto the pile. I cannot take my eyes off of my dress. I stand there, with Ma and Pa on either side of me. My insides are tied up in knots, a scream claws its way up my throat but I push it all down. "No! Not my dress. What have I done to you?" I scream in my head, tears welling up in my eyes. "Please help me! I don't know if I can handle it anymore! I don't understand why you hate me so much!" I grind my teeth so hard the pain in my throat moves up to my temples. My hands clench in fists; I continue to stare at my dress. I do not see the soldier's hand reach into his pocket and retrieve from it a box of matches. I do not hear his fingers strike a match against the side of the box. The next thing I know the pile of clothes bursts into flames and my red dress melts like plastic in the fire.

"Wearing colorful clothes is forbidden. You will take off the clothes you have on and burn those as well. Bright colors only serve to corrupt your mind. You are no different from anyone else here and from now on will dress in black pants and shirts. A new set will be issued to you once a month." To drive

Children suffered terribly under the rule of the Khmer Rouge. Children were regularly used as slave labor or executed. Other children were taken from their parents to be raised as fanatical followers and soldiers of the Khmer Rouge.

> **Summarize**
> In a word or phrase, describe how the author is feeling in this scene.

corrupt (v.) to cause someone to behave in a dishonest way

his point home, the chief paces around, looking the new people in the eye, pointing his long index finger at them.

"In Democratic Kampuchea," the chief continues, "we are all equal and do not have to cower to anyone. When the foreigners took over Kampuchea, they brought with them bad habits and fancy titles. The Angkar has expelled all foreigners so we no longer have to refer to each other using fancy titles. From now on, you will address everyone as 'Met!' For example, he is Met Rune, she is Met Srei. No more Mr., Mrs., Sir, Lord, or His Excellency."

"Yes, comrade," we reply collectively.

"The children will change what they call their parents. Father is now 'Poh' and not Daddy, Pa, or any other term. Mother is 'Meh.'" I hold on to Pa's finger even tighter as the chief rants off other new words. The new Khmer have better words for eating, sleeping, working, stranger; all designed to make us equal.

"In this village, as in the whole of our new and pure society, we all live in a communal system and share everything. There is no private ownership of animals, land, gardens, or even houses. Everything belongs to the Angkar. If the Angkar suspects you of being a traitor, we will come into your home and go through whatever we like."

The Khmer Rouge's policies of extermination, torture, and forced labor caused the deaths of an estimated two million people, about one-fifth of the population of Cambodia.

---

cower (v.) to lower the head or body in fear

LITERARY ANALYSIS

Description: Sensory Details

Review the paragraphs that describe the destruction of Loung's dress. <u>Underline</u> sensory details the author uses.

- Choose one underlined detail that appeals to each of these senses:

Sight: _____

_____

_____

Sound: _____

_____

_____

Touch: _____

_____

_____

CRITICAL THINKING

Analyze

What do you think the burning of Ung's dress represents?

_____

_____

_____

[21] SMALL GROUPS/INDEPENDENT

COLLABORATE

Evaluate How do the stated values of the Khmer Rouge differ from their actions? Discuss what this tells you about the leaders of the Khmer Rouge and their vision of society.

COMMUNICATE

React and Write Imagine you are Loung Ung. Record some notes about your experiences. Use your notes to write a journal entry about your first encounter with the Khmer Rouge.

Under the Khmer Rouge, urban populations were uprooted and forced into rural labor camps. In the city of Phnom Penh alone, more than two million people were displaced in forced evacuations.

Each family will be assigned a house in the village. Those who do not get a house today will be built one tomorrow.

"The Angkar will provide you with everything you need. You new people will eat your meals together. Meals will be served from 12 to 2 P.M., and from 6 to 7 P.M. If you come late, you will get nothing. Your meal will be rationed to you; the harder you work, the more you'll eat. After dinner each night, I will let you know whether or not there will be meetings. The base people and our comrade soldiers will patrol your work area. If they see you neglecting your duties and report that you are lazy, you will get nothing to eat." My eyes follow the chief as he paces around the circle of people. I pray that I will remember all he has said.

"You must follow all the rules set for you by the Angkar. This way, we will never have to deal with the crimes and corruption of the city people."

"Yes, comrade," the new people echo in unison.

"Each family will be assigned a house in the village. Those who do not get a house today will be built one tomorrow. Your first work assignment is to build houses for each other!"

"Yes, comrade."

in unison (adv.) at the same time

"Children in our society will not attend school just to have their brains cluttered with useless information. They will have sharp minds and fast bodies if we give them hard work. The Angkar cannot tolerate laziness. Hard work is good for everyone. Any kind of schooling carried out by anyone without the government's approval is strictly forbidden."

"Yes, comrade."

Though we are all supposed to be equal, there are nonetheless three levels of citizenship in the village. The first-class citizenry **comprises** the chief, who has authority over the whole village, his aides, and the Khmer Rouge soldiers. They have the power to teach, police, judge, and execute. They make all decisions: work details, food **rations** per family, severity of punishment. They are the eyes and ears of the Angkar at the local level. They report all activities to the Angkar and have full power to enforce the Angkar's law.

Then there are the base people. If the first-class citizens are the all-powerful brutal teachers, the base people are the bullies who work closely with them.

The new people are considered the lowest in the village structure. They have no freedom of speech and must obey the other classes. The new people are those who lived in cities and have been forced out to the villages. They cannot farm like the rural people. They are suspected of having no **allegiance** to the Angkar and must be kept under an ever-watchful eye for signs of rebellion. They have led corrupt lives and must be trained to be productive workers. To instill a sense of loyalty to the Angkar and break what the Khmer Rouge views as an inadequate urban work ethic, the new people are given the hardest work and the longest hours.

> **Visualize**
> **Describe your idea of how the village society is organized.**

After the chief issues us our meal bowls and spoons and assigns us our hut, we have only minutes to settle down before the 6 P.M. bell rings, signaling mealtime. Gripping my wooden bowl and spoon, I run with my family to the communal kitchen. The kitchen is nothing but a long table, with no chairs or benches, and under a thatched roof with no walls. In the middle of the open hall, there are a few brick ovens and one long table but no chairs or benches. On the long table sit two pots, one full of rice and the other salted grilled fish. There are six or seven base women stirring and scooping food from the pots. A long line of new people has already formed around the table. Like us, they have all changed from their city clothing into their black pajama pants and shirts, the only clothes we will wear from now on.

> **instill** (v.) to put an idea in someone's mind so that it influences their thinking and behavior
>
> **inadequate** (adj.) not enough

Read and Synthesize

LITERARY ANALYSIS

Description: Sensory Details
In the chart below, list one vivid detail from these pages that appeals to each sense.

Sight:
Taste:
Sound:
Touch:

CRITICAL THINKING

Analyze
Review Ung's explanation on page 211 of the three levels of citizenship in the village. What does this tell you about the leaders of the Khmer Rouge?

_____

_____

_____

COMPREHENSION

Draw Conclusions
Review the description of the village. What conclusion can you draw about the family's future?

_____

_____

_____

_____

_____

_____

A Refugee in Her Own Country (211)

Due to inadequate food and transportation, several thousand Cambodians died during the forced evacuations before ever reaching the labor camps.

Though the Angkar says we are all equal in Democratic Kampuchea, we are not. We live and are treated like slaves.

My heart lurches as I see the long line in front of me. Eyeing the many black pots filled with steamy food on the ground, I tell my stomach to be calm. The line moves quickly and silently. Under my breath I count the heads before me, eliminating them one by one, anxiously waiting for my turn. Finally, it is Ma's turn. She puts Geak down and holds up two bowls. She bends her head and shoulders so she is lower than the cook, and quietly says, "Please comrade, one for me and one for my three-year-old daughter." The woman looks down blankly at Geak, who barely reaches Ma's thigh and puts two scoops of rice and two fish into Ma's bowl and one of each in Geak's bowl. Ma lowers her head and thanks the woman and walks away with her food, Geak trailing behind her.

My stomach growls loudly as I step up to the table. I cannot see into the pot and my mouth salivates at the smell of the rice and fish. I raise my bowl to my eye level to make it easier for the comrade to serve me. I dare not look up at her, afraid she might become angry with me for staring and not give me my food. Eyes focused on my bowl, I see her hand dump some rice in my bowl and drop a whole fish on top of it. Somehow, I manage to whisper, "Thank you, comrade" and walk away, praying that I won't fall and spill my food.

Sitting in the shade underneath a tree, our family eats the food together. Though it is the most food we have eaten in a long time, before nightfall we are all hungry again. Realizing we have to find a way to get more food, Pa somehow arranges for Kim to work at the chief's house as his errand boy. The next night, Kim comes home with leftovers.

*   *   *

Day after day we work, seven days a week. Some months, if we have been very productive workers, we are given half a day to rest. In those hours,

lurches *(v.)* makes a sudden move
salivates *(v.)* produces saliva in the mouth in preparation for eating

Ma and us girls wash our clothes in a nearby stream, but without detergent they are not very clean. I look forward to those hours off as our special time together. Of the five hundred or so new people in our village, there are only two or three babies among the families. Although I cannot fully understand her words, I overhear Ma say women are so overworked, underfed, and filled with fear that most cannot become pregnant anymore. Even when they do, many suffer miscarriages. Most newborn babies do not survive more than a couple of days. Pa says there will be a generation of children completely missing from our country. Shaking his head, he looks at Geak. "The first victims are always the children."

> **Predict**
> **What do you think will happen to Geak?**

Pa says Geak will not become the Khmer Rouge's next victim because the chief likes him. The chief allows Kim to bring extra food home, and he knows that things are easier for us because of that. Pa works harder and longer than anyone else in the village. Because of his humble upbringing, Pa has many skills and can do anything the chief asks of him. He is a skilled carpenter, builder, and farmer. Pa is always quiet and even seems enthusiastic about the work—a trait which proves to the chief that Pa is an uncorrupted man. He picks Pa to be the leader of the new people, a position that comes with a raise in the food ration.

Though the Angkar says we are all equal in Democratic Kampuchea, we are not. We live and are treated like slaves. In our garden, the Angkar provides us with seeds and we may plant anything we choose, but everything we grow belongs not to us but to the community. The base people eat the berries and vegetables from the community gardens, but the new people are punished if they do. During harvest season the crops from the fields are turned over to the village chief, who then rations the food to the fifty families.

As always, no matter how plentiful the crops, there is never enough food for the new people. Stealing food is viewed as a heinous crime and, if caught, offenders risk either getting their fingers cut off in the public square or being forced to grow a vegetable garden in an area near identified minefields. The Khmer Rouge soldiers planted these land mines to protect the provinces they took over from the Lon Nol army during the revolution. Since the Khmer Rouge planted so many land mines and drew no maps of where these mines are, now many people are injured or killed traversing these areas. People who work in these areas do not come back to the village. If people step on one and their arms or legs are blown off, they are no longer of any value to the Angkar. The soldiers then shoot them to finish the job. In the new pure agrarian society, there is no place for disabled people.

---

heinous *(adj.)* very bad and shocking
agrarian *(adj.)* dependent on farming

VOCABULARY/WORD ANALYSIS

Denotation and Connotation
Find the word *dump* in the second paragraph on page 212.

denotation of *dump*: _____

_____

_____

connotation of *dump*: _____

_____

_____

Why does Ung choose to use the word *dump*?

_____

_____

_____

_____

LITERARY ANALYSIS

Description: Sensory Details
Review the second paragraph on page 212. How does Ung use sensory details to help you feel how hungry she is?

_____

_____

_____

_____

_____

_____

_____

_____

COMPREHENSION

Fact and Opinion
On page 213, Pa gives his opinion that there will be a generation of children completely missing from the country. (Circle) the evidence in the first paragraph that supports his opinion.

"This is where the gods live," he said quietly.

The Khmer Rouge government also bans the practice of religion. Kim says the Angkar do not want people worshipping any gods or goddesses that might take away devotion to the Angkar. To ensure that this rule is enforced, the soldiers destroyed Buddhist temples and worshipping sites throughout the country with major destruction done to the area known as Angkor Wat, an ancient religious site important in Kampuchean history.

Covering more than twenty-five miles of temples, Angkor Wat was built by powerful Khmer kings as monuments of self-glorification in the ninth **century** and completed three hundred years later. In the fifteenth century, Angkor Wat was abandoned to the jungles after an invasion by Siam and forgotten about until French explorers rediscovered it in the nineteenth century. Since then, the battle-scarred temples with their beautiful statues, stone sculptures, and multilayered towers remain one of the seven man-made wonders of the world.

I remember clutching tightly to Pa's finger as we walked along wide crumbling corridors. The temple walls are decorated with magnificent detailed carvings of people, cows, wagons, daily life, and battle scenes from long ago. Guarding the ancient steps are giant granite lions, tigers, eight-headed snakes, and elephants. Next to them, sandstone gods with eight hands who sit cross-legged on lotus flowers watch over the temple ponds. On the walls beneath the jungle vines, thousands of beautiful apsara goddesses wearing only short wraparound skirts smile at visitors.

Completed in the early 12th century, Angkor Wat was created by king Suryavarman II. Although much of the building was left to decay after the 15th century, the temple was never completely abandoned by monks.

Pa led me to a temple area where the trees were so tall that they seemed to reach the heavens. Their twisted trunks, roots, and vines wrapped themselves around the ruins like gigantic boa constrictors, crushing and swallowing the overturned stones. He lifted me over the wobbly steps to the dark mouth of the temple cave. "This is where the gods live," he said quietly, "and if you call out to them, they will answer." Anxiously, I wet my lips and yelled, "*Chump leap sursdei, dthai pda!*" ("Hello, gods!") Then wrapped my arms around Pa's leg when the gods answered me: "*Dthai pda! Dthai pda! Dthai pda!*"

At the temples in this area, my sixteen-year-old brother, Khouy, says the soldiers mutilated its animal guards, and either knocked or shot off the stone heads of the gods, riddling the sacred bodies with bullets. After they destroyed the temples, the soldiers roamed the country searching for monks and forced them to convert to the Angkar. Those monks who refused were murdered or made to work in minefields. To escape extermination, many monks grew their hair and went into hiding in the jungle. Although these monks maintained and took care of the temples, now they are left to the jungle once again. I wonder where the gods go now that their homes have been destroyed. ■

> **Summarize**
> **Describe in one or two sentences what has happened to the author's culture.**

Loung Ung

AUTHOR FILE

BORN 1970 in Phnom Penh, Cambodia

ACTIVISM Today, Ung is a human rights activist and a national spokesperson for the Campaign for a Landmine Free World. She worked with the International Campaign to Ban Landmines, which received the Nobel Peace Prize in 1997.

FAMILY Ung is one of seven children, but many of her relatives died in the Cambodian genocide. At age ten, along with her older brother and his wife, Ung fled Cambodia by stowing away in a fishing boat bound for Vietnam. Later, they traveled in a houseboat to Thailand. In June of 1980, they received sponsorship to come to the United States.

EDUCATION As a sophomore in high school, Ung received a high grade in her English class for an essay about her experiences growing up in Cambodia. Encouraged by her teacher, she began keeping a journal and writing more about her life and family in Cambodia.

---

mutilated (*v.*) damaged severely

convert (*v.*) to change beliefs or allegiance

> **LITERARY ANALYSIS**

Description: Sensory Details

What single sensory detail best communicates the emotions Angkor Wat evokes in the author? Explain your answer.

_____

_____

_____

_____

_____

_____

> **COMPREHENSION**

Fact and Opinion

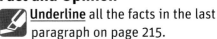 **Underline** all the facts in the last paragraph on page 215.

• Based on these facts, what is your opinion of the monks?

_____

_____

> **21** **SMALL GROUPS/INDEPENDENT**

> **COLLABORATE**

Design Create a poster for the International Campaign to Ban Landmines, alerting people to the dangers of minefields and the need to keep from creating new ones.

> **COMMUNICATE**

Discuss and Write Discuss how another member of Ung's family, such as Pa, might have felt about life under the Khmer Rouge. Jot down your ideas. Then write a journal entry from the other family member's point of view.

W

> **READ ONLINE**

expert space
Go to **www.expert21.com/student** to learn more about Khmer Rouge; Pol Pot; Cambodia.

ONE GIANT LEAP FOR HUMANKIND

By Andrés Eloy Mendoza Rodriguez

On July 16, 1969, the Apollo XI space mission blasted off from the Kennedy Space Center in Florida. Four days later, six hundred million people around the world—one-fifth of the world's population—watched on TV as humans walked on the moon for the first time. Here is one viewer's account of watching the takeoff, the moonwalk, and the July 24 splashdown on Earth.

Propelled by a powerful Saturn V rocket, the Apollo XI space mission launches from the John F. Kennedy Space Center in Florida.

In this iconic image, astronauts Neil Armstrong and Buzz Aldrin place an American flag on the moon.

I am from Barquisimeto, Venezuela. With the broadcast via satellite of the Apollo XI mission, Venezuela inaugurated its first satellite tracking station, which was installed precisely for everyone to be a witness to this great human feat.

On July 16, 1969, I remember I got to school late. The reason? I was watching the launching of Apollo XI. By the way, I was not the only kid late for school that morning. As the majestic Saturn V lifted off from launchpad 39A, you could hear the people in the neighborhood clapping and cheering, excited by what they were watching on their TV sets. As the Saturn V rocket catapulted mankind into the future, I remember the late [television news anchor] Renny Ottolina saying that we were watching a "huge bird made out of steel and built by man."

Finally the day came when Neil Armstrong would step on the moon. My father had a shortwave radio, and he tuned in the Armed Forces of the USA. I already spoke English at the time, and I lowered the volume on the TV while I listened to the radio. I kept listening to the radio while watching the TV until Armstrong was about to come out of the *Eagle* [the detachable vehicle in which Armstrong and fellow astronaut Buzz Aldrin left the main ship, *Columbia*, and landed on the moon's surface].

All of a sudden I felt the urge to look at the moon again. I went to the yard and looked at it. Something was telling me that I wouldn't look at the moon in the same manner again. The mysticism about our only natural satellite was about to change forever. There was not a single car in the streets. It was as if the whole world had stopped to witness the

feat *(n.)* an impressive achievement
mysticism *(n.)* vague thoughts and ideas, not based on reality

greatest adventure of man. I went back to the living room, and everyone was mute. You could hear our hearts beat. I couldn't believe what I was watching. There was so much I didn't know. What would happen? Was the moon full of quicksand? Would Armstrong sink into the moon sand? Would Aldrin be able to rescue Armstrong?

Finally Armstrong began coming down the ladder. As he got to the foot of the ladder our excitement grew to a level that I can't describe. And when he said those famous words "It's one small step for man, one giant leap for mankind," again you could hear the cheers of the neighbors. As Armstrong began to walk on the moon, the fear of something terrible happening began to fade away. We watched the whole moonwalk, and afterwards they were showing replays in all channels. That went on practically until the day of the splashdown in the Pacific.

That was again an exciting moment [on July 24], when finally the capsule [returned to Earth and] appeared on our TV screen and the parachutes were patiently bringing down the three heroes and gently placing them in the waters of the North Pacific Ocean [hundreds of miles from land]. Humankind's greatest adventure was over, and I was thankful to live in a country that was able to witness the whole thing live.

Humans will go to Mars one day, and to other distant places in the Cosmos, but as U.S. President Nixon said the night of the moonwalk: "For one priceless moment, in the whole history of man, all the people on this Earth are truly one."

I doubt humankind will ever again be as united as we were at that point. That was not a triumph of the United States, or of the free world, or of NASA, although undoubtedly they all have reasons for believing that. I think that was a triumph of man's intelligence and perseverance and it showed us what humans can accomplish when we all work towards one goal. THAT WAS A TRIUMPH OF THE HUMAN RACE! ∎

---

undoubtedly *(adv.)* definitely; without doubt
triumph *(n.)* victory; success

NAVIGATING TEXT

Primary Sources

Remember that a primary source is a firsthand account of an experience.

- (Circle) a detail in the introduction that shows the reading is a primary source.
- What sort of details does this account provide that a secondary source—such as a history text—might not?

_____

_____

_____

_____

_____

_____

COMPREHENSION

Fact and Opinion

Label each statement **F** for fact or **O** for opinion.

1. Apollo XI launched on July 16, 1969. ____
2. The *Eagle* landed on the Moon's surface. ____
3. Humankind will never again be as united as we were at that point. ____
4. Humankind's greatest adventure was over. ____

- Now give your opinion. Decades later, do you agree that the moon landing was humankind's greatest adventure? Explain.

_____

_____

_____

_____

READ ONLINE

expert space
Go to **www.expert21.com/student** to learn more about Apollo Program; Moon; Neil Armstrong.

Think Across Texts

Organize and Synthesize

1. Complete this chart using information from "No More Strangers Now," "A Refugee in Her Own Country," and "One Giant Leap for Humankind."

	Bandile Mashinini and Mark Abrahamson	Loung Ung	Andrés Eloy Mendoza Rodriguez
How has the historical event each person experienced affected his or her view of the world?			

Compare and Evaluate

2. Compare and contrast "No More Strangers Now" and "A Refugee in Her Own Country" by completing the chart below.

"No More Strangers Now"   Both   "A Refigee in Her Own Country"

3. Choose one person from these selections and describe how they work to make the world a better place.

_____

_____

_____

4. Which of these selections was most meaningful to you? Give reasons for your choice.

_____

_____

_____

_____

_____

_____

_____

_____

Discuss and Write

5. With a partner, discuss how the three readings in "Lessons from History" helped you understand how ordinary people experience historical events. Take notes as you talk. Then use your notes to write a response to the question: *Can history be a life lesson?*

Apply Word Knowledge

Word Lab

1. **Answer it.**

- When are **atrocities** likely to happen?

_____

_____

- Is a **fugitive** likely to live a **solitary** life? Explain why or why not.

_____

_____

2. **Circle it.** Imagine that someone drank your glass of milk. Which of the following would be the most **incriminating** sight?

- someone eating a peanut butter sandwich

- someone pouring a glass of milk

- someone with a milk mustache

3. **Select one.** Study the statements below. Which one would a **capitalist** agree with?

- Ⓐ The economy works best without government interference.

- Ⓑ Businesses should be controlled by the government.

4. **Describe them.**

- How does someone who is **paranoid** act?

_____

- How do students **assess** their work?

_____

_____

_____

5. **Complete it.** Complete these sentences with the following words: **comprise, ration,** and **relocation.**

- Refugees often undergo frequent _____.

- Beans, rice, an apple, and a glass of water

   _____ today's meal.

- The expedition leaders will _____ our

   food, because there is not much left.

Word Analysis

6. Rewrite these sentences so the underlined word is replaced by a word with a positive or neutral connotation.

The farmer's toil kept him busy throughout the day.

_____

_____

The servant lived a life of drudgery.

_____

_____

The student completed the task quickly.

_____

_____

7. Match each of the underlined words above with its denotation.

toil	hard physical labor
task	boring or unpleasant work
drudgery	assignment

21

Play a Role

Playing the role of someone else can help you see things in a new way. The role may be someone from history, a current figure, or just someone other than you. It also stretches your understanding and your creative thinking skills.

Role Play: The Fall of the Berlin Wall

▶ **Examine this role-playing activity. See how each student plays a role.**

MARK IT

(Circle) the words the American visitor uses to show her point of view.

Put a **star** ★ by the detail the older German gives that shows facts about her life.

Scenario: Several East and West Berlin residents are invited to be on a talk show to share their reactions to the fall of the Berlin Wall—one week after the fall of the wall.

So, tell me, what were your impressions of what happened to our country these last few days?

I always thought the wall would be permanent. I never imagined it would be torn down by people in the street.

Talk show host

student #1

student #2

American visitor to Berlin

How about you, sir?

I'm amazed by what I'm seeing in West Berlin. Even the supermarkets are amazing. There's so much stuff!

student #3

East German resident, never left East Berlin before

Ma'am, this event must have special meaning for you.

The last time I saw my sister we were teenagers in the 1960s. I can't believe how different our lives have been. It is extraordinary.

student #4

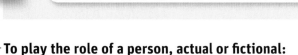
West German resident—her sister was across the wall for 28 years

Here's How ▶ **To play the role of a person, actual or fictional:**

Step 1 Understand the scenario. Where are you in time and in the world? Make sure you understand the facts of the situation.

Step 2 Study your role. What facts would this person know? What is their perspective on the situation? Take some notes before you begin the role-playing activity.

Step 3 Play your role. Speak in the first person. You need to walk, talk, listen, respond, and interact in character with your team—also in character.

Step 4 Reflect. After the role-playing activity, think about what new insights each of you learned about your role—and each other.

Apply: Act It Out

▶ Examine this role-play scenario, then follow the steps to play out roles with a group.

Role Play: 1969 Moon Landing

Group: 4 People

Scenario: It is one week after the moon landing. A group of people discuss their reactions on a talk show.

TV talk show host

NASA scientist

13-year-old student

70-year-old American

1. **Understand the scenario.** What facts do you know about the topic?

_____

_____

_____

2. **Study your role.** Place a check beside the role you are taking. Write notes about that character's perspective on the event. Create a name card for your character.

   ❏ the TV talk show host   ❏ a 13-year-old student

   ❏ a scientist who works for NASA   ❏ a 70-year-old American

   _____

   _____

   _____

3. **Present your role.** Act out the situation. The talk show host is responsible for welcoming everyone to the show, and for asking questions of the guests.

4. **Reflect.** How did the role-playing activity change what you thought about the moon landing?

   _____

   _____

   _____

Traits of Writing

Traits of Writing is a model for assessing and teaching. The traits work within the writing process to support revision and editing.

Each puzzle piece below represents one of the **traits** that define good writing.

Each trait is made up of four **key qualities.** The trait that you will focus on in this lesson is Sentence Fluency.

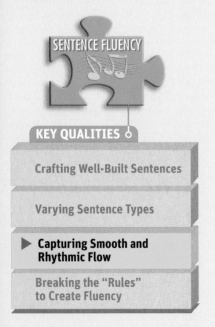

SENTENCE FLUENCY

KEY QUALITIES

Crafting Well-Built Sentences

Varying Sentence Types

► **Capturing Smooth and Rhythmic Flow**

Breaking the "Rules" to Create Fluency

Research Paper

A research paper presents information based on facts gathered from different sources. Research papers are found in scientific journals, government reports, health newsletters, and in many other places.

In this writing workshop, you will write a research paper about an historic event, citing your sources. You also have the option of writing a first-person historical narrative, using researched facts to add details.

Example: This biography cites factual information from NASA.

> Neil Armstrong was a research pilot testing high-speed aircraft on May 25, 1961 when President John F. Kennedy pledged to put a man on the moon before 1970. The following year he was transferred to astronaut status. Then on July 21, 1969, he became the first person to set foot on the moon and fulfilled Kennedy's promise. (NASA, Biography of Neil Armstrong)

BIOGRAPHY:
Neil Armstrong

► **Analyze Features** **A strong research paper has the following features:**

FEATURE	🖊 MARK IT
Look for these features in the Student Model on the next page.	Mark the features as you read the Student Model.
1. A **topic statement** that says what the paper is going to be about. (Ideas)	<u>Underline</u> the topic sentence.
2. **Subtopics** that break the topic into parts. (Ideas)	Circle the subtopics.
3. **Focus Trait: Sentence Fluency** Sentences that flow well together.	Check ✓ examples of transitions that help sentences flow smoothly.
4. **Sources** of information cited within the text. (Presentation)	Star ★ the sources cited.
5. A strong **conclusion** that ties up the information presented. (Organization)	Draw a box around how the information is summed up in the conclusion.

► **Read Anna's research paper about Cesar Chavez leading farm workers to fight for their rights.**

STUDENT MODEL

By Cesar's Side
By Anna Blair

Cesar Chavez organized farm workers to protest against unfair treatment by farm owners. In 1965 he organized a boycott that helped change things for the better.

Migrant farm labor has a long history. The first generation of migrant workers from Mexico came to the United States through the Bracero program. That program allowed Mexican workers to enter the U.S. to work in the fields. But, in 1964, the program ended (Marentes, "The Bracero Project," par. 4).

However, younger generations came to the U.S. after that, often illegally. Many worked picking fruit. The pay was barely enough to live on. Many children worked alongside their parents and did not go to school. Many migrants lived without running water or indoor toilet (Oliver, "La Causa," par. 6).

In 1965, in Delano, California, Cesar Chavez organized workers and convinced them to join his organization, the National Farm Workers Association (NFWA). Chavez held a meeting and asked Mexican laborers to join Filipino workers in a strike. He gave a speech and said, "Si se puede," words of encouragement that mean "yes we can." Some farmers sprayed striking workers with pesticides. However, Chavez made a pledge to remain nonviolent. He admired men like Martin Luther King, Jr. and Mohandas Gandhi ("Cesar E. Chavez," par. 12).

Soon, other unions began to support the migrant workers. People sent food. The dockworkers refused to load grapes picked by strikebreakers. Finally, people all over the country began a boycott of products in support of the strike. That gave the migrant workers the opportunity to join the United Farm Workers ("Delano Grape Boycott Readings," par. 10). Things didn't change overnight. But, thanks to Chavez, that victory became the first step on the way to a better life.

► **Read Anna's notes about how she worked on her research paper.**

ORGANIZATION

At first I started my essay with facts about the boycott, but then I revised it so that the events were told in chronological order, making it easier to follow.

SENTENCE FLUENCY

When I revised my essay, I added more transitions, such as "however," "finally," "soon," and "and," to keep my sentences flowing and my details in order.

► **Analyze how Anna organized her ideas. Fill in the missing parts of the outline.**

Topic Statement: Cesar Chavez's Grape Boycott fought for migrant rights.

   I. Older generation came to U.S. under Bracero program.

       A. worked hard

       B. program ended

   II. Younger generation came to U.S. illegally.

       A. worked hard under terrible conditions

       B.

   III. People joined the strike.

       A.

       B.

How Do I Get Started?

Your Topic:

Assignment: Research Paper or Historical Narrative
Purpose: To write about an historical event
Audience: Your classmates and teacher

Ideas: Developing the Topic

Developing your topic deepens what you have to say. Use these Think-Abouts as you work on your ideas:

- Am I sure my information is right? *The writer of the Student Model did careful research to find details that showed that migrant workers in California lived without running water.*
- Are my details chock-full of interesting information?
- Have I used details that show new thinking about this idea?
- Will my reader believe what I say about this topic?

IDEAS

KEY QUALITIES

Finding a Topic

Focusing the Topic

▶ **Developing the Topic**

Using Details

▶ **Model** Go back to Reading 1, "The Diary of a Young Girl," in this workshop. List some details that create a picture in the reader's mind of Anne's daily life.

▶ **Practice** Find one interesting detail you definitely want to include in your research paper.

Topic:_____

Interesting Detail:_____

_____

▶ **Plan Your Research Paper** Use the outline below to plan your research paper. Revise as necessary.

expert space
www.expert21.com/student

▶ **Go to Expert Space to use these tools that will help you write a research paper.**

- Notes, Note Organizer & Citations
- Bibliography
- Outline

Topic Statement: _____

I._____

   A._____

   B._____

II._____

   A._____

   B._____

III._____

   A._____

   B._____

How Do I Get Organized?

ORGANIZATION

Organization: Structuring the Body

Good writers show sequences and transition in their work. Ask yourself these Think-Abouts as you improve your organization.

- Have I shown the reader where to slow down and where to speed up? *The Student Model quickly moves through the Bracero program, because it's not critical to the main topic.*
- Do all the details fit where they are placed?
- Will the reader find it easy to follow my ideas?
- Does the organization help the main idea stand out?

○ KEY QUALITIES

Creating the Lead

Using Sequence Words and Transition Words

▶ Structuring the Body

Ending With a Sense of Resolution

▶ **Model** Go back to Reading 2, "The Fall of the Wall," and describe how the author organizes Gillian's eyewitness experience.

▶ **Practice** Think about how to show the reader when to speed up. Rewrite the third paragraph of the Student Model in three sentences.

_____

_____

_____

_____

_____

_____

▶ **Write a Paragraph** Use the information you have learned in your research to write a first draft of one of your paragraphs here.

_____

_____

_____

_____

_____

▶ **Draft Your Research Paper** Write a first draft.

Quick Check

▶ Check how well you structured the body of your research paper. Have a writing partner rate it, too.

6 = Expert   **3** = Making Strides

5 = Well Done   **2** = On the Way

4 = Almost There   **1** = Getting Started

Organization

1. Have I shown the reader where to slow down and where to speed up?

Self   ① ② ③ ④ ⑤ ⑥
Partner   ① ② ③ ④ ⑤ ⑥

2. Do all the details fit where they are placed?

Self   ① ② ③ ④ ⑤ ⑥
Partner   ① ② ③ ④ ⑤ ⑥

3. Will the reader find it easy to follow my ideas?

Self   ① ② ③ ④ ⑤ ⑥
Partner   ① ② ③ ④ ⑤ ⑥

4. Does the organization help the main idea stand out?

Self   ① ② ③ ④ ⑤ ⑥
Partner   ① ② ③ ④ ⑤ ⑥

How Do I Capture Smooth and Rhythmic Flow?

FOCUS TRAIT

Sentence Fluency: Capturing Smooth and Rhythmic Flow

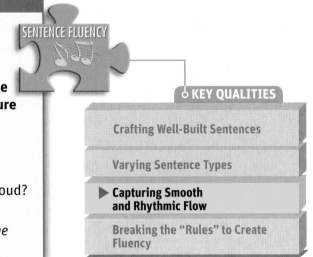

Good writers think about how their writing sounds and if the sentences flow together. Use these Think-Abouts to make sure the sentences in your research paper have a rhythmic flow.

◆ KEY QUALITIES

- Is it easy to read my entire piece aloud?

- Do my sentences flow easily from one to the next?

- Do I have phrases that sound smooth when I read them aloud?

- Do my sentences have a pleasing tempo? *Read the second paragraph from the Student Model out loud. Listen to how the rhythm is accented by natural sounding pauses.*

Crafting Well-Built Sentences

Varying Sentence Types

▶ Capturing Smooth and Rhythmic Flow

Breaking the "Rules" to Create Fluency

▶ **Model** Go back to Reading 3, "From Iraq With Love," and read one of the letters out loud. How does the writer make the letter sound as though someone is speaking?

▶ Read Ruth Culham's writing blog below to get advice on improving your writing.

Ask the Expert: Ruth Culham

Ruth Culham, an award-winning teacher, is the author of *6+1 Traits of Writing: The Complete Guide for Middle School* and other books on writing.

Q & A: Capturing a Smooth and Rhythmic Flow

Solomon Smooth Writes:

I'm sure that my sentences are working fine because I jot them down fast and I always write in sentences because my teachers tell me to use sentences so I'm not sure why my sentence fluency score is not the best of all the trait scores I get. Do you know?

Dear Solomon Smooth:
When you write your ideas down quickly, it's easy to forget to read aloud to check how the writing sounds. If you have to stop and take a breath, your sentence is too long. Break it down into shorter ones of differing lengths. You'll like the result! And your new and improved sentence fluency score.

Posted by: Ruth Culham | April 3 at 8:30 A.M.

▶ **Practice** Read the sample paragraphs and think about which one varies sentence patterns to make the writing more fluent.

<u>Underline</u> the run-on and rushed sentences.

Ⓒircle the sentences that sound smooth.

Star ★ the passage that shows a smooth and rhythmic flow.

Sample 1: The Beginning of the Terror

It was all very scary one day we were all friends and then the next day there were these new rules that forced all the Jewish people to wear yellow stars on their coats. After that the Jewish students were not allowed to go to school at all and I even saw a good friend of mine being dragged out of her home with her family and I don't know where they went.

Sample 2: The Beginning of the Terror

It was all very scary. All of us were friends, and we never thought about the difference in our religion. Then a new law passed and all the Jewish students had to sew yellow stars on their coats. Before long, they weren't even allowed to go to school. One day I saw a friend of mine being dragged from her home with her family. I wonder where they were being taken.

▶ **Revise** Now try to capture a smooth and rhythmic flow in your writing. Choose a paragraph from your first draft and revise it below. Remember to read your sentences out loud to hear how they sound.

_____

_____

_____

_____

_____

_____

_____

_____

_____

_____

_____

Quick Check

▶ **Check your research paper for how well you captured a smooth and rhythmic flow. Then have a writing partner rate it, too.**

6 = Expert **3** = Making Strides

5 = Well Done **2** = On the Way

4 = Almost There **1** = Getting Started

Sentence Fluency

1. Is it easy to read my entire piece aloud?
Self ① ② ③ ④ ⑤ ⑥
Partner ① ② ③ ④ ⑤ ⑥

2. Do my sentences flow easily from one to the next?
Self ① ② ③ ④ ⑤ ⑥
Partner ① ② ③ ④ ⑤ ⑥

3. Do I have phrases that sound smooth when I read them aloud?
Self ① ② ③ ④ ⑤ ⑥
Partner ① ② ③ ④ ⑤ ⑥

4. Do my sentences have a pleasing tempo?
Self ① ② ③ ④ ⑤ ⑥
Partner ① ② ③ ④ ⑤ ⑥

Revise With Technology Use the Expert Space tutorials and tools to help you through the steps of the research process, such as searching, note-taking, outlining, and citing sources.

How Can I Finish a Great Paper?

Grammar: Phrases and Clauses

A clause has a subject and predicate, but it can only stand alone if it expresses a complete thought. A phrase is a group of words that lack a subject and a predicate.

CONVENTIONS

- Subordinate clauses: do not express a complete thought.

Example: It will be exciting to witness history when the country **elects a woman president.**

- Gerund phrases: begin with a verb in the *–ing* form used as a noun.

Example: Studying history allows you to imagine the past.

▶ **Practice** Rewrite this paragraph correctly below.

People were worried about nuclear war. When Reagan first became president. But we didn't know how quickly things would change. Bankrupting the Soviet Union. Caused the communist government to collapse.

_____

_____

_____

Mechanics: Using Commas with Phrases and Clauses

Use commas after a subordinate clause or a phrase that begins a sentence.

CONVENTIONS

Example: <u>Before the Civil Rights movement began</u>, segregation was legal. (subordinate clause)

<u>Through legal action</u>, the movement was able to change laws. (phrase)

▶ **Practice** Rewrite this formal paragraph correctly below.

When Anne Frank's diary was published the world was amazed. By recording her daily thoughts Anne had shown her humanity.

_____

_____

_____

▶ **Proofread** **Find and correct any errors in your research paper. Put a check beside the types of errors you find. Then write three corrected sentences below.**

❑ using phrases and clauses

❑ using commas with phrases and clauses

❑ using modifiers correctly

❑ using colons, semi-colons, and parentheses correctly

❑ misspellings

❑ other: _____

1. _____

_____

2. _____

_____

3. _____

_____

PUBLISH/PRESENT

▶ **Write Your Final Draft** **Now, using your edited draft, begin creating a final draft for presentation.**

Use word processing software to type your final draft. Make sure to format your margins and spacing according to your teacher's request.

Check your final draft against the Traits of Writing Scoring Guide on pages 336–339 and correct any errors before you present it.

Be sure to use the proper citation form that your teacher requests. For help formatting your citations and bibliography, go to Expert Space.

▶ **Beyond the Classroom** **Extend your finished research paper.**

Look online for a blog, message board, magazine, or newspaper where you could publish your research paper.

List two places you could upload or share your research paper for publication.

_____

_____

Quick Check

▶ Check your research paper for correct use of conventions. Then have a writing partner rate it, too.

6 = Expert   **3** = Making Strides

5 = Well Done   **2** = On the Way

4 = Almost There   **1** = Getting Started

Conventions

1. Did I use phrases and clauses correctly?
Self   ① ② ③ ④ ⑤ ⑥
Partner ① ② ③ ④ ⑤ ⑥

2. Did I use commas correctly?
Self   ① ② ③ ④ ⑤ ⑥
Partner ① ② ③ ④ ⑤ ⑥

3. Did I use modifiers correctly?
Self   ① ② ③ ④ ⑤ ⑥
Partner ① ② ③ ④ ⑤ ⑥

4. Is the spelling in the research paper correct?
Self   ① ② ③ ④ ⑤ ⑥
Partner ① ② ③ ④ ⑤ ⑥

READ ONLINE
expert space
Go to **www.expert21.com/ student** to get help writing a bibliography.

21

Expert Reading

You have learned about eyewitness accounts of history. Now apply your Expert Reading strategies to the following essay written by a teen reporter assigned to write about September 11, 2001. ▶

REMEMBERING 9/11

As a second grader at a downtown New York public school, teen reporter Juliette Kessler became an eyewitness to one of the most tragic and terrifying events in American history. In this essay, she shares her memories of September 11, 2001.

By Juliette Kessler

New York, September 10, 2007

Six years ago, I was lining up in the hallway to begin my third day of second grade at PS 234, an elementary school a few blocks from the World Trade Center.

"Glenda!" There was a shout from down the hallway, and a friend's dad came running, addressing my teacher. "A plane," he was panting, "has just crashed into the World Trade Center. We need to get these children to safety."

At the time, I didn't understand what was going on. I remember pretending to cry like all the other children around me. I remember the voice of our principal, Anna, coming through the public announcement system, telling the teachers to lower the window shades. I remember my mother running into the classroom, taking my hand and pulling me out.

She picked me up and put my head on her shoulder to block out what was happening. People were running, some screaming, some just standing still, stupefied, staring in eerie silence. I remember looking up from her shoulder and seeing the two burning towers looming over us.

So, I hesitated when asked if I would like to visit the remains of the World Trade Center to write this anniversary essay. I wasn't sure if I wanted to revive that memory.

stupefied *(adj.)* too surprised to think clearly
surreal *(adj.)* very strange, like something from a dream

The Better Memories

As time goes on, 9/11 has become more of a surreal dream for me than a crisp memory. I sometimes forget that it ever happened. But then I'll walk by a construction site and the smell of concrete dust and burning metal revives the visions from that time.

Six years later I am now 13, and I have done a very good job of blocking those memories. Not that I want to forget completely, but it's hard to think about how my neighborhood became a battlefield with battered fire trucks and Army tanks parked on my street. People wore face masks to protect their lungs from the toxic air. My school was closed for five months. Life was chaotic. The smell lingered for months.

But something else happened too.

Inside the war zone that the area near Ground Zero had become, neighbors were reaching out to each other and to the rescue workers.

Families volunteered to peel and chop vegetables at Bouley, a neighborhood restaurant that was feeding the workers. The hotel next to my house, the Tribeca Grand, took in displaced families and their pets. Everyone in my building shared what was in our refrigerators because the local shops were closed. It was New York at its best—people of all kinds coming together.

Those are some of the better memories.

Preserving the Pieces

I visited Hangar 17 at JFK Airport in a part of New York City named Queens, with my editor Suzanne Freeman and Sonnet Takahisa, the director of education for the National September 11 Memorial & Museum at the World Trade Center site. Peter Gat, an objects conservator, showed us around the 80,000 square feet of 9/11 artifacts, which is not open to the public.

As we entered the enormous space, my heart skipped.

People created memorials like this one, located at Ground Zero, for the victims of the September 11th attacks.

Inside were rows and rows of iron bars, strips of long twisted metal, bent in ways that they shouldn't have been, like a dislocated shoulder. There were twisted bicycles still locked to a bike rack. And stone benches, where I used to sit and eat ice cream at the World Trade Center plaza. Some beams had the word "SAVE" spray painted on them, sending an ironic message. While ironworkers used machinery to cut through the rubble at Ground Zero, other experts were picking and choosing pieces to preserve.

Steel beams and concrete blocks have been sorted, numbered, and catalogued. Sections are divided by wide walkways marked with white tape. While my neighborhood was a messy battlefield after the attacks, this place is extremely neat. I felt as though we had entered a morgue.

We went into a special climate-controlled room with more of the buildings' remains. Steel beams showed cutouts of crosses, stars of David, and police badges. The shapes were polished by ironworkers and rescue crews to give to volunteers and family members of those who died there.

Another climate-controlled room is lined with damaged fire trucks, ambulances, motorcycles, and Port Authority cars. Some cars are too crushed and rusted to identify. In another room, objects that had been in the World Trade Center's underground shopping mall have been preserved. Some were disturbingly whole: a doll covered in gray September 11th dust was laid out on a shelf. A giant plastic bunny dressed as a businessman with a briefcase and cell phone stood in a corner smiling at us.

These sad objects are all being carefully preserved. Some will be loaned to the Memorial Museum at Ground Zero for the public to see. Some are now being shown across the U.S. to help raise money to build a memorial at the site. According to Takahisa, they are a tragic but important piece of our history, a reminder of what happened that day.

For me personally, they are also a reminder of what happened afterward: New Yorkers of all kinds, from all different races and religions, from all different parts of the world, came together to help each other. So, when I was asked to take this assignment, I said yes. I knew it wouldn't be easy, but I accepted because I am a New Yorker and because I love this city. ■

Reflect

1. Circle all the expert strategies you used while reading this essay.

   A. Summarize

   B. Question

   C. Other: _____

   D. Other: _____

   E. Other: _____

2. Use the letters above to label where in the essay you applied the expert strategies.

3. Select one expert strategy you used. Explain why you applied that strategy where you did.

   _____
   _____
   _____
   _____
   _____
   _____

RESEARCH ONLINE

expert space
Go to **www.expert21.com/student** to learn more about 21st Century News Stories; September 11, 2001; The Global Financial Crisis.

---

morgue *(n.)* a building where dead bodies are kept before they are buried or burned
stars of David *(n.)* symbols of Judaism

PROJECT
RESEARCH

EYEWITNESS TO THE PRESENT DAY

THE SITUATION

The Event: Your town or city is celebrating its 100th anniversary next month and is planning an event to mark the moment.

The Plan: As part of the festivities, the mayor would like to display a time capsule—a time pod—to represent what the United States and your town is like at this moment in history, in the early decades of the 21st century. She has put out a call to all citizens asking for suggestions for the time pod.

YOUR CHALLENGE

With a group of classmates, you will choose eight items to represent this moment in time. You will then present your ideas to the mayor's committee and provide a rationale for your choices.

To choose a list, you will

- make inferences.
- record observations.
- review resources.
- brainstorm objects.
- choose objects for the time pod.
- plan and present your rationale.

CAREER CONNECTION
Education and Training
www.careerclusters.org

Go to [21] ToolKit Expert File 6.20 to learn about historians.

1 Make inferences about American eras.

Look back at the readings in this workshop. What objects from each reading might be a good item to include in a time capsule for that era?

"The Diary of a Young Girl": _____

_____

"The Fall of the Wall": _____

_____

"From Iraq With Love": _____

_____

"No More Strangers Now": _____

_____

2 Record observations.

You can also make inferences about our own era. Spend a few minutes with your group discussing what each of the following objects tells you about what we value today. Write your inferences below.

- cell phones
- PDAs
- SUVs
- hybrid or electric cars

From these things, I can infer that people

today _____

_____

_____

_____

3 Review resources.

Go to the **Resource Bank** to look at sample time capsules from the 1920s and 1960s. Discuss how each item represents the era and why it might have been included. Write down some of the different types of objects and media that were included:

_____

_____

_____

4 Brainstorm ideas.

Look at each category below. What items, people, events, or ideas might represent each category at this moment in history? Use **Expert Space** to research your ideas.

Science and Technology

Fashion

Politics and Public Life

Music, Art, and Literature

Family and Home Life

Pop Culture and Sports

5 Create your time pod.

Place a star by your top 5 choices in the chart. Then, turn the page to complete your project. Finally, use **21** **Tool**Kit **Expert File 1.11** to create a multimedia presentation explaining your choices.

THE 1920s

A new generation of young women, called "flappers," began to wear short dresses, bob their hair, listen to jazz, and otherwise shake things up.

flapper dress

The Roaring Twenties were brought to a dramatic halt with the Great Crash of 1929, the most devastating stock market crash in history.

front-page news

In 1923, baseball great Babe Ruth helped the Yankees win the World Series; in 1927, he became the first player to hit 60 home runs in one season.

baseball signed by Babe Ruth

In 1927, Charles Lindbergh became the first person to fly solo across the Atlantic Ocean.

Lindbergh's flight goggles

signed poetry collection

American poet, writer, and playwright Langston Hughes is known for his work during the Harlem Renaissance, an African American cultural movement of the 1920s and '30s.

> From these items, what inference can you make about life in the 1920s before the Great Crash of 1929?

_____

_____

THE 1960s

pen used by President Johnson to sign the 1964 Civil Rights Act

The Civil Rights Movement of the 1960s, led by Dr. Martin Luther King, Jr. and many other inspiring men and women, sought to abolish racial discrimination against African Americans and restore their voting rights.

U.S. involvement in the Vietnam War peaked in the late 1960s, as did protests against the war.

anti-war pins

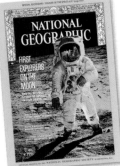

National Geographic from December 1969

On July 20, 1969, more than 600 million people around the world watched astronaut Neil Armstrong on their TV sets, as he became the first man to walk on the moon.

In the 1960s, Barbie dolls—first marketed as teenage fashion models—became all the rage.

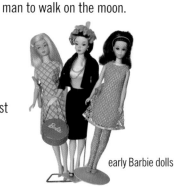

early Barbie dolls

a boycott sign from a march for farm workers

In 1962, Cesar Chavez founded the National Farm Workers Association (later the United Farm Workers of America) to fight for fair wages, medical coverage, humane living conditions, and other protections for hundreds of thousands of farm workers.

> What do these items tell you about the 1960s?

_____

_____

Discuss how you can best represent the entries you starred in the chart on page 235. For example, if you want to include information about a historic election, you might include a clip from a newscast, audio from a campaign rally, or photos. Use the chart below to organize your ideas.

What things have we chosen?	How will we represent them?	Why are we including them?
1.	1.	1.
2.	2.	2.
3.	3.	3.
4.	4.	4.
5.	5.	5.

Strategy Check

Use your knowledge and strategies from the workshop to answer these questions.

COMPREHENSION

Fact and Opinion

1. Review the following statements from the workshop readings. Write F for "fact" or O for "opinion" next to each statement.

_____ After World War II, East Germany sealed Berlin's border and built a wall that became known as the Berlin Wall.

_____ "So much has happened, it is just as if the world had turned upside down."

_____ In 1921, Adolf Hitler became the leader of the Nazi party.

_____ Ninety percent of those who died in the Soweto Uprisings were under the age of 23.

_____ "The ANC were the good guys."

Make Inferences

2. Based on what you read in "No More Strangers Now," you can reasonably infer that

Ⓐ most black South Africans want to take revenge on the whites who supported apartheid.

Ⓑ South Africans who fought against apartheid during their teen years regret having given up their youth.

Ⓒ teens living in South Africa during apartheid had different experiences, depending on their skin color.

State evidence from the text and from your own knowledge that you used to make this inference.

_____

_____

_____

_____

LITERARY ANALYSIS

Author's Voice

3. The voice writers use can reveal information about who they are and how they feel. Read the following sentence from "A Refugee in Her Own Country." Then fill in the circle next to the word that best describes the author's voice.

I don't understand why they are looking at me as if I am a strange animal, when in reality, we look very much the same.

Ⓐ bewildered   Ⓑ optimistic

Ⓒ sarcastic   Ⓓ determined

Description: Sensory Details

4. Read this description. Then fill in the chart with sensory details from the paragraph.

"The children here run about in just a thin blouse and clogs; no coat, no hat, no stockings.... Their tummies are empty; they chew an old carrot to stay the pangs, go from their cold homes into the cold street...."

Sense	Details
sight	
sound	
feeling	
taste	

NAVIGATING TEXT

Primary Sources

5. Check two items below that are examples of primary sources.

_____ news report   _____ textbook article

_____ letter   _____ diary entry

Base Words

6. Read the words in the box below. Circle each base word and underline each prefix or suffix.

misrepresent	courageously
uncommon	semicircle

Denotation and Connotation

7. Identify the connotation of these words. Write *neutral*, *negative*, or *positive* next to each word.

cheering _____

screeching _____

wreckage _____

remains _____

aroma _____

odor _____

stench _____

Analyze

8. Many of the people you have read about in this workshop faced terrible and sometimes life-threatening situations with courage and resolve. What other personal qualities allowed these people to cope with their experiences? What qualities do you think they have in common? Include evidence from at least two of the readings to support your response.

_____

_____

_____

_____

_____

_____

_____

_____

_____

_____

_____

_____

_____

_____

? EXPERT QUESTION

What was it like to be there?

9. Use what you learned in this workshop to answer the Expert Question. Jot down some notes here. Then use a separate sheet of paper to write your response.

_____

_____

_____

DO THE RIGHT THING

 Expert Question:
What values do we live by?

Explore the Expert Question

 **Expert Knowledge**

Watch the Anchor Media!

PAGE **242**

An audiovisual introduction to **Do the Right Thing**.

Explore Expert Space

PAGE **243** **expert space**

See **Do the Right Thing** online at **www.expert21.com/student**.

Meet the Expert

Jill Bargonetti: Genetic Scientist

PAGE **244** This scientist does genetic research and mentors students to change the world for the better.

Read and Synthesize

Inquiry 1 — Classic Questions

Reading 1 — SHORT STORY

The Lady, or the Tiger?

By Frank R. Stockton, adapted by Joy Nolan

Girl meets boy. Girl and boy fall in love. Girl's father forbids the love and presents a life-or-death choice.

PAGE **248**

Reading 2 — SHORT STORY

A Retrieved Reformation

By O. Henry

Jimmy Valentine, a reformed bank robber, is earning an honest living in a quiet town. Then one day, he is faced with a crucial decision in front of a bank vault.

PAGE **254**

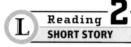

Reading 3 — NEWS ARTICLE

New Brand of High-Seas Pirates Lurks Off Somali Coast

By Alex Seitz

Old-fashioned high-seas swashbuckling has made an alarming 21st century resurgence in parts of the world, and for mariners, the threat of pirates is real.

PAGE **264**

Area of major pirate activity

21st Century Skills

Make Decisions

PAGE **268**

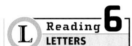
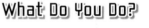

That's totally unfair. You should treat us both the same.

Rita, as long as you are under my roof, you have to follow my rules. And my rules are that you need to be home by 10.

21] What values do we live by?

Almost every day we make decisions based on our—and society's—ideas of what is right and wrong. How do we know we're doing the right thing?

▶ Anchor Your Knowledge

Watch the Anchor Media, "Do the Right Thing," and meet Jill Bargonetti, who conducts genetic research and mentors students to change the world for the better.

WORKSHOP GOALS

To gain expert knowledge about ethics, you will

- study **informational texts** about the rules we live by.

- read **literature** about people who must make tough moral decisions.

- learn **important skills and strategies** to help you understand what you read.

- develop **21st Century Skills** to **make decisions** and **examine multiple perspectives.**

- write a **persuasive essay** about an issue you care about.

- complete a **multimedia presentation** about your view on a moral dilemma.

▶ Opinionaire

An opinionaire is a list of statements that you can agree or disagree with. **Before** reading this workshop, put a check mark to the left of each statement you agree with. Then, come back **after** the workshop is completed to see if you have changed your mind.

BEFORE		TOPIC: **Values**	AFTER	
Y	N		Y	N
		If you see someone being bullied, you shouldn't do anything—it's not your business.		
		Breaking the law is never okay, no matter the circumstances.		
		Sometimes it's hard to choose between doing what's right and doing what you want.		
		You should always help a person in need.		
		People who have ethical objections to scientific breakthroughs like genetic engineering are silly.		
		Shoplifting is barely a crime and is not worth worrying about.		
		People don't get all their values from their parents.		

Preview the Expert Project

Preview the **Expert Project** on pages 316–319. At the end of this workshop, you'll complete a multimedia presentation that takes a side on such important 21st century ethical issues as the right to privacy, cloning, animal rights, and capital punishment.

FAIRNESS VS. EMPATHY
Your best friend is terrible at math. He tries really hard and studies all the time, but he just doesn't get it. He asks if he can look at your paper during the next math test. You don't want him to fail . . . again. What do you do?

AMBITION VS. LOYALTY
You make extra money mowing lawns. Your best friend wants to work, too. He's not a very hard worker, though. Do you let him work with you?

SHORT-TERM VS. LONG-TERM
Your family doesn't have a lot of money, and you are expected to save your paper-route earnings for college. However, you are active and athletic and love skateboarding—you really want to buy a skateboard of your own. It's your money, after all. Do you spend it?

SECURITY VS. JUSTICE
There's a nation in another part of the world where a minority group is being killed in large numbers. The U.S. military is already overstretched. Should we intervene in another country's problem?

▶ What will you need to know or do to complete the Expert Project?

_____

_____

_____

_____

Explore Expert Space

Go to **www.expert21.com/student** to learn more about the topics in this workshop.

DISCOVER ONLINE
- Careers in Genetic Research
- Genetic Engineering
- Ethics

READ ONLINE
- O. Henry
- Modern Pirates
- Mary Shelley
- Cyber-Bullying

RESEARCH ONLINE
- Human Behavior
- Social Psychology
- Values

Personal Inquiry

Explore the topic of values and ethical dilemmas by asking your own questions. Return to add questions as you continue reading Workshop 8. Plan to revisit your questions.

21

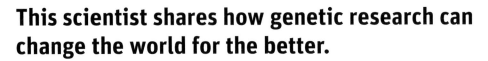

Jill Bargonetti: Genetic Scientist

This scientist shares how genetic research can change the world for the better.

"In scientific research, you go to school for a long time, and you don't earn a lot of money. But every decision can't be driven by money."

Dr. Jill Bargonetti works at the City University of New York studying the p53 gene, which plays a key role in 70 percent of cancers. Bargonetti experiments on human cancer cells and worms, but eventually the therapies she discovers may be tested on humans. Find out what ethical issues are important to a genetic scientist—and what inspires her to keep searching for a cure.

FACTS AND STATS

NAME: Jill Bargonetti

HOMETOWN: New York City

JOB: Professor and principal investigator of molecular genetics and biochemistry

EDUCATION: Ph.D., Molecular Biology; M.S., Molecular Biology; B.A., Biology

WORKPLACE: Hunter College and the Graduate Center at the City University of New York

SKILLS: Collaboration; understanding multiple perspectives; using scientific technology; finding mentors; leading a team

SALARY: $60,000–$100,000

CAREER CONNECTION **Health Science**
www.careerclusters.org

Go to 21 ToolKit **Expert File 6.23** to learn more about careers in health science.

RELATED JOBS: lab assistant, medical assistant, home health care attendant

Q: What is the p53 gene?

A: The p53 gene helps keep tumors from forming. In 70 percent of cancers, that gene isn't working properly. We look at ways to make the gene work or to kill cells in which it isn't functioning. We also try to understand why p53 does not always kill cancer cells.

Q: What is a typical day of research for you and the p53 gene?

A: Each graduate student who works with me has his or her own part of the project. I help them design their experiments. We study human cancer cells from patients and the germ cells in microscopic worms. Germ cells are a special type of cell that divides quickly, like cancer cells do. We treat the worms with drugs to see how those drugs affect the germ cells. Then we study whether the P53 gene makes those cells die.

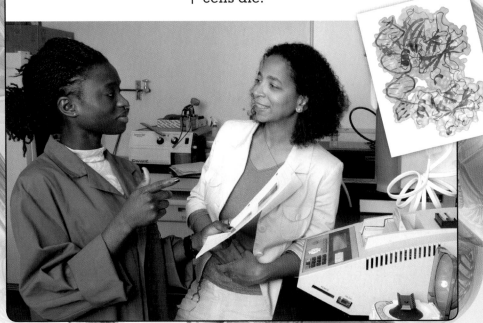

Q: Eventually, a successful result in your lab will mean that the drug will be tested on humans, not just on worms. How can you test drugs on human beings in an ethical way?

A: There are trial designs that make testing drugs in sick patients ethical. It is amazing how selfless some terminally ill patients are. However, it is only okay to try things that we all feel are going to deliver more benefit than harm. Therefore, testing on an animal model first is absolutely essential.

Q: What inspired you to become a researcher?

A: After high school, I became a counselor at a camp for children who were disabled or had birth defects. It was the hardest experience of my life. I could find ways to make them slightly more comfortable, but I couldn't change their situations or the rest of their lives. So, I became more interested in doing research that could change their situations.

Q: Gene therapy—which is basically "fixing" genes so that they work properly—is a way to help people with illnesses and birth defects. But we don't know all the consequences of this work. How do you decide what is ethical research to do?

A: These decisions have to be made on a case-by-case basis. We need groups of people from many walks of life to be educated in the science and human aspects of gene therapy. Those people need to be at the table making decisions like these—especially if the decisions are going to be written into the laws of the land. We need teamwork to address these types of issues!

Q: You could have gone to any institution in the world but chose to teach in an urban public college. What values prompted you to do that?

A: I didn't come from a scientific academic family, but two professors during my undergraduate years were mentors to me. They put the application for graduate school in front of me and made me fill it out. Today, I want to be a mentor, too. I thought it would be especially good for students of color to see someone like me in a role as a researcher, geneticist, and teacher.

ANALYZE WORKPLACE SKILLS

1. Lead a Team
How does Dr. Bargonetti lead her team? What does she do with her students?

_____

_____

_____

2. Analyze Multiple Perspectives
What is the perspective of each group on conducting clinical trials in humans? Dr. Bargonetti and other scientists:

_____

_____

Terminally ill patients:

_____

_____

3. Find Mentors
How did mentors help Dr. Bargonetti find her career?

_____

_____

_____

Why do you think Dr. Bargonetti mentions that she doesn't come from an academic family?

_____

_____

_____

DISCOVER ONLINE

 expert space
Go to **www.expert21.com/student** to learn more about Careers in Genetic Research; Genetic Engineering; Ethics.

Short Story

the LADY, or the TIGER?

How do we make terribly difficult decisions? In this story, a woman is faced with a wrenching test of the heart. What will she decide?

Have you ever been faced with a difficult choice? Describe the choice you faced, and explain how you reached a decision.

Theme LITERARY ANALYSIS

A story's theme is a message about life or human nature that the writer wants to share with the reader.

To find a story's theme, think about what the main character learns as a result of his or her experience.

▶ **Read the start of the tale "A Mysterious Heart." Then complete the chart.**

A Mysterious Heart

When Princess Keira met Sir Alberto, it was love at first sight. She knew right away that he was the most wonderful man she had ever met. Others saw something odd about him, though. Sir Alberto never spoke about friends, family, or the past. People wondered: Where was Sir Alberto from? What was in his past? Princess Keira's brother, Prince Kevin, was older than his sister and trusted people less than she did. He told Keira his doubts about Alberto, but she did not listen. Princess Keira liked the air of mystery surrounding Alberto. To her brother's dismay, Keira and Alberto quickly got engaged to marry.

What is the princess like?	What are possible consequences of her actions?

Given what you know about Princess Keira's character, what do you think the story's themes might be about?

Problem and Solution COMPREHENSION

Most stories focus on a **problem** that the characters face. Events in the story and the characters' actions and decisions may lead to a **solution** to the problem.

The characters' traits can help shape both the problem and its solution.

In "A Mysterious Heart," what problem does Prince Kevin, Keira's brother, face?

_____

Think about what Prince Kevin is like. Then describe one possible way in which he might try to solve his problem.

_____

_____

_____

_____

Academic Language VOCABULARY

▶ Rate your knowledge of each word. Then write its meaning and an example sentence.

Word	Meaning	Example
EXPERT WORDS *Use these words to write and talk about the workshop topic.*		
dilemma di•lem•ma *(noun)* ① ② ③ ④	a hard choice between two difficult alternatives	The imprisoned duke's dilemma was this: should he starve or eat the poisoned apple?
perception per•cep•tion *(noun)* ① ② ③ ④		
ACADEMIC WORDS *Use these words in all your subject classes.*		
fateful fate•ful *(adjective)* ① ② ③ ④	having an important and usually unpleasant effect on future events	
prior pri•or *(adjective)* ① ② ③ ④		
SELECTION WORDS *These words are key to understanding this selection.*		
agony ag•o•ny *(noun)* ① ② ③ ④		Jay is so shy that speaking in public causes him agony.
despise de•spise *(verb)* ① ② ③ ④		
devious de•vi•ous *(adjective)* ① ② ③ ④		
interfere in•ter•fere *(verb)* ① ② ③ ④		

Rating Scale   ① I don't know the word.   ② I've seen it or heard it.   ③ I know its meaning.   ④ I know it and use it.

Word Families WORD ANALYSIS

A word family is a group of words that share the same base word. Words in the same word family have related meanings. For example:

fate *(noun)*, meaning "the force some people believe determines events"

fated *(adjective)*, meaning "determined by fate"

fateful *(adjective)*, meaning "having an important and usually unpleasant effect on future events"

▶ **Three of the words below are in the same word family. Circle them.**

exit   excitement

excitable   excel

excite   excuse

the LADY, or the TIGER?

By Frank R. Stockton, adapted by Joy Nolan

Girl meets boy. Girl and boy fall in love. Girl's father forbids the love and presents a life-or-death choice.

In the very olden time, there lived an excitable and semi-barbaric king. He was happiest when things did not go as they should, for nothing pleased him more than to use his power to crush down trouble where he found it. His methods were strange and sometimes cruel, but he was king, and all did his bidding.

When one of his subjects was accused of a crime of sufficient importance to interest the king, the accused person would be judged publicly in the royal arena by chance. All the people in the kingdom would gather in the arena, as the king, surrounded by his court, sat upon his throne. At his signal, a door beneath him opened, and the accused man stepped out and bowed to the king. Directly across from the man, on the other side of the enclosed space, were two identical doors, side by side. The man on trial had to decide his fate by opening one. He could open either door. If he opened one door, a fierce, hungry tiger would spring out and tear him to pieces as punishment for his guilt. When a man's fate was decided thus, iron bells clanged, wails went up from the assembled crowd, and the vast audience, with bowed heads and downcast hearts, walked slowly homeward, mourning greatly that one so young and fair, or so old and respected, should have deserved so wretched an end.

However, if the accused man opened the other door, a beautiful maiden would come forth, and he would immediately marry her, as a reward for his innocence. It did not matter that he might already have a wife and family; the king allowed no such **prior** arrangements to **interfere** with his plan. The wedding would take place then and there, in the arena. A priest, followed by a band of singers and dancing maidens playing joyous wedding songs on golden horns, would marry the pair. After the wedding, brass bells would ring out in celebration as the people shouted glad hurrahs, and the innocent man would walk on a bed of flowers to take his new bride home.

> **clanged** *(v.)* made a loud ringing sound
> **wails** *(n.)* loud cries of sadness

This was the king's method of administering justice. It was perfectly fair. The accused did not know which door would lead to the lady, nor to the tiger. He opened the door of his choice, without having the slightest idea whether, in the next instant, he was to be devoured or married.

When the people gathered for a trial, they never knew whether they would witness a bloody killing or a joyous wedding. This uncertainty made the occasion twice as riveting. The custom was very popular, and the thoughtful citizens of the kingdom could bring no charge of unfairness against it; for did not the accused decide his own fate?

This king had a daughter who was as lively and untamed as he was. He loved her above all else.

In his court worked a young man of humble origins. He was unusually handsome and brave, as is common among romantic heroes who court royal maidens, and this royal maiden adored the young man. Their love deepened as time passed, until one day the king learned of their devotion to each other. The youth was immediately cast into prison, and a day was set for his trial in the arena. Never before had such a case occurred; never before had a subject dared to love the daughter of the king.

The enraged king ordered that the land be searched for the fiercest tiger that could be found, and the maidens throughout the land be carefully surveyed in order that the young man might have a fitting bride, should he live. Of course, he was guilty of the deed with which he was charged. He indeed loved the princess, and neither he, she, nor anyone else thought of denying the fact; but the king did not think of allowing this certainty to interfere with the workings of the court, in which he took such great delight and satisfaction. The youth would be disposed of one way or the other—he would be dead or married—and the king would take pleasure in making it happen.

The appointed day arrived. From far and near the people gathered and filled the arena. Crowds, unable to gain admittance, massed against its outside walls. The king and his court were in their places, opposite the **fateful** twin doors.

riveting *(adj.)* exciting
disposed of *(v.)* gotten rid of

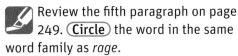

COMPREHENSION

Problem and Solution

Underline the problem the king discovers.

• How does the king plan to solve this problem?

_____

_____

_____

VOCABULARY/WORD ANALYSIS

Word Families

Review the fifth paragraph on page 249. (Circle) the word in the same word family as *rage*.

• What is the meaning of *enraged*?

_____

• Why was the king enraged?

_____

_____

_____

_____

LITERARY ANALYSIS

Theme

Based on the king's character traits and his behavior so far, what can you predict about the story's theme? Complete the chart.

What the king is like: _____

_____

_____

The king's actions: _____

_____

_____

The story's theme probably involves

_____

_____

All was ready. The signal was given. A door beneath the royal party opened, and the young man walked out. His appearance spurred a hum of admiration and anxiety. Many in the audience had not known so grand a youth had lived among them. No wonder the princess loved him! How terrible for him to be there!

As the youth advanced into the arena he turned, according to custom, to bow to the king, but his eyes were fixed upon his princess, who sat beside her father. Any lady more tender would not have been able to bear being present, but this princess could not stay away. She was terribly interested. From the moment the decree had gone forth that her beloved should meet his fate in the king's arena, she had thought of nothing else, night or day.

Through the power of her own will, and a hefty sum of gold, she had learned the secret of the day. She knew what lay behind each door: the tiger chosen for its ferocity and the lady chosen for her beauty and charm. Through these thick, heavily curtained doors, it was impossible that any noise or hint should come from within to the person outside who was to choose.

Not only did she know in which room stood the lady, but she knew who the lady was—one of the loveliest damsels of the court. The princess **despised** her. She had often seen, or imagined, this fair creature glancing at her beloved, and sometimes she thought he saw her loving looks, and even returned them. Now and then she had seen them talking, only for a moment, but much can be said in a moment. With all the intensity of the savage blood of her family line, the princess hated the lady who trembled behind that silent door.

When her beloved's eye met hers in the arena that day, he saw, by that power of quick **perception** between two souls who are one, that she knew behind which door crouched the tiger, and behind which stood the lady. He had expected her to know it. He understood her nature, and had known that she would never rest until

she learned this secret fact, hidden to all other onlookers, even to the king.

His nervous glance asked, "Which?" It was as plain to her as if he shouted it from where he stood. The question was asked in a flash; it must be answered in another.

Her right arm lay on the cushioned wall before her. She raised her hand and made a slight, quick movement toward the right. No one but her beloved saw her. Every eye was fixed on the man in the arena.

He turned, and with a firm and rapid step, strode across the empty space. Every heart stopped beating, every breath was held. Without hesitation, he went to the door on the right and opened it.

Now, the point of the story is this: Did the tiger come out of that door, or did the lady?

She had lost him, but who should have him?

The more we ponder this question, the harder it is to answer. It involves a study of the human heart, which leads us through **devious** mazes of passion, out of which it is difficult to find our way.

Consider, dear reader, not what you would have done, but instead that hot-blooded, semi-barbaric princess, her soul suffering the combined fires of despair and jealousy. She had lost him, but who should have him?

How often she had imagined in horror her beloved opening the door to meet the cruel fangs of the tiger!

And how much oftener had she imagined him at the other door! How she had gnashed her teeth and torn her hair when she saw his start of delight as he opened the door of the lady! How her soul had burned in **agony** when she had seen him rush to lead forth that damsel, his whole frame lit with the joy of recovered life; when she had heard the wild ringing of the happy bells; when she had seen them made man and wife, and watched them walk away together upon their path of flowers, followed by the tremendous shouts of the joyful multitude, in which her one despairing shriek was lost and drowned!

---

decree (n.) an official order given by a leader
beloved (n.) someone who is loved romantically by someone else

Would it not be better for him to die at once? And yet, that awful tiger, those shrieks, that blood!

The princess considered her **dilemma** for what seemed like eternity. Her decision had been made after days and nights of anguished deliberation. She had known she would be asked, she had decided how to respond, and, without hesitation, she had moved her hand to the right.

The question of her decision is not to be considered lightly, and I shall not presume to present myself as the one person able to answer it. And so I leave it with all of you: Which came out of the opened door: the lady, or the tiger? ■

> **Predict**
> **What do you think happens next?**

anguished *(adj.)* suffering from pain and sadness
deliberation *(n.)* careful decision making

Read and Synthesize

CRITICAL THINKING

Analyze
Think about the princess's actions before and during the trial. What do they tell you about her character?

_____

_____

_____

LITERARY ANALYSIS

Theme
Describe the dilemma the princess faces within her own heart.

_____

_____

How does the princess's dilemma reflect the theme of the story?

_____

_____

[21] SMALL GROUPS/INDEPENDENT

COLLABORATE

Examine Perspectives Imagine the young man's thoughts as he approaches the two doors. Which door do you think he hopes to open?

COMMUNICATE

Discuss and Write With a partner, discuss whether you think the princess directed the young man to the lady or to the tiger. Jot down your thoughts. Then write a paragraph expressing your view.

W

READ ONLINE

expert space
Go to **www.expert21.com/student**
to learn more about Frank R. Stockton;
The Judicial System; Criminal Justice.

Short Story

A RETRIEVED REFORMATION

Jimmy Valentine, a former bank robber, is out of jail and trying to lead an honest life. Has Jimmy really changed his ways, or is he putting on a show?

[W] **QuickWrite**

What's your opinion: Can people change their behavior so much that they become like different people, or are such changes never true and lasting? Support your opinion with reasons and examples.

Plot and Character   LITERARY ANALYSIS

The series of events in a story is called the plot.

The elements of a plot include

- a **conflict**, or struggle.
- a **resolution**, or outcome.

Often a plot will focus on one main **character**. The character's **traits** are revealed by

- the conflict he or she faces.
- the way he or she resolves the conflict.

▶ **Read this passage from "A Retrieved Reformation." Then complete the activities.**

> A guard came to the prison shoe shop, where Jimmy Valentine was assiduously stitching uppers, and escorted him to the front office. There the warden handed Jimmy his pardon, which had been signed that morning by the governor. Jimmy took it in a tired kind of way. He had served nearly ten months of a four-year sentence. He had expected to stay only about three months, at the longest. When a man with as many friends on the outside as Jimmy Valentine had is received in the "stir" it is hardly worthwhile to cut his hair.
>
> "Now, Valentine," said the warden, "you'll go out in the morning. Brace up, and make a man of yourself. You're not a bad fellow at heart. Stop cracking safes, and live straight."
>
> "Me?" said Jimmy, in surprise. "Why, I never cracked a safe in my life."

What conflict has Jimmy Valentine been facing?

_____

What does this conflict reveal about Jimmy?

_____

Sequence of Events   COMPREHENSION

The events in a story help to move the plot along. Their **sequence** is often important to the plot.

In a story, the author usually tells the events in the order they happen. However, sometimes the author includes **flashbacks**, or scenes from the past, to give the reader background information.

▶ **Put the events below in sequence by numbering them from 1 to 5.**

____ John dropped his ticket on the floor during lunch.

____ Tom was sad when tickets for the game sold out.

____ Tom listened to John brag about getting a ticket to the game.

____ Tom finds the ticket and must decide whether to keep it or return it to John.

____ Tom had been saving money for weeks to buy a ticket to the game.

Academic Language VOCABULARY

▶ Rate your knowledge of each word. Then write its meaning and an example sentence.

Word	Meaning	Example
EXPERT WORD *Use this word to write and talk about the workshop topic.*		
retribution *ret•ri•bu•tion (noun)* ① ② ③ ④	punishment that is deserved	The thief escaped retribution for stealing the car.
ACADEMIC WORDS *Use these words in all your subject classes.*		
interval *in•ter•val (noun)* ① ② ③ ④		
leisurely *lei•sure•ly (adverb)* ① ② ③ ④		
SELECTION WORDS *These words are key to understanding this selection.*		
elusive *e•lu•sive (adjective)* ① ② ③ ④		
eminent *em•i•nent (adjective)* ① ② ③ ④		The eminent football hero visited Eric's school and gave his team a pep talk.
genially *ge•nial•ly (adverb)* ① ② ③ ④		
saunter *saun•ter (verb)* ① ② ③ ④		
swiftly *swift•ly (adverb)* ① ② ③ ④	in a very fast manner; quickly	

Rating Scale ① I don't know the word. ② I've seen it or heard it. ③ I know its meaning. ④ I know it and use it.

Word Families WORD ANALYSIS

A group of words sharing a common base word is called a **word family**.

Recognizing word families can help you figure out the meanings of unfamiliar words.

What base word do the words *disprove* and *provable* share?

_____

One meaning of the prefix *dis–* is "do the opposite of." What does *disprove* mean?

_____

The suffix *–able* means "capable of being." What does *provable* mean?

_____

Jimmy Valentine, a reformed bank robber, is earning an honest living in a quiet town. Then one day, he is faced with a crucial decision in front of a bank vault.

A RETRIEVED REFORMATION

By O. Henry

A guard came to the prison shoe shop, where Jimmy Valentine was assiduously stitching uppers, and escorted him to the front office. There the warden handed Jimmy his pardon, which had been signed that morning by the governor. Jimmy took it in a tired kind of way. He had served nearly ten months of a four-year sentence. He had expected to stay only about three months, at the longest. When a man with as many friends on the outside as Jimmy Valentine had is received in the "stir" it is hardly worthwhile to cut his hair.

"Now, Valentine," said the warden, "you'll go out in the morning. Brace up, and make a man of yourself. You're not a bad fellow at heart. Stop cracking safes, and live straight."

"Me?" said Jimmy, in surprise. "Why, I never cracked a safe in my life."

"Oh, no," laughed the warden. "Of course not. Let's see, now. How was it you happened to get sent up on that Springfield job? Was it because you wouldn't prove an alibi for fear of compromising somebody in extremely high-toned society? Or was it simply a case of a mean old jury that had it in for you? It's always one or the other with you innocent victims."

"Me?" said Jimmy, still blankly virtuous. "Why, warden, I never was in Springfield in my life!"

"Take him back, Cronin," smiled the warden, "and fix him up with outgoing clothes. Unlock him at seven in the morning, and let him come to the bull-pen. Better think over my advice, Valentine."

At a quarter past seven on the next morning Jimmy stood in the warden's outer office. He had on a suit of the villainously fitting, ready-made clothes and a pair of the stiff, squeaky shoes that the state furnishes to its discharged compulsory guests.

---

assiduously (adv.) in a hardworking way
compulsory (adj.) required

The clerk handed him a railroad ticket and the five-dollar bill with which the law expected him to rehabilitate himself into good citizenship and prosperity. The warden shook his hand. Valentine, prisoner #9762, was chronicled on the books "Pardoned by Governor," and Mr. James Valentine walked out into the sunshine.

Disregarding the song of the birds, the waving green trees, and the smell of the flowers, Jimmy headed straight for a restaurant. There he tasted the first sweet joys of liberty in the shape of a chicken dinner. From there he proceeded **leisurely** to the depot. He tossed a quarter into the hat of a blind man sitting by the door, and boarded his train. Three hours set him down in a little town near the state line. He went to the café of one Mike Dolan and shook hands with Mike, who was alone behind the bar.

"Sorry we couldn't make it sooner, Jimmy, my boy," said Mike. "But we had that protest from Springfield to buck against, and the governor nearly balked. Feeling all right?"

"Fine," said Jimmy. "Got my key?"

He got his key and went upstairs, unlocking the door of a room at the rear. Everything was just as he had left it. There on the floor was still Ben Price's collar-button that had been torn from that **eminent** detective's shirt-band when they had overpowered Jimmy to arrest him.

Pulling out from the wall a folding-bed, Jimmy slid back a panel in the wall and dragged out a dust-covered suitcase. He opened this and gazed fondly at the finest set of burglar's tools in the East. It was a complete set, made of specially tempered steel, the latest design in drills, punches, braces and bits, jimmies, clamps, and augers, with two or three novelties, invented by Jimmy himself, in which he took pride. Over nine hundred dollars they had cost him to have made at ——, a place where they make such things for the profession.

In half an hour Jimmy went downstairs and through the café. He was now dressed in tasteful and well-fitting clothes, and carried his dusted and cleaned suitcase in his hand.

"Got anything on?" asked Mike Dolan, **genially.**

"Me?" said Jimmy, in a puzzled tone. "I don't understand. I'm representing the New York Amalgamated Short Snap Biscuit Cracker and Frazzled Wheat Company."

> *Jimmy slid back a panel in the wall and dragged out a dust-covered suitcase. He opened this and gazed fondly at the finest set of burglar's tools in the East.*

> **Make Inferences**
> What do these details reveal about Jimmy Valentine's personality?

This statement delighted Mike to such an extent that Jimmy had to take a seltzer-and-milk on the spot.

---

pardoned *(v.)* granted release
augers *(n.)* drill-like tools

A week after the release of Valentine, 9762, there was a neat job of safe-burglary done in Richmond, Indiana, with no clue to the author. A scant eight hundred dollars was all that was secured. Two weeks after that a patented, improved, burglar-proof safe in Logansport was opened like a cheese to the tune of fifteen hundred dollars, currency; securities and silver untouched. That began to interest the rogue catchers. Then an old-fashioned bank-safe in Jefferson City became active and threw out of its crater an eruption of banknotes amounting to five thousand dollars. The losses were now high enough to bring the matter up into Ben Price's class of work. By comparing notes, a remarkable similarity in the methods of the burglaries was noticed. Ben Price investigated the scenes of the robberies, and was heard to remark:

"That's Dandy Jim Valentine's autograph. He's resumed business. Look at that combination knob—jerked out as easy as pulling up a radish in wet weather. He's got the only clamps that can do it. And look how clean those tumblers were punched out! Jimmy never has to drill but one hole. Yes, I guess I want Mr. Valentine. He'll do his bit next time without any short-time or clemency foolishness."

Ben Price knew Jimmy's habits. He had learned them while working up the Springfield case. Long jumps, quick getaways, no confederates, and a taste for good society—these ways had helped Mr. Valentine to become noted as a successful dodger of **retribution**. It was given out that Ben Price had taken up the trail of the **elusive** cracksman, and other people with burglar-proof safes felt more at ease.

One afternoon Jimmy Valentine and his suitcase climbed out of the mail hack in Elmore, a little town five miles off the railroad down in the blackjack country of Arkansas. Jimmy, looking like an athletic young senior just home from college, went down the board sidewalk toward the hotel.

A young lady crossed the street, passed him at the corner, and entered a door over which was the sign "The Elmore Bank." Jimmy Valentine looked into her eyes, forgot what he was, and became another man. She lowered her eyes and colored slightly. Young men of Jimmy's style and looks were scarce in Elmore.

Jimmy collared a boy that was loafing on the steps of the bank as if he were one of the stockholders, and began to question him about the town, feeding him dimes at **intervals**. By and by the young lady came out, looking royally unconscious of the young man with the suitcase, and went her way.

"Isn't that young lady Miss Polly Simpson?" asked Jimmy, with specious guile.

---

clemency (n.) mercy shown toward the accused
specious (adj.) seemingly good, but with false intentions

VOCABULARY/WORD ANALYSIS

Word Families

Review the first paragraph on page 256. (Circle) the word that is in the same word family as *prospering*, which means "being successful."

- What base word do these words share?

_____

- How would the law expect Jimmy to achieve prosperity?

_____

_____

_____

LITERARY ANALYSIS

Plot and Character

<u>Underline</u> the details on page 257 that explain why Ben Price suspects Jimmy of robbing banks again.

- What does Ben Price's statement tell you about his character?

_____

_____

_____

_____

- How might these character traits advance the story's plot?

_____

_____

_____

_____

_____

COMPREHENSION

Sequence of Events

Review page 257. Draw a box around the paragraph that contains a flashback explaining how Ben Price knows Jimmy Valentine.

"Naw," said the boy, "She's Annabel Adams. Her pa owns this bank. What'd you come to Elmore for? Is that a gold watch-chain? I'm going to get a bulldog. Got any more dimes?"

Jimmy went to the Planters' Hotel, registered as Ralph D. Spencer, and engaged a room. He leaned on the desk and declared his platform to the clerk. He said he had come to Elmore to look for a location to go into business. How was the shoe business, now, in the town? He had thought of the shoe business. Was there an opening?

The clerk was impressed by the clothes and manner of Jimmy. He, himself, was something of a pattern of fashion to the thinly gilded youth of Elmore, but he now perceived his shortcomings. While trying to figure out Jimmy's manner of tying his four-in-hand, he cordially gave information.

Yes, there ought to be a good opening in the shoe line. There wasn't an exclusive shoe store in the place. The dry-goods and general stores handled them. Business in all lines was fairly good. Hoped Mr. Spencer would decide to locate in Elmore. He would find it a pleasant town to live in, and the people very sociable.

Mr. Spencer thought he would stop over in the town a few days and look over the situation. No, the clerk needn't call the boy. He would carry up his suitcase, himself; it was rather heavy.

Mr. Ralph Spencer, the phoenix[1] that arose from Jimmy Valentine's ashes—ashes left by the flame of a sudden and alterative attack of love—remained in Elmore, and prospered. He opened a shoe store and secured a good run of trade.

> **Clarify**
> **Why does the author refer to Ralph Spencer as "the phoenix"?**

Socially he was also a success and made many friends. And he accomplished the wish of his heart. He met Miss Annabel Adams and became more and more captivated by her charms.

At the end of a year the situation of Mr. Ralph Spencer was this: he had won the respect of the community, his shoe store was flourishing, and he and Annabel were engaged to be married in two weeks. Mr. Adams, the typical, plodding country banker, approved of Spencer. Annabel's pride in him almost equaled her affection. He was as much at home in the family of Mr. Adams and that of Annabel's married sister as if he were already a member.

---

[1] A phoenix is a mythical bird that burns itself at the end of its life and is born again from the ashes.

> **platform** *(n.)* the aims of a person or a group
> **alterative** *(adj.)* having the ability to make someone or something change

COMPREHENSION

Sequence of Events

Underline the sentence that tells you how much time has passed between Jimmy first seeing Annabel and the end of the page. Why did the author condense so much time into such a short space?

_____

_____

_____

_____

LITERARY ANALYSIS

Plot and Character

What do Ralph Spencer's experiences in Elmore tell you about his character?

_____

_____

_____

_____

• How does this contribute to the plot?

_____

_____

_____

_____

21 SMALL GROUPS/INDEPENDENT

COLLABORATE

Make Decisions Do you think Jimmy should tell Annabel and her family the truth about his past? Discuss your opinion and reasons with a partner.

COMMUNICATE

React and Write Do you think a person can change his or her life by assuming a new identity? Jot down ideas. Then write a paragraph expressing your view.

One day Jimmy sat down in his room and wrote this letter, which he mailed to the safe address of one of his old friends in St. Louis:

> *"I'm making an honest living, and I'm going to marry the finest girl on Earth two weeks from now."*

Dear Old Pal:

I want you to be at Sullivan's place, in Little Rock, next Wednesday night, at nine o'clock. I want you to wind up some little matters for me. And, also, I want to make you a present of my kit of tools. I know you'll be glad to get them—you couldn't duplicate the lot for a thousand dollars. Say, Billy, I've quit the old business—a year ago. I've got a nice store. I'm making an honest living, and I'm going to marry the finest girl on Earth two weeks from now. It's the only life, Billy—the straight one. I wouldn't touch a dollar of another man's money now for a million. After I get married I'm going to sell out and go West, where there won't be so much danger of having old scores brought up against me. I tell you, Billy, she's an angel. She believes in me; and I wouldn't do another crooked thing for the whole world. Be sure to be at Sully's, for I must see you. I'll bring along the tools with me.

Your old friend,

Jimmy

On the Monday night after Jimmy wrote this letter, Ben Price jogged unobtrusively into Elmore in a livery buggy. He lounged about town in his quiet way until he found out what he wanted to know. From the drugstore across the street from Spencer's shoe store he got a good look at Ralph D. Spencer.

Make Inferences
Why is Ben Price in Elmore?

"Going to marry the banker's daughter are you, Jimmy?" said Ben to himself, softly. "Well, I don't know!"

The next morning Jimmy took breakfast at the Adamses. He was going to Little Rock that day to order his wedding suit and buy something nice for Annabel. That would be the first time he had left town since he came to Elmore. It had been more than a year now since those last professional "jobs," and he thought he could safely venture out.

duplicate *(v.)* make a copy	
unobtrusively *(adv.)* without attracting attention	

After breakfast quite a family party went downtown together—Mr. Adams, Annabel, Jimmy, and Annabel's married sister with her two little girls, aged five and nine. They came by the hotel where Jimmy still boarded, and he ran up to his room and brought along his suitcase. Then they went on to the bank. There stood Jimmy's horse and buggy and Dolph Gibson, who was going to drive him over to the railroad station.

All went inside the high, carved oak railings into the banking room—Jimmy included, for Mr. Adams's future son-in-law was welcome anywhere. The clerks were pleased to be greeted by the good-looking, agreeable young man who was going to marry Miss Annabel. Jimmy set his suitcase down. Annabel, whose heart was bubbling with happiness and lively youth, put on Jimmy's hat and picked up the suitcase. "Wouldn't I make a nice drummer?" said Annabel. "My! Ralph, how heavy it is. Feels like it was full of gold bricks."

"Lot of nickel-plated shoehorns in there," said Jimmy, coolly, "that I'm going to return. Thought I'd save express charges by taking them up. I'm getting awfully economical."

The Elmore Bank had just put in a new safe and vault. Mr. Adams was very proud of it, and insisted on an inspection by everyone. The vault was a small one, but it had a new, patented door. It fastened with three solid steel bolts thrown simultaneously with a single handle, and had a time lock. Mr. Adams beamingly explained its workings to Mr. Spencer, who showed a courteous but not too intelligent interest. The two children, May and Agatha, were delighted by the shining metal and funny clock and knobs.

While they were thus engaged Ben Price **sauntered** in and leaned on his elbow, looking casually inside between the railings. He told the teller that he didn't want anything; he was just waiting for a man he knew.

Suddenly there was a scream or two from the women, and a commotion. Unperceived by the elders, May, the nine-year-old girl, in a spirit of play, had shut Agatha in the vault. She had then shot the bolts and turned the knob of the combination as she had seen Mr. Adams do.

The old banker sprang to the handle and tugged at it for a moment. "The door can't be opened," he groaned. "The clock hasn't been wound nor the combination set."

Agatha's mother screamed again, hysterically.

"Hush!" said Mr. Adams, raising his trembling hand. "All be quiet for a moment. Agatha!" he called as loudly as he could. "Listen to me." During the following silence they could just hear the faint sound of the child wildly shrieking in the dark vault in a panic of terror.

> **courteous** *(adj.)* polite and considerate
> **commotion** *(n.)* a noisy disturbance

VOCABULARY/WORD ANALYSIS

Word Families

 Circle the word *unperceived* in the sixth paragraph on page 261.

• What is the base word?

_____

• What does the base word mean?

_____

• What does "unperceived by the elders" mean?

_____

LITERARY ANALYSIS

Plot and Character

Reread the last four paragraphs on page 261. What event creates a conflict in the story?

_____
_____
_____
_____
_____
_____
_____

• How does this external conflict create an internal conflict for Jimmy?

_____
_____
_____
_____
_____
_____
_____
_____

"My precious darling!" wailed the mother. "She will die of fright! Open the door! Oh, break it open! Can't you men do something?"

"There isn't a man nearer than Little Rock who can open that door," said Mr. Adams, in a shaky voice. "My God! Spencer, what shall we do? That child—she can't stand it long in there. There isn't enough air, and, besides, she'll go into convulsions from fright."

Agatha's mother, frantic now, beat the door of the vault with her hands. Somebody wildly suggested dynamite. Annabel turned to Jimmy, her large eyes full of anguish, but not yet despairing. To a woman nothing seems quite impossible to the powers of the man she worships.

"Can't you do something, Ralph—try, won't you?"

He looked at her with a strange, soft smile on his lips and in his keen eyes.

"Annabel," he said, "give me that rose you are wearing, will you?"

Hardly believing that she heard him right, she unpinned the bud from the bosom of her dress, and placed it in his hand. Jimmy stuffed it into his vest pocket, threw off his coat and pulled up his shirt sleeves. With that act Ralph D. Spencer passed away and Jimmy Valentine took his place.

"Get away from the door, all of you," he commanded, shortly.

He set his suitcase on the table, and opened it out flat. From that time on he seemed to be unconscious of the presence of anyone else. He laid out the shining implements **swiftly** and orderly, whistling softly to himself as he always did when at work. In a deep silence and immovable, the others watched him as if under a spell.

In a minute Jimmy's pet drill was biting smoothly into the steel door. In ten minutes—breaking his own burglarious record—he threw back the bolts and opened the door.

Agatha, almost collapsed but safe, was gathered into her mother's arms.

Jimmy Valentine put on his coat and walked outside the railings toward the front door. As he went he thought he heard a faraway voice that he once knew call "Ralph!" But he never hesitated.

> **Make Inferences**
> Which character would call out "Ralph!" and why?

At the door a big man stood somewhat in his way.

---

convulsions *(n.)* uncontrolled spasms
immovable *(adj.)* unmoving

"Hello, Ben!" said Jimmy, still with his strange smile. "Got around at last, have you? Well, let's go. I don't know that it makes much difference, now."

And then Ben Price acted rather strangely.

"Guess you're mistaken, Mr. Spencer," he said. "Don't believe I recognize you. Your buggy's waiting for you, ain't it?"

And Ben Price turned and strolled down the street. ■

CAREER CONNECTION **Finance**
www.careerclusters.org

Go to **21 ToolKit Expert File 6.21** to learn more about careers in finance.

WHO O. Henry, born William Sidney Porter

BORN September 11, 1862, in Greensboro, North Carolina

ADVICE TO WRITERS "Write what you like; there is no other rule."

AUTHOR FILE

FAMILY He was the only child of Algernon Sidney Porter, a physician, and Mary Jane Virginia Swaim Porter. His mother died of tuberculosis when he was only three years old. Porter married Athol Estes, and they had a daughter, Margaret. His wife also died of tuberculosis in July 1897.

CAREER Pharmacist, draftsman (person who makes technical drawings for architects and engineers), bank teller, cartoonist, editor, column writer.

BIG BREAK After serving three years in prison for embezzling money from First National of Austin, the bank where he worked, Porter wrote and published one short story per week under the pen name O. Henry. His work was in high demand among New York publishers, allowing him to have a successful and lasting career as an author.

embezzling *(v.)* taking money that isn't yours that you are supposed to be protecting

---

Read and Synthesize

LITERARY ANALYSIS

Plot and Character

After opening the safe, why do you think Jimmy begins to walk away and ignore Annabel?

_____

_____

_____

_____

CRITICAL THINKING

Analyze

At the end of the story, do you think Ben Price did the right thing?

_____

_____

_____

_____

_____

21 SMALL GROUPS/INDEPENDENT

COLLABORATE

Examine Perspectives With a group, role-play a conversation that might take place between Jimmy and the Adamses right after the story ends.

COMMUNICATE

React and Write Do you feel that Jimmy still has a chance to live a good, honest life? After outlining your thoughts, write a short paragraph that supports your opinion with reasons and examples.

W

READ ONLINE

**expert space**
Go to **www.expert21.com/student** to learn more about O. Henry; O. Henry Award; Phoenix.

Adapted from PBS.org

New Brand of High-Seas Pirates Lurks Off Somali Coast By Alex Seitz

Old-fashioned high-seas swashbuckling has made an alarming 21ˢᵗ century resurgence in parts of the world, and for mariners, the threat of pirates is real.

It's not a Hollywood movie or a 19ᵗʰ century novel: pirates have attacked hundreds of ships in recent times. In April 2009, they hijacked an American cargo ship and held its captain, Richard Phillips, hostage for five days before snipers from the U.S. Navy SEALS were able to shoot down three of the hijackers and rescue Phillips.

In 2007, pirates attacked 263 ships, held more than 150 sailors hostage, and killed more than a dozen people, according to the International Maritime Bureau (IMB).

Pirates Thrive Off Chaos

Nowhere is the pirate problem worse than in waters off the coast of Somalia in East Africa. The war-torn country, located at the entrance to one of the world's busiest shipping lanes, has been without a functioning government since 1991. With no authority to rein in rogue ships, attacks have become increasingly brazen in recent years. While pirates used to simply raid ships for the cash kept in onboard safes, they have begun capturing entire boats and holding the crews hostage for ransom.

Somali pirates search for their next victims.

The world's most pirated waters are off the coast of Somalia in East Africa.

Area of major pirate activity

SAUDI ARABIA

YEMEN

ERITREA

Red Sea

SUDAN

Gulf of Aden

ETHIOPIA

INDIAN OCEAN

SOMALIA

KENYA

---

rogue *(adj.)* behaving in an abnormal, destructive way
brazen *(adj.)* obvious; bold

Pirate "Mother Ships"

Modern pirates use modern weapons like assault rifles and rocket-propelled grenades to hold ships hostage.

Pirates have also begun using other captured boats as "mother ships" from which to launch attacks hundreds of nautical miles offshore. The hijackers then steer the captured ships into Somali waters so they cannot be pursued.

Pirates have used distress flares to lure ships close to shore, and out of international waters, before ambushing them. Seafaring gunmen have even attacked boats bringing much-needed aid to poverty- and famine-stricken Somalia itself.

Not Like Johnny Depp

Observers warn that modern pirates are very different from fictional characters, like Johnny Depp's popular Jack Sparrow character from the *Pirates of the Caribbean* franchise.

"These are ruthless people who are heavily armed," said the director of the IMB, Captain Pottengal Mukundan. "There's nothing romantic about piracy."

Most pirates claim they are wrongly accused. They say they are local protectors trying to support their villages. "We were forced into this role," say Somali pirate Ali Sugule. "We were fishermen. But ships from other countries fish our coasts illegally, destroy our nets, and fire on whoever approaches them. They even dump toxic waste. We couldn't work. So we decided to defend ourselves."

Most observers are not convinced. Juman Muita was a crew member on a boat captured by Somali pirates. "[They] are better armed, and they want ransom, not just our goods," Muita warns. "These pirates are worse than the pirates we read about in history books." ■

Modern pirates are very different from fictional characters such as Johnny Depp's Jack Sparrow.

CRITICAL THINKING

Analyze

Ali Sugule states that the Somali pirates were forced into their role and were capturing boats and demanding ransom for sailors to feed their villages. However, Somali pirates have attacked ships carrying food aid meant for the country. What do you think is the reason for the increase in piracy along Somalia's coast?

_____
_____
_____
_____
_____
_____
_____
_____
_____
_____
_____

NAVIGATING TEXT

Text Features and Visual Features

Look at the map on page 264. How does this visual feature contribute to your understanding of the text?

_____
_____
_____
_____
_____
_____
_____
_____
_____
_____

READ ONLINE

expert space
Go to **www.expert21.com/student** to learn more about Modern Pirates; Somalia.

Think Across Texts

Organize and Synthesize

1. Complete this chart using information from "The Lady, or the Tiger?" and "A Retrieved Reformation."

	Describe the dilemma each character faces
The princess in "The Lady, or the Tiger?":	
Jimmy Valentine in "A Retrieved Reformation":	

Compare and Evaluate

2. Think about Jimmy Valentine in "A Retrieved Reformation" and the pirates in "New Brand of High-Seas Pirates Lurks Off Somali Coast." How are they alike in their behavior? How are they different? Fill in the chart below.

Jimmy Valentine	Both	The pirates
	Steal what isn't theirs	

3. In the three readings in this inquiry, which offers the most ethical model of behavior? Select a fictional character you read about or one of the Somali pirates, and explain why this person's sense of ethics is most correct.

_____

_____

_____

4. Each selection presents ideas about what is right and wrong. For each one, write a sentence that sums up each view of right and wrong.

"The Lady, or the Tiger?"

_____

_____

_____

"A Retrieved Reformation":

_____

_____

_____

"New Brand of High-Seas Pirates":

_____

_____

_____

Discuss and Write

5. Discuss how the three readings in "Classic Questions" helped you understand what it means to live ethically. Then write a response to the question *What rules should we live by?*

Apply Word Knowledge

Word Lab

1. **Name it.** Think of an object or activity you **despise**. Describe it, and explain why you feel this way.

_____

_____

2. **Describe them.** Give an example of each.

• an occasion when you might **saunter**

_____

• something that might fill a person with **agony**

_____

3. **Check it.** What would be likely to interfere with your ability to do homework **swiftly**? Check two.

❏ a dictionary or thesaurus
❏ a ringing cell phone
❏ the television
❏ a sharp pencil

4. **Think about it.** Imagine that someone has hurt your best friend's feelings. Would you want that person to face **retribution**? Why or why not?

_____

_____

_____

5. **Select one.** If someone has excellent **perception,** he or she

Ⓐ tends to be imaginative and artistic.

Ⓑ notices and understands things quickly.

Ⓒ always has a great sense of humor.

Ⓓ is very good at making friends.

6. **Finish them.** Complete the sentences below with the words **eminent, prior,** and **elusive.**

The _____ biologist Dr. Sonia Semenovsky flew to South America. She was searching for an _____ butterfly species that lived only in the Amazon rain forest. _____ to Dr. Semenovsky's trip, scientists had not seen the butterfly for almost twenty years.

Word Analysis

7. What is the root word of _leisurely_?

_____

• Meaning: _____
• How does adding the suffix -_ly_ change the part of speech?

_____

_____

8. Circle at least three words below that are in the same word family.

ingenuity   congenial   genius

genial   congeal   genially

What base word do all three words share?

_____

Make Decisions

CAREER CONNECTION Human Services
www.careerclusters.org

Go to **21** ToolKit **Expert File 6.25** to learn more about jobs that help people make decisions.

You will face dilemmas, or difficult choices, throughout your life. Thinking through the situation and looking at your options can help you decide.

Resolving a Dilemma

▶ **Erika had to resolve a dilemma. See how she did it below.**

Situation: Erika and her friend Kevin are in the local pharmacy. Erika likes the owner; they've known each other for years. Erika buys a magazine, and then she and Kevin leave. Then Kevin pulls a pair of sunglasses out of his pocket.

"Where did that come from?" Erika asks.

"I took it," Kevin says.

"That's not right," Erika says.

"Whatever," Kevin says. "It's called the five-finger discount. I do it all the time."

This store is monitored by Closed Circuit TV Cameras

SHOPLIFTING: Should I Report My Friend For Stealing?

Pros	Cons
I know it's not right to shoplift; I have to do something about it.	It's just $10 sunglasses. It's not worth upsetting Kevin or the store owner.
Kevin isn't going to stop, because he admits that he does it all the time.	There are other ways to deal with the problem, like shaming Kevin into returning them.
Kevin might start committing more serious crimes if no one stops him from committing a small crime.	It would be personally embarrassing for me, and Kevin would tell people that I told on him.

Questions to Consider:
Could I live with myself if I didn't turn Kevin in?
Would I be helping or hurting Kevin by turning him in?
Is there a better way to help Kevin correct his behavior?

ERIKA'S DECISION: Erika reviews the pros and cons and thinks about the answers to her questions. She decides that she will turn Kevin in because she doesn't think it is right for people to steal. If anyone tells her she was wrong, she'll explain that she believes stealing is worse than telling on someone, even a friend.

Here's How ▶ **Follow these steps to help make a decision:**

Step 1 **Identify the situation.** What decision do you have to make?

Step 2 **List arguments for and against.** Think about the pros and cons of each choice. If appropriate, ask: What do experts or other people believe?

Step 3 **Ask yourself questions.** Think about the issues that are important to you.

Step 4 **Make the best decision.** Review the pros and cons and the answers to the questions you asked. Think about whether the positive effects outweigh any negative ones. You may have to think of another option if you can't make a decision.

Apply: Resolving a Dilemma About Winning

▶ Christy has just won the Washburn High annual poetry contest. All 700 students in the school were required to enter. So she should be thrilled to win—but she's not. She hadn't had time to write her own poem, and her cousin had written one for her.

1. **Identify the situation.** What choice is Christy faced with?

_____

_____

2. **List arguments for and against.** Complete the chart with the pros and cons of each option.

CHOICES	PROS	CONS

3. **Ask yourself questions.** List three questions that Christy should ask herself.

_____

_____

_____

4. **Make the best decision.** If you were Christy, how would you resolve the dilemma?

_____

_____

Explain why you made that decision.

_____

_____

Magazine Article

To **CHEAT** or **NOT** To **CHEAT**

With students facing ever-increasing pressure to excel in school, the temptation to cheat can be strong. What can be done to stop cheating? Read this article to find out.

 **QuickWrite**

Is cheating ever acceptable, or is it always wrong, no matter what the circumstances? Give specific reasons or examples to support your response.

Problem and Solution COMPREHENSION

Writers of nonfiction often present a **problem** and one or more **solutions**.

As you read, analyze the causes of problems. Evaluate solutions by asking yourself these questions:

- Will each solution work? Why or why not?

- Is there a better solution?

▶ **Read this passage from "To Cheat or Not to Cheat." Then respond to the questions that follow.**

> Low-tech tactics work in the classroom, too. In a 1998 study conducted at two public colleges, Oregon State University economics professor Joe Kerkvliet found that students were 31 percent more likely to cheat in courses taught by teaching assistants—graduate students or adjunct professors—than those taught by tenured or tenure-track faculty. . . . By offering multiple versions of the same test, so students can't share answers with friends in different sections, adding extra proctors, and giving verbal warnings that cheaters will be punished, Kerkvliet has reduced cheating in his classes to practically zero.

- **Underline two solutions to the problem of cheating.**
- **Which other solutions do you think might work?**

_____

_____

_____

Evaluate Evidence NAVIGATING TEXT

Evidence is information used to support points. Writers may present several types of evidence:

- **facts**

- **statistics** (facts expressed as numbers or percentages)

- **examples**

- **expert opinions**

To evaluate evidence, ask yourself: Is the evidence reliable? Does it support the writer's point?

▶ **According to the passage above, in what kinds of classes are students more likely to cheat?**

_____

What evidence does the author present to support this point?

_____

Do you think this evidence is reliable? Why or why not?

_____

_____

_____

Academic Language `VOCABULARY`

▶ **Rate your knowledge of each word. Then write its meaning and an example sentence.**

Word	Meaning	Example
EXPERT WORD *Use this word to write and talk about the workshop topic.*		
integrity in·teg·ri·ty *(noun)* ① ② ③ ④	honesty	Leon's refusal to lie about his mistake was proof of his integrity.
ACADEMIC WORDS *Use these words in all your subject classes.*		
erosion e·ro·sion *(noun)* ① ② ③ ④		
implement im·ple·ment *(verb)* ① ② ③ ④	to put a plan or an idea into action	
SELECTION WORDS *These words are key to understanding this selection.*		
customize cus·tom·ize *(verb)* ① ② ③ ④		
eligible el·i·gi·ble *(adjective)* ① ② ③ ④		
pervasiveness per·va·sive·ness *(noun)* ① ② ③ ④		The pervasiveness of the flu meant that several students were absent from school this week.
plagiarize pla·gia·rize *(verb)* ① ② ③ ④		
quandary quan·da·ry *(noun)* ① ② ③ ④		

Rating Scale ① I don't know the word. ② I've seen it or heard it. ③ I know its meaning. ④ I know it and use it.

Multiple-Meaning Words `WORD ANALYSIS`

A **multiple-meaning word** has more than one meaning.

For example, the word *implement* can be a verb meaning "to put a plan or an idea into action" or a noun meaning "a tool, instrument, or utensil."

To figure out which meaning of a word is being used in a sentence, look for context clues.

▶ **In the sentence below, underline the context clues that point to the meaning of *implement*.**

The scientist replaced his old microscope with a new underline{implement} to use in experiments.

Which meaning of *implement* is used in the sentence?

_____

A faxed copy of the exam

$150

Professor Davis, who has gathered data on more than *Seventeen Thousand* students, notes that 50 years ago, only about one in five college students admitted to having cheated in high school.

In·teg·ri·ty
rigid adherence to a code of behavior; probity

pla·gia·rize
to use and pass off (the ideas or writings of another) as one's own

20%
of parents say doing a child's homework is okay

papers for twenty basketball players between 1993 and 1998

400

A former tutor for the University of Minnesota revealed that she had written

Ninety percent say cheaters never pay the price

Students say they cheat because of

Parental Pressure	Peer Pressure	Technology
40%	**40%**	**20%**

1 in 4
adults believes they have to cheat to get ahead

Over 90% of college students say
- **Politicians**
- **The Media**
- **High Schoolers**
often cheat

To CHEAT or NOT to CHEAT

By Carolyn Kleiner and Mary Lord from *U.S. News & World Report*

Kids do it. Adults do it. Even politicians do it. But that still does not make cheating right.

Umpteen pages to plow through for English, anatomy, and U.S. history. ... Geometry problems galore. ... It was a typical weeknight for high school sophomore Leah Solowsky. Before tackling her first assignment—a Spanish essay on healthy eating—the honor-roll student logged on to her computer to chat with pals. Suddenly, it hit her: Perhaps she could download some of her workload.

Solowsky cruised to the AltaVista search engine, clicked on "Spanish," and typed in "la dieta." Fifteen minutes later, she had everything she needed to know about fruits, vegetables, and grains—all in flawless español. She quickly retyped the information and handed in her paper the next day. "I had a ton of homework, I wasn't doing that well in the class, and I felt, hey, this is one way to boost my grade," explains Solowsky, now a junior with a B-plus average at the highly competitive Gulliver Preparatory School in Miami. "I didn't think it was cheating because I didn't even stop to think about it."

A Widespread Issue

Every day across America, millions of students from middle school to medical school face similar ethical **quandaries**—and research indicates that most choose to cheat. In a recent survey conducted by *Who's Who Among American High School Students,* 80 percent of high-achieving high schoolers admitted to having cheated at least once; half said they did not believe cheating was necessarily wrong—and 95 percent of the cheaters said they have never been caught. According to the Center for Academic Integrity at Duke University, three quarters of college students confess to cheating at least once. And a new *U.S. News* poll found 90 percent of college kids believe cheaters never pay the price.

> **galore** *(adj.)* in large amounts or numbers
> **flawless** *(adj.)* perfect, with no mistakes

Read and Synthesize

NAVIGATING TEXT

Evaluate Evidence

Review the third paragraph on page 273. <u>Underline</u> the evidence the authors give to support their claim that cheating is a widespread issue.

- How does providing the example of Leah Solowsky support the evidence?

_____

_____

_____

_____

_____

_____

- Imagine you are a teacher. Describe one way you would try to solve the problem of students using technology to cheat.

_____

_____

_____

_____

_____

_____

_____

COMPREHENSION

Make Inferences

Based on what you have read so far, what can you conclude about the ethical beliefs of most high school and college students?

_____

_____

_____

_____

_____

_____

Crib sheets and copying answers are nothing new, of course. What's changed, experts maintain, is the scope of the problem: the technology that opens new avenues to cheat, students' boldness in using it, and the **erosion** of conscience at every level of education. "I'm scared to death," says Emporia State University psychology professor Stephen Davis, who recently expanded his study of cheating to graduate students—including those in medical school. "I hope I never get a brain disease."

Academic fraud has never been easier. Students can tamper electronically with grade records, transmit quiz answers via pager or cell phone, and lift term papers from hundreds of Web sites. At the same time, an overload of homework combined with intense pressure to excel in school, from hard-driving peers and parents, makes cheating easy to justify—and hard to resist. Valedictorians are as likely to cheat as laggards, and girls have closed the gap with boys. In fact, the only thing that makes Leah Solowsky's case unusual is that she got caught—earning a zero on her Spanish paper and getting barred from the National Honor Society.

Most alarming to researchers is the **pervasiveness** of cheating among adolescents. What begins as penny-ante dishonesty in elementary school—stealing Pokemon cards or glancing at a neighbor's spelling test—snowballs into more serious cheating in middle and high school, as enrollments swell and students start moving from class to class, teacher to teacher. Professor Davis, who has gathered data on more than 17,000 students, notes that 50 years ago, only about 1 in 5 college students admitted to having cheated in high school. Today, a range of studies shows that figure has exploded, to anywhere from three quarters of students to an astonishing 98 percent.

The notion that schools are awash with cheaters doesn't always square with what administrators say goes on in their classrooms and corridors. "My goodness, the students are 12-, 13-, 14-year-old kids, and sometimes they make a bad decision," says Gary McGuigan, principal of the H. E. Huntington Middle School in San Marino, California. "But [cheating] isn't rampant." Sunny Hills High School in nearby Fullerton weathered two major cheating scandals in two years involving more than a dozen honor-roll students, yet principal Loring Davies insists these are "isolated" incidents.

High-Tech Cheating

The pressure to succeed, particularly on high-stakes tests, can drive students to consider extreme measures. Two months ago, nothing mattered more to Manuel than doing well on the SAT. "If your score is high, then you get into [a good school] and scholarships come to you," explains the high school senior from Houston, who is going to have to cover half of his college expenses himself. "If not, then you go to some community college, make little money, and end up doing nothing important the rest of your life." Desperate for a competitive edge, he started poking around the Net and soon stumbled upon an out-of-the-way message board where students bragged about snagging copies of the test. Manuel posted his own note, begging for help; he says he got a reply offering a faxed copy of the exam for $150 but ultimately chickened out.

While crib notes and other time-honored techniques have yet to go out of style, advanced technology is giving slackers a new edge. The Internet provides seemingly endless opportunities for cheating, from online term-paper mills to chat rooms where students can swap science projects and math solutions. They also share test questions via email between classes and hack into school mainframes to alter transcripts; they use cell phones to dial multiple-choice answers into alphanumeric

> **So where, exactly, does teamwork end and cheating begin?**

laggards (n.) people who fail to keep up
awash (adj.) having too much of something

pagers and store everything from algebra formulas to notes on *Jane Eyre* in cutting-edge calculators. Some devices even have infrared capabilities, allowing students to zap information across a classroom. "I get the sense there's a thrill to it, that 'my teachers are too dumb to catch me,'" says English teacher Connie Eberly.

Reasonably priced surveillance equipment, including hidden cameras and tape recorders, is taking cheating to a whole new level. "If [students] spent as much time on their studies as they do on cheating, we'd be graduating rocket scientists all over the place," says Larry McCandless, a science teacher at Hardee Junior High in Wauchula, Florida, who recently caught his students using sign language to signal test answers to each other.

Mixed Messages

If students do spend homeroom copying assignments from one another, it may be because schools send such mixed messages about what, exactly, constitutes crossing the line. Mark, a senior at a Northeastern boarding school, doesn't believe that doing homework with a friend—or a family member—is ever dishonest and blames the people at the head of the classroom for any confusion over collaboration. "I mean, some of my teachers say you can't do it, some say two minds are greater than one," he explains, breaking into a laugh. "I obviously agree with the latter."

He isn't the only one. In a new study of 500 middle and high school students, Rutgers University management professor Donald McCabe, a leading authority on academic dishonesty, found that only one third said doing work with classmates was cheating, and just half thought it was wrong for parents to do their homework. So where, exactly, does teamwork end and cheating begin? It's not always that clear, even for grown-ups. According to the *U.S. News* poll, 20 percent of adults thought that doing homework for a child was fair. It's no wonder that teachers see students of every age handing in essays that contain words they can't pronounce, much less define.

Sue Bigg, a college consultant outside Chicago, often sees the hand of pushy parents. "I am beginning to think of myself in the role of 'integrity police,'" she says, relating countless stories of college application essays that have been "edited" by Mom or Dad—and often for the worse, as big words replace any shred of youthful personality.

> **Clarify**
> What does it mean when someone plays the role of "integrity police"?

> **consultant** (n.) a person whose job is to give advice on a particular area of expertise

COMPREHENSION

Problem and Solution
According to the first paragraph on page 274, why has cheating recently become a bigger problem? List three factors.

1. _____

_____

2. _____

_____

3. _____

_____

VOCABULARY/WORD ANALYSIS

Multiple-Meaning Words
Look at the final sentence of the third paragraph on page 274. What does *quarters* mean here?

Ⓐ coins worth 25¢ each

Ⓑ measurements of one-fourth

Ⓒ places where people live

• **Underline** the context clues that helped you figure out the word's meaning.

NAVIGATING TEXT

Evaluate Evidence
Underline evidence in the "Mixed Messages" section that supports the claim that adults aren't always clear about what constitutes cheating.

• Does this evidence provide reasonable proof for the authors' claim? Explain.

_____

_____

_____

_____

_____

_____

_____

_____

_____

"I'm afraid a lot of this cheating comes from home, where the parents' modus operandi is success at any cost." Edit-happy adults are part of the reason why schools across the country are having students do much of their writing in class nowadays. (It also prevents them from pulling papers off the Web.)

A Society of Cheaters?

The *U.S. News* poll found that 1 in 4 adults believes he has to lie and cheat to get ahead, and it seems this mentality is communicated to children. "Students see adults—parents, businessmen, lawyers—violating ethical standards and receiving a slap on the wrist, if anything, and quickly conclude that if that's acceptable behavior in the larger society, what's wrong with a little cheating in high school or college?" says Rutgers professor McCabe. "Too often the messages from parents and teachers come off as, 'You need to do everything you can, at all costs, to get to the top.' You never see any gratification for being a good person anymore," says Audrey James, a senior at the North Carolina School of Science and Mathematics in Durham. "Once you get to high school, it's all about who has the grades and who's going to get the most scholarships."

> **Make Connections**
> **Describe an example in history or current events where someone violated ethical standards.**

Some blame schools, not parents or students, for the cheating epidemic. "We should look at the way we run our institutions and the way those institutions tolerate, or at the very least, make cheating easy," says Theodore Sizer, a longtime educator and coauthor of *The Students Are Watching: Schools and the Moral Contract,* citing teachers with too-large classes and too little time to get to know students or to create new assignments that cannot be pulled off the Internet.

Sometimes the schools are directly responsible. In the midst of March Madness last spring, a former tutor for the University of Minnesota revealed that she had written 400 papers for 20 basketball players between 1993 and 1998; four athletes were suspended, and the team was upset in the first round of the NCAA tournament. "You can talk to any academic adviser [for a sports program], and they will tell you that there have been times when coaches have put pressure on them to do anything it takes to keep an athlete **eligible**," says Richard Lapchick, director of the Center for the Study of Sport in Society at Northeastern University. He claims that in the past year alone, he has counseled tutors and former players at six different schools to report cheating, only to have every athletic director—and one college president—investigate and deny there was a problem.

It's clear that when students really care about learning, they're much less likely to cheat. Take Bob Corbett, for example. Though he details his years of making cheat sheets and paying people to take his AP exams in *The Cheater's Handbook: The Naughty Student's Bible,* Corbett insists that he never cheated in any subject he really cared about or in classes with inspiring instructors. In fact, he dedicated his book to the eleventh-grade teacher who "did such a wonderfully engaging job that he destroyed any shred of desire I may ever have had to cheat in English thereafter. ... "

Combating the Problem

It's early in November, SAT day, and Ray Nicosia is on the prowl. The director of test security for the Educational Testing Service, Nicosia is making the rounds at a high school test center that has had a string of recent security problems, to guarantee things go smoothly this time—or take steps to shut the site down. He cruises the corridors, a vision of calm amid the throngs of edgy students, and runs through a mental checklist: He verifies that test booklets are kept in a secure storage area, far away from the probing eyes—and fingers—of students, until the very last minute. He glances in classrooms, making sure that proctors follow the rules, checking and double-checking valid forms

---

proctors *(n.)* people assigned to keep watch over students taking exams

of identification, randomly assigning students to desks at least 4 feet apart, filling out a seating chart (a permanent record of who sat next to whom), and then strolling about the room during the exam, searching out wandering eyes and other suspicious activity.

To combat a scourge some deem as pernicious as underage drinking, educators are **implementing** such countermeasures as character education programs, honor codes, and strict academic integrity policies. "I'm not saying it's impossible to cheat, but we're taking a lot of steps to secure our tests," says Nicosia. In recent years, ETS [Educational Testing Service], which administers some 11 million standardized tests a year and questions less than 1 percent of scores, has boosted prevention efforts, aiming to thwart impersonators, thieves, and copycats either before or during the act. Even the simplest precautions, from better training for proctors to a free hotline for reporting shady activity, can make a huge difference. In 1996, for example, ETS began shrink-wrapping the essay section of Advanced Placement exams, to stop students from sneaking a look during the first part of the test; peeking is now virtually nonexistent.

pernicious *(adj.)* destructive

COMPREHENSION

Fact and Opinion

Identify each statement as a fact or an opinion. Write F for fact or O for opinion.

____ A tutor for the University of Minnesota wrote 400 papers for 20 athletes.

____ You never see any gratification for being a good person anymore.

• Explain how you identified each as either a fact or an opinion.

_____

_____

_____

_____

_____

_____

_____

NAVIGATING TEXT

Evaluate Evidence

How do the authors support the assertion that "when students really care about learning, they're much less likely to cheat"?

_____

_____

_____

_____

_____

_____

• Is this evidence convincing? Why or why not?

_____

_____

_____

_____

_____

_____

Low-tech tactics work in the classroom, too. In a 1998 study conducted at two public colleges, Oregon State University economics professor Joe Kerkvliet found that students were 31 percent more likely to cheat in courses taught by teaching assistants—graduate students or adjunct professors—than those taught by tenured or tenure-track faculty. (Typically, 1 in 8 students will cheat on at least one exam in any given class.) By offering multiple versions of the same test, so students can't share answers with friends in different sections, adding extra proctors, and giving verbal warnings that cheaters will be punished, Kerkvliet has reduced cheating in his classes to practically zero.

Just talking about the problem can be enough to stop it. Sohair Ahmadi used to regularly cut corners back in the ninth and tenth grades—trading test answers in biology, copying homework like mad—and no one seemed to care. In her junior year, she switched schools, to the North Carolina School of Science and Mathematics, where teachers discuss academic integrity from the outset, outlining why it's important and detailing a laundry list of unacceptable behaviors. "They make it clear that cheating will not be tolerated," says Ahmadi, 18, who not only shed her habit but now heads a committee dedicated to starting a school honor code.

High-tech countermeasures are also on the rise. From the moment a student walks into ETS's computer-based testing center at George Mason University in Fairfax, Virginia, for example, it's clear that Big Brother is watching. A digital camera stands in one corner, ready to snap a test-day photo for posterity; five video cameras record each student's every move; the 15 computers run **customized** exams, with the order and type of questions determined by a test taker's previous answers. At the moment, ETS is working toward adding a biometric scan (using, say, thumbprints to identify students) to the check-in process.

Stumbling Blocks and Lessons Learned

The biggest stumbling block, however, may be that when cheaters do get busted, the penalties are rarely harsh. Last year, for instance, the valedictorian at Brea Olinda High School in Southern California was caught electronically altering a course grade. His punishment: being banned from the graduation ceremony. Cheat on the SAT and your score will be canceled; but you can take a retest. It's often true that getting caught cheating "doesn't have the terrifically terrible college ramifications you might think," says Don Firke, academic dean at Choate Rosemary Hall, a boarding school in Wallingford, Connecticut. "If a college really wants a kid, they're going to find a way to take him." Once on campus, a cheater is apt to find similarly lax discipline. With the exception of a handful of schools like the University of Virginia, which have one-strike-and-you're-out honor-code policies, the vast majority simply dole out zeros for an assignment or course in which a student has been found cheating.

Still, a growing number of institutions are trying to turn discipline into a teachable moment. At the University of Maryland–College Park, for example, students caught cheating must attend a seven-week ethics seminar.

> You're going to have to think about this behavior and what danger it poses to you and the larger society.

Summarize
Why do students cheat, and what are schools doing about the problem?

---

tenured *(adj.)* able to stay permanently in a teaching job at a university
ramifications *(n.)* consequences

"We're not trying to mar someone's life, but we are saying, 'You're going to have to think about this behavior and what danger it poses to you and the larger society,'" says Gary Pavela, director of judicial programs and student ethical development.

Do the cheaters actually mend their ways? Leah Solowsky isn't glad she was caught **plagiarizing** last year, but she acknowledges that the experience did teach her a thing or two. "I learned that teachers aren't as stupid as some people think they are," she says with just a hint of humor. Pausing to think for a moment, she adds: "I mean, cheating should affect your conscience, because you are doing something wrong." Solowsky vows she's sworn off cheating for good—no matter how much loathsome Spanish homework piles up every night. ■

COMPREHENSION

Problem and Solution

What two problems are solved by having students do most writing in class? Complete the chart.

Problem 1:
_____
_____

Problem 2:
_____
_____

Solution:
Students do most writing assignments in class.

[21] SMALL GROUPS/INDEPENDENT

COLLABORATE

Create Criteria As a group, brainstorm and then draft two rules or policies that could be included in or added to your school's honor code.

COMMUNICATE

Discuss and Write With a partner, discuss Gary Pavela's question: What danger does cheating pose to society at large? Jot down three ways you think cheating is harmful. Then write a paragraph expressing your view.

W

READ ONLINE

expert space
Go to **www.expert21.com/student** to learn more about Cheating; Honor System; SAT.

PLAY: CLASSIC RETELLING

Frankenstein

What would it be like to create a monster? In this stage version of the famous story of Dr. Frankenstein, a scientist is horrified and grief-stricken when he realizes what he has done.

W **QuickWrite**

Today, scientists can already clone, or copy, some life forms. Do you think it is wise to create clones? Support your opinion with reasons.

Dramatic Elements   LITERARY ANALYSIS

A **drama**, or play, is a story written to be performed before an audience.
It includes

- a **cast of characters:** a list of who is in the play.
- **acts:** groups of scenes.
- **scenes:** parts of the play that take place in one location.
- **settings:** descriptions of where and when scenes take place.
- **stage directions:** text that tells what the characters do and where they are onstage.
- **dialogue:** words spoken by characters.

▶ **Read the following excerpt from "Frankenstein." Then answer the question.**

SETTING: *a ship in the Arctic Sea, north of Russia, July 1797*

CAPTAIN WALTON *is in his study addressing a letter home.*

CAPTAIN WALTON: My dear sister, strange events have occurred since my last letter. Some days ago, as my crew and I continued on our arduous journey toward the North Pole, we beheld the oddest sight. A man, half-dead, lay in a sledge, stranded by the ice.

Underline the setting. What does the stage direction add to your understanding of Captain Walton's speech?

_____

_____

_____

_____

Sequence of Events   COMPREHENSION

In literary works, writers sometimes present events out of **sequence**, or order.

They may use **flashbacks**, or scenes that interrupt the current action to show events from the past.

As you read a drama, look for time clues in the setting and in the characters' dialogue. Think about why the writer presents events out of sequence.

▶ **In the excerpt above, the author uses a letter rather than a flashback to give readers information about past action. How much time has passed between Walton's seeing the half-dead man and his writing the letter?**

_____

Circle the words that tell you this.

Academic Language VOCABULARY

▶ Rate your knowledge of each word. Then write its meaning and an example sentence.

Word	Meaning	Example
ACADEMIC WORDS *Use these words in all your subject classes.*		
enormity e•nor•mi•ty *(noun)* ① ② ③ ④	the quality of being very wicked or evil	Everyone was horrified by the enormity of the villain's crimes, but he didn't feel guilty at all.
undertaking un•der•tak•ing *(verb)* ① ② ③ ④		
CONTENT AREA WORDS *Use these words to talk and write about social studies.*		
desolate des•o•late *(adjective)* ① ② ③ ④	empty; deserted	
nurture nur•ture *(verb)* ① ② ③ ④		
SELECTION WORDS *These words are key to understanding this selection.*		
arduous ar•du•ous *(adjective)* ① ② ③ ④		
engrossed en•grossed *(adjective)* ① ② ③ ④		Engrossed in a video game, Yin did not hear the telephone ring.
repulse re•pulse *(verb)* ① ② ③ ④		
revulsion re•vul•sion *(noun)* ① ② ③ ④		

Rating Scale ① I don't know the word. ② I've seen it or heard it. ③ I know its meaning. ④ I know it and use it.

Multiple-Meaning Words WORD ANALYSIS

Words with more than one meaning are called multiple-meaning words.

Remember that the different meanings of these words may be different parts of speech. For example, the word *desolate* can be an adjective meaning "empty; deserted." It can also be a verb meaning "to ruin or lay waste."

▶ **Write the meaning and part of speech of the word *desolate* as it is used in the sentence below.**

People feared that the scientist was creating a new weapon that would <u>desolate</u> cities.

_____

_____

Frankenstein

By Mary Shelley, adapted by Sunita Apte

Scientist Victor Frankenstein has the power to create life. Will it bring him glory—or something else?

CAST OF CHARACTERS

CAPTAIN WALTON, THE CAPTAIN OF A SHIP IN THE ARCTIC

DR. FRANKENSTEIN, THE NARRATOR, A SCIENTIST AND PASSENGER ON THE SHIP

YOUNG VICTOR, FRANKENSTEIN WHEN HE WAS YOUNGER

ELIZABETH, HIS FIANCÉE

HENRY CLERVAL, HIS BEST FRIEND

FATHER, HIS FATHER

CREATURE, FRANKENSTEIN'S MONSTER

MR. DELACEY, AN OLD BLIND MAN

AGATHA, DELACEY'S DAUGHTER

FELIX, DELACEY'S SON

ACT 1

Act I, Scene 1

SETTING: a ship in the Arctic Sea, north of Russia, July 1797

CAPTAIN WALTON is in his study addressing a letter home.

CAPTAIN WALTON: My dear sister, strange events have occurred since my last letter. Some days ago, as my crew and I continued on our **arduous** journey toward the North Pole, we beheld the oddest sight. A man, half-dead, lay in a sledge, stranded by the ice. I ordered my men to help the poor wretch on board the ship. There I proceeded to administer to his comforts as he lay sick and feverish abed.

For many a day he was too ill to speak, but yesterday I found him sufficiently recovered. As I sat with him in the evening, he began to relay to me his wretched tale of woe.

sledge *(n.)* a sleigh
woe *(n.)* sadness

Act I, Scene 2

SETTING: Geneva, Switzerland, some years before

DR. FRANKENSTEIN: My name is Victor Frankenstein. My family is one of the most distinguished in Geneva, and it is there that I spent my youth, surrounded by the love of my family. How, you might wonder, did I come from such a place as that to this one? It is a sad and unlikely tale. Take heed, so that you might learn from my mistakes. At 17, I left the loving comfort of my family and went to Germany to study at the university there. I took leave of my fiancée, Elizabeth.

ELIZABETH: Victor, my love. Study hard and come back soon.

YOUNG VICTOR: I will, my dearest Elizabeth. Write me often.

ELIZABETH: Oh Victor, I will miss you so!

YOUNG VICTOR: And I will miss you. And Father, and William. It's hard to believe my little brother is growing so fast.

ELIZABETH *(looking sad)*: If only your dear mother were still alive to see you off!

At the mention of his mother, YOUNG VICTOR's face falls. He struggles not to cry.

YOUNG VICTOR: Oh Elizabeth, I miss Mother more than words can say. Without you and Father and William, I don't think I could have gone on after she died. And it is the thought of you here waiting for me that will keep me going at university.

DR. FRANKENSTEIN: One day I would marry my Elizabeth, beloved by me from childhood. But first, I needed to quench my thirst for scientific knowledge. I would spend my time unlocking nature's secrets. Then I would use them for the greater glory of all humankind. Only after that would I be able to return to Geneva and my family.

Act I, Scene 3

SETTING: YOUNG VICTOR's lab at Ingolstadt

DR. FRANKENSTEIN: Once at the university, I wasted no time in attending lectures and setting up my own lab. Soon, I was fully **engrossed** in my studies—perhaps too engrossed. Two years passed in this way. My dear friend, Henry Clerval, was a student at the same university, but I rarely saw him. One day, I returned home to find Henry in my laboratory.

HENRY: Victor, you don't look well. Whatever is the matter? Aren't you sleeping?

YOUNG VICTOR: My dear Henry, sleep can wait. My studies are too important.

HENRY *(looking around)*: What studies are you pursuing, Victor?

YOUNG VICTOR: Henry, you are a man of arts and letters, not a scientist. I feel that my explanations would bore you.

HENRY stares keenly at YOUNG VICTOR, sensing that Victor is lying. HENRY begins to walk around the lab, examining everything in great detail. Then, with a cunning look, he addresses YOUNG VICTOR, trying to trap his friend into revealing what he has been doing.

HENRY: Goodness, Victor, my eyes must be playing tricks on me. I thought I saw a human head floating in that tank. But I know no such thing is possible. You are not the sort of man to dabble in that kind of science.

> **Clarify**
> **What is Henry trying to get Victor to do?**

YOUNG VICTOR, wounded by HENRY's words, falls right into the trap. Angrily, he shouts at his friend.

YOUNG VICTOR: That kind of science? You mean the kind that holds the secret, the very elixir, of life itself? Yes, I have been dabbling in "that kind of science." Not just dabbling, my friend, but making great strides. You will one day find Victor Frankenstein's name alongside

quench *(v.)* satisfy
elixir *(n.)* a potion that prolongs life

those of all the great scientists of history. For, you see, I have discovered a way to give life.

HENRY looks at YOUNG VICTOR for a long moment without speaking. A flash of terror crosses HENRY's eyes. Then he composes himself and glances around the lab once more.

HENRY: I pray, Victor, that my thoughts are in error. But at this moment I can only suspect that you intend to bring one who has been dead back to life. I beseech you to reconsider your path. Such a thing should not be attempted by any man!

YOUNG VICTOR: Not one who has been dead, Henry, but a person of my own creation. And why should I not? That way of thinking is for cowards! What is the use of science if we shy away from its power, like frightened little children? Down my path lies glory and the future of humankind!

HENRY: Victor, you are my dearest friend. I urge you to think very carefully about what you are doing. Once you have crossed the line between death and life, there will be no turning back. In your rush to glory, have you not stopped to consider what will happen once you have created life?

YOUNG VICTOR: That is my affair, Henry, not yours. I beg you to keep my secret! A scientist must be allowed to do his work without fear of judgment.

HENRY *(looking extremely unsettled)*: All right, old friend, I will keep your secret. And remember, I am here for you if I am needed.

HENRY shakes YOUNG VICTOR's hand and leaves the lab.

DR. FRANKENSTEIN: How I wish I had heeded the advice of my friend! But at the time I was unable to. I was too caught up in the feverish excitement of my discovery. I would not be stopped by the reasonable objections of an old friend.

Act I, Scene 4

SETTING: YOUNG VICTOR's lab at Ingolstadt some weeks later

DR. FRANKENSTEIN: In the next few weeks I worked feverishly to finish. I had been haunting graveyards and morgues for months, gathering parts for my creature. In my haste I decided to make my creature very large. This would make the various parts I had gathered easier to connect. Finally, late one November night, all was ready.

YOUNG VICTOR *(to himself)*: Steady, Victor. In a moment, you will accomplish something no one else has ever done.

beseech *(v.)* to plead with
feverishly *(adv.)* with constant intensity and excitement

Read and Synthesize

LITERARY ANALYSIS

Drama Elements

How are Dr. Frankenstein and Young Victor related? Why are they onstage at the same time?

_____

_____

_____

_____

_____

_____

_____

_____

COMPREHENSION

Sequence of Events

(Circle) the lines that show the play is shifting back in time.

• Explain what is happening in Young Victor's life at this point in the play.

_____

_____

_____

_____

CRITICAL THINKING

Analyze

Draw one line under Victor's argument in favor of creating human life. Draw two lines under Henry's argument against creating human life.

• What do you think is at the heart of this conflict?

_____

_____

_____

_____

_____

YOUNG VICTOR, heart beating wildly, flips some switches and turns some dials. There is a long pause. Then, slowly, the CREATURE comes to life, rising from the table. It is monstrous, over eight feel tall with dull eyes, yellow skin, and black lips. YOUNG VICTOR backs away, terrified.

YOUNG VICTOR *(to himself)*: What have I done? I had thought I was making something beautiful, but instead it is monstrous—monstrous!

Unable to bear it, YOUNG VICTOR rushes from the lab and throws himself on his bed. He sleeps fitfully and finally startles awake to see the CREATURE, staring down at him in the moonlight, grinning.

YOUNG VICTOR *(flailing at the CREATURE)*: Oh no! Go away! Leave me be!

With a cry, YOUNG VICTOR rushes from his bedchamber. He ends up in the courtyard, where he spends the rest of the night pacing. HENRY discovers him there in the morning.

HENRY: Victor, whatever is the matter? You look awful.

YOUNG VICTOR *(troubled and obviously lying)*: It's nothing, Henry. I was just up late, working on a problem.

DR. FRANKENSTEIN: The creature was gone, and there I hoped the matter would end. But deep down inside, I knew it would not be so simple. I had given it life and then turned my back on it. For that, I sensed I would somehow pay. I just never realized how dearly.

ACT 2

Act II, Scene 1

SETTING: On the road from Ingolstadt to Geneva

DR. FRANKENSTEIN: The next few months went well and I almost forgot about my horrible creation. Henry was my constant companion. We decided to travel back to Geneva together. The journey was stormy and the road rough. On the second night, nearing Geneva, I glanced out of the carriage into the rainy darkness and gasped.

HENRY: What is it Victor? Have you seen something outside? Is it bandits?

YOUNG VICTOR *(obviously shaken)*: No, Henry, it's nothing. I am just tired, that's all.

> **Make Inferences**
> Why doesn't Victor tell his best friend Henry the truth?

DR. FRANKENSTEIN: But I was lying to my friend yet again. For when I looked out the window, a flash of lightning had lit up the sky. And there, by the road, watching the carriage, stood my creature—my monstrous creature.

Act II, Scene 2

SETTING: The FRANKENSTEIN home in Geneva

DR. FRANKENSTEIN: The sight of the creature unsettled me. But I put it out of my mind. I only wanted to go home. How I longed to see my family and my sweet Elizabeth. Imagine my surprise when I arrived to find Elizabeth in tears and my father's face white with grief.

YOUNG VICTOR: What is it? Father? Elizabeth? What has happened?

FATHER: Oh, my dear Victor. After so long, you come home to heartbreak and tragedy. Your younger brother, William, has been murdered.

YOUNG VICTOR: William, murdered? But he was only a boy—a sweet angelic boy. Who would do such a thing?

A sudden knowledge causes YOUNG VICTOR to freeze. He knows with certainty that his CREATURE had done this deed.

ELIZABETH: Victor, things are even worse than that. Not only is our sweet, lovely William gone, but Justine has been arrested for his murder.

YOUNG VICTOR: Justine arrested? But she is innocent, I am sure of it.

ELIZABETH: As am I. But the court has decided otherwise. She is sentenced to be hanged.

fitfully *(adv.)* restlessly

LITERARY ANALYSIS

Drama Elements

Circle details that describe the Creature.

10 feet tall	8 feet tall
yellow face	green face
red lips	black lips

- **Underline** the stage directions on page 286 that support your answers.

VOCABULARY/WORD ANALYSIS

Multiple-Meaning Words

Circle the word *matter* in Henry's last lines of dialogue in Act I, Scene 4. Then **circle** the word *matter* in Dr. Frankenstein's dialogue at the end of Act I, Scene 4.

- What does *matter* mean in each sentence? Draw lines to match the word with its meanings.

When Henry uses *matter*:   a problem

When Dr. Frankenstein uses *matter*:   an issue

What matter did Dr. Frankenstein hope would end?

_____

_____

_____

_____

_____

_____

COMPREHENSION

Sequence of Events

How much time goes by between the moment Young Victor chases the Creature away and the next time he sees the Creature? Put a box around the clues that help you.

DR. FRANKENSTEIN: Who can understand my rage and grief? Justine had lived and worked in our house for many years. She had nursed my mother during her final illness. One innocent soul killed, another about to be, all because of me. I thought about going to the police and telling them my story, but quickly realized I would be thought a madman. I had no way of saving Justine.

Act II, Scene 3

SETTING: The Swiss mountains

DR. FRANKENSTEIN: After Justine's execution, the whole house was filled with grief. Father decided to take us on holiday to the mountains, to distract us. It worked for a while, until one afternoon when I hiked alone up a hillside.

YOUNG VICTOR *(to himself)*: Now which of these paths is the right one? Oh look, there is another hiker in the distance. I shall ask him.

YOUNG VICTOR waits for the hiker, who appears larger and larger as he comes closer, until it is obvious the hiker is no human being, but his CREATURE. Seeing him, YOUNG VICTOR begins to tremble, full of fear and rage.

YOUNG VICTOR *(shouting)*: Leave me alone! Or better yet, stay so that I can kill you. I only wish your death could bring back your two victims.

CREATURE: I feared that you would greet me this way. But how can you, my creator, hate me?

YOUNG VICTOR: I should not have created you. It was not my place to give life. I thought only of my glory and not of the **enormity** of what I was **undertaking.**

YOUNG VICTOR tries to attack the monster but is unable. The CREATURE has a strength much greater than an ordinary man's.

CREATURE *(standing over YOUNG VICTOR)*: You created me. You were my mother and father. But you thought me a monster and sent me away. You, who should have **nurtured** and taught me. And now you wish me dead?

YOUNG VICTOR: You are a murderer, a monster. You have taken innocent lives!

CREATURE: All of you humans abhor me on sight. Am I so wrong to hate back? I was created with a good heart but have turned to evil. You may ask why, and I can give you an answer. To understand, you will have to hear my story.

DR. FRANKENSTEIN: I had no choice but to listen as the creature told his tale. He told me that after I shunned him, he left my apartment and went into the hills. He tried to make contact with other people, but they were all terrified of him.

Act II, Scene 4

SETTING: The German countryside, months earlier

CREATURE: One day I found an empty shed next to an old farmhouse. I took refuge there. An old blind man named Mr. DeLacey lived in the farmhouse with his children, Agatha and Felix. I spied on the family, watching and listening to everything they did. In this way, I learned to speak. I even learned to read.

The CREATURE pauses, clearly moved by the memory.

CREATURE: I came to love the DeLacey family. I was sure that they would love me back if only they got to know me. So I waited, until one day the blind father was home alone. Since he could not see my horrible appearance, I thought he wouldn't run from me, terrified. If I could win his friendship, then perhaps the rest of the family would welcome me. Trembling, I knocked on his door.

MR. DELACEY: Who is it? Come in, please.

CREATURE: Hello, sir. I am a weary traveler in want of a little rest.

MR. DELACEY: By all means, come in and sit by the fire. Where are you traveling?

CREATURE: I am journeying to meet some family friends. They have never set eyes on me, so I am a little nervous about meeting them. I am worried that they will dislike me and reject my friendship.

> **abhor** *(v.)* to hate intensely
> **refuge** *(n.)* protection

MR. DELACEY: Don't be afraid. These friends are almost certainly good people. I'm sure they will welcome you dearly.

CREATURE: My heart filled with joy at the old man's words and I went to hug him. But at that moment, I heard footsteps. Felix and Agatha opened the cottage door. When they saw me, their faces twisted in **revulsion.**

AGATHA: Aagh! A monster, a hideous monster!

CREATURE: Felix darted forward and pulled me away from Mr. DeLacey.

FELIX: Get away from my father, you brute!

CREATURE: I could have killed Felix most easily. But instead I ran from the farmhouse into the hills. It was then that I knew there was no hope for me among the human race.

> **Make Connections**
> **How would you feel in the Creature's situation?**

Act II, Scene 5

SETTING: Back in the Swiss mountains

DR. FRANKENSTEIN: After he left the DeLacey farmhouse, the creature began to search for me. He had taken a letter from my lab, and he used the address on it to follow me to Geneva.

CREATURE: Although I hated you for sending me away, I knew that you were the only one who could help me.

YOUNG VICTOR: Help you! This is how you ask for help—by murdering my beloved brother?

CREATURE: At first I only meant to seize the child and keep him for a friend. I thought perhaps an innocent child would not be **repulsed** by me. But he began screaming and calling me a monster and an ugly wretch. He said his brother, Mr. Frankenstein, would save him.

YOUNG VICTOR (*shuddering at the thought of what happened next*)**:** Poor, innocent William!

CREATURE: When I heard your name, I was taken by rage. I grasped his throat to silence him and in a moment he lay dead at my feet. I gazed at my victim, and my heart swelled with triumph. I thought of you and how this death would cause you despair and how I would create a thousand other miseries to torment you.

YOUNG VICTOR: Torment me? Aye, you have succeeded. But what do you want from me now?

Read and Synthesize

CRITICAL THINKING

Evaluate

Did Frankenstein do the right thing by not trying to save Justine? Give reasons to support your answer.

_____

_____

_____

_____

_____

_____

LITERARY ANALYSIS

Drama Elements

How does Victor look and behave during his conversation with the Creature?

_____

_____

- <u>Underline</u> the part of the play that tells you this.

[21] SMALL GROUPS/INDEPENDENT

COLLABORATE

Solve the Problem In a group, discuss the problem the Creature faces as he tries to make friends. Come up with two or three possible solutions for his problem. Vote on which one you think would be best.

COMMUNICATE

React and Write The Creature says that Dr. Frankenstein should have nurtured and taught him. Do you think Dr. Frankenstein is responsible for turning the Creature into a monster? Jot down some notes based on details in the story. Then write a paragraph explaining your views.

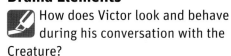

CREATURE: I am alone and miserable. No humans will associate with me. But one as deformed and horrible as myself would not refuse to keep me company. I would like a companion, a bride with whom to share my days. This being you must create.

YOUNG VICTOR: I will never create another like yourself. Bring another wicked creature into this world? Impossible!

CREATURE: You are in the wrong. I am wicked because I am miserable. Am I not shunned and hated by all mankind? You, my creator, would tear me to pieces and then be happy. Tell me, why should I pity humans more than they pity me? You would not call it murder if you could kill me right now. Shall I respect humans, when they condemn me?

YOUNG VICTOR: Most humans have not done the evil things that you have done.

CREATURE: Oh creator, have pity on me! Have you brought me into this world solely to be wretched and miserable? Only you have the power to make me happy. Please do not deny me my request.

YOUNG VICTOR's face softens and he paces a few steps. It is obvious that he is pondering the CREATURE's request, weighing the consequences.

CREATURE *(searching his master's face)***:** Do not worry. If you agree, no one shall ever see my companion and me again. We will quit the human world for good.

YOUNG VICTOR: All right. I will consent to your demand. But you must promise to leave my family alone forever.

CREATURE: I promise. Please go now, and begin your work. I will watch its progress from afar, and when you are almost done, I shall appear.

DR. FRANKENSTEIN: Saying this, he suddenly left me. I hiked home with a heavy heart. What terrible thing had I promised? What monstrous bargain had I made? To give life again to another creature? I shuddered from the very thought of it. And yet, I knew I had no choice. I had to begin my work at once.

condemn *(v.)* to judge as guilty
consent *(v.)* to agree to

ACT 3

Act III, Scene 1

SETTING: A cottage on a Scottish island

DR. FRANKENSTEIN: The idea of making a bride for the creature disgusted me. Yet I knew it was the only way to rid myself of him. I rented a small cottage on a **desolate** island in Scotland and began my work. One night, as I was almost finished, I had a most terrifying thought.

YOUNG VICTOR *(to himself):* What if the two creatures have children of their own? They might create a whole population of monsters! I can't take that chance!

In a fit of rage and fear, YOUNG VICTOR tears the still-lifeless new monster apart. As he does so, he glances up at the window. The CREATURE is there, watching him, his hideous face filled with a mixture of anger and despair.

YOUNG VICTOR *(to himself):* It is impossible! I can never bring myself to do this.

YOUNG VICTOR paces and mumbles incoherently to himself. He waits and looks out the window, searching. He paces some more until he hears footsteps in the hall. He stands defiantly as the door to the lab opens.

CREATURE: You have broken your promise and betrayed me!

YOUNG VICTOR: Begone! I do break my promise. Never will I create another like yourself, equal in hideous wickedness.

CREATURE: Remember, my creator, that I have power. You believe yourself miserable now, but I can make you so wretched that even the very light of day will be hateful to you. You are my creator, but I am your master. You must obey me!

YOUNG VICTOR: Your threats cannot move me to an act of wickedness. Shall I set loose upon the earth another like you? No, I will not! Begone, I say!

CREATURE: So you think it fair that every creature on earth should have love and companionship, except for me? Very well, I shall go. But remember this before I take my leave. I shall be with you on your wedding night!

DR. FRANKENSTEIN: The creature's words sent fear through my heart.

> **Predict**
> **What do you think will happen next?**

---

incoherently *(v.)* in a confused manner

COMPREHENSION

Sequence of Events

What important plot events led up to Dr. Frankenstein's meeting with the Creature?

1. _____

_____

2. _____

_____

LITERARY ANALYSIS

Drama Elements

Dialogue moves the plot along, and it also tells you a lot about the characters. What does Dr. Frankenstein promise the Creature he will do in Act II, Scene 5?

_____

_____

- (Circle) the lines on page 290 in which the Creature persuades Frankenstein.

CRITICAL THINKING

Synthesize

- What are the Creature's reasons for wanting a bride?

_____

_____

_____

- Why does he think Dr. Frankenstein owes him this?

_____

_____

_____

LITERARY ANALYSIS

Drama Elements

Why does Victor break his promise to the Creature in Act III, Scene 1?

_____

_____

_____

Act III, Scene 2

SETTING: The FRANKENSTEIN home in Geneva

DR. FRANKENSTEIN: I was full of fear, yet also felt a kind of relief. The creature would kill me on my wedding night. Why then not hasten death? I would wed my sweet Elizabeth as soon as possible. Once the creature was done with me, she and my family would be left to live in peace. I departed for Geneva, but I had underestimated the monster's evil intentions. Once again, I arrived home to grief and sorrow.

ELIZABETH: Oh Victor, have you not heard? Henry Clerval has been found murdered.

YOUNG VICTOR: Henry murdered! No, that can't be. Oh Elizabeth, please say it isn't so.

ELIZABETH: Oh my love, I'm afraid I cannot say that, for it is so. Poor Henry. He was such a dear friend to you, and loved by everyone. Who could have wanted him dead?

YOUNG VICTOR lets ELIZABETH console him. Then, he suddenly squares his shoulder and displays a face of resolute determination. He takes ELIZABETH's hands and falls to his knees in a proposal.

YOUNG VICTOR: Oh Elizabeth, could we not get married soon, very soon? My grief is so great that only life with you will keep me going.

ELIZABETH: Of course, my dear Victor. We will get married as soon as possible.

DR. FRANKENSTEIN: My final meeting with the creature could not come quickly enough.

Act III, Scene 3

SETTING: A hotel in Evian, France, a week later

DR. FRANKENSTEIN: And so Elizabeth and I were wed. On our wedding night, we went to a hotel in France. I knew the creature would find a way to join us. I was prepared for my fate, but I vowed not to go down without a fight. If only I had realized then the monster's unspeakable plan.

ELIZABETH: Victor, my husband, aren't you tired?

YOUNG VICTOR: No, I will stay up awhile. You go to bed without me, my love.

ELIZABETH leaves and YOUNG VICTOR wanders the halls of the hotel, alternately angry and scared, awaiting the appearance of the CREATURE and his fate. Suddenly, a woman's shrill scream pierces the air.

YOUNG VICTOR: Elizabeth! No! Oh no!

YOUNG VICTOR rushes upstairs to find ELIZABETH lying on the bed in their room, dead. Like a madman, he races out into the hall.

YOUNG VICTOR *(shouting)*: Come out, wherever you are. You have taken my Elizabeth from me. I will tear you from limb to limb!

No one appears. YOUNG VICTOR falls to his knees, overcome by grief.

YOUNG VICTOR: Foul villain! I will kill you! If I have to travel to the ends of the earth, I will find you!

> **Make Inferences**
> **What details reveal that Victor Frankenstein is ready to face the Creature?**

DR. FRANKENSTEIN: From that moment I accepted my fate and vowed to avenge the death of my dear Elizabeth no matter the cost.

underestimated *(v.)* to judge a value lower than it is
shrill *(adj.)* high-pitched and piercing

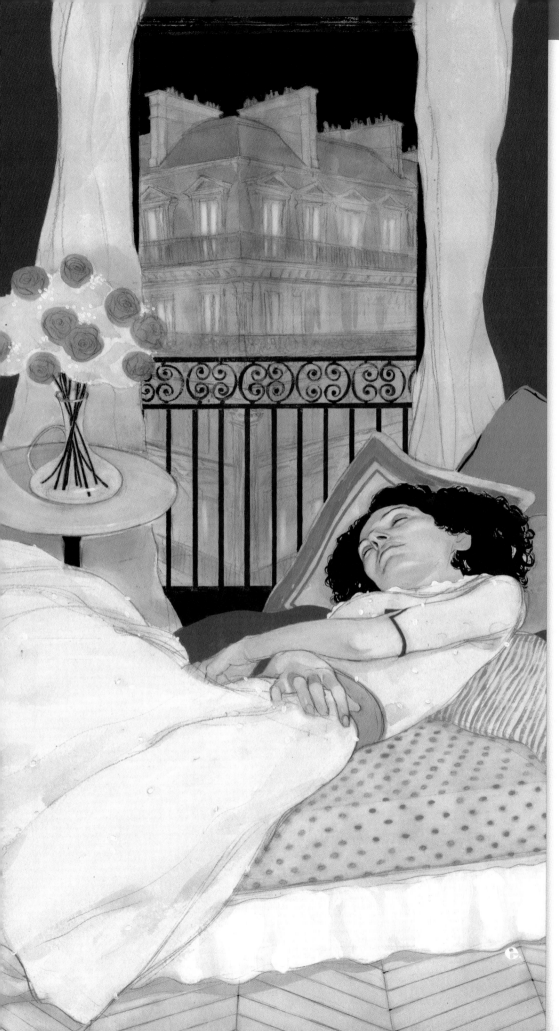

Make Inferences

What inference does Dr. Frankenstein make about the Creature's plans for revenge?

_____

_____

_____

_____

_____

_____

_____

Multiple-Meaning Words

Reread the stage directions in Act III, Scene 2. What does the word *console* mean here?

   a small table designed to stand against a wall

   a panel for electrical equipment

   to give comfort

• <u>Underline</u> the context clues that helped you figure this out.

Drama Elements

Look at the stage directions in Act III, Scene 2. What information do they provide that the dialogue of the play does not?

_____

_____

_____

_____

_____

_____

_____

_____

Act III, Scene 4

SETTING: CAPTAIN WALTON's ship in the Arctic, August 1797

DR. FRANKENSTEIN: So that is my story. My father died soon after Elizabeth, overtaken by grief. And I, I have been chasing the creature ever since. I have followed him all through Europe and up here onto the ice. He toys with me, leaving me clues every now and then, just often enough so that I don't lose his trail. And now, now I lie dying, having still not found him. The wretch is even at this moment out there, able to do evil.

CAPTAIN WALTON: Rest easy, friend. You might yet recover and capture your monster.

DR. FRANKENSTEIN: I'm not afraid of dying. I have no one left to live for, now. And perhaps dying is my just reward. I have failed everyone. I failed my creature whom I brought into this world. And then, when he turned to evil, I failed to protect those I loved.

CAPTAIN WALTON: Not all is bad. You made a great scientific discovery. To you goes the glory of finding the secret of eternal life.

DR. FRANKENSTEIN: Glory yes, but at what price? The secret will die with me because I cannot chance having someone else repeat my mistakes. Promise me that if you ever see the creature, you will kill him. Promise me that. It will bring peace to my poor soul.

Act III, Scene 5

SETTING: Still onboard ship, September 10, 1797

CAPTAIN WALTON: My dear sister, I write with some sad and disturbing news. Victor Frankenstein died last night. My sorrow at the passing of my friend was enormous. At first, I couldn't bring myself to view his body. But when finally I entered his cabin to prepare him for burial, I encountered the most surprising scene. The creature, the monstrous creature, was there, standing over his dead creator, his face made even more hideous by grief. He addressed me, saying that he came to bid his creator farewell.

Said he, "I condemned him to misery, but his life has been no more miserable than my own. You may hate me, but not as much as I hate myself. I have done horrible things but will do them no more."

So saying, he sprung from the cabin window onto a raft of ice. He was soon carried away by the waves and was lost in the darkness and distance. ■

> **Question**
> **What questions do you have about the end of this play?**

Mary Shelley

AUTHOR FILE

BORN: August 30, 1797, in London, England

FAMILY: Mary Shelley was the daughter of two of England's most respected writers, Mary Wollstonecraft Godwin and William Godwin. Her mother died from complications after Mary's birth, leaving her father to raise her and her two sisters. She married Percy Bysshe Shelley, another famous writer, who had been her father's student.

INSPIRATION: Shelley wrote this story when her husband and the great poet Lord Byron proposed that each of them write a ghost story. She began writing *Frankenstein* at the age of nineteen.

OTHER JOBS: Her final novel, *The Last Man,* was a science fiction epic set in a postapocalyptic, disease-ravaged world. The main character is said to be a glorified version of her then-deceased husband.

Scientific Breakthrough or Human Arrogance?

It is now scientifically possible to clone certain animals. But is it the right thing to do?

Dolly the Cloned Sheep

Scotland, 1996 > Scientists created the world's first cloned mammal: Dolly the lamb. They put the nucleus [the cell part that contains DNA] of an udder cell from one sheep into the hollowed-out egg cell of another. Then they implanted the egg cell into a third sheep, who acted as the surrogate mother. So, technically, Dolly had no father.

Ethical Debate > The cloning technique could be used to produce genetically identical animals to benefit research on human diseases. Critics point out that cloned animals are usually unhealthy and that the technique could lead to human cloning.

Mira the Cloned Pet

United States, 1998 > Lou Hawthorne took his family dog, Missy, to Texas A&M University, where scientists preserved the animal's DNA. This marked the start of the Missyplicity Project, the first time scientists cloned a family pet. Missy died in 2002, and five years later, her clone was born. The puppy, Mira, was soon joined by two other puppies cloned from Missy's DNA.

Ethical Debate > Some people believe that cloning animals could benefit humanity. For example, scientists want to clone Trakr, a search-and-rescue dog who found survivors of the September 11 terrorist attacks. However, cloning can be expensive: It can cost more than $100,000 to have a beloved pet cloned. In addition, the cloned animals are never identical to the original. In fact, Lou Hawthorne's mother stated that the cloned puppy was nothing like Missy and insisted on getting herself a "real" dog. Animal welfare advocates also point to the huge number of pets living in shelters who are in need of a good home.

---

cloned *(adj.)* copied exactly from the cells of another animal or plant

implanted *(v.)* put into someone's body through a medical procedure

---

LITERARY ANALYSIS

Drama Elements

 Where do the last two scenes of the drama take place?

___ on a raft of ice

___ at Victor's lab at Ingolstadt

___ on Captain Walton's ship

● (Circle) the setting notes that tell you this.

CRITICAL THINKING

Synthesize

Read the text and look at the images on page 295. Then write a statement that synthesizes what all of the examples show about cloning.

_____

_____

_____

_____

_____

_____

21 SMALL GROUPS/INDEPENDENT

COLLABORATE

Debate In a group, debate whether people should attempt to modify life by cloning, replacing one human face for another, or creating "Frankenfoods."

COMMUNICATE

Discuss and Write With a partner, discuss who was more at fault in this story, Frankenstein or the Creature. Jot down your ideas, and then write them in a paragraph.

READ ONLINE

expert space
Go to **www.expert21.com/student** to learn more about Mary Shelley; Frankenstein; English Literature; Cloning.

Dear Olivia:
Letters to a Bullied Girl

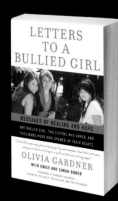

By Olivia Gardner, with
Emily and Sarah Buder

Small acts of kindness by complete strangers gave Olivia Gardner reason to hope again.

For Olivia Gardner, the bullying began in middle school in California. It took the form of name-calling after she suffered an epileptic seizure in front of her peers. Olivia was singled out as different, rejected by her classmates, and tormented in the hallways and on the Internet by an "Olivia Haters" Web site created by some students at her school. Her bullies dragged her backpack through mud, taunted her in school, and wore "I Hate Olivia" bracelets. The bullying went on for two years in three different schools. With each incident, Olivia withdrew further. Eventually, she fled the school environment and rarely left her home.

In March 2007, sisters Emily and Sarah Buder read about Olivia's story in the *San Francisco Chronicle*. They felt her pain and took action by mobilizing a letter-writing campaign called "Olivia's Letters" to draw attention to bullying and its consequences. Below are some of these letters.

Former Bullies Speak Up

Dear Olivia,

I have been on both sides of the bully fence. I was a skinny, self-conscious 12-year-old. I hated the way I looked and endured many taunts and lots of comments about my body! Somewhere in my self-loathing I turned on another friend and verbally abused her and convinced other friends to taunt her, too. She was a good person, and she and I made amends soon after and we are still close friends. But not a year goes by that I don't think of that and feel ashamed. How could I be so awful? How could I become the bully I myself so hated?

I think some bullies are people who don't like themselves. They attack others to make themselves feel better. Maybe those people who are so mean to you are not very happy themselves. . . .

Jessica

Dear Olivia,

My name is Lindsey. I'm so sorry people were so mean to you. Bullies can be mean but deep down we are all good people. . . . Sometimes I bully myself about my insecurities, but then I have to remember that everyone is beautiful in their own way. . . .

Your friend,

Lindsey

---

endured *(v.)* withstood
insecurities *(n.)* things that make people feel bad about themselves

---

COMPREHENSION

Cause and Effect

What happened as a result of Jessica being bullied? Write the missing effects in the causal chain.

Cause: Jessica was bullied.

Jessica felt ashamed of her actions.

LITERARY ANALYSIS

Author's Voice

How would you describe the voice of the first letter writer, Jessica? Circle any words that apply.

compassionate   thoughtful

angry   gentle   resentful

CRITICAL THINKING

Evaluate

Do you agree with Jessica's opinion that bullies hurt other people in order to feel better about themselves?

Parents Take Action

Dear Olivia,

Your story has really brought to light a problem that needs much more attention. As the parent of a bully, I admit to being caught completely off guard when I received a call about my son's bullying behavior at school. The call was from the parent of another child at school. She told me that my son and his friends had been calling her son names and throwing food at him in the cafeteria. She said he "often" wound up with nothing to eat for lunch. I was just horrified and upset. Often? How long had this been going on? Apparently, when the boy asked for his food back, my son and his friends threw it back to him chicken nugget by chicken nugget, grape by grape, with much of it landing on the floor.

I never imagined in a million years that my son would behave in this foolish way. He was a good kid and did not show any signs of this behavior at home. I was aware that bullying is a problem in our school system, but I never thought to ask him about it. Well, I learned a lesson . . . bring up the subject with your children. Let them know you are aware and watching!

My husband came home from work early the day I received the call so the three of us could have a chat about the problem. My son first denied it, but then his face turned red and he started to get upset. He finally spilled the beans and admitted the truth. Olivia, I cannot begin to tell you how hard it was to hear that your child has brought pain to another child. We felt anger, shame, disappointment, disbelief, and confusion toward our own son and sadness for the boy he taunted.

I am writing because I felt this same sadness for you. I know this was a difficult experience for you to go through, but it can lead to important changes. Olivia, I believe you have the strong will and the capacity to turn the pain you've experienced into positive action.

In our situation, we insisted that the parents and the other boys who were involved be brought in to the principal's office to discuss the situation. None of the boys were able to explain why they bullied this boy. Was it a feeling of power? The ability to get away with something? Group-think? Experimenting with being naughty? What we do know is that it had nothing to do with the boy who was bullied and everything to do with our son's (and his friends') poor judgment. What was illuminating to all of the adults in this meeting was that these kids just seemed ignorant about the concept of bullying, what it consists of and how deeply targets of bullying are affected by it. We all decided that what was sorely needed was ACTION.

Each of the boys went over to the child's home to apologize to him, and they took turns making his lunches for a month. They also formed a committee, supervised by the principal, to find local experts on bullying and invite them to come to the school for assemblies. The teachers reinforced what the kids learned about bullying by asking them to write papers on bullying that were hung in the school hallways for all to read. Posters about tolerance and respect were also put up around the school. A parent volunteer program was started to supervise the students during lunch and recess. The school really took charge, and the bullying stopped.

Olivia, my son is very remorseful about being a bully, and I know he will never forget the big lesson he learned from all this. I hope that one day your bullies will get to the same point. I am glad that your message is one of love and not hate. Thanks to you and the Buder sisters for being such strong beacons of light to many others.

Keep up the good work.

Maggie (a former bully's mother)

capacity *(n.)* the ability
reinforced *(v.)* made stronger

Bullied No More

Dear Olivia,

I grew up in the South and was made fun of for being half-Hispanic by non-Hispanics and for being half-Hispanic by Hispanics. I was made fun of for being poor by rich kids and for where I lived by everyone. I was made fun of for wearing clothes my classmates recognized as having been given away and I was made fun of for being smart. . . . Why do I tell you these things? Because you have the building blocks to take control and prove who you are. . . . Where will life take you? Where do you want to go? I participated in as many activities in high school as I was able. I went to competitions for my singing, was a National Merit Scholar, and, as non-athletic as I was, I even lettered in football. I even sang with a rock band. I went to college and became a veterinarian. I have been in almost forty countries. I have been nationally recognized for my achievements and have a wonderful family and friends who know what true friendship means. . . . Believe me when I say things will get far better.

Be strong,
Rick

Dear Olivia,

I was very disheartened to hear about your ordeal and all of the suffering that you had to endure. Unfortunately, as you have no doubt become aware, this sort of thing has gone on long before the invention of the Internet. When I grew up, I experienced bullying and prejudice when my family moved from San Francisco to the suburbs of the East Bay. I was the smallest in almost every grade and one of the only Asians at school.

The thing is, over the years, I realized that kids and adults alike will always find something to pick on and attack, whether it's race, height, weight, religion, money, or poverty. . . . Be confident in who you are and know that you are making a difference in speaking out to other kids.

Sincerely,
Curtis

> **disheartened** (adj.) saddened and disappointed
> **ordeal** (n.) a difficult or painful experience

COMPREHENSION

Sequence of Events

Review Maggie's letter. **Number** the following events to show the order in which they happened:

____ Maggie asked the principal to act.

____ Maggie's son bullied another student.

____ Maggie got a call from another parent.

____ Bullying in the school was reduced.

____ Maggie's son admitted to the bullying.

____ Maggie confronted her son.

NAVIGATING TEXT

Author's Style

Underline all the sentences in Rick's letter that begin with the words "I was made fun of ..."

• What effect does this repetition have on Rick's argument?

_____

_____

_____

CRITICAL THINKING

Evaluate

Think about the possible solutions to the problem of bullying that were offered in these letters. Which solution do you think would be most beneficial and why?

_____

_____

_____

_____

_____

_____

_____

_____

_____

READ ONLINE

expert space
Go to **www.expert21.com/student** to learn more about Cyber-Bullying; Epilepsy.

Think Across Texts

Organize and Synthesize

1. Complete this chart using information from "To Cheat or Not to Cheat," "Frankenstein," and *Dear Olivia: Letters to a Bullied Girl*.

	Ethical Dilemma (What is the heart of the issue)	Ethical Lessons Learned
"To Cheat or Not to Cheat"		
"Frankenstein"		
Dear Olivia: Letters to a Bullied Girl		

Compare and Evaluate

2. Why is cheating so harmful? Think about all the people it affects. Use examples from the selection to support your answer.

_____

_____

_____

_____

3. What turned Dr. Frankenstein's fictional Creature into something similar to a real-life bully? What traits might school bullies have in common with Frankenstein's Creature? Explain.

_____

_____

_____

_____

4. Do you think it is important for everyone in a school community—students, parents, teachers, and administrators—to be involved in the effort to stop bullying? Give examples from the selections to support your answer.

_____

_____

_____

_____

_____

_____

_____

_____

React and Write

5. With a partner, discuss and take notes on how the three readings in Inquiry 2 helped you understand ethics. Then write a response to the question *How do we decide what really matters?*

Apply Word Knowledge

Word Lab

1. **Explain it.** List two things a person with **integrity** would do.

_____

_____

2. **Describe it.** What would an **arduous** journey through a **desolate** place be like?

_____

_____

_____

3. **Name them.** What is something that **repulses** you?

_____

What is something that might put you in a **quandary**?

_____

_____

What is a project you would **undertake** enthusiastically?

_____

_____

4. **Describe it.** If you could **customize** a bicycle in any way you wished, what would you do to it?

_____

_____

5. **Circle them.** Which would you do to **nurture** a pet?

| give it food | talk to it | play with it | train it |
| give it water | sell it | give it baths | ignore it |

Word Analysis

6. Read each sentence below. Circle the meaning of the underlined word. Then underline the context clues that revealed the meaning of the word as it is used in each sentence.

The sloppy picnickers left cans, bags, and other <u>refuse</u> all around the picnic table.

garbage   to say no

7. Bill used a sharp <u>implement</u> to get the can open.

to carry out   a tool

8. The moon rock damaged the <u>integrity</u> of the space ship.

honesty or fairness   soundness or wholeness

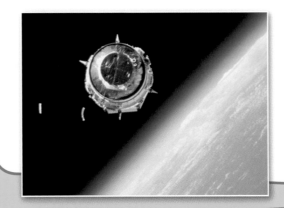

21

Examine Multiple Perspectives

Everyone has their own perspective, or way of looking at issues and ideas. When people make the effort to understand each other's perspectives, it is easier to settle differences, solve problems, and reach agreement.

Understand Two Viewpoints

▶ Anita and Greg disagree about a topic—the salaries of major league ballplayers. Read their emails. Remember, with email the first email below is the response.

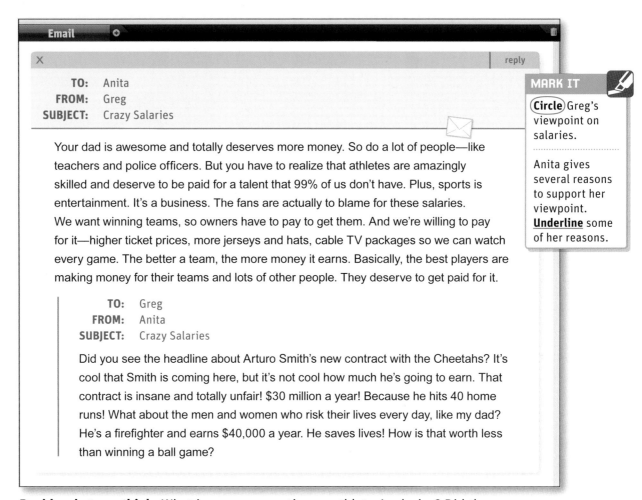

Email

TO: Anita
FROM: Greg
SUBJECT: Crazy Salaries

Your dad is awesome and totally deserves more money. So do a lot of people—like teachers and police officers. But you have to realize that athletes are amazingly skilled and deserve to be paid for a talent that 99% of us don't have. Plus, sports is entertainment. It's a business. The fans are actually to blame for these salaries. We want winning teams, so owners have to pay to get them. And we're willing to pay for it—higher ticket prices, more jerseys and hats, cable TV packages so we can watch every game. The better a team, the more money it earns. Basically, the best players are making money for their teams and lots of other people. They deserve to get paid for it.

TO: Greg
FROM: Anita
SUBJECT: Crazy Salaries

Did you see the headline about Arturo Smith's new contract with the Cheetahs? It's cool that Smith is coming here, but it's not cool how much he's going to earn. That contract is insane and totally unfair! $30 million a year! Because he hits 40 home runs! What about the men and women who risk their lives every day, like my dad? He's a firefighter and earns $40,000 a year. He saves lives! How is that worth less than winning a ball game?

MARK IT

(Circle) Greg's viewpoint on salaries.

Anita gives several reasons to support her viewpoint. **Underline** some of her reasons.

Decide what you think: What is your perspective on athletes' salaries? Did the reasons Anita and Greg gave affect your perspective?

[Here's How] ▶ **Follow these steps to examine multiple perspectives:**

Step 1 Identify the different viewpoints. What does each person or group believe? What points do they disagree on? Are there any points on which they agree?

Step 2 Think about the people involved. Ask yourself how a person's values, culture, background, or experiences might affect his or her perspective.

Step 3 Decide what you think. Consider each viewpoint and how well the reasons support it. Decide which viewpoint you agree with and why. You may not agree with either perspective.

Step 4 Go beyond. Think about other perspectives on the issue. Have any viewpoints been overlooked? If so, does the new information lead you to change your opinion? Why?

Apply: Examine Multiple Perspectives

▶ **Rita wants to be able to stay out late with her friends. Her mother doesn't agree. Read the following discussion. Follow the steps to analyze the two perspectives and decide what you think.**

1. **Identify the different viewpoints.** State each person's point of view.

Rita: _____

Mom: _____

2. **Think about the people involved.** What makes Rita think she should have a later curfew?

_____

_____

What factors influence Rita's mom's opinion?

_____

_____

3. **Decide what you think.** Whom do you agree with? Explain.

_____

_____

4. **Go beyond.** Have any viewpoints been overlooked? Would those viewpoints change your mind?

_____

_____

Persuasive Essay

A persuasive essay states a thesis, point of view, or opinion, and then gives reasons that are supported by facts, logic, and examples. Persuasive writing is used in advertising, political speeches, and in many other places.

In this writing workshop, you will write a persuasive essay about a value you feel deeply about, for example, promoting peace.

Example: This blog writer uses persuasive text to convince people to recycle.

> Many people realize that recycling is important for the environment because it helps keep trash out of landfills. But did you know recycling is also good for the economy? According to the National Recycling Coalition's Web site, recycling provides jobs for 1.1 million workers!

Traits of Writing

Traits of Writing is a model for assessing and teaching. The traits work within the writing process to support revision and editing.

Each puzzle piece below represents one of the **traits** that define good writing.

Each trait is made up of four **key qualities.** The trait you will focus on in this lesson is Word Choice.

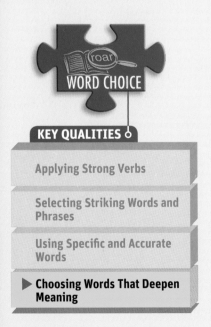

WORD CHOICE

KEY QUALITIES

Applying Strong Verbs

Selecting Striking Words and Phrases

Using Specific and Accurate Words

▶ **Choosing Words That Deepen Meaning**

▶ **Analyze Features** A persuasive essay has the following features:

FEATURE	✏ MARK IT
Look for these features in the Student Model on the next page.	**Mark the features as you read the Student Model.**
1. An **introduction** that explains the issue and states the writer's opinion. (Organization)	Draw a box around the thesis, point of view, or opinion that the writer gives.
2. One or more reasons backed by evidence that argue in favor of this opinion. (Ideas)	Circle the reasons and evidence that argue for this opinion.
3. Focus Trait: Word Choice Carefully chosen **words that deepen meaning.** (Organization)	Check ✓ examples of carefully chosen words.
4. A good **counterargument** for a different opinion and a reason that the writer is against the counter-argument. (Ideas)	Star ★ the counterargument for a different opinion.
5. A strong **final statement** that leaves the reader with something to think about. (Organization and Ideas)	Underline the thought-provoking sentence in the last paragraph.

▶ **Read Chris's persuasive speech about treating farm animals with compassion.**

STUDENT MODEL

Kindness for Farm Animals
By Chris Morgan

Most people think that cruel treatment of animals is wrong. In Texas, abuse of pets can land you in jail for a year. Sports such as dogfighting are illegal in all 50 states. However, many of the animals raised for food are treated terribly. This is wrong—society should treat farm animals with compassion.

Many farms keep animals in small, crowded cages. These poor beasts never see the light of day. Animals obviously feel physical pain. But research shows that animals also feel happiness, sadness, and stress. Confining animals in this harsh way is unfeeling. Why do we limit our caring about animals to pets?

There are also health reasons to support better treatment of farm animals. Farm animals in cramped cages filled with waste are given antibiotics in their feed to prevent them from becoming ill and spreading disease to the other animals. Seventy percent of all antibiotics in the U.S. go to healthy livestock. This practice creates "superbugs" that are resistant to antibiotics. These "superbugs" could infect humans.

In 2008, California passed the Prevention of Farm Animal Cruelty Act. Today, in that state, calves raised for veal, egg-laying hens, and pregnant pigs can be confined only in ways that allow these animals to lie down, stand up, fully extend their limbs, and turn around freely. This law should be enacted in all 50 states.

If we treat animals more humanely, the costs of meat and poultry will rise. Meat that comes from well-treated animals, often at organic farms, can cost almost twice as much as regular farmed meat in some parts of the country. Some say it's not worth it. However, despite the cost, we must have laws that follow our value of compassion.

Think about your values. Then, look at your diet. If you are what you eat, and you care about kindness, you should not eat meat from animals raised in evil ways.

▶ **Read Chris's notes about how he worked on his persuasive essay.**

When I edited this essay, I added some details explaining the new law in California, because it's not obvious how the law can help.

When I revised my essay, I used the words "unfeeling," "harsh," and "evil," instead of using the word "cruel" four times.

▶ **Analyze how Chris developed and organized his ideas.**

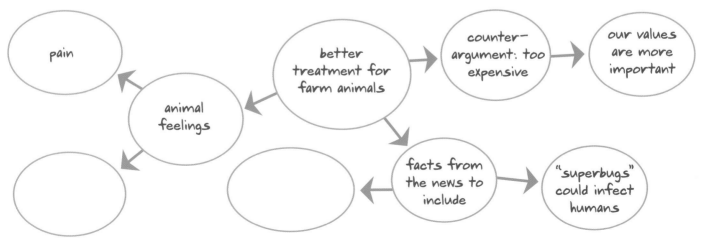

How Do I Get Started?

Your Topic:

Assignment: Persuasive Essay

Purpose: To write a persuasive essay about a value you feel deeply about

Audience: Student's choice

Ideas: Using Details

Using details deepens what you have to say. Use these Think-Abouts as you work on your ideas:

- Did I create a picture in the reader's mind?
- Did I use details that draw upon the five senses (sight, touch, taste, smell, hearing)? *For example, the third paragraph of the Student Model gives a detail about crowded cages full of waste so you can imagine the way it looks and smells.*
- Do my details stay on the main topic?
- Did I stretch for details beyond the obvious?

IDEAS

○ **KEY QUALITIES**

Finding a Topic

Focusing the Topic

Developing the Topic

▶ Using Details

▶ **Model** Go back to Reading 2, "A Retrieved Reformation," in this workshop. List some sensory details that create a picture in the reader's mind.

▶ **Practice** Draw upon one or more of the five senses with a detail.

Your Topic: _____

A detail that draws on the senses: _____

_____

▶ **Plan Your Persuasive Essay** Use the organizer below to jot down ideas for your essay.

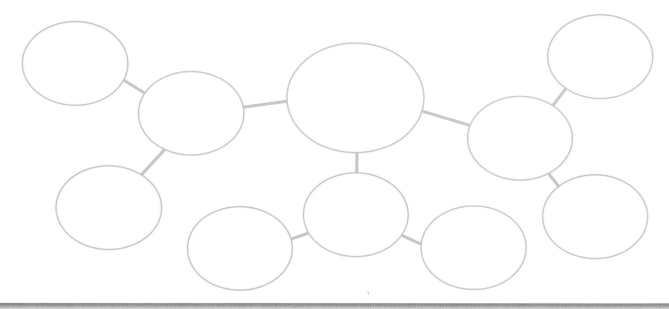

How Do I Get Organized?

ORGANIZATION

Organization: Ending With a Sense of Resolution

Good writers end their essays with a sense of resolution. Ask yourself these Think-Abouts as you work on your organization.

- Have I wrapped up all the loose ends?
- Have I ended at the best place?
- Do I have an ending that makes my writing feel finished?
- Did I leave the reader with something to think about? *The Student Model ends with a challenge about the reader's diet.*

KEY QUALITIES

Creating the Lead

Using Sequence Words and Transition Words

Structuring the Body

▶ **Ending With a Sense of Resolution**

▶ **Model** Go back to Reading 1, "The Lady, or the Tiger?" and explain how it felt to read a story where the loose ends were not wrapped up.

▶ **Practice** Rewrite the last paragraph from the Student Model. Remember, you can wrap up the loose ends in different ways. You can also leave the reader with something different to think about.

_____

_____

_____

_____

_____

▶ **Write a Paragraph** Practice ending your persuasive essay with a sense of resolution as you write a first draft of your conclusion here.

_____

_____

_____

_____

_____

▶ **Draft Your Persuasive Essay** Write a first draft.

Quick Check

▶ Check how well you ended your persuasive essay with a sense of resolution. Have a writing partner rate it, too.

6 = Expert   **3** = Making Strides

5 = Well Done   **2** = On the Way

4 = Almost There   **1** = Getting Started

Ideas

1. Have I wrapped up all the loose ends?
Self ① ② ③ ④ ⑤
Partner ① ② ③ ④ ⑤

2. Have I ended at the best place?
Self ① ② ③ ④ ⑤
Partner ① ② ③ ④ ⑤

3. Do I have an ending that makes my writing feel finished?
Self ① ② ③ ④ ⑤
Partner ① ② ③ ④ ⑤

4. Did I leave the reader with something to think about?
Self ① ② ③ ④ ⑤
Partner ① ② ③ ④ ⑤

How Do I Choose Words That Deepen Meaning?

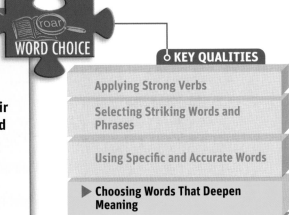

FOCUS TRAIT

Word Choice: Choosing Words That Deepen Meaning

Good writers think about the words that will best express their meaning. Use these Think-Abouts to make sure you make word choices that deepen meaning in your essay.

- Did I choose words that show I really thought about them?
- Have I tried to use words without repeating myself?
- Do my words capture the reader's imagination? *The Student Model uses the phrase "poor beasts" to generate sympathy.*
- Have I found the best way to express myself?

⚬ KEY QUALITIES

Applying Strong Verbs

Selecting Striking Words and Phrases

Using Specific and Accurate Words

▶ **Choosing Words That Deepen Meaning**

▶ **Model** Go back to Reading 3, "New Brand of High-Seas Pirates Lurks Off Somali Coast," and circle word choices that help deepen meaning.

▶ Read Ruth Culham's writing blog below to get advice on improving your writing.

Ask the Expert: Ruth Culham

Ruth Culham, an award-winning teacher, is the author of *6+1 Traits of Writing: The Complete Guide for Middle School* and other books on writing.

Q & A: Choosing Words That Deepen Meaning

<u>Winnefred Word</u> Writes:

I think that word choice is a pretty easy trait because everyone knows you need words. Words can be long or short. Words are interesting, but why not just use the words that you use all the time? What's the big deal about meaningful words?

Dear Winnefred Word:
Words rock the writer's world. Did you know that there are synonyms for *words*, such as *language, vocabulary, terms,* and *expressions*? There are so many similar words to choose from, choose the perfect ones for your ideas.

Posted by: Ruth Culham | December 22 at 4:30 P.M.

▶ **Practice** **Read the sample paragraphs and think about which one uses words carefully to deepen meaning.**

<u>Underline</u> the words that deepen meaning.

(Circle) the repetitive words.

(Circle) the sample that uses words to deepen meaning.

Sample 1: Peer Pressure

Peer pressure can be fine, like when peers tell you to listen to a cool new band. However, the pressure of peers can become worse when it involves activities that are ethically bad or against the law. Peers might try to pressure you to do drugs, shoplift, or cheat.

Sample 2: With Friends Like These...

Peer pressure can be harmless, like when friends tell you to listen to an innovative new band. However, the influence of other teens can become dangerous when it involves activities that are ethically wrong or against the law. Friends might try to force you to do drugs, shoplift, or cheat.

▶ **Revise** **Now make thoughtful word choices in your writing. Choose a paragraph from your first draft and revise it below. Remember to avoid repeating the same word, and use words that capture the reader's imagination.**

_____

_____

_____

_____

_____

_____

_____

_____

_____

_____

Quick Check

▶ **Check your essay for how well you deepened meaning with word choice in your writing. Then have a writing partner rate it, too.**

6 = Expert   **3** = Making Strides

5 = Well Done   **2** = On the Way

4 = Almost There **1** = Getting Started

Word Choice

1. Did I choose words that show I really thought about them?
Self   ① ② ③ ④ ⑤
Partner   ① ② ③ ④ ⑤

2. Have I tried to use words without repeating myself?
Self   ① ② ③ ④ ⑤
Partner   ① ② ③ ④ ⑤

3. Do my words capture the reader's imagination?
Self   ① ② ③ ④ ⑤
Partner   ① ② ③ ④ ⑤

4. Have I found the best way to express myself?
Self   ① ② ③ ④ ⑤
Partner   ① ② ③ ④ ⑤

Revise With Technology Use the thesaurus feature of the word processing program to be sure to avoid repeating the same words over and over.

How Can I Finish a Great Paper?

Grammar: Common Confusions

It is easy to confuse words that sound the same or similar or have similar meanings. Choose the right word based on meaning or the grammar of the sentence.

Examples: Accept: I was happy to accept help with my homework.

Except: He helped me with all the math problems except one.

Between: We had $2.35 between the two of us.

Among: They had $17.45 among all their classmates.

Too/two/to: The two books were too heavy to carry.

▶ **Practice** **Rewrite this paragraph correctly below.**

Some students except cheating and say it doesn't effect anyone else. However, cheating isn't just among to people. It is a a problem between everyone in the class.

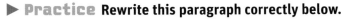

_____

_____

Mechanics: Spelling Confusions

You can use some spelling rules to help you avoid common confusions.

- drop final –*e* when adding the endings -*ing*, -*ed*, -*able*, -*ity*, -*ible*, -*est*, -*ive*.
- do not drop final –*e* when adding the endings -*ment*, -*less*, -*ly*, -*ful*, -*like*, -*ship*.
- put *i* before *e* except after *c* or when the vowel team forms **/ā/** (with these exceptions: *neither, leisure, foreign*).

Example: I was **hoping** their **excitement** about travel would help them **perceive** the value of learning a **foreign** language.

▶ **Practice** **Rewrite this formal paragraph correctly below.**

Law enforcment is not just prisoners recieving punishment. Some people think prison is just a place for warehouseing people who break the rules. However, it can also be a place for self-improvment.

_____

_____

_____

▶ **Proofread** Find and correct any errors in your essay. Put a check beside the types of errors you find. Then write three corrected sentences below.

❏ using similar words correctly

❏ using spelling words correctly

❏ using phrases and clauses correctly

❏ using commas in phrases and clauses correctly

❏ misspellings

❏ other: _____

1. _____

   _____

2. _____

   _____

3. _____

   _____

PRESENTATION

PUBLISH/PRESENT

▶ **Write Your Final Draft** Now, using your edited draft, begin creating a final draft for presentation.

🖥 Use word processing software to type your final draft. Make sure to format your margins and spacing according to your teacher's request.

Check your final draft against the Traits of Writing Scoring Guide on pages 336–339 and correct any errors before you present it.

▶ **Beyond the Classroom** Extend your finished persuasive essay.

List two ideas for photos that could illustrate your persuasive essay:

_____

_____

Look online for a blog, message board, magazine, or newspaper where you could publish your persuasive essay.

List two places where you could upload or share your essay for publication.

_____

_____

Quick Check

▶ **Check how well you used conventions in your essay. Then have a writing partner rate it, too.**

6 = Expert   **3** = Making Strides

5 = Well Done   **2** = On the Way

4 = Almost There   **1** = Getting Started

Conventions

1. Did I use similar words correctly?
Self ① ② ③ ④ ⑤ ⑥
Partner ① ② ③ ④ ⑤ ⑥

2. Did I use spelling rules correctly?
Self ① ② ③ ④ ⑤ ⑥
Partner ① ② ③ ④ ⑤ ⑥

3. Did I use phrases and clauses correctly?
Self ① ② ③ ④ ⑤ ⑥
Partner ① ② ③ ④ ⑤ ⑥

4. Did I use commas in phrases and clauses correctly?
Self ① ② ③ ④ ⑤ ⑥
Partner ① ② ③ ④ ⑤ ⑥

READ ONLINE

expert space Go to **www.expert21.com/ student** to find photographs and other visuals to illustrate your persuasive essay.

You have learned what it takes to do the right thing—and what happens when people do the wrong thing. Now apply your expert reading strategies to the following article about a social experiment designed to explore how people respond to a stranger in need. ▶

SOMEONE FALLS DOWN ON THE SIDEWALK WHAT DO YOU DO?

By Geoff Martz and Anna Norman, from **ABC NEWS**

If you saw someone collapse in front of you on your way to school or work, would you come to his or her aid or just walk on by? It seems like a simple question, and we all like to think that we would do the right thing, but sometimes there's evidence to the contrary.

In 2008, shocking surveillance footage of a woman's death on the floor of a New York hospital waiting room made news across the country as people questioned why she was left to die. In the video, released by the New York Civil Liberties Union, hospital staff apparently ignored her as she lay on the floor for 45 minutes, until it was too late.

And just last month in Washington, D.C., a homeless man was attacked and left on the sidewalk for 19 minutes before anyone called the police. A security camera was rolling as numerous people stopped to look and then passed right on by. Eventual attempts to help the man were too little and too late, and he later died.

But regardless of incidents like these, wouldn't the average person step in to help someone in need? "What Would You Do?" went to New Jersey with hidden cameras to find out.

Rush Hour Test

We chose a busy street, planning to catch people at the peak of rush hour as they hurried to the nearby train station. But the morning commute was anything but ordinary. Suddenly, a woman fell to the ground right in the flow of pedestrian traffic, apparently unconscious.

What the commuters didn't know was that this woman was not really in danger. She was stuntwoman Stephanie Stokes-Smyj, hired by the "What Would You Do?" team for this ethical dilemma. Would people stop to help her, even if it meant arriving late to work and possibly putting themselves in harm's way?

A few people walked right by after she hit the ground, but within seconds, concerned commuters rushed to her aid. Diane Coward hurried over to Stokes-Smyj and knelt down beside her.

"Hello? Are you all right? Miss? Miss?" she said as she leaned over our actor. She pulled out her cell phone to call 911. "What Would You Do?" had already alerted 911 operators to disregard calls related to this ABC News ethical dilemma.

A crowd quickly formed, all offering assistance.

"I Didn't Want to Take Chances"

When anchor John Quinones approached Coward, he asked why she would take so much time out of her morning to help a stranger.

"She fell and she was hurt, and I didn't want to take chances," Coward said. "It doesn't make any difference if you're a stranger. You know, you're supposed to take care of anybody."

Time after time, people rushed to Stokes-Smyj's aid within seconds. She barely hit the ground before people were at her side trying to help. Some tried to assess her medical needs, taking her pulse and listening to her breathing. Others simply offered comfort.

"Honey, sweetie, you OK?" asked Carmen Cordero, who jumped out of her car and rushed to Stokes-Smyj's side. "Stay there, I know it hurts. Help is coming. Help is on the way, sweetie."

Cordero said people's caring reactions to the scenario are a testament to her strong community. "Around here, I don't know, we stick up for each other," she said. "We look out for each other. It doesn't matter who it is."

---

commute (*n.*) the trip made to work or school every day
disregard (*v.*) to ignore something in a way that makes it seem unimportant

Helping the Homeless

We were impressed with everyone's generosity and concern, but we wondered what would happen if, instead of a well-dressed businesswoman, the person in need was a homeless man.

It was time to send in Mick O'Rourke, a stuntman dressed in tattered, dirty clothing. Just like Stokes-Smyj, he fell to the ground in front of a stream of pedestrians. But while help was instantaneous before, no one was quite as eager to step in this time around.

A young woman stared over her shoulder as she walked by.

"I'm scared, I don't know. It's not safe," she told Quinones after she left the scene. "I would probably stay out of this. I'll just look and leave."

One man said that if he'd decided to get involved, he may have put himself in danger.

"Especially in this area, you don't know," said Peter McKnight. "People come up with all kinds of scams, all kinds of situations to try and take advantage of being nice. And therefore, you have to be very careful."

It took several minutes, but eventually people did step up to the plate. While many called 911, a few people even searched through O'Rourke's tattered clothes to find his medicine.

"It shouldn't matter—people, you've got to help them," said Charles Mobley, who came to our actor's rescue. "They need help, help them. Just reach out. What if it was you? What if it was me?"

> "The good part about human beings is that we have a capacity to connect and experience concern and sympathy for others. The bad part is we often decide who's worth caring about."

Homeless Not Considered "Fully Human"?

While bystanders rushed to the side of our female stuntwoman in mere seconds, it took much longer for anyone to help the homeless man.

We asked social psychologist Jack Dovidio of Yale University why people reacted so differently.

"The good part about human beings is that we have a capacity to connect and experience concern and sympathy for others. The bad part is we often decide who's worth caring about," Dovidio explained.

"And in this case, a homeless person is a member of a group that we don't care about, that we don't see as fully human. And therefore, we don't respond the way we would to other people."

The Last Hurdle

At the end of the day, we decided to give our unknowing passersby one more test. If they thought this homeless man had been drinking, and perhaps was at fault for his own situation, would they still be moved to help?

O'Rourke collapsed on the ground again, but this time he had a beverage can in his hand. Immediately, two men walked right past him. One spat on the ground as he went by.

"Wow, a beautiful view of New Jersey," said another woman sarcastically as she stepped around him and continued down the street.

Eleven minutes ticked by and in total, 88 people walked right past.

---

instantaneous *(adj.)* happening immediately
sarcastically *(adv.)* in an ironic way that is meant to be unkind or bitter

An Unexpected Hero

Just as it began to look as if no one would ever step in we saw a disabled woman limping slowly down the street toward our actor.

Linda Hamilton, who police told us is sometimes homeless herself, tried to get others to help. She didn't have a cell phone, but Hamilton made her presence known, standing right next to O'Rourke for several minutes, trying to get others to stop and call 911.

"Excuse me, could you please call an ambulance?" she repeated as person after person passed by. Shockingly, 26 people walked by, ignoring her simple plea for help. Hamilton even took the can out of our actor's hand and threw it away, perhaps hoping this would convince others to step in.

Finally, Hamilton's courageous example helped turn the tide. As she stayed by our actor's side, one woman heard her and stopped to call for an ambulance. A few moments later, another man, Bill Donzeiser, joined in, sliding a piece of cardboard under O'Rourke's head to make him more comfortable.

At one point, Hamilton checked O'Rourke's pulse. When she saw that he was still alive, she said, "Billy, open your eyes. You're still here." Hamilton did not know O'Rourke, but she named him "Billy" and tried to comfort him until help arrived.

"By giving him the name Billy, she really created a personal connection," Dovidio said. "She had a bond with that person that nobody else was willing to consider."

"You Should Help People in Need"

"I was kind of surprised when I came walking along. Nobody seemed to be caring," Donzeiser said. "There are a lot of people that need help, and there are a lot of us that are fortunate enough to be able to help. And I always think you should help people in need."

Hamilton, asked why she stopped and stayed by the man for so long, said, "I'm disabled. If I was out in the street like that I'd want someone to help me."

When we asked her how she felt as she watched people walk right by, her response was simple.

"I cried," she said. "I cried."

And then this quiet and unassuming woman, our hero of the day, slowly hobbled away down the street, inviting us all to consider what we ourselves would do. ■

> **unassuming** *(adj.)* quiet and showing no desire for attention
> **hobbled** *(v.)* walked with difficulty

Reflect

1. Circle all the expert strategies you used while reading this article.
   A. Clarify
   B. Make Connections
   C. Other: _____
   D. Other: _____
   E. Other: _____

2. Use the letters above to label where in the article you applied the expert strategies.

3. Select one expert strategy you used. Explain why you applied that strategy where you did.

   _____
   _____
   _____
   _____

RESEARCH ONLINE

expert space
Go to **www.expert21.com/student** to learn more about Human Behavior; Social Psychology; Values.

PROJECT
SOCIAL ACTION

What Would You Do?

THE SITUATION

When faced with a decision between right and wrong, most people try to choose the right path. But sometimes the right choice is not clear, or both choices are "right" in their own way. Tough decisions require you to examine your values and think critically about your choices.

YOUR CHALLENGE

With a group of classmates, you will review some ethical dilemmas—tough choices that cause you to examine your values today—and decide which one to discuss. Then, you must make a choice about the ethical dilemma you picked and create a multimedia presentation about it.

To create the presentation, you will

• Review the ethical dilemmas, and choose one to focus on.

• Identify your choices.

• Think through justifications.

• Think about how to share your message.

CAREER CONNECTION Arts, A/V Technology, and Communications
www.careerclusters.org

Go to 21 ToolKit Expert File 6.18 to learn more about jobs and careers in presenting information.

1 Review dilemmas.

With your group, spend a few minutes discussing how your values help you make decisions. Refer to **Expert Space** on the subject of ethics and values. First, mark "yes" or "no" to each question below. Then, discuss your justifications with the group.

Yes	No	
		Is lying always wrong?
		Is it okay to encourage a child to believe in the tooth fairy?
		Is it okay to lie to spare someone's feelings?
		Would you stand up to a bully who was picking on another kid?
		What if the bully was really mean and might turn on you?
		Would you help someone in need?
		If a homeless person asked you for money, would you give it?
		Can two people have opposite opinions and both still be right?

2 Choose your dilemma.

Look at the ethical dilemmas on pages 318–319. Take a few moments to talk about each dilemma and decide which you want to focus on. If there is a dispute over which dilemma to pick, elect one person as the arbitrator, or judge. After listening to all sides, the arbitrator will choose the situation. Write it here:

_____

VS.

_____

3 Identify the choices.

Each dilemma suggests two different ways you might handle the situation. What are your options? Write them here:

OPTION 1 _____

_____

_____

OPTION 2 _____

_____

_____

4 Think through justifications.

Use the chart below to record arguments for each option. Circle the choice you want to present for the video, or pick another option that isn't mentioned.

Option 1	Option 2

Storyboard

5 Share your message.

Now create a video essay that gives students advice about what to do if faced with such a situation. You can even be funny if you think it will help your message. Include a slogan to sum up your recommended action. Use [21] ToolKit **Expert File 2.9** to learn how to create a storyboard and **Expert File 4.4** to learn about multimedia presentations. Use this space to plan your brief video essay. Your message:

_____

_____

_____

Shot 1

Visual: _____

Audio: _____

Shot 2

Visual: _____

Audio: _____

Shot 3

Visual: _____

Audio: _____

Ethical Dilemmas

FITTING IN VS. STANDING UP

A girl in your class sent an unflattering picture of another girl to everybody in the class. Do you do anything about it?

FAIRNESS VS. EMPATHY

Your best friend is terrible at math. He tries really hard and studies all the time, but he just doesn't get it. He asks if he can look at your paper during the next math test. You don't want him to fail . . . again. What do you do?

> What else could you do to help your friend besides letting him cheat off your paper?
>
> _____
> _____
> _____
> _____

DUTY VS. FUN

Every Saturday you volunteer at a soup kitchen, but this week you've been invited to a party. You really want to go to the party, but there is no one to cover for you at the soup kitchen. Still, no one there will be angry with you for skipping it this one time. What do you do?

AMBITION VS. LOYALTY

You make extra money mowing lawns. Your best friend wants to work, too. He's not a very hard worker, though. Do you let him work with you?

> If the person were not your friend, would your decision be easier? Explain why or why not.
>
> _____
> _____
> _____
> _____

PATRIOTISM VS. FRUGALITY

You need new shoes. You can buy cheap shoes made in a country where people live in fear of their government. The shoes that are made in the U.S. are expensive, but the company that makes them gives Americans jobs. Which shoes do you buy?

SHORT-TERM VS. LONG-TERM

Your family doesn't have a lot of money, and you are expected to save your paper-route earnings for college. However, you are active and athletic and love skateboarding—you really want to buy a skateboard of your own. It's your money, after all. Do you spend it?

Explain what you would gain in the short term if you spent the money and what you would gain in the long term if you save it.

Short Term: _____

_____

Long Term: _____

_____

HONESTY VS. CASHING IN

You buy something at the store and the clerk gives you too much change. She mistook a $20 bill for a $1 bill, so you are now $19 richer! Do you keep it?

SECURITY VS. JUSTICE

There's a nation in another part of the world where a minority group is being killed in large numbers. The U.S. military is already overstretched. Should we intervene in another country's problem?

Explain how this situation sets our national self-interest against our national values.

_____

_____

_____

Strategy Check

Use your knowledge and strategies from the workshop to answer these questions.

Problem and Solution

1. In *Dear Olivia*, a former bully's mother lists ways to solve the problem of bullying in school. Describe two of those solutions in the chart.

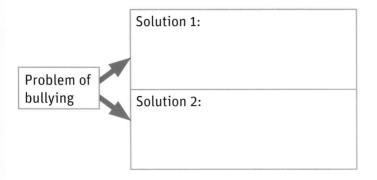

Problem of bullying

Solution 1:

Solution 2:

• In your opinion, which solution is better? Why?

_____

_____

Sequence of Events

2. Read the following passage from "Frankenstein."

Young Victor (*troubled and obviously lying*)**:** *It's nothing, Henry. I was just up late, working on a problem.*

Dr. Frankenstein: *The creature was gone, and there I hoped the matter would end. But deep down inside, I knew it would not be so simple. I had given life and then turned my back on it. For that, I sensed I would somehow pay. I just never realized how dearly.*

Why are Young Victor and Dr. Frankenstein onstage at the same time? How does this help to clarify the play's sequence of events?

_____

_____

_____

Theme

3. How do Ben Price's actions at the end of "A Retrieved Reformation" contribute to the story's theme? Complete the chart.

How Ben Price acts:

The consequences of his action:

How this contributes to the theme:

Plot and Character

4. In "The Lady, or the Tiger?" the princess goes to great lengths to find out which doors the lady and the tiger are behind.

• What do the princess's actions show about her character?

_____

_____

_____

• How do the princess's actions make the plot more exciting?

_____

_____

_____

_____

NAVIGATING TEXT

Evaluate Evidence

5. Read the following claim about pirates:

Today pirates are once again a serious problem at sea, threatening commercial ships.

- Which statement below provides the best evidence to support the claim above?

   Ⓐ Piracy sharply increased in the 1900s.

   Ⓑ In 2005, pirates attacked a cruise ship off Somalia.

   Ⓒ The International Maritime Bureau logged 239 pirate attacks in 2006.

   Ⓓ Captain Jack says, "We hear about pirate attacks all the time."

VOCABULARY/WORD ANALYSIS

Word Families

6. Which of the words below are in the same word family? Circle four.

customize	custard	customization
discussed	custom	customary

Multiple-Meaning Words

7. Use context clues to figure out the meaning of *bow* as it is used in this sentence. Then fill in the circle next to the correct answer.

*The branches of the tree **bow** under the weight of the snow.*

   Ⓐ lower the head in respect

   Ⓑ droop or curve downward under a burden

   Ⓒ knot usually having two loops

   Ⓓ weapon used to shoot an arrow

CRITICAL THINKING

Analyze and Evaluate

8. Based on what you have read in this workshop, do you think that choosing between right and wrong is always an easy decision with an obvious answer? Support your response with details from at least two selections. Include examples from your own experiences.

_____

_____

_____

_____

_____

_____

_____

_____

? EXPERT QUESTION

What values do we live by?

9. Use what you learned in this workshop to answer the Expert Question. Jot down some notes here. Then use a separate sheet of paper to write your response.

_____

_____

Glossary

A glossary is a useful tool found at the back of many books. It contains information about key words in the text. Look at the sample glossary entry below.

This is an **entry word** — the word you look up. It is divided into syllables.

This tells you the **part of speech** of the entry word.

mem•o•rize
(**mem**-uh-rize) *verb*　To learn by heart.

The **pronunciation** appears below the entry word in parentheses. Letters and letter combinations stand for different sounds. The accented syllable is in boldfaced type.

Look here to find the **meaning** of the entry word.

ab•stract
(**ab**-strakt *or* ab-**strakt**) *adjective* Showing imagined things rather than what people or objects actually look like.

ac•cess
(**ak**-sess) *noun*　The ability to enter a place or use something.

ac•com•mo•date
(uh-**kom**-uh-date) *verb*　To make space for.

ac•cus•tomed
(uh-**kuss**-tuhmd) *adjective*　To be familiar with something and accept it as normal.

Prefixes

Unaccustomed begins with the prefix *un-*, meaning "not" or "the opposite of." A **prefix** is a letter or letter group added to the beginning of a word to change its meaning. **Unaccustomed** means "not used to" or "the opposite of accustomed."

ac•quire
(uh-**kwire**) *verb*　To obtain or get something.

ad•e•quate
(**ad**-uh-kwit) *adjective*　Enough, or just what is needed.

ad•min•is•tra•tion
(ad-min-uh-**stray**-shuhn) *noun*　The people in the executive branch of government during a certain president's term.

a•dore
(uh-**dor**) *verb*　To worship or love a lot.

ad•van•tage
(ad-**van**-tij) *noun*　A benefit; something that helps you get ahead.

ad•vise
(ad-**vize**) *verb*　To guide; to suggest something.

af•firm
(uh-**furm**) *verb*　To approve something or say it is true.

ag•o•ny
(**ag**-uh-nee) *noun*　Great pain or suffering.

al·le·giance
(uh-**lee**-junss) *noun*   Loyalty; obedience.

al·ter·nate
(**awl**-tur-nit) *adjective*   Every second time.

am·bush
(**am**-bush) *verb*   To attack by surprise from a hidden place.

angst
(**angst**) *noun*   A feeling of anxiety.

ap·point
(uh-**point**) *verb*   To choose someone for a position or job.

ap·pre·hen·sive
(ap-ri-**hen**-siv) *adjective*   Nervous or uneasy about a future event.

ap·ti·tude
(**ap**-ti-tood) *adjective*   Having to do with the natural ability to do well.

ar·du·ous
(**ar**-joo-uhss) *adjective*   Very difficult; demanding great effort.

ar·id
(**ar**-id) *adjective*   Very dry, without much rainfall.

ar·ro·gance
(**a**-ruh-guhnss) *noun*   Behavior that is conceited or too proud.

as·sess
(uh-**sess**) *verb*   To evaluate.

as·ter·oid
(**ass**-tuh-roid) *noun*   A piece of rock that orbits the sun.

a·troc·i·ty
(uh-**tross**-uh-tee) *noun*   A terrible cruelty done to a person or group.

at·tend·ant
(uh-**ten**-duhnt) *noun*   Someone who serves or waits on people.

au·di·tion
(aw-**dish**-uhn) *verb*   To try out for a role or part by giving a performance.

a·wry
(uh-**rye**) *adverb*   Wrong; amiss.

bit·ter·sweet
(**bit**-ur-sweet) *adjective*   Producing both pain and happiness.

brace
(**brayss**) *verb*   To prepare for something unpleasant, usually by tightening your muscles.

bur·den
(**bur**-duhn) *noun*   Something that is heavy and hard to carry.

cap·i·tal·ist
(**kap**-uh-tuh-list) *noun*   A person who favors a society in which most goods and property are owned by individuals, not the government.

cap·tor
(**kap**-tuhr) *noun*   A person who takes someone as a prisoner.

car·a·van
(**kar**-uh-van) *noun*   A group of people, animals, or vehicles carrying cargo and traveling as a group.

> ### Noun Endings
>
> To make most nouns plural, add an *s*, as in ***caravans***. But nouns that already end in *s* need –*es*, as in ***losses***. Nouns that end in *y* need –*ies*, as in ***casualties***.

cas·u·al·ty
(**kazh**-oo-uhl-tee) *noun*   Death or injury that occurs as a result of war.

cat·a·pult
(**kat**-uh-puhlt) *verb*   To cause something to rise forcefully and suddenly.

cen·tu·ry
(**sen**-chuh-ree) *noun*   A period of 100 years.

cha·os
(**kay**-oss) *noun*   A state of total disorder and confusion.

char·is·mat·ic
(ka-riz-**mat**-ik) *adjective*   Having a powerful ability to charm and influence people.

clut·tered
(**kluht**-urd) *adjective*   Crowded, messy, and disorderly.

col·league
(**kol**-eeg) *noun*   A coworker or fellow member of an organization.

col·lec·tive·ly
(kuh-**lek**-tiv-lee) *adverb*   Together as a whole.

com·et
(**kom**-it) *noun*   Chunks of rocks, frozen gas, and ice that orbit the sun.

com·pact
(**kom**-pakt) *adjective*   Designed to take up very little space.

com·pas·sion
(kuhm-**pass**-shuhn) *noun*   A feeling of sympathy for and a desire to help someone who is suffering.

com·po·si·tion
(kom-puh-**zish**-uhn) *noun*   Something whole formed in a certain way from parts.

com·prise
(kuhm-**prize**) *verb*   To consist of; to be made up of.

con·cen·tra·tion
(kon-suhn-**tray**-shuhn) *noun*   Focusing your thoughts and attention on something.

con·du·cive
(kuhn-**doo**-siv) *adjective* Tending to bring about a particular result.

con·sole
(kuhn-**sole**) *verb* To comfort; to try to make someone feel better.

con·struc·tive
(kuhn-**struhk**-tiv) *adjective* Useful; helping with improvement.

con·tour
(**kon**-toor) *noun* The outline or edge of an object, or a line that represents it.

con·vert
(kuhn-**vert**) *verb* To change into another form.

co·or·di·nate
(koh-**or**-duh-nate) *verb* To move or work together smoothly and easily.

co·or·di·na·tion
(koh-or-duh-**nay**-shuhn) *noun* The act of working together smoothly.

cor·po·ra·tion
(kor-puh-**ray**-shuhn) *noun* A company or other business group.

course
(**korss**) *noun* A class or series of classes in a subject.

Idioms

When something is **"par for the course"** it is typical or expected. This expression is an **idiom**, a phrase that means something different from the meanings of its separate words.

cun·ning·ly
(**kuhn**-ing-lee) *adverb* In a clever, sneaky way.

cus·tom·ize
(**kuhss**-tuh-mize) *verb* To prepare something to meet a particular need or requirement.

cyl·in·der
(**sil**-uhn-dur) *noun* A shape like a tube or can.

dec·ade
(**dek**-ayd) *noun* A period of ten years.

de·cep·tive·ly
(di-**sep**-tiv-lee) *adverb* In a way that is misleading or false.

de·cline
(di-**kline**) *verb* To turn something down or refuse it.

de·flect
(di-**flekt**) *verb* To make something go in a different direction.

de·ject·ed
(di-**jekt**-id) *adjective* Unhappy, disappointed, or sad.

de·mise
(di-**mize**) *noun* Death or disappearance.

de·pict
(di-**pikt**) *verb* To show something in a picture or with words.

de·port
(di-**port**) *verb* To send people back to the country of their birth.

de·prive
(di-**prive**) *verb* To prevent someone from having something, especially something necessary.

des·o·late
(**dess**-uh-luht) *adjective* Empty; deserted.

de·spise
(di-**spize**) *verb* To greatly dislike someone or something.

de·tect
(di-**tekt**) *verb* To discover or notice something.

de·vice
(di-**visse**) *noun* An object or mechanism used for a particular purpose.

de·vi·ous
(**dee**-vee-uhss) *adjective* Winding or roundabout; deceitful or tricky.

de·void
(di-**void**) *adjective* Without something or empty of something.

dig·it·al
(**dij**-uht-uhl) *adjective* Relating to electronic or computer-based technology.

di·lem·ma
(duh-**lem**-muh) *noun* A hard choice between two difficult alternatives.

di·men·sion
(duh-**men**-shuhn) *noun* A measurement of space; in science fiction, a universe.

di·min·ish
(duh-**min**-ish) *verb* To decrease or to become decreased.

dis·card·ed
(diss-**kard**-ed) *adjective* Thrown away or abandoned.

dis·creet
(diss-**kreet**) *adjective* Showing good judgment in the way information is shared.

dis·dain
(diss-**dayn**) *verb* To treat with lack of respect; to look down on something.

dis·perse
(diss-**purss**) *verb* To break up or scatter in various directions.

dome
(**dohm**) *noun* A round structure shaped like half of a sphere.

drought
(**drout**) *noun* An unusually long period of time without rain.

ech·o
(**ek**-oh) *verb*   To be repeated or heard over and over.

ef·fi·cient
(uh-**fish**-uhnt) *adjective*   Wasting as little time, energy, and effort as possible.

ef·fi·cient·ly
(uh-**fish**-uhnt-lee) *adverb*   In a way that gets the best results with the least waste of time or effort.

el·i·gi·ble
(**el**-uh-juh-buhl) *adjective*   Having the right qualifications for something.

e·lu·sive
(i-**loo**-siv) *adjective*   Difficult to find or catch.

em·brace
(em-**brayss**) *noun*   A hug.

em·i·nent
(**em**-uh-nuhnt) *adjective*   Well-known and respected.

e·mis·sion
(i-**mish**-uhn) *noun*   Something that is released into the atmosphere.

en·cir·cle
(en-**sur**-kuhl) *verb*   To form a circle around.

en·crust·ed
(en-**kruhst**-ed) *verb*   Covered with a hard coating.

en·gi·neer
(en-juh-**nihr**) *noun*   A professional trained to use math and science to design machines and buildings.

en·grossed
(en-**grohst**) *adjective*   Wholly absorbed.

e·nor·mi·ty
(i-**nor**-muh-tee) *noun*   The quality of being very wicked or evil.

en·vi·sion
(en-**vi**-zhuhn) *verb*   To imagine something.

e·ro·sion
(i-**roh**-zhuhn) *noun*   The gradual wearing away of something.

etch
(**ech**) *verb*   To impress strongly.

e·val·u·ate
(i-**val**-yoo-ate) *verb*   To look at and judge the worth or quality of something.

e·voke
(i-**voke**) *verb*   To call to mind a certain feeling or idea.

ex·ceed
(ek-**seed**) *verb*   To be greater or better than something else.

ex·cel
(ek-**sel**) *verb*   To do something very well.

ex·change
(eks-**chaynj**) *verb*   To give something to someone and receive something in return.

ex·clu·sive
(eks-**kloo**-siv) *adjective*   Limited; private; restricted.

ex·hi·bi·tion
(eks-uh-**bish**-uhn) *noun*   A public display of works of art or objects of special interest.

ex·pan·sive
(eks-**pan**-siv) *adjective*   Grand or large in scale.

ex·ter·nal·ly
(ek-**stur**-nuhl-lee) *adverb*   Having to do with the outside of something.

ex·tract
(**ek**-strakt) *noun*   A selection or excerpt.

ex·tra·cur·ric·u·lar
(ek-struh-kuh-**rik**-yuh-lar) *adjective*   Connected with a school but not an academic class.

fate·ful
(**fayt**-fuhl) *adjective*   Having an important and usually unpleasant effect on future events.

fi·er·y
(**fye**-ree *or* **fye**-uh-ree) *adjective*   Full of emotion; enthusiastic and energetic.

fil·ter
(**fil**-tur) *verb*   To pass liquid or gas through an object to strain out larger particles.

fore·front
(**for**-fruhnt) *noun*   The most important or noticeable position.

foun·da·tion
(foun-**day**-shuhn) *noun*   The base or basis of something.

fric·tion
(**frik**-shuhn) *noun*   The rubbing of two objects against each other.

fu·gi·tive
(**fyoo**-juh-tiv) *noun*   A person who is running from the law.

func·tion
(**fuhngk**-shuhn) *noun*   The assigned job or duty of something.

fun·da·men·tal
(fuhn-duh-**men**-tuhl) *adjective*   Basic and necessary.

fu·tur·is·tic
(fyoo-chur-**iss**-tik) *adjective* Relating to the future.

gap·ing
(**gape**-ing) *adjective* Wide open.

ge·nial·ly
(**jeen**-yuhl-ee) *adverb* In a friendly and welcoming manner.

gru·el·ing
(**groo**-uh-ling) *adjective* Tiring and difficult.

haul
(**hawl**) *verb* To drag or pull something heavy.

haz·ard·ous
(**haz**-urd-uhss) *adjective* Dangerous.

hol·o·gram
(**hol**-uh-grahm) *noun* A three-dimensional image created by laser beams.

Root Words

The word **hologram** comes from the Greek root *holo* which means "whole" or "complete." A **root** is a word or word part from another language that is the basis of an English word.

hos·tile
(**hoss**-tuhl) *adjective* Threatening or aggressive.

im·pact
(**im**-pakt) *noun* The effect that something has.

im·pend·ing
(im-**pend**-ing) *adjective* Upcoming; going to happen very soon.

im·per·so·nate
(im-**pur**-suh-nayt) *verb* To pretend to be someone else.

im·ple·ment
(**im**-pluh-ment) *verb* To put a plan or an idea into action.

im·press
(im-**press**) *verb* To make people think highly of you.

in·come
(**in**-kuhm) *noun* The amount of money a person earns.

in·crim·i·nat·ing
(in-**krim**-uh-nate-ing) *adjective* Evidence that makes someone look guilty.

in·ev·i·ta·ble
(in-**ev**-uh-tuh-buhl) *adjective* Impossible to prevent.

in·flict
(in-**flikt**) *verb* To make someone else experience something unpleasant.

in·her·ent·ly
(in-**her**-ent-lee) *adjective* Basically; by nature.

in·no·va·tive
(**in**-uh-vay-tiv) *adjective* Completely new.

in·stance
(**in**-stuhnss) *noun* One case or example of something.

in·su·la·tion
(in-suh-**lay**-shuhn) *noun* Material used to prevent the passage of heat into or out of something.

in·teg·ri·ty
(in-**teg**-ruh-tee) *noun* Honesty.

in·tel·lec·tu·al
(in-tuh-**lek**-choo-uhl) *adjective* Involving thought or reason.

in·ter·ac·tion
(in-tur-**ak**-shuhn) *noun* The activity of talking with other people and working together with them.

in·ter·fere
(in-tur-**fihr**) *verb* To prevent something from happening; to get in the way of something.

Synonyms

To **interfere** is "to prevent something from happening" or "to get in the way." To **hinder** is "to make something difficult for someone to do." These words are **synonyms**, words that have the same or similar meanings.

in·ter·mit·tent
(in-tur-**mit**-uhnt) *adjective* Starting and stopping, over and over.

in·ter·nal
(in-**tur**-nuhl) *adjective* Located on the inside.

in·tern·ship
(**in**-turn-ship) *noun* A job a student works at in order to gain work skills and experience.

in·ter·val
(**in**-tur-vuhl) *noun* A period of time between two events or activities.

in·tol·er·a·ble
(in-**tol**-ur-uh-buhl) *adjective* Impossible to endure or experience.

in·tri·cate
(**in**-truh-kit) *adjective* Having a lot of fine detail; complex.

in·vig·o·ra·ting
(in-**vig**-uh-ray-ting) *adjective* Energizing.

ir·rev·o·ca·ble
(ihr-**rev**-oh-kuh-buhl) *adjective* Unable to be taken back, changed, or stopped.

jus·ti·fy
(**juhss**-tuh-fye) *verb* To show that something is fair or reasonable.

jux·ta·pose
(juhk-stuh-**poze** or **juhk**-stuh-poze) *verb* To place side by side for the purpose of comparing and contrasting.

lad·en
(**layd**-uhn) *adjective* Loaded or weighed down.

le·git·i·mate
(luh-**jit**-uh-mit) *adjective* Lawful and reasonable.

lei·sure·ly
(**lee**-zhur-lee) *adverb* In an unhurried or relaxed manner.

ma·neu·ver
(muh-**noo**-ver) *verb* To carefully direct or steer.

mech·a·nism
(**mek**-uh-nizm) *noun* A system of moving parts inside a machine.

mem·o·rize
(**mem**-uh-rize) *verb* To learn by heart.

me·te·or
(**mee**-tee-ur) *noun* A bright streak caused by a space rock entering Earth's atmosphere.

mo·bile
(**moh**-buhl) *adjective* Capable of moving.

mod·i·fy
(**mod**-uh-fye) *verb* To change or alter in some way.

mo·men·tous
(moh-**men**-tuhss) *adjective* Of great importance.

mo·ti·vate
(**moh**-tuh-vate) *verb* To encourage to do something; inspire.

na·tive
(**nay**-tiv) *adjective* Originally from a certain place.

net·work·ing
(**net**-wurk-ing) *adjective* Related to sharing interests and making connections.

nom·i·nate
(**nom**-uh-nate) *verb* To recommend someone for an award, honor, or job.

nur·ture
(**nur**-chur) *verb* To bring up; to take care of someone's needs, especially a child.

o·a·sis
(oh-**ay**-siss) *noun* A small area in a desert where water rises to ground level.

ob·jec·tive
(uhb-**jek**-tiv) *noun* A goal one plans to achieve; the job at hand.

ob·sta·cle
(**ob**-stuh-kuhl) *noun* Something that blocks a path or gets in the way.

op·pres·sion
(uh-**press**-shuhn) *noun* The placement of unfair burdens and restrictions on a person or group.

o·ri·en·ta·tion
(or-ee-uhn-**tay**-shuhn) *noun* A course introducing a new situation or environment.

o·ver·all
(oh-vur-**awl**) *adjective* In all; including everything.

par·a·noid
(**pa**-ruh-noid) *adjective* Believing unreasonably that you cannot trust people or that they are trying to harm you.

pe·cu·liar
(pi-**kyoo**-lyur) *adjective* Strange, unfamiliar, or slightly surprising.

per·cep·tion
(pur-**sep**-shuhn) *noun* Understanding; awareness.

per·va·sive·ness
(pur-**vay**-siv-niss) *noun* The state of being extremely common or widespread.

pla·gia·rize
(**play**-juh-rize) *verb* To steal another person's words or ideas and pass them off as your own.

pop·u·lar·ize
(**pop**-yuh-lur-ize) *verb* To make popular and well-known.

por·trait
(**por**-trit) *noun* A drawing, painting, or photograph of a person.

pre·fer
(pri-**fur**) *verb* To like better than something else.

pre·sump·tion
(pri-**zuhmp**-shuhn) *noun* Something you think must be true.

pri·or
(**prye**-ur) *adjective* Done or planned earlier than something else.

pri·va·cy
(**prye**-vuh-see) *noun* Freedom from unwanted exposure.

pro·found
(pruh-**found**) *adjective* Far-reaching and very significant.

pro·hib·it·ed
(proh-**hib**-it-ed) *adjective* Forbidden by law or authority.

prom·i·nent
(**prom**-uh-nuhnt) *adjective* Obvious and easily visible.

prop·a·gan·da

(prop-uh-**gan**-duh) *noun* Incomplete or biased information designed to influence the way people think.

pro·pel

(**pruh**-pel) *verb* To cause something to move.

pro·por·tion

(pruh-**por**-shuhn) *noun* A certain part or fraction of a whole.

pros·per·ous

(**pross**-pur-uhss) *adjective* To be successful; to have wealth.

pur·sue

(pur-**soo**) *verb* To try to accomplish or obtain.

quan·da·ry

(**kwahn**-duh-ree) *noun* A state of confusion or uncertainty.

ral·ly

(**ral**-lee) *verb* To gather together with others to support a common purpose.

ra·tion

(**rash**-uhn) *verb* To distribute sparingly.

re·cit·al

(ri-**sye**-tuhl) *noun* A music or dance performance.

re·cruit

(ri-**kroot**) *noun* Someone who has recently joined a group or team.

reg·u·la·tion

(reg-yuh-**lay**-shuhn) *noun* A rule or law.

re·ject

(ri-**jekt**) *verb* To refuse to accept something.

re·lo·ca·tion

(ri-loh-**kay**-shuhn) *noun* A move to a new place.

rep·re·sent

(rep-ri-**zent**) *verb* To serve as an excellent example.

re·pulse

(ri-**puhlss**) *verb* To make someone feel sick or disgusted.

re·quire·ment

(ri-**kwire**-ment) *noun* Something you need to do or have.

re·sist·ance

(ri-**ziss**-tuhnss) *noun* The act of resisting or fighting against something.

re·stric·tion

(re-**strikt**-shuhn) *noun* Something that limits or takes away rights.

ret·ri·bu·tion

(ret-trib-**yoo**-shuhn) *noun* Punishment that is deserved.

re·volt

(ri-**vohlt**) *noun* A rebellion.

rev·o·lu·tion

(rev-uh-**loo**-shuhn) *noun* A sudden, sometimes violent change in government.

> ## Multiple-Meaning Words
>
> ***Revolution*** means "a sudden, sometimes violent change in government." It also means "the orbiting of one body in space around another." **Multiple-meaning words** are words that have more than one meaning.

re·vul·sion

(ri-**vuhl**-shuhn) *noun* A strong feeling of disgust.

rig·or

(**rig**-ur) *noun* Strict devotion to something.

rue·ful·ly

(**roo**-fuhl-lee) *adverb* In a way that shows shame or regret.

rum·mage

(**ruhm**-ij) *verb* To search through, especially by moving, turning, or looking through the contents of a container.

sal·vage

(**sal**-vij) *noun* Something that has been saved from destruction or loss.

sat·el·lite

(**sat**-uh-lite) *noun* A machine sent into space to orbit Earth, used for radio, television, and other electronic communication.

saun·ter

(**sawn**-tur) *verb* To walk in a slow or casual way.

schol·ar·ship

(**skol**-ur-ship) *noun* Money given to a student to pay for school.

scope

(**skohp**) *verb* To look at, often for the purpose of evaluation.

sculp·ture

(**skuhlp**-chur) *noun* A three-dimensional work of art made by carving, modeling, or constructing.

seep

(**seep**) *verb* To flow or trickle slowly.

se·mes·ter

(suh-**mess**-tur) *noun* Half of the school year, usually about four months long.

sen·sa·tion

(sen-**say**-shuhn) *noun* A feeling that comes from heightened interest or emotions.

sen·sor
(**sen**-sur) *noun*   A device that scans an object and senses its characteristics.

shun
(**shun**) *verb*   To deliberately avoid something or someone.

> ### Antonyms
>
> *Shun* means "to deliberately avoid something or someone." *Welcome* means "to greet in a friendly way." These words are **antonyms**, words that have opposite meanings.

sol·i·ta·ry
(**sol**-uh-teh-ree) *adjective*   Completely alone; without human contact.

spe·ci·fic
(spi-**sif**-ik) *adjective*   Particular.

spon·sor
(**spon**-sur) *verb*   To help and support, often in an official and/or financial way.

sta·tion·a·ry
(**stay**-shuhn-eh-ree) *adjective*   Not moving or not able to be moved.

ster·ile
(**ster**-uhl) *adjective*   Free from bacteria or other germs.

strat·e·gy
(**strat**-uh-jee) *noun*   Plan of action.

sub·se·quent
(**suhb**-suh-kwuhnt) *adjective*   Coming after; next.

suc·ces·sion
(suhk-**sesh**-shuhn) *noun*   A series of events that happen one after the other.

sup·port·ive
(suhp-**port**-iv) *adjective*   Ready to help out; understanding.

sus·pend
(suhs-**pend**) *verb*   To stop something for a short time.

sus·pense·ful
(suhs-**penss**-ful) *adjective*   Filled with excitement over an uncertain outcome.

swift·ly
(**swift**-lee) *adverb*   In a very fast manner; quickly.

tran·sit
(**tran**-zit) *noun*   Related to a system of buses or trains that moves people or goods.

tran·si·tion
(tran-**zi**-shuhn) *noun*   Movement from one place to another or from one lifestyle to another.

trau·ma
(**traw**-muh) *noun*   Serious physical, mental, or emotional damage.

tra·verse
(tra-**verss**) *verb*   To travel across.

un·der·foot
(uhn-der-**fut**) *adverb*   In the way.

> ### Compound Words
>
> *Underfoot* is a compound word. A **compound word** is made up of two smaller words, like *under* + *foot*.

un·der·tak·ing
(**uhn**-dur-tayk-ing) *verb*   To commit oneself to and begin.

u·ni·ver·sal
(yoo-nuh-**vur**-suhl) *adjective*   Common to everyone or everything.

un·prec·e·dent·ed
(un-**press**-uh-dent-id) *adjective*   Never seen or done before.

up·roar
(**uhp**-ror) *noun*   State of disturbance.

van·dal·ize
(**van**-duhl-ize) *verb*   To harm or destroy property that belongs to someone else.

var·si·ty
(**var**-si-tee) *noun*   The main team that represents a school in a sport.

vi·o·la·tion
(**vye**-uh-lay-shuhn) *noun*   An action that breaks a rule.

vir·tu·al
(**vur**-choo-uhl) *adjective*   Generated by a computer; not real.

vul·ner·a·ble
(**vuhl**-nur-uh-buhl) *adjective*   Able to be harmed or damaged.

wince
(**winss**) *verb*   To flinch; to draw back from as if in pain.

with·er
(**with**-ur) *verb*   To dry up and shrivel from lack of water.

wretch·ed
(**rech**-id) *adjective*   Extremely unpleasant or miserable.

Glossary of Literary Terms

alliteration
The repetition of initial (beginning) consonant sounds in a string of words. Notice the alliteration in this line: *a sweet, sad song.*

assonance
The repetition of vowel sounds within non-rhyming words. The repetition of the "aw" sound in the following line is an example: *the soft wings of the moth.*

author's perspective
A writer's way of looking at a topic. Perspective is usually influenced by the author's background and experiences.

author's purpose
A writer usually writes for one or more of these purposes: to express thoughts or feelings, to inform or explain, to persuade, or to entertain.

autobiography
A writer's account of his or her own life. It is usually told from the first-person point of view.

biography
The true account of a person's life, written by another person. Biographies are usually told from a third-person point of view. The writer of a biography researches his or her subject through interviews, primary sources, and/or reference materials.

cast of characters
A list of all the characters in a play, usually in order of appearance. It appears at the beginning of a script, and may contain a brief description of each character.

character
The people, animals, or imaginary creatures in a work of literature.
main character Main characters are the most important characters in literary works.
minor characters The less important characters in a literary work are known as minor characters.
dynamic character A dynamic character is one who changes over the course of a story.
static character A static character is one who stays the same throughout a story, no matter what experiences he or she has.

characterization
The way a writer creates and develops characters. There are five basic methods of characterization:
- The story's narrator makes direct comments about a character.
- The writer describes the character's physical appearance.
- The writer presents the character's own thoughts, speech, and actions.
- The writer shows how other characters think about or interact with the character.
- The writer reveals a character's motivation, or the reason why the character acts a certain way.

See also **character; character traits.**

character traits
The character's qualities. These qualities may include physical traits (strength) as well as personality traits (stubbornness).

climax
The point of greatest interest in a story. At the climax, the outcome of the plot usually becomes clear.

See also **plot.**

conflict

A struggle between opposing forces. Almost every story has a main conflict that is the focus of the story.

external conflict A struggle between a character and a force outside him or herself: nature, a physical obstacle, another character, or society.

internal conflict A struggle that occurs within a character; for example, deciding whether to betray a friend.

consonance

The repetition of consonant sounds within and at the ends of words: *on a lonely afternoon.*

See also **alliteration.**

dialect

A variation on a language spoken in a particular place or by a particular group of people. Dialects may feature unique pronunciations, vocabulary, and grammar.

dialogue

Written conversation between two or more characters. Writers use dialogue to bring characters to life and move the story's action along.

diary

A daily record of a person's experiences and feelings, written by that person. The terms *diary* and *journal* are often used to mean the same thing.

drama

A form of literature meant to be performed by actors in front of an audience. In a drama, the characters' dialogue and actions tell the story. The written form of a play is known as a script. A script usually includes a cast of characters, dialogue, and stage directions. Dramas are usually divided into acts and scenes.

epic

A long narrative poem on a serious subject. It is usually written in formal style and tells the adventures of a great hero whose actions reflect the ideals of his or her society. *Beowulf* and *The Odyssey* are examples.

essay

A short work of nonfiction that deals with a single subject. An *expository essay* presents or explains information and ideas. A *personal essay* usually tells about the writer's experiences, feelings, and beliefs. A *persuasive essay* attempts to convince the reader to take action or accept a certain opinion.

exposition

The first stage of a typical story plot. The exposition introduces the setting and the important characters. The exposition may also introduce the story's conflict.

fable

A brief tale told to illustrate a moral or teach a lesson. Often the moral of a fable is directly stated near the tale's beginning or end.

falling action

The stage of the plot in which the story begins to come to a close. The falling action comes between the climax and the resolution. Events in the falling action begin to show the results of an important decision or action that happened at the climax.

See also **climax; plot.**

fiction

Writing that tells an imaginary story. It includes both short stories and novels. The writer of a fictional work might invent all the events and characters or might base parts of the story on real people and events. The basic elements of fiction are *plot, character, setting,* and *theme.*

See also **novel; short story.**

figurative language

Words or phrases that go beyond the literal meanings of words. Writers use figurative language to create a picture in readers' minds, to emphasize ideas, and to create strong emotion.

See also **metaphor; onomatopoeia; personification; simile.**

first-person point of view

See **point of view**.

flashback

Interrupts the sequence of events to tell about something that took place at an earlier time. A flashback provides information that can help a reader better understand a character's current situation.

folk tale

A story that has been passed from generation to generation originally by word of mouth. Folk tales often take place in the distant past and involve supernatural events. Characters may be animals, people, or superhuman beings.

foreshadowing

Provides hints about what will happen in a story. Foreshadowing creates suspense and makes readers eager to find out what will happen.

form

The structure or organization of a piece of writing. The form of a poem, for example, includes the arrangement of its words and lines on the page.

genre

A category, or group, in which a work of literature is classified. The major genres in literature are fiction, nonfiction, poetry, and drama.

graphic story

A story that combines text and visuals and tells the plot through a series of panels. Graphic stories often include speech bubbles to convey dialogue and captions to present information to the reader.

hero

A main character in a story. In older literary works, the heroes are often courageous, strong, honorable, and intelligent. In today's stories, a hero may be an ordinary person with ordinary problems.

historical fiction

A short story or a novel set in the past which includes real places and real events.

hyperbole

Figurative language in which the truth is exaggerated for emphasis or humorous effect: *I tried a million times, but I could not do that puzzle.*

idiom

An expression with a meaning different from the meaning of its individual words. For example, if a job is said to be "a piece of cake," it can be done easily.

imagery

Descriptive words and phrases that appeal to one or more of the five senses—sight, hearing, smell, taste, and touch. Writers use imagery to help readers picture what the writers describe.

interview

A conversation between a writer or reporter and another person in which the writer asks questions to gather facts and information. Interviews may be recorded, broadcast, or published.

journal

See **diary**.

legend

A story handed down from the past about a hero or someone who has achieved something great. Legends usually have some basis in historical fact.

line

The core unit of a poem. In a poem, lines may end, or break, at the end of a phrase or in the middle of one.

memoir

A form of autobiographical writing in which a writer shares his or her personal experiences and observations.

See also **autobiography**.

metaphor

A comparison of two things that are different but have some qualities in common. Unlike a simile, a metaphor does not include the words *like* or *as*. If a person is described as "a beast," he probably is big and mean.

See also **figurative language; simile.**

meter

In poetry, the repeated pattern of rhythm in a poem.

See also **rhythm**.

mood

The feeling or atmosphere that a writer creates in a piece of writing. For example, *gloomy, lighthearted,* or *suspenseful* could be the mood of a piece.

See also **tone**.

moral

A lesson that a story teaches. A moral is often stated at the end of a fable. A reader must often infer a story's moral from what happens to the characters.

See also **fable**.

motivation
See **characterization**.

myth

Stories that explain the creation of the world or something in nature, such as the changing seasons. They often focus on both gods and mortals, and in ancient times were used to comment on personality traits and human behavior.

narrative poetry

Poetry that tells a story. Like fiction, a narrative poem contains characters, a setting, and a plot.

narrator

The voice that tells a story. Sometimes the narrator is a character in the story. At other times, the narrator is an outside voice created by the writer. The narrator is not the same as the writer. In drama, the narrator is a character who explains the action in the play to the audience.

See also **point of view**.

nonfiction

Writing that tells about real people, places, and events. Nonfiction is mainly written to communicate facts and information. Nonfiction includes a wide range of writing: newspaper articles, Web sites, biographies, essays, movie reviews, speeches, blogs, and more.

See also **fiction**.

novel

A long, complex work of narrative fiction, usually divided into chapters. Novels most often feature invented characters and events, but sometimes include characters based on real people and events drawn from history or the news. Novels include the basic elements of fiction: *plot, character, setting,* and *theme*.

See also **fiction**.

omniscient point of view
See **point of view**.

onomatopoeia

A word that sounds like the action it describes. An example is the word *buzz*.

See also **sound devices**.

oral literature

Stories that have been passed down by word of mouth from generation to generation. Oral literature includes folk tales, legends, and myths.

personification

The giving of human qualities to an animal, object, or idea. For example, the wind is personified in this poem by James Stephens: *The wind stood up and gave a shout./He whistled on his fingers and/kicked the withered leaves about.*

See also **figurative language**.

play
See **drama**.

plot

The series of events in a story. The plot usually centers on a conflict, or struggle, faced by the main character. The main stages of a plot include exposition, rising action, climax, falling action, and resolution.

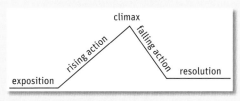

See also **climax; conflict; exposition; falling action; resolution; rising action**.

poetry

Literary works in which words are chosen and arranged in rhythmic verses that express emotions and ideas in imaginative ways.

point of view

The method of narration used in a short story, novel, narrative poem, or work of nonfiction.

first-person point of view

The narrator is a character in the story and refers to himself or herself as "I."

second-person point of view

The main character is presented using "you" as the main pronoun.

third-person point of view

The narrator is outside of the action, and is not one of the characters.

third-person omniscient

or all-knowing point of view: The narrator sees into the minds of all characters.

third-person limited point of view

The narrator tells what only one character thinks, feels, and observes.

protagonist

The main character in a story, play, or novel. The protagonist is involved in the main conflict of the story.

repetition

A technique in which a sound, word, phrase, or line is repeated. Repetition helps to emphasize meaning and create an appealing rhythm in a speech or poem. For example, the phrase "I have a dream" is repeated throughout Dr. Martin Luther King, Jr.'s most famous speech.

See also **alliteration; sound devices.**

resolution

See **falling action.**

rhyme

Similar or identical sounds at the end of two or more words, such as *beat, heat,* and *complete.* Lines in a poem often end with rhyming words.

rhyme scheme

A pattern of end rhymes in a poem. A letter of the alphabet is assigned to each line. Lines that rhyme are given the same letter. Notice the rhyme scheme in this poem by Christina Rosetti:

Is the moon tired? she looks so pale *a*
Within her misty veil; *a*
She scales the sky from east to west *b*
And takes no rest, *b*

rhythm

A pattern of stressed and unstressed syllables in a line of poetry. Poets use rhythm to bring out the musical quality of language and to create moods. Outside of poetry, rhythm refers to the repetition of specific phrases, images, or ideas.

See also **meter.**

rising action

The stage of the plot that develops the conflict, or struggle. The events in the rising action build toward the climax, or turning point.

See also **plot.**

script

The text of a play, film, or broadcast.

second-person point of view
See **point of view**.

sensory details

Words and phrases that appeal to the reader's senses of sight, hearing, touch, smell, and taste.

See also **imagery.**

setting

The time and place of the action. Elements of setting include location, historical period (past, present, or future), season, time of day, and culture.

short story

A brief work of fiction that centers on a single idea. Generally, a short story has one main conflict that involves the characters and keeps the story moving.

See also **fiction.**

simile

A way of describing something by comparing it with something else, using the words *like* or *as*. For example, "This pillow is as light as a snowflake."

See also **figurative language; metaphor.**

sound devices

Words used to appeal to the sense of hearing. Some common sound devices include *alliteration, assonance, consonance, meter, onomatopoeia, repetition, rhyme,* and *rhythm.*

speaker

The voice an author uses to tell a story or present a poem to the reader.

speech

A talk or public address given to a group of people.

stage directions

The instructions to the actors, director, and stage crew in the script of a play. Stage directions often appear in parentheses and in italic type.

stanza

One of the groups of lines into which a poem or song is divided.

static character

See **character.**

style

A way of writing. It involves how something is said, rather than what is said. For example, a writer may use sentence fragments, repetition, and unusual words, or may prefer long sentences and poetic language.

surprise ending

An unexpected plot twist at the end of a story. The surprise may be a sudden turn in the action or a new piece of information.

suspense

The growing tension and excitement felt by a reader. A writer creates suspense by raising questions in the reader's mind. The use of foreshadowing is one way that writers create suspense.

See also **foreshadowing.**

symbol

A person, a place, an object, or an activity that stands for something beyond itself. For example, a white dove is a bird that represents peace.

tall tale

A humorous, exaggerated story about impossible events. Stories about folk heroes such as Pecos Bill and Paul Bunyan are typical tall tales.

theme

The main subject or idea of a piece of writing. For example, the theme of *Barrio Boy* is finding pride in one's heritage and culture.

third-person point of view

See **point of view.**

tone

The writer's attitude toward his or her subject. *Angry, sad,* and *humorous* are examples of different tones.

See also **author's perspective; mood.**

traits

See **character traits.**

turning point

See **climax.**

voice

The writer's unique use of language that allows a reader to "hear" his or her personality.

word choice

The use of clear, specific, and strong words by an author to create certain effects for the reader.

Traits of Writing Scoring Guide

Traits of Writing is a model for assessing and teaching. The traits work within the writing process to support revision and editing. Each puzzle piece below represents one of the traits that define good writing.

▶ **Use the scoring guides on the following pages to assess your own work against these traits.**

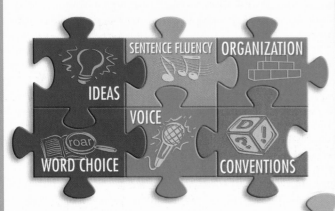

Ideas: The content of the piece, its central message and the details that support it.

Organization: The internal structure of the piece—the thread of the logic, the pattern of meaning.

Voice: The personal stamp of the writer, which includes tone, is achieved through a strong understanding of purpose and audience.

Word Choice: The specific vocabulary the writer uses to convey meaning and enlighten the reader.

Sentence Fluency: The way words and phrases flow through the piece. It is an auditory trait, and is therefore "read" with the ear as much as the eye.

Conventions: The mechanical correctness of the piece. Correct use of conventions (spelling, capitalization, punctuation, paragraphing, and grammar and usage) guides the reader through text easily.

Presentation: This trait addresses how the writing looks to the reader. This includes spacing, handwriting or font, formatting, and images.

IDEAS

 SCORE 6 EXPERT

 SCORE 5 WELL DONE

My topic is well-developed and focused. My piece contains specific, interesting, and accurate details, and new thinking about this topic.

- I have a clear, central theme or a simple, original story line.
- I've narrowed my theme or story line to create a piece that is focused and a pleasure to read.
- I've included original information to support my main idea.
- I've included clear, accurate details that will create pictures in the reader's mind.

 SCORE 4 ALMOST THERE

 SCORE 3 MAKING STRIDES

My writing includes many general observations about the topic, but lacks focus and clear, accurate details. I need to elaborate.

- I've stayed on the topic, but my theme or story line is fairly general.
- I haven't dug into the topic in a logical, focused way.
- My unique perspective on this topic is not coming through as clearly as it could.
- The reader may have questions after reading this draft because my details don't provide answers.

 SCORE 2 ON THE WAY

SCORE 1 GETTING STARTED

I'm still thinking about my theme or story line for this piece. So far, I've only explored possibilities.

- I've jotted down some ideas for topics, but it's a hodgepodge.
- Nothing in particular stands out as important in my piece.
- I've not written much. I may have just restated the assignment.
- My details are thin and need to be checked for accuracy.

ORGANIZATION

SCORE 6 EXPERT

My details unfold in a logical order. The structure makes reading my piece a breeze.

- My beginning grabs the reader's attention.
- I've used sequence and transition words to guide the reader.
- All of my details fit logically and my pacing is smooth.
- My ending gives the reader a sense of closure and something to think about.

SCORE 5 WELL DONE

SCORE 4 ALMOST THERE

My piece's organization is pretty basic and predictable. I have the essential ingredients: beginning, middle, and end, but that's about it.

- My beginning is clear, but too obvious. I've used a technique that writers use all too often.
- I've used simple sequence and transition words that stand out too much.
- A few details need to be moved around to create a more logical flow of ideas.
- My ending needs work; it's pretty canned.

SCORE 3 MAKING STRIDES

SCORE 2 ON THE WAY

My piece doesn't make much sense because I haven't figured out a way to organize it. My details are jumbled together at this point.

- My beginning doesn't indicate where I'm going next.
- I've not grouped ideas nor connected them using sequence and transition words.
- With no sense of order, it will be a challenge for the reader to sort out how ideas relate.
- I haven't figured out how to end this piece.

SCORE 1 GETTING STARTED

VOICE

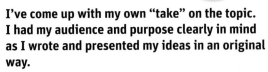

SCORE 6 EXPERT

I've come up with my own "take" on the topic. I had my audience and purpose clearly in mind as I wrote and presented my ideas in an original way.

- My piece is expressive, which shows how much I care about my topic.
- The purpose for this piece is clear, and I've used a tone and tenor that is appropriate for that purpose.
- There is no doubt in my mind that the reader will understand how I think and feel about my topic.
- I've expressed myself in some new, original ways.

SCORE 5 WELL DONE

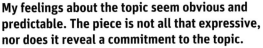

SCORE 4 ALMOST THERE

My feelings about the topic seem obvious and predictable. The piece is not all that expressive, nor does it reveal a commitment to the topic.

- In a few places, my authentic voice comes through, but only in a few.
- My purpose for writing this piece is unclear to me, so the tone feels off.
- I've made little effort to connect with the reader; I'm playing it safe.
- This piece sounds like lots of others on this topic. It's not very original.

SCORE 3 MAKING STRIDES

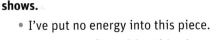
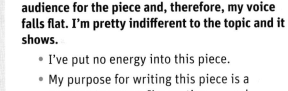

SCORE 2 ON THE WAY

I've not thought at all about my purpose and audience for the piece and, therefore, my voice falls flat. I'm pretty indifferent to the topic and it shows.

- I've put no energy into this piece.
- My purpose for writing this piece is a mystery to me, so I'm casting around aimlessly.
- Since my topic isn't interesting to me, chances are, my piece won't be interesting to the reader. I haven't thought about my audience.
- I have taken no risks. There is no evidence of my feeling about or interest in this topic.

SCORE 1 GETTING STARTED

WORD CHOICE

SCORE 6 EXPERT

SCORE 5 WELL DONE

The words and phrases I've selected are accurate, specific, and natural-sounding. My piece conveys precisely what I want to say because I use powerful language.

- My piece contains strong verbs, which bring it alive.
- I stretched by using the perfect words and phrases to convey my ideas.
- I've used content words and phrases with accuracy and precision.
- I've picked the best words and phrases, not just the first ones that came to mind.

SCORE 4 ALMOST THERE

SCORE 3 MAKING STRIDES

My words and phrases make sense but aren't very accurate, specific, or natural-sounding. The reader won't have trouble understanding them, but may find them uninspiring, except perhaps for one or two.

- I've used passive voice. I should rethink those passages that contain it and add "action words."
- I haven't come up with new ways to say obvious things.
- My content words and phrases are accurate, but general. I might have used too much jargon. I need to choose more precise words.
- I need to revise this draft by replacing many of the words and phrases with stronger ones.

SCORE 2 ON THE WAY

SCORE 1 GETTING STARTED

My words and phrases are so unclear the reader may wind up more confused than entertained, informed, or persuaded. I might need to expand writing vocabulary to improve my piece.

- My verbs are not strong. I've used passive voice throughout this piece.
- I've used bland words and phrases throughout—or the same words and phrases over and over.
- My content words are not specific or accurate enough to make the meaning clear.
- My words and phrases are not working; they distract the reader rather than help him or her.

SENTENCE FLUENCY

SCORE 6 EXPERT

SCORE 5 WELL DONE

My piece is strong because I've written a variety of well-built sentences. I've woven those sentences together to create a smooth-sounding piece.

- I've constructed my sentences for maximum impact and used transitions effectively.
- I've varied my sentence lengths and types— short and long, complex and simple.
- When I read my sentences aloud, they are pleasing to the ear.
- I've broken the "rules" at points to create impact and interest.

SCORE 4 ALMOST THERE

SCORE 3 MAKING STRIDES

My sentences lack variety or creativity, but most of them are grammatically correct. Some of them are smooth, while others are choppy and awkward.

- I've written solid shorter sentences. Now I need to try some longer ones.
- I've created different kinds of sentences, but the result is uneven.
- When my sentences are read aloud, the reader will stumble in only a few places.
- Any sentences that break the "rules" are accidental and don't work well.

SCORE 2 ON THE WAY

SCORE 1 GETTING STARTED

My sentences are choppy, incomplete, or rambling. I need to revise my piece extensively to make it more readable.

- Many of my sentences don't work because they're poorly constructed.
- I've used the same sentence lengths and types over and over again.
- When I try to read my piece aloud, I stumble in many places.
- If I've broken any "rules," it's not for stylistic reasons. It's because I may not understand those rules.

CONVENTIONS

My piece proves I can use a range of conventions with skill and creativity. It is ready for its intended audience.

- My spelling is strong. I've spelled almost all the words accurately.
- I've used punctuation creatively and correctly, and begun new paragraphs in the right places.
- I've used capitals in the right places throughout my piece, even in tricky places.
- I've taken care to apply standard English grammar and usage.

SCORE 5
WELL DONE

SCORE 4
ALMOST THERE

My writing still needs editing for many problems in one convention or a variety of smaller problems in several conventions. I've stuck to the basics and haven't tried anything challenging.

- I've misspelled some words that I use all the time, as well as complex words that I don't use as often.
- My punctuation is basically strong. I should review it one more time. I indented the piece's first paragraph, but not others.
- I've used capitals in obvious places, but not in others.
- Even though my grammar and usage are not 100 percent correct, my audience should be able to read my piece.

SCORE 3
MAKING STRIDES

SCORE 2
ON THE WAY

The problems I'm having in conventions make this piece challenging to read, even for me! I've got lots and lots of work to do before it's ready for its intended audience.

- Extensive spelling errors make my piece a challenge to read and understand.
- I haven't punctuated or paragraphed the piece well, which is necessary to guide the reader.
- My use of capitals is so inconsistent it's distracting.
- I need to clean up the piece considerably for grammar and usage.

SCORE 1
GETTING STARTED

PRESENTATION

SCORE 6
EXPERT

My piece's appearance makes it easy to read and enjoy. I've taken care to create a piece that is pleasing to my reader's eye.

- I've written very clearly and legibly. My letters, words, and spaces between them are uniform.
- My choice of font style, size, and/or color make my piece a breeze to read.
- My margins frame the text nicely. There are no tears, smudges, or cross-outs.
- Text features such as bulleted lists, charts, pictures, and headers are working well.

SCORE 5
WELL DONE

SCORE 4
ALMOST THERE

My piece still looks like a draft. Many visual elements should be cleaned up and handled with more care.

- My handwriting is readable, but my letters, words, and the spaces between them should be treated more consistently.
- My choice of font style, size, and/or color seem off—inappropriate for my intended audience.
- My margins are uneven. There are some tears, smudges, or cross-outs.
- I've handled simple text features well, but am struggling with the more complex ones.

SCORE 3
MAKING STRIDES

SCORE 2
ON THE WAY

My piece is almost unreadable because of its appearance. It's not ready for anyone but me to read.

- My handwriting is so hard to read it creates a visual barrier.
- All the font styles, sizes, and/or colors I've used are dizzying. They're not working.
- My margins are uneven or nonexistent throughout, making the piece difficult to read.
- I haven't used text features well, even simple ones.

SCORE 1
GETTING STARTED

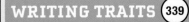

Author and Title Index

HAIM POTOK [1929 – 2002]   MARGARET PETERSON HADDIX [1964 –]   MARY SHELLEY [1797 – 1851]   NEIL DEGRASSE TYSON [1958 –]   KATHERINE PATERSON [1932 –]   RAY BRADBURY [1920 –]   SUZANNE FISHER STAPLES [1945 –]

ARTHUR C. CLARKE [1917 – 2008]

ANNE FRANK [1929 – 1945]

JACK LONDON [1876 – 1916]

LOUNG UNG [1970 –]

WALTER DEAN MYERS [1937 –]

O. HENRY [1862 – 1910]

Acknowledgments

Grateful acknowledgment is made to the following sources for permission to reprint from previously published material. The publisher has made diligent efforts to trace the ownership of all copyrighted material in this volume and believes that all necessary permissions have been secured. If any errors or omissions have inadvertently been made, proper corrections will gladly be made in future editions.

Caldecott Medal and Newbery Medal seals reprinted by permission of the American Library Association. All rights reserved.

WORKSHOP 5
iSHOWCASE

"Sounds of Success" adapted from "Nuttin But Success" by Christy Damio from *Scholastic Action* magazine, December 10, 2007, and "The Sound of Success" by Christy Damio from *Scholastic Action* magazine, September 15, 2008. Copyright © 2007, 2008 by Scholastic Inc. All rights reserved.

"Behind the Lens" from "Stories Behind the Lens - Profiles: Jacob Foko" from the Brooks Institute Web site (www.brook.edu). Copyright © 2007 by Brooks Institute of Photography. Reprinted by permission of Brooks Institute of Photography.

"Zebra" from ZEBRA AND OTHER STORIES by Chaim Potok. Copyright © 1998 by Chaim Potok. Published by Alfred A. Knopf, a division of Random House, Inc. Reprinted by permission of The William Morris Agency, LLC.

From LETTERS TO A YOUNG ARTIST by Anna Deavere Smith. Copyright © 2006 by Anna Deavere Smith. Cover photo copyright © Janette Beckman. Reprinted by permission of Anchor Books, a division of Random House, Inc. All rights reserved.

"If I Were a Poem" from CHICKS UP FRONT: POEMS by Sara Holbrook. Copyright © 1998 by Sara Holbrook. Reprinted by permission of Cleveland State University Poetry Center.

"I Want to Write" from THIS IS MY CENTURY: NEW AND COLLECTED POEMS by Margaret Walker. Copyright © 1989 by Margaret Walker Alexander. Reprinted by permission of the University of Georgia Press.

"Introduction to Shelf Life" from SHELF LIFE: STORIES BY THE BOOK edited by Gary Paulsen. Copyright © 2003 by Gary Paulsen. Reprinted by permission of Simon & Schuster Books for Young Readers.

WORKSHOP 6
SPACE INVADERS

From "Zero Hour" by Ray Bradbury. Copyright © 1947 by Ray Bradbury. Reprinted by permission of Don Congdon Associates Inc.

Adapted from "Crash Course?" by Nancy Honovich from *Science World* magazine, December 12, 2005. Copyright © 2005 by Scholastic Inc. All rights reserved.

"Bizarre Beings From Beyond" adapted from BARLOWE'S GUIDE TO EXTRATERRESTRIALS by Wayne Douglas Barlowe, Ian Summers, and Beth Meacham. Copyright © 1979 by Wayne Douglas Barlowe and Ian Summers. Art copyright © 1979 by Wayne Douglas Barlowe. Reprinted by permission of Workman Publishing Company, Inc. All rights reserved.

"Who's There?" from OF TIME AND STARS by Arthur C. Clarke. Copyright © 1972 by Arthur C. Clarke. Published by Penguin Group (USA) Inc. Reprinted by permission of the author and the author's agents, Scovil Galen Ghosh Literary Agency, Inc.

"The Case for Space" adapted from "Reaching for the Stars" by Neil deGrasse Tyson from *Natural History* magazine, April 2003. Copyright © 2003 by Natural History Magazine, Inc. Reprinted by permission of Natural History Magazine, Inc. All rights reserved.

"Elegy for Challenger" from JAGUAR OF SWEET LAUGHTER: NEW AND SELECTED POEMS by Diane Ackerman. Copyright © 1993 by Diane Ackerman. Reprinted by permission of Random House, Inc. All rights reserved.

"Postcards From Space: True Stories From Space Tourists" from "Very Stunning, Very Space, and Very Cool" by Adam Fisher from *Technology Review* magazine, January/February 2009. Copyright © 2009 by Technology Review. Reprinted by permission of Technology Review.

WORKSHOP 7
EYEWITNESS TO HISTORY

From Anne Frank: The Diary of a Young Girl by Anne Frank. Copyright © 1952 by Otto H. Frank, copyright © 1967 by Doubleday, a division of Random House, Inc. Cover photo copyright © 1986 by Anne Frank-Fonds Basel/Cosmopress SA, Geneva, Switzerland. Reprinted by permission of Random House, Inc.

"The Fall of the Wall" from "Berlin Wall Account" by Gillian Cox from the Cold War Museum Web site (www.coldwar.org). Copyright © The Cold War Museum. Reprinted by permission of The Cold War Museum.

"From Iraq With Love" from "The Smell of Fresh Paint" by Sgt. Tina M. Beller from Operation Homecoming: Iraq, Afghanistan, and the Home Front, in the Words of U.S. Troops and Their Families edited by Andrew Carroll. Copyright © 2006 by Tina Beller. Published by Random House, Inc. Reprinted by permission of the author. All rights reserved.

"To the Fallen" by Sgt. John McCary from Operation Homecoming: Iraq, Afghanistan, and the Home Front, in the Words of U.S. Troops and Their Families edited by Andrew Carroll. Copyright © 2006 by John McCary. Published by Random House, Inc. Reprinted by permission of the author. All rights reserved.

From No More Strangers Now: Young Voices From a New South Africa by Tim McKee. Copyright © 1998 by Timothy Saunders McKee. Reprinted by permission of Dorling Kindersley Ltd.

"A Refugee in Her Own Country" from First They Killed My Father by Loung Ung. Text and cover photo copyright © 2000 by Loung Ung. Reprinted by permission of HarperCollins Publishers. All rights reserved.

"One Giant Leap for Humankind" excerpt by Andrés Eloy Mendoza Rodriguez. Copyright © Andrés Eloy Mendoza Rodriguez. All rights reserved.

"Remembering 9/11" by Juliette Kessler from Scholastic News Online. Copyright © by Scholastic Inc. All rights reserved.

WORKSHOP 8
DO THE RIGHT THING

Adapted from "The Lady, or the Tiger?" by Frank R. Stockton.

"A Retrieved Reformation" by O. Henry.

"New Brand of High-Seas Pirates Lurks Off Somali Coast" by Alex Seitz Wald from Online News Hour Extra (www.pbs.org). Copyright © MacNeil/Lehrer Productions. Reprinted by permission of MacNeil/Lehrer Productions.

"To Cheat or Not to Cheat?" from "The Cheating Game" by Carolyn Kleiner and Mary Lord from U.S. News and World Report, November 14, 1999. Copyright © 1999 by U.S. News and World Report, LP. Reprinted by permission of U.S. News and World Report, LP.

Adapted from "Frankenstein" from Scholastic Scope magazine, October 16, 2006, based on the novel by Mary Shelley. All rights reserved.

"Dear Olivia" from Letters to a Bullied Girl by Olivia Gardner with Emily and Sarah Buder. Copyright © 2008 by Olivia Gardner with Emily and Sarah Buder. Reprinted by permission of HarperCollins Publishers. All rights reserved.

"Someone Falls Down on the Sidewalk: What Do You Do?" by Geoff Martz and Anna Norman from the ABC News Web site, March 13, 2009 (www.abcnews.go.com). Copyright © 2009 by ABCNEWS VideoSource. Reprinted by permission of ABCNEWS VideoSource.

Credits